ABORIGINAL CANADA REVISITED

N

ABORIGINAL CANADA REVISITED

Kerstin Knopf, Editor

UNIVERSITY OF OTTAWA PRESS

The University of Ottawa Press acknowledges with gratitude the support extended to its publishing list by Heritage Canada through its Book Publishing Industry Development Program, by the Canada Council for the Arts, by the Canadian Federation for the Humanities and Social Sciences through its Aid to Scholarly Publications Program, by the Social Sciences and Humanities Research Council, and by the University of Ottawa.

We also gratefully acknowledge Gesellschaft für Kanada-Studien whose financial support has contributed to the publication of this book.

LIBRARY AND ARCHIVES CANADA CATALOGUING IN PUBLICATION

Aboriginal Canada revisited / Kerstin Knopf, editor.

Includes bibliographical references and index.
ISBN 978-0-7766-0679-8

1. Native peoples--Canada. 2. Native peoples in literature. 3. Native peoples in mass media. I. Knopf, Kerstin

E78.C2A137 2008 971.004'97 C2008-903526-7

PRINTED AND BOUND IN CANADA

For Hartmut Lutz

Contents

Print Media and Film

Preface and Acknowledgements

This collection of essays contains the proceedings from the third Interdisciplinary Graduate Studies Symposium entitled "Aboriginal Peoples in Canada in the 21st Century" and held in April 2005 at the University of Greifswald in Germany. The conference was dedicated to Professor Dr. Hartmut Lutz as a "present" to commemorate his sixtieth birthday.

Since the early 1970s Hartmut Lutz has taught, researched, and lived Native American and Native Canadian Studies and has been instrumental in establishing these fields within German academia. For most of his academic career he has written on various topics within Native Studies, in particular on the "imaginary and ideological Indian" with his study of the genesis and dissemination of Indian stereotypes in American and German public and literary discourses (*"Indianer" und "Native Americans": Zur sozial- und literaturhistorischen Vermittlung eines Stereotyps*); articles on the representations of Native people in German children's and juvenile literature and in Hollywood movies; and with groundbreaking research on the phenomenon that he calls German "Indianthusiasm"—the Germans' enthusiastic infatuation with Native people. In addition, he has edited various books on Native history, politics, and literature. He founded the OBEMA-series, and together with friends, colleagues, and students, he translated and published compilations of poetry and stories by such Native American authors as Joseph Bruchac and Lance Henson as well as an anthology of Native Canadian authors, including Lenore Keeshig-Tobias and Daniel David Moses, among others. Hartmut Lutz has written extensively on Native literature, including chapters in a German history of Canadian literature, several encyclopaedia entries on Native authors, and afterwords for two Native novels translated into German: Jeannette Armstrong's *Slash* and Beatrice Culleton's *In Search of April Raintree (Halbblut: Das Mädchen April Raintree)*. A collection of interviews with a number of high-calibre Canadian Native authors (*Contemporary Challenges: Conversations with Canadian Native Authors*) and another with Native individuals from the USA (*Achte Deines Bruders Traum! Gespräche mit nordamerikanischen Indianern 1978–1985*) who talk about Native identity, education, residential school experiences, political struggles, oral tradition, religion, and Christianization continue his formidable catalogue of scholarly work. As contributor to the appropriation and impostor debate that started in the late 1980s, Hartmut Lutz has discussed cultural imperialism and cultural appropriation. Together with two Saskatoon colleagues, he created a collection of writings of, and about, his late friend, the political activist and writer Dr. Howard Adams, entitled *Howard Adams: Otapawy!* Last but not least, Hartmut Lutz has, together with a group of Greifswald students, translated, edited, and put into historical context the diary of Abraham Ulrikab (*The Diary of Abraham Ulrikab: Text and Context*), one member of a group of eight Inuit from Labrador who were taken to Germany to be exhibited in zoos and public shows and who all died within a few months. Abraham Ulrikab wrote this diary in Inuktitut, which was translated into German by a German missionary in Labrador. In order to return this intellectual property to the Inuit, and because the Inuktitut original is now lost, they have translated the German version to English. His work does not end here however, as he has an ambitious project planned for the future: a comprehensive history of Native literature in Canada.

Hartmut Lutz has been honoured with various awards and scholarships that have enabled his research, among them the Harris German-Dartmouth

Distinguished Visiting Professorship in 2001 and in 2003, the John G. Diefenbaker Award—a prestigious endowment awarded by the Canada Council for the Arts. In addition to his scholarly work, Hartmut Lutz has ambitiously, tirelessly and enthusiastically "spread the word" through his teaching of Native Studies in Germany, Poland, Denmark, Finland, Iceland, Norway and Spain, and at North American colleges and universities including Deganawidah-Quetzalcoatl University in Davis, California; the First Nations University of Canada in Regina, Saskatchewan; Dartmouth College in Hanover, New Hampshire; and Widener University in Chester, Pennsylvania. Through his teaching, he has "hooked" numerous students and colleagues in the field. Many a German high school teacher of English graduating from the universities of Köln. ln, Osnabrück, and Greifswald has developed a sensibility to Native issues, culture, and literature in their teaching curricula. Similarly, many former students continue their research in this field and contribute to the academic discourse, including seven finished dissertations in Native studies so far (Briese, Eigenbrod, Episkenew, Erf, Haible, Knopf, and von Berg). Hartmut, in the name of all the people who learned and benefitted from your work, I wish to most gratefully thank you and dedicate this book to you!

I would also like to thank each of the contributors to this edition, who, with their research, have enhanced the conference and the book so well. Nearly half of the participants were from Canada and came up with the travel costs themselves; so thanks to all of you for taking the effort to raise this money and to travel to Germany. This book would not have become what it is without the very energetic and supportive work of Lee Blanding, who, as participant of the International Council for Canadian Studies Internship Program, spent six months at the department of North American Studies at the University of Greifswald and helped with qualitative advice, research, and formal editing; thanks Lee. I also wish to take this opportunity to thank Foreign Affairs Canada, the Canadian Embassy in Berlin, and the German Association for Canadian Studies (GKS) for generously supporting the conference and the publication of this edition.

Kerstin Knopf
Greifswald, December 2006

Kerstin Knopf

Introduction: Aboriginal Canada Revisited

Today, at the beginning of the 21st century, it has been more than five hundred years since the "discovery" and beginning of the European conquest of North America—the "new world." The term new world itself betrays the European ideological framework of the late 15th and 16th century that included the desire to explore another "new" non-European world, the divine and political right to the conquest and domination thereof, and the perceived European cultural and intellectual supremacy over the inhabitants of this 'new' continent. Colonial European discourse deemed them uncivilized primitives—noble, and mystical wo/men of the woods at best, and cruel, bloodthirsty, and cannibalistic savages at worst.

The perspective of the original inhabitants of this new world is a different one. Wherever first contact took place, the Europeans must have appeared as strange and 'other' to Aboriginal people, not fathomable as equal human beings. To Native people, their world was not new and they, in all probability, did not feel discovered. The European first-comers must have seemed visitors, even pitiful at times, who had to be fed and helped through the first years, as in the case of the Jamestown settlement. In the situation of contact between two worlds unknown to each other, who has the right to define his/her own culture as the norm and the encountered world as the 'other' and inferior culture? The Europeans' self-proclaimed natural, divine, and political right to invade these new territories quickly solved that question. The pervasive usage of terms like "discovery" and "new world" betrays contemporary power relations in North America and the ongoing ideological and discursive fortification of Eurocentric cultural and political hegemony, as can be seen in the recently released feature film *The New World* (2005).

Today, the Native inhabitants of Canada and the USA are still internally colonized peoples. They belong to the Fourth World—nations subjected to imperial domination within the nations that colonized their traditional territories (Manuel/Posluns 1974). In Canada, politics, economics, judicial and social systems, museum culture, arts, print media, and electronic media have remained dominated by the Canadian mainstream throughout the 20th century. However, Aboriginal[1] visual artists, intellectuals, politicians, lawyers, entrepreneurs, writers and other professionals have been claiming positions in these areas and in the past few years have begun to actively participate in the Canadian mainstream and in the shaping of public discourses. This volume looks critically at the state of Aboriginal Canada at the beginning of the new millennium and asks: How much has the status of Aboriginal peoples within the nation and their relation to mainstream Canada changed? How much have Aboriginal people been able to decolonize Canadian institutions and public discourses? What has been achieved on the way toward emancipation of Aboriginal Canada?

Aboriginal Protest against Colonial Domination

The "Oka crisis" in Quebec in 1990 certainly was the trigger for a new Aboriginal self-consciousness and a turn in Canadian-Aboriginal relations. It was the climax of a series of events that started with Trudeau's unsuccessful White Paper in 1969 and escalated to the bringing down of the Meech Lake

Accord in 1990 by Elijah Harper. On the one hand, the Mohawks' stand for their sacred burial ground fortified antagonisms between mainstream and Aboriginal Canada. This was largely due to the overreaction of the Quebec provincial, and later the federal government, as well as the criminalization of the initially peaceful blockaders, not to mention the biased Canadian media coverage of this conflict, and the media construction of the "gun-toting, militant, terrorist Mohawk warriors" (Guthrie Valaskakis 2005, 39). However, the conflict did force the Canadian public and government to acknowledge Canadian colonial history and the subsequent political, economic, and social domination of Aboriginal people.

The crisis over the Pines and a golf course evolved to a crisis in Aboriginal-Canadian relations and compelled Canada to address Aboriginal issues on a much broader and more serious basis. Again and again simmering conflicts over Aboriginal and treaty rights became politicized on the national level, with Aboriginal people protesting continuous violations of their rights and exploitation of their resources by mainstream industry.

In the spirit of Oka, they have asserted and defended Aboriginal and treaty rights—from continual large-scale road blockades against logging and clear-cutting of forests in British Columbia[2] and Grassy Narrows, Ontario,[3] to the occupation of Ipperwash Provincial Park in Ontario in 1995, where they protested against the destruction of a sacred burial ground at the park and strove to initiate negotiation for the return of traditional lands at nearby Camp Ipperwash. Similarly, the Mi'kmaq in Burnt Church, New Brunswick, exercised their rights to fish for lobster, which resulted in a war-like confrontation between the Mi'kmaq, local non-Aboriginal fishermen and federal fishery officers in 2000, and became, in a sense, the first "Oka" of the 21st century. The Aboriginal protest that began in February 2006 against a residential development on unceded Six Nations land in Caledonia, Ontario, is the latest example of such struggles, and they point to ongoing problems over jurisdiction and a lack of clarity over Aboriginal title. Moreover, they reveal that Aboriginal Canada is moving in a direction where historical injustices and colonial atrocities are fought with self-assured determination.

Aboriginal Statistics

At the turn of the century, the colonial legacy still rendered Aboriginal people the most distressed group in Canadian society, afflicted by large-scale poverty, residential school traumas, low education levels, high incarceration and suicide rates, family violence, poor health, and almost epidemic diabetes, alcoholism, and substance addiction.

The majority of the Aboriginal population lives at or below the poverty line. In major Western cities, the rate of Aboriginal people below the poverty line is four times that of the non-Aboriginal population (INAC "Health and Social Indicators," online). As of 1991, the general Aboriginal unemployment rate was 19.4 percent, almost the double of that of non-Aboriginal Canadians. Just 53.2 percent of registered Indians on reserve and 42.7 percent of registered Indians off-reserve aged between fifteen and sixty-four were in the labour force, while 43.5 percent Inuit and 40.9 percent Métis participated. The average Aboriginal income was only 70.1 percent of that of the non-Aboriginal population, with the average income of registered individuals on reserves being only 43.5 percent of the national average (INAC "Highlights," online). In 2001, the average income of registered Aboriginal individuals rose slightly to 44.9 percent of that of the Canadian reference population (Cooke/Beavon/McHardy, 8–9, online). As of 1996–97, only 71 percent of Aboriginal students remained in school until grade twelve (INAC "Health and Social Indicators," online), although between 1981 and 2001, the gap in educational attainment between registered Indians and other Canadians was reduced from 0.23 to 0.11 (Cooke/Beavon/McHardy, 9, online).

Life expectancy for registered Indians in 2001 was roughly six years lower than that of other Canadians (Cooke/Beavon/McHardy, 8, online). In 1990, suicide rates of registered Indian youth (aged fifteen to twenty-four) were eight times the national average for men and five times for women, whereas the registered Indian birth rate was twice the Canadian average (2.7 percent to 1.3 percent). Infant mortality rates had fallen but still doubled that of the national rate.

Sixty-two percent of registered Indians aged fifteen and over stated that alcohol abuse is a problem in their communities, and 48 percent saw drug abuse as an issue. Twenty-two percent of First Nations youth reported as chronic solvent users and came "from homes where there is financial hardship, neglect, family conflict or child abuse" (INAC "Health and Social Indicators," online). By 1995, AIDS/HIV infection was increasing for the Aboriginal population, while it was decreasing for the rest of the Canadian population. Thirty-nine percent of Aboriginal adults perceived family violence, including sexual abuse and rape, as social problems in their communities.

Incarceration rates of Aboriginal people were five to six times the national average, reaching 80 percent in the Northwest Territories and 50 percent in the Prairie Provinces. The rates for urban Aboriginal perpetrators were four and a half times higher than those for non-Aboriginal perpetrators in Calgary and twelve times higher in Regina and Saskatoon. In 1996–97, 20 percent of houses on reserves were overcrowded. Nevertheless, it is encouraging that 92 percent of Aboriginal people aged fifteen and over stated that they have someone to call for help, 54 percent reported being involved in some form of physical activity and social sport, and 51 percent said that they participate in traditional activities (INAC "Health and Social Indicators," online).

The research of the Royal Commission on Aboriginal People (hereafter RCAP) has revealed, "The overall policy process with respect to Aboriginal peoples has improved somewhat in the last decade; however, it has been a decade of small gains in the normal (non-constitutional) policy process set against a 200-year history of losses" (RCAP, vol. 1, part 2, chapter 8, "False Assumptions," online).

The Canadian government itself expressed to the UN Human Rights Committee in 1999 that the situation of Aboriginal people is "'the most pressing human rights issue in Canada.' Despite this admission, Canada has been repeatedly criticized by UN treaty bodies [...] for its failure to implement comprehensive reforms identified as critical by its own Royal Commission on Aboriginal Peoples" (Amnesty International 2004, 34-35, online). Canada was one of the four settler nations (including Australia, New Zealand, and the USA) that voted against the United Nations Declaration on the Rights of Indigenous Peoples when it was adopted on 13 September 2007, apparently motivated by a refusal to acknowledge Indigenous sovereignty rights.

This refusal is a slap in the face of Aboriginal Canada, and it renders the recommendations of the RCAP and the small gains in policy processes almost ludicrous. In this light, the above statement by the Canadian government and other declarations of good intentions appear as plain *maquillage*.

Aboriginal Political Emancipation and Legal Battles

Despite the distressing state of Aboriginal Canada and the official nonrecognition of Indigenous rights, more progress is becoming visible at the onset of the new millennium. We can witness a growing Aboriginal presence in and influence on many aspects of Canadian society. In terms of politics and Aboriginal governance, for example, the Assembly of First Nations (AFN), in its function as representative of Aboriginal people at a national level, has the power to profoundly influence Canadian Aboriginal politics; it recently negotiated a financial compensation package for each residential school survivor. Likewise, the Native Women's Association of Canada (NWAC), and provincial and territorial organizations such as the Federation of Saskatchewan Indian Nations and the Inuit Tapiriit Kanatami, are potent lobbyists and negotiation partners.

In addition to political developments, Aboriginal protest, and seminal court decisions, the creation and financing of the Royal Commision on Aboriginal Peoples in 1991, as well as the government's formal response to the release of its five-volume report – *The Report of the Royal Commision on Aboriginal Peoples* – in 1996, the *Statement of Reconciliation*, negotiated with Phil Fontaine, grand chief of the AFN (Miller 2000, 388) in 1998, were achievements of determined political work of Aboriginal organizations. Additionally, the number of Aboriginal politicians in Ottawa is on the rise: 2.9 percent of Canadian Members of Parliament are Aboriginal, which almost corresponds to the Aboriginal population in Canada (roughly 3 percent). Of the 108 current senators, seven are of Aboriginal ancestry (6.7 percent), and of the 308 current members of the House of Commons, five are Aboriginal (1.6 percent) (Parliament of Canada "Aboriginal Senators," online; Parliament of Canada "Aboriginal Members," online). As early as 1974, the Honourable Ralph Steinhauer became the first Canadian Aboriginal lieutenant governor in Alberta, in 2002, the Honourable James K. Bartleman was appointed the first Aboriginal lieutenant governor of Ontario (Lieutenant governor of Ontario "The First Aboriginal," online) and in October 2007, the Honourable Steven L. Point was sworn in as the first Aboriginal lieutenant governor of British Columbia.

The first modern land claim settlements are the *James Bay and Northern Quebec Agreement* (JBNQA) and the *Northeastern Quebec Agreement* (NEQA), signed in 1975 and 1978 respectively. They granted the Quebec government, the James Bay Energy Corporation, Hydro-Québec, and the James Bay Development Corporation rights to the development of water resources and, in turn, self-government and participation in environmental and social protection, education, and wildlife harvesting regulation to the Cree, Inuit, and Naskapi of Northern Quebec (INAC "The James Bay," online).

Similarly, the Nisga'a Treaty, ratified between 1998 and 2000, secures the Nisga'a control over roughly 2000 square kilometres of their traditional land in British Columbia, and jurisdiction over forest management, taxation, law enforcement, and self-government (Government of British Columbia "The Nisga'a," online).

The creation of Nunavut in 1999, the first and only Aboriginal territory of Canada, followed the *Nunavut Land Claims Agreement* of 1992, the largest land claim settlement in Canada to this day. Nunavut has an area of 2 million square kilometres and 85 percent of its population is Inuit. This self-government agreement provides the Inuit, among other things, with a share of resource royalties, wildlife harvesting rights, and increasing responsibility for economic development, land management, and environmental protection. As the only Aboriginal territorial government, the government of Nunavut applies Inuit traditional knowledge and values, philosophies, attitudes, and practices of

Nunavut's Inuit majority in its decision-making processes (Privy Council Office "The Creation," online; Government of Nunavut "Government of Nunavut," online).

Canadian Aboriginal politics are highly conditioned by legal decisions; many Aboriginal-Canadian conflicts, unfortunately, have not been negotiated between the Canadian government and Aboriginal officials, but were fought in provincial courts and the Supreme Court of Canada. Many of these legal battles were successes for Aboriginal people and led to recognition of Aboriginal and treaty rights. Major landmark decisions include the Delgamuukw decision of the Supreme Court of Canada in 1997. It turned out to be a mammoth victory, not only for the Gitxzan but for all future Aboriginal litigants and claimants, because it "upheld the validity and appropriateness of oral history evidence, ordering courts in future to take it into consideration along with other form of evidence" (Miller 2000, 373).

That this ruling was a pivotal turning point in legal decision-making becomes obvious in view of the earlier land claim negotiations of the Gitxzan and Wet'suwet'en nations of British Columbia in the Delgamuukw case in 1991 before the Supreme Court of British Columbia, where they sought "to achieve recognition of ownership, jurisdiction and self-government of their traditional territories from the governments of Canada and B.C." (Gitxzan Chiefs Office "The Delgamuukw Court Action," online). In 1991, they brought forward oral accounts about the boundaries of trails through their traditional territories as evidence of physical occupation, and the court dismissed their arguments using racist language (Cruikshank 1994, 413; Lischke/McNab 2005, 7; Miller 2000, 372–373).

Another landmark was the 1999 Marshall decision of the Supreme Court, which granted the Mi'kmaq Donald Marshall Junior the right to fish eel for commercial purposes, thereby acknowledging the 1760 treaty with the Mi'kmaq in Nova Scotia. Like the Delgamuukw decision, it was relevant for future decisions, as the court ruled that Aboriginal and treaty rights must not be narrowly defined on the basis of written records and treaty documents, but that oral accounts and the historical context of treaty negotiations must be weighted equally with written records (Lischke/McNab 2005, 7–8). The Delgamuukw decision of 1997 was also instrumental for its expansive definition of Aboriginal title (373). Seminal court rulings that clarified Aboriginal rights were, for example, the 1973 Calder case and the 1996 Van der Peet, Gladstone, and N.T.C. Smokehouse Ltd. decisions (Government of British Columbia "Landmark Cases," online).

Economics, Health and Social Situation

The most pressing issue is the intolerable economic situation of many Aboriginal people. The RCAP states, "The legacy of history is economies that are dependent rather than self-reliant and that offer labour force participation rates, incomes and levels of business development far below Canadian averages. In the absence of new approaches to economic development, this situation is not likely to improve" (RCAP, vol. 2, part 2, chapter 5, "Economic Development," online).

Aboriginal economic development is of utmost importance for Aboriginal local, provincial, and territorial government bodies, and some local Aboriginal economies are on their way to becoming flourishing and successful. There are now a number of Aboriginal-owned companies, such as Umingmak Supply Ltd. in Rankin Inlet, Nunavut; Aboriginal Engineering Ltd. in Yellowknife; First Nations OWEESTA; Air Inuit and Air Creebec; as well as joint-venture companies like Tahltan Nation Development Corporation (TNDC) and Northern Resource Trucking (NRT) (Natural Resources Canada "Community Capacity," online). First Nations casinos; independent media production companies, such as Big Soul productions, Blue Hill Productions, and Turtle Night Productions; and a variety of Aboriginal-run holiday resorts, art galleries, and design businesses bear witness to this positive economic development.

Health and social services for First Nations on-reserve and Inuit are the responsibility of the federal government, while provincial and territorial governments provide services elsewhere. This has created a gap in service provision for urban Aboriginal people, who have access to general health

-care programs, which "are not necessarily aligned" to their specific needs "or delivered in a culturally appropriate way" (Amnesty International 2004, 20, online). The RCAP assessed the health-care situation as follows:

- Aboriginal people with serious illnesses were often sent, unaccompanied, to distant medical facilities for treatment in strange and sometimes hostile environments.

- In their own communities, Aboriginal people were offered health care services that had no foundation in local values, traditions or conditions. At worst, a few were forced (or convinced) to suffer invasive medical procedures, including sterilization.

- Virtually all providers of health and social services were non-Aboriginal, many with little interest in the cultural practices or values of their Aboriginal clients. Encounters were often clouded by suspicion, misunderstanding, resentment and racism.

- Indigenous healing skills and knowledge of herbal medicines and other traditional treatments were devalued by medical personnel and hidden by those who still practised or even remembered them. Much knowledge was eventually lost (RCAP, vol. 3, chapter 3, "Health and Healing," online).

In order to curb the problem of inappropriate health-care programs and health-care administrators' inability to meet the culture-specific needs of Aboriginal patients, the federal government has promoted and supported the transfer of control of health service programs to First Nation and Inuit organizations. By 1996, 141 First Nations communities had adopted administrative responsibility for health-care services, and 237 were in the pre-transfer process (INAC "Aboriginal Health," online). One example of such a transfer is the creation of the Ahousaht Holistic Society in a remote community in Clayoquot Sound in 1990, where social and health services are provided in an

Aboriginal, holistic, and culturally appropriate way, as discussed in Marlene Atleo's essay later in this volume.

Earlier examples of Aboriginal communities taking control over health services, without the encouragement of the federal government, are the Kateri Memorial Hospital Centre in Kahnawake, established in 1955; the first independent Aboriginal health and service boards as part of the 1975 *James Bay and Northern Quebec Agreement* (JBNQA); the 1979 Labrador Independent Health Commission (LIHC); and the 1981 Alberta Indian Health Commission (AIHCC). Anishnawbe Health Toronto became the first multi-service urban community health centre in 1988, providing services to off-reserve, non-status, and Métis Toronto residents (RCAP, vol. 3, chapter 3, "Health and Healing," online).

A 2003 study estimated that as a result of poverty, substance abuse, and family problems Aboriginal children are four to six times more likely than non-Aboriginal children to be removed from their families and placed in foster care (Amnesty International 2004, 16–17, online). In 1996, the RCAP report stated that the rate of Aboriginal children in the care of public agencies was six times that of children from the general population (RCAP, vol. 3, chapter 2, "The Family," online). This situation is all the more reason to transfer child welfare responsibilities to Aboriginal organizations and communities. In 1981, the first agreement to transfer authority for child welfare services to an Aboriginal agency was signed, and since then the delegation of child welfare responsibilities to First Nations and Métis communities has been progressively increased. Most Aboriginal child welfare agencies have placement protocols that prioritize placement of children first within the extended family, second with Aboriginal members of the community, third with other alternative Aboriginal caregivers, and last with non-Aboriginal foster parents. Aboriginal placement agencies have been able to considerably expand the number of Aboriginal foster parents, while provincial agencies have had difficulties in locating appropriate caregivers. "Despite these welcome reforms, and modest successes in placing children in Aboriginal foster homes, which have stemmed the flow of Aboriginal children out of their communities and nations," the RCAP contends, "It is evident that services to care for neglected and abused children are insufficient to repair the ills plaguing Aboriginal families" (RCAP, vol. 3, chapter 2, "The Family," online).

Colonial Representation and Aboriginal Self-Representation

Physical and empirical realities condition the state of Aboriginal Canada to a large degree, but epistemologies, such as the representation of Aboriginal cultures in various discourses, condition this state on another level. Gretchen Bataille explains,

> Native Americans have been mythologized by anthropologists and ethnographers, by tourists and the tourist industry, and through art and literature. Both the popular media and scholars have participated in creating the 'Indian that never was.' Indian images reflected the creators of those images more than the people themselves, and the images have changed through time, with portrayals of vanishing Indians, primitives, half-breeds, squaws, warriors and militants taking their turn in the foreground during various historical periods. (Bataille 2001, 4)

The creation of the various "ideological Indians," according to the taste and wants of the day, and the professed notion of Aboriginal Cultures as inferior to European ones was not simply a random exercise but had tangible motives. "Representations of others are usually social and political acts," as Ute Lischke and David McNab pointedly state (Lischke/McNab 2005, 3). With the construction of the "bloodthirsty savage," the "untameable man of the wilderness," the "noble and vanishing Indian," the "tawny temptress" and "squaw drudge," and the "heathen idolaters," Eurocentric discourses legitimized conquest and colonial politics that latently carried 'manifest destiny' ideology. Moreover, they created colonized minds that would not question the status quo.

Aboriginal people would appropriate and internalize this Western construct about their cultures through historical, cultural, political, ethnic, aesthetic, academic, and sociological discourses. They would see themselves through the colonizer's ideological framework and produce collective identities that were alienated from Aboriginal cultures and philosophies. Colonialist ideas and principles disseminated through discourse practices influenced their thought structures, ideas about their own cultures, and their understanding of power relations, subsequently producing colonized minds. Stuart Hall summarizes, "They had the power to make us see and experience ourselves as 'Other'" (Hall 1989, 71). Lischke and McNab also make the point that Aboriginal peoples always represented themselves within Aboriginal contexts, but that recipients of these self-representations were ignorant and/ or negligent of these contexts and replaced them with the European imperial context (2005, 4). Consequently, all Aboriginal representation, whether Aboriginal or European/Western, is read/seen within a Eurocentric context.

By the end of the last century, a substantial group of Aboriginal scholars, authors, artists, and media-makers had begun to represent Aboriginal cultures themselves within Aboriginal frameworks. With their works, they offer Aboriginal contexts for representation, they decolonize Aboriginal representation from within, and they create discourses responsive to the existing Eurocentric ones. They battle the mental adaptation to colonialist thought structures and work toward the decolonization of those minds.

In academia, for example, Olive Patricia Dickason, the renowned Canadian Aboriginal historian, writes Aboriginal historiography from an Aboriginal perspective and Armand Garnet Ruffo explores and explains the mind set of the impostor Archie Belaney and creates poetical Aboriginal-Canadian history. Similarly, Georges E. Sioui authors Wendat history and philosophy and revises Aboriginal-Canadian history from a new perspective; hence the title *For an Amerindian Autohistory*. Janice Acoose traces the genesis of Aboriginal women's stereotypes through discourses and discusses Aboriginal women's images in Canadian literary texts. Hereditary Chief Umeek/Richard E. Atleo introduces an alternative Aboriginal philosophy—"Tsawalk," based upon Nuu-chah-nulth oral traditions—that combines Western and Aboriginal perspectives. With her edition *Looking at the Words of our People*, Jeannette Armstrong offers vistas on Aboriginal literature and the publishing industry from Aboriginal perspectives and inscribes Aboriginal literary criticism into academic discourse. Writer Thomas King and playwright Tomson Highway enter the ivory towers of non-Aboriginal academia by presenting the prestigious Massey and Charles R. Bronfman lectures. In the same vein, Aboriginal poets, playwrights, and novelists have contributed substantially to Canadian literature: Maria Campbell, Beth Cuthand, Lee Maracle, Monique Mojica, Daniel David Moses, Drew Hayden Taylor, Richard Wagamese, Emma Lee Warrior, and Jordan Wheeler—to name but a few—add to those already mentioned. Playwright Ian Ross was the first Aboriginal author to win the Governor General's Award for Drama in 1997 with *fareWel.*

Within the media-scape, Aboriginal Canada has begun to take a stand. There are a considerable number of Aboriginal newspapers, such as *Windspeaker, Grassroots News, Nunatsiaq News, Raveneye, Anishinabek News,* and the magazines *Aboriginal Voices* and SAY *Magazine.* Aboriginal radio stations, such as Native Communication, Inc. (NCI) in Winnipeg, which reaches 95 percent of the province of Manitoba, and Aboriginal Voices Radio, based in Toronto and soon to be nationwide, have been successful. They broadcast news, popular music, event coverage and announcements, and cultural programming, partly in Aboriginal languages, in order to "counteract some of the effects of mass culture and to encourage their people to work through problems using the media as a means of communication," in the words of David McLeod, CEO of NCI Winnipeg.[4]

The Aboriginal Peoples Television Network (APTN), which began as TeleVision Northern Canada, has a national broadcast license and is the first television channel created and operated by Aboriginal people in the world. With this television channel, Aboriginal mediamakers now have an outlet where they can contest the "ideological and imaginary Indian" constructed in Western media discourse; they have qualitative and quantitative control over the representation of Aboriginal culture, politics, languages, and traditions. The production of Aboriginal electronic media presents contrastive perspectives in terms of politics and culture, applying program policies that are shaped according to the respective local and cultural needs. On the one hand, APTN and Aboriginal radio stations create sites for intercultural understanding and cultural exchange. On the other, the production and broadcast of self-controlled, anticolonial media works toward a gradual decolonization of North American airwaves.

Similarly, Canada's documentary landscape, largely carried by the National Film Board of Canada and shaped by Griersonian documentary and film ethics, allows an increasing number of Aboriginal filmmakers, such as Gil Cardinal, Barb Cranmer, Loretta Todd, Brion Whitford, Christine Welsh, and others, to represent Aboriginal culture, history, politics, art, and contemporary issues from within their ranks. Without doubt, Alanis Obomsawin is the pioneer among Aboriginal documentarists; her seminal *Kanehsatake: 270 Years of Resistance* and a number of her other documentaries have helped to provide insight into Aboriginal viewpoints within political conflict. Similarly, the works of other independent filmmakers, such as Marjorie Beaucage, Maria Campbell, Doug Cuthand, Lloyd Martell, Evelyn Poitras, and Rodger Ross, contribute to a documentary mediascape that looks at Aboriginal issues from an inside perspective.

The Canadian feature film industry is more reluctant than Europe and Hollywood to issue biased cinematic historiography such as *1492: Conquest of Paradise* (1992) and *The New World* (2005)—films that do nothing more than legitimize colonial conquest and fortify 'manifest destiny' ideology. The Canadian cinematic equivalent, *Black Robe* (1991), attempts to be historically accurate and lacks the other two films' heroic conquest mythology and sweet sexualized exoticism. Nevertheless, told from the European perspective, it remains within the ideological framework of the historical "inevitability" of colonial conquest and its divine legitimation. Aboriginal filmmakers tap into the industry and create self-controlled dramatic films that represent Aboriginal history and contemporary reality. The CBC two-part-series *Big Bear* (1998) and the three-hour feature film *Atanarjuat: The Fast Runner* (2001) were the first major films directed and produced by Aboriginal people in Canada to receive national and international attention. Independent dramatic films like *Honey Moccasin* and *Suite: Indian* by Shelley Niro; *Bearwalker* and *Johnny Tootall* by Shirley Cheechoo; *Laurel* and the television series *Moccasin Flats* by Jennifer Podemski and Laura Milliken; *Tkaronto* by Shane Belcourt; as well as numerous short films created by young Aboriginal talent contribute to a fast-growing Canadian Aboriginal film discourse. These films usually screen at national and international (Aboriginal) film festivals and, unfortunately, do not receive major distribution, so the Canadians do not have much knowledge of what is going on in the Aboriginal film industry. Nevertheless, Aboriginal media creators are moving ahead, thus initiating Aboriginal *self*-representation as well as correcting and responding to mainstream/colonial (*mis*)-representation.

Aboriginal art, be it sculptures, paintings, installations, photography, or cartoons, has come to be a major pillar of Canadian art. Artists like Rebecca Belmore, George Littlechild, Jim Logan, Gerald McMaster, Kent Monkman, Shelley Niro, Edward Poitras, Jane Ash Poitras, Bill Reid, Allan Sapp, Alfred Young Man, and Lawrence Paul Yuxweluptun come to mind. Art works of Carl Beam, Bob Boyer, Norval Morrisseau, and Joane Cardinal-Schubert and a substantive collection of Inuit art, for example, belong to the permanent collection of the National Gallery of Canada in Ottawa. Art seems to be the form of Aboriginal cultural expression most easily accepted as constituting part of the Canadian national self-image—it has become a standard practice to exhibit Aboriginal art in official buildings and at international fairs and festivals presenting Canada. A practice that promotes Aboriginal art and economically benefits the artists.[5] Yet this open embrace of Aboriginal art seems at times to be a tokenizing act, an act that could mitigate collective colonial guilt and gloss over more pressing political and economic issues that need to be acted upon.

Aboriginal Canada Revisited

This collection of articles helps to assess the state of Aboriginal Canada at the beginning of the new millennium: to highlight areas where colonial legacy still takes its toll, to acknowledge the variety of Aboriginal cultural expression, and to demonstrate where Aboriginal and non-Aboriginal people are starting to find common ground.

The first five contributions are concerned with Aboriginal politics, education, and health and social issues. Providing a historical perspective, Marlene

Atleo outlines the effects of colonization and the subsequent disadvantages and marginalization of Aboriginal people, as well as the devastating assimilation policies enforced through the residential school system. With the example of the Ahousaht Holistic Society in Nuu-chah-nulth Territory at Clayoquot Sound in British Columbia, she delineates the development of decolonized legal, health, and social services. Informed by government-mandated service structures and an Indigenous value system, it embeds the people in their own culture, traditions, territory, and history. Falko Brede also takes issue with the status of Aboriginal health care and discusses the reform proposals of the Romanow report—most of which, however, have not (yet) been implemented for various reasons. To improve the health of Aboriginal people in Canada, he argues for increased funding and a new infrastructure for health service provision, including the training of more Aboriginal physicians. Moreover, he calls for politicians from various areas within the health-care sector to "develop a concerted approach to improve the social determinants of health." Antino Spanjer and Mansell Griffin discuss the Nisga'a treaty as one of the first major successful land claim negotiations where Aboriginal people gained self-governance and control a part of their traditional lands. The Common Bowl concept—"all Nisga'a lands and resources are common property"—is the basis of modern Nisga'a administration and Nisga'a philosophy; it underlies the negotiation process and the treaty, and it is thus defined as both traditional philosophy and political tool.

In her article on Métis scholarship, Tricia Logan makes clear that Métis face a double marginalization: because they do not belong to the mainstream centre on a national level and because they do not belong to the pan-Aboriginal centre, Métis scholarship faces the dilemma that it has a weaker position than First Nations scholarship in competing for funding and research. It is often lumped in with the latter as First Nations-informed research methods are dominant and applied to Métis research as well. Consequently, Logan calls for progressive research methods, "separate from both mainstream and Aboriginal methods, taking into account Métis history and culture." Barbara Walberg addresses the need to decolonize education and to reform the Aboriginal post-secondary education system in order to create a new paradigm of learning that integrates Indigenous knowledge and more traditional Western knowledge. Drawing on Paulo Freire's pedagogy for people recovering from oppression, the Negahneewin College of Indigenous Studies at the Confederation College of Applied Arts and Technology in Thunder Bay developed a degree-level program in Indigenous Leadership that draws from both world views and combines theoretical and experiential, active learning. In this way, the college explored one of the ways of "moving forward in the future which are more inclusive, equitable and sustainable."

Other contributions are concerned with the presentation and representation of Aboriginal people in public, literary, and art discourses. Geneviève Susemihl takes issue with the "imaginary indian" and analyses the representation of Aboriginal people in contemporary German children's and juvenile literature and finds that these books almost exclusively repeat devastating clichés that are being widely, and in part, successfully, contested in other literary areas. The stereotypical image of Aboriginal peoples among German children and youth is that of a Plains Indian, a "mounted warrior and buffalo hunter, who rides through the endless prairies, wearing war paint and a headdress, dwells in a tipi and sits around the campfire in a dignified manner, smoking a peace pipe ... and frequently brandish[es] tomahawks." This image is derived from, and in turn reinforced in, numerous books and toys that usually repeat and make use of the pan-Indian Plains warrior of the past, thereby homogenizing the hugely diverse Native American and Native Canadian cultures. Such books hardly go beyond the "Pan-Indian Mash" (Lutz 2002, 53), do not address contemporary Native experience, issues, and problems, and thus freeze the "Indian" in a suspended past. Moreover, such books treat "Indianness" as a role in society and not as ethnic identity. Susemihl demands that the children and youth book and toy industry reconsider their view and representation of Native cultures, that "parents and teachers must become aware of their role in facilitating and preventing the development of prejudices," and that extensive empirical studies on the effects of stereotypes in racist children and youth literature be undertaken.

Siobhán Smith discusses practices of inclusion and exclusion of Aboriginal art works in the Canadian artscape and specifically those of the McMichael

Canadian Art Collection (hereafter MCAC) in Kleinburg, Ontario. First Nations and Inuit Art, having been one cornerstone of the collection's exhibition until the 1990s, was later consciously neglected in the collection's mandate and acquisition policies; furthermore, legislative changes to the *McMichael Act* that oversees these practices were implemented. This article offers an in-depth analysis of MCAC's legislated collecting policies and the changing status of Aboriginal art from inclusion to exclusion in its mandate, which Smith defines as cultural racism. She calls for a revision of MCAC's legislation and mandate and for a return to a long-term commitment to Aboriginal art because "[i]nstitutions such as the MCAC, the Art Gallery of Ontario, and the National Gallery of Canada, with their commitment to collect Canadian artworks and their status as cultural authorities, are central in the construction of Canadian art history and culture." Consequently, as Smith makes clear, these institutions need to "move beyond Eurocentric definitions of 'Canadian Art.'"

The four articles on Aboriginal literature deal with various strategies of representing Aboriginal culture and experience. Nancy Grimm discusses Aboriginal drama and its decolonizing potential, and in particular Drew Hayden Taylor's *Only Drunks and Children Tell the Truth*. She outlines the play's complex reflection of Nativeness, its capacity to decolonize the mind, as well as the semantics and functions of irony that carry the play's intercultural dialogue. She concludes "Taylor's play is based on versatile approaches towards both Native and non-Native cultures and calls for both sides to question simplistic perceptions of either the Native or the non-Native culture." Also using Aboriginal humour and irony as reference points, Eva Gruber introduces and theorizes "restorification"—the way in which texts may reintroduce history to the realm of story and expose the constructedness of history in a humorous way—and looks at a variety of Aboriginal texts that contest Euro-Canadian historiography and employ Aboriginal-informed restorification. Humour in these texts acquires a didactic, diplomatic, disruptive, confrontational, and/or therapeutic function. Contemporary Aboriginal literature revises the grand narratives of Western supremacy and Western historiography with lots of humour, as Gruber says, thus "freeing both Native and Euro-Canadian readers from their conventional frames of reference and the corresponding historical paradigms in which Western superiority appears as a given, while Native perspectives are still repressed or relegated to the margin."

Thomas Rüdell examines constructions of the Native in Canadian mainstream texts before venturing into analysis of Thomas King's texts as responding to these constructions. King breaks down stereotypes of the Indian frozen in the past, of the stoic and monosyllabic Indian, of the spiritual Indian, and of the Indian as victim by creating modern Native characters as strong members of contemporary communities, who balance the traditional and modern, the reservation and the urban, the spiritual and physical, and the serious and humorous/subversive. Thus, he metadiscursively comments on and ridicules Western discourses; the reader "is thus compelled by King to revise his or her own view of the Native." Besides humour and subversive play, the integration of oral tradition is another characteristic feature of Aboriginal literature. This tradition also informs Ruby Slipperjack's texts as explored by Katarzyna Juchnowicz. She holds "In the post-colonial literary world of Native North America, storytelling has taken the direction of storywriting, marking thus a new means for the preservation and continuation of oral traditions." With implicit and explicit references to oral storytelling interwoven into her characters' lives, Slipperjack illustrates how this tradition is still strongly persistent in contemporary Aboriginal lives on various levels and how "storytelling adjusts to the passing of time." In this way, Juchnowicz says "Contemporary Native North American fiction is a hybrid fiction, consisting of both the oral and the written."

The next two contributions examine the (opposing) contemporary print media discourses about and by Aboriginal people. In an article outlining the results of a 2004 study of representations of Aboriginal child welfare services in the news in British Columbia, Robert Harding notes that between 1993 and 2003 there was an overall increase of stereotypes in the news coverage, an emergence of new stereotypes as well as an overwhelmingly negative and hostile tone. This phenomenon "has occurred during a time in which Aboriginal people have increasingly been challenging the status quo and taking control over institutions that have a decisive impact on their lives."

Aboriginal autonomy over child welfare poses a challenge to hegemonic Euro-Canadian values and views to which the print media has reacted. Harding argues that only comprehensive background information about the history and context of such complex issues would "create a genuine opportunity for news audiences to understand the structural inequality facing Aboriginal people in general as well as specific Aboriginal attempts to seek redress." In her study of Aboriginal news discourse, specifically the newspapers *First Nations Messenger* and *Anishinabek News,* Steffi Retzlaff crystallizes several Aboriginal discursive models, derived from traditional discourses, that are employed in order to project Aboriginal cultural values into contemporary discourses and to positively (re)affirm Aboriginal identities. These properties include cultural address markers, the concept of 'family' and emphasis on future generations, the appeal to authority by referring to elders as well as references to the medicine wheel. Other discursive strategies are engagement with Aboriginal humour and the introduction of Aboriginal terminology in order to construct collective and national identities and to counter hegemonic discursive practices. She concludes, "The evolving status and acknowledgement of Aboriginal people as distinct peoples with a right to self-determination, land and resources, and treaty concessions is mediated through" this "powerful Aboriginal discourse in Canada."

Finally, Kerstin Knopf's article takes issue with the despicable economic situation of many Indigenous women in Canada, the constant threats of misogynist violence that they face, and the horrific cases of sexist- and racist-motivated murders outlined in Amnesty International's Human Rights report "Stolen Sisters." It analyzes how this topic is reflected in Audrey Huntley's documentary *Go Home, Baby Girl,* Nathaniel Geary's feature film *On the Corner,* and Jennifer Podemski's short drama film *Laurel.* Knopf concludes, "By translating these issues into film, the filmmakers battle against the public apathy and indifference towards the plight of Indigenous sex trade workers," and "they appeal to the public Canadian conscience and call for awareness about the human tragedies that happen daily at the margins of a rich First World country."

Endnotes

1 Following the *Constitution Act* of 1982, the term "Aboriginal" as used in this book includes non-status and status Indians, Inuit, and Métis.

2 In February 2006, environmental organizations, the forest industry, Aboriginal communities, and the Provincial Government of British Columbia reached an agreement on the future forestry use and protection of the Great Bear Rainforest region, stretching from the North of Vancouver Island to the Alaska Panhandle (Hume "Years of tension end with 'unique' B.C. rain forest deal," online).

3 Since December 2002, Grassy Narrows band members maintain a continuous blockade camp at Slant Lake. They also "sometimes show up unannounced on other bush roads, blocking logging equipment with their vehicles, campfires and bodies. These 'roving blockades' usually last a few days and disrupt timber operations with their unpredictability" (Christian Peacemaker Teams – "Grassy Narrows [Asubpeeschoseewagong]," online).

4 This quotation is taken from a speech by David McLeod on NCI Winnipeg at a CRTC hearing in Toronto in 2003.

5 Cf., for example, Bill Reid's sculpture at the Canadian Embassy in Washington, D.C.

Bibliography

Acoose, Janice. (1995). *Iskwewak. Kah' Ki Yaw Ni Wahkomakanak: Neither Indian Princesses Nor Easy Squaws.* Toronto, ON: Women's Press.

Armstrong, Jeannette, ed. (1993). *Looking at the Words of our People: First Nations Analysis of Literature.* Penticton, BC: Theytus Books.

Atleo, Richard E. (2004). *Tsawalk: A Nuu-chah-nulth Worldview.* Vancouver, BC: University of British Columbia Press.

Bataille, Gretchen M. (2001). "Introduction." In *Native American Representations: First Encounters, Distorted Images, and Literary Appropriations,* ed. Gretchen M. Bataille. Lincoln, NE: University of Nebraska Press, 1–7.

Cruikshank, Julie. (1994). "Oral Tradition and Oral History: Reviewing Some Issues." *Canadian Historical Review,* 75:3, 403–418.

Dickason, Olive Patricia. (2002). *Canada's First Nations: A History of Founding Peoples from*

Earliest Times. 3rd ed. Don Mills, ON: Oxford University Press Canada.

Guthrie Valaskakis, Gail. (2005). *Indian Country: Essays on Contemporary Native Culture*. Waterloo, ON: Wilfrid Laurier University Press.

Hall, Stuart. (1989). "Cultural Identity and Cinematic Representation." *Framework: A Film Journal, 36*, 68–81.

Highway, Tomson. (2003). *Comparing Mythologies*. Charles R. Bronfman Lecture. Ottawa, ON: University of Ottawa Press.

King, Thomas. (2003). *The Truth about Stories: A Native Narrative*. Massey Lecture. Toronto, ON: Anansi Press.

Lischke, Ute, and David McNab. (2005). "Introduction." In *Walking a Tightrope: Aboriginal People and Their Representations*, eds. Ute Lischke and David McNab. Waterloo, ON: Wilfrid Laurier University Press, 1–17.

Lutz, Hartmut. (2002). "'Indians' and Native Americans in the Movies: A History of Stereotypes, Distortions, and Repression." In *Approaches: Essays in Native North American Studies and Literatures*, ed. Hartmut Lutz. Augsburg: Wißner Verlag, 48–61.

Manuel, George, and Michael Posluns. (1974). *The Fourth World: An Indian Reality*. Don Mills, ON: Collier-Macmillan Canada, Ltd.

Miller, J. R. (2000). *Skyscrapers Hide the Heavens: A History of Indian-White Relations in Canada*. 3rd ed. Toronto, Buffalo, London: U of Toronto Press.

Ross, Ian. (2002). *fareWel*. 6th ed. Winnipeg, MB: J. Gordon Shillingford Publishing Inc.

Ruffo, Armand Garnet. (1996). *Grey Owl: The Mystery of Archie Belaney*. Regina, SK: Coteau Books.

Sioui, Georges E. (1992). *For an Amerindian Autohistory*, trans. Sheila Fischman. Montreal, QC and Kingston, ON: McGill-Queen's University Press.

Filmography

Belcourt, Shane, dir./writ./prod. *Tkaronto*. The Breath Films.

Beresford, Bruce, dir. (1991). *Black Robe*. Writ. Brian Moore. Alliance Communications.

Cheechoo, Shirley, dir./writ. (2000). *Bearwalker [Backroads]*. Girls from the Backroads Productions.

———, dir. (2005). *Johnny Tootall*. Writs. Shirley Cheechoo and Andrew Genaille. Kitchen Sink Entertainment.

Cardinal, Gil, dir. (1998). *Big Bear*. Prod. Doug Cuthand. Writs. Gil Cardinal and Rudy Wiebe. Télé-Action Bear Inc./Big Bear Films.

Kunuk, Zacharias, dir. (2001). *Atanarjuat: The Fast Runner*. Writs. Paul Apak Angilirq and Norman Cohn. Igloolik Isuma Productions.

Malick, Terrence, dir./writ. (2005). *The New World*. New Line Cinema.

Niro, Shelley, dir./writ. (1998). *Honey Moccasin*. Turtle Night Productions.

———, dir./writ. (2005). *Suite: Indian*. Shelley Niro Production.

Obomsawin, Alanis, dir./co-prod./writ. (1993). *Kanehsatake: 270 Years of Resistance*. National Film Board of Canada.

Podemski, Jennifer, and Laura Milliken, prods. (2001). *Laurel*. Writ. Patrick Tenascon. Big Soul Productions.

———, prods. (2004–2006). *Moccasin Flats*. Dirs. Dwayne Beaver, Gil Cardinal, Lorne Cardinal, Stacey Steward Curtis, and Rob King. Writs. Darrell Dennis, Penny Gummerson, Karen Hill, Laura Milliken, Jennifer Podemski, and Patrick Tenascon. Big Soul Productions, Television series.

Scott, Ridley, dir. (1992). *1492: Conquest of Paradise*. Writ. Roselyne Bosch. Canal and Droits Audiovisuels.

Internet Sources

Amnesty International. (October 2004). "Canada: Stolen Sisters – A human rights response to discrimination and violence against Indigenous women in Canada." http://www.amnesty.ca/stolensisters/amr2000304.pdf [consulted February 12, 2006].

Christian Peacemaker Teams. "Grassy Narrows (Asubpeeschoseewagong)." http://www.cpt.org/gallery/view_album.php?set_albumName=grassy_narrows [consulted December 11, 2006].

Cooke, Martin, Daniel Beavon, and Mindy McHardy. (October, 2004). "Measuring the Well-Being of Aboriginal People: An Application of the United Nation's Human Development Index to Registered Indians in Canada 1981–2001." http://www.ainc-inac.gc.ca/pr/ra/mwb/mwb_e.pdf [consulted March 24, 2006].

Gitxsan Chiefs Office. "The Delgamuukw Court Action: A Brief History." http://www.gitxsan.com/html/delga2.htm [consulted March 24, 2006].

Government of British Columbia. "Landmark Cases." http://www.gov.bc.ca/arr/treaty/

landmark_cases.html#aboriginal_rights [consulted March 24, 2006].

Government of British Columbia. "The Nisga'a Final Agreement." http://www.gov.bc.ca/arr/negotiation/nisgaa/docs/newbrief.htm [consulted March 24, 2006].

Government of Nunavut. "Government of Nunavut." http://www.gov.nu.ca/Nunavut/English/about/cg.pdf [consulted March 24, 2006].

Hume, Mark. (2006, 8 February). "Years of tension end with 'unique' B.C. rain forest deal." *Globe and Mail*, A7. http://monado2.blogspot.com/2006/02/unique-agreement-saves-rain-forest-in.html [consulted March 24, 2006].

Indian and Northern Affairs Canada. "Aboriginal Health: What Health Coverage Is Available?" http://www.ainc-inac.gc.ca/pr/pub/ywtk/index_e.html#hcca [consulted March 24, 2006].

Indian and Northern Affairs Canada. (October 1995). "Health And Social Indicators." http://www.ainc-inac.gc.ca/gs/soci_e.html [consulted March 24, 2006].

Indian and Northern Affairs Canada. "Highlights of Aboriginal Conditions 1991, 1986: Demographic, Social and Economic Conditions." http://www.ainc-inac.gc.ca/pr/sts/hac/hilts_e.pdf [consulted March 24, 2006].

Indian and Northern Affairs Canada. "The James Bay and Northern Quebec Agreement and the Northeastern Quebec Agreement." http://www.ainc-anac.gc.ca/pr/info/info14_e.html [consulted March 24, 2006].

Lieutenant Governor of Ontario. "The First Aboriginal Lieutenant Governor." http://www.lt.gov.on.ca/sections_english/history/history_middle_frame/history_facts.html [consulted March 24, 2006].

Natural Resources Canada. "Community Capacity Building." http://www.nrcan.gc.ca/mms/socíprac/cap_e.htm [consulted March 24, 2006].

Parliament of Canada. "Aboriginal Members of the House of Commons." http://www.parl.gc.ca/information/about/people/key/Aboriginal.asp?Language=E&Hist=Y&leg=H [consulted March 24, 2006].

Parliament of Canada. "Aboriginal Senators." http://www.parl.gc.ca/information/about/people/key/Aboriginal.asp?Language=E&leg=S [consulted March 24, 2006].

Privy Council Office. "The Creation of Nunavut." http://www.pco-bcp.gc.ca/AIA/default.asp?Language=E&Page=federation&Sub=TheCreationofNunavut [consulted March 24, 2006].

The Royal Commission on Aboriginal Peoples. (Updated 2006, August 2). "False

Assumptions and a Failed Relationship." Vol. 1, part 2, chapter 8. http://www.ainc-inac.gc.ca/ch/rcap/sg/sg21_e.html#67 [consulted March 24, 2006].

———. (Updated 2006, August 2). "The Family." Vol. 3, chapter 2 http://www.ainc-inac.gc.ca/ch/rcap/sg/si4_e.html#2.3%20Child%20Welfare%20Reform [consulted March 24, 2006].

———. (Updated 2006, August 2). "Health and Healing." Vol. 3, chapter 3. http://www.ainc-inac.gc.ca/ch/rcap/sg/si12_e.html#1.%20The%20Burden%20of%20Ill%20Health [consulted March 24, 2006].

———. (Updated 2006, August 2). "Economic Development." Vol. 2, part 2, chapter 5. http://www.ainc-inac.gc.ca/ch/rcap/sg/sh70_e.html#1.2%20Contemporary%20Aboriginal%20Economies [consulted March 24, 2006].

HEALTH
SOCIAL ISSUES
POLITICS

Marlene Atleo

De-colonizing Canadian Aboriginal Health and Social Services from the Inside Out: A Case Study—The Ahousaht Holistic Society

Introduction

The colonization of Aboriginal bodies and life-worlds has been a long-term assimilation project that began legislatively with the British North America Act (BNA Act) of 1867—to which the Indian nations whose inherent rights had been recognized in the Royal Proclamation of 1763 were not party (Morse 1999, 16–19). Subsequent to the BNA Act, the new settler government in 1876 drafted the Indian Act, which gave the federal government fiduciary responsibility for Indian nations. Without consultation, the Indian Act turned Native people into wards of the state, excluding Inuit and Métis by definition (Morse 1999). It was not until the revisions to the Indian Act in 1952 that a few small restrictions in wardship were lifted (Henderson, online), an interesting parallel to the post-WWII zeitgeist that demanded democracy for the oppressed. While the Indian Act was not repealed, established BNA relationships were acknowledged and a new relationship was proclaimed through the Constitution Act of 1982, which repatriated the Canadian Constitution from Great Britain. In this Act, Aboriginal and treaty rights of First Nations, Inuit and Métis were recognized and guaranteed equally to men and women in the Dominion of Canada. In light of almost 400 years of engagement with English and French forces, resulting in Aboriginal colonization, this reversal of assimilationist policy is very recent. Consequently, the current process of decolonization of the life-world of Canadian Aboriginal people is an arduous process both for Aboriginal and non-Aboriginal people alike—arduous because it requires a mutual self-consciousness about the challenges created by the very processes of colonization that, in turn, requires a cooperative deconstruction of the institutionalizations of that process and a creation of institutional forms that are more appropriate and mutually beneficial. The cultural dialectic (Read 1995) that exists for First Nations today involves the interplay between Aboriginal cultures and the overlay of imposed culture. The processes involved in the renegotiation of First Nations' social institutions in the context of reclaiming the self-determination of their cultural life-worlds is painstakingly difficult, because such processes reach into the dark shadows of historical assumptions and motives and require a conscious probing by all citizens to begin to come to terms with the past in a good way.

This paper is a product of my observation of and participation in a de-colonizing process that involved the creation of the Ahousaht Holistic Society in British Columbia and describes some of my experiences as a participant in the healing journey of one Canadian Aboriginal community.

In this instance, de-colonizing includes claiming a rightful place through the testimonies of members and stories of Nuu-chah-nulth history that celebrates and affirms the survival of a people. Through the remembering of what was, there is an opportunity to see more clearly what is, to intervene in the oppressive forces, and move to revitalize cultural practices in the context of social and health programming in ways that reconnect people to the past in the realities of the present. Such a process comes about through a critical interrogation of present institutions through the input of Indigenous scholarship and activism that represents the vision of a people in a grounded manner. Taking charge in such a way requires a reframing of social issues that reflects a local cultural reality. It is illuminated by a critical consciousness of colonialization in ways that permit the restoration of life-worlds remembered, as well as a return to the territories and a repatriation of artifacts scattered through colonial edicts. A process of democratizing and networking can permit gender barriers to fall, and in the process of naming, protect and recreate a cultural legacy steeped in millennia. By sharing this project of decolonization with Indigenous people around the world, it can be consolidated, strengthened, and constructed in a mutually beneficial way.

As a member of the Ahousaht First Nation, Nuu-chah-nulth, I embarked on post-secondary studies late in life, with a view to discovering ways and means to untangle the oppression of mainstream programs and institutions in a manner that values Nuu-chah-nulth culture and history. Post-secondary education permits a glimpse into the formal life-world of mainstream society on which social policy and programming of the federal and provincial governments is based. The theories, histories, and methodologies that form the assumptions of federal and provincial programming are, for the most part, understandable only with advanced education in the disciplines, wherein strategic cultural and scientific knowledge becomes revealed. I was determined to bring the understandings achieved through my undergraduate and master's degree studies in Family Science for service in the community, and to participate in community rebuilding. Consequently, from January 1995 to September 1996, I acted as the executive director and program coordinator of the Ahousaht Holistic Society.

The Colonization

The colonization of Aboriginal bodies and minds has been a long-term strategy of successive governments in Canadian territories to assimilate First Nations people (Aboriginal Healing Foundation, online). Over more than a hundred years, federal Canadian government policy favoured settlers and excluded Aboriginal people from legal, social, political, and economic life in ways that privileged the Canadian majority while disadvantaging and assimilating Aboriginal people (Ing 2001).

The systematic nature of the assimilation process has been illustrated by the role of the residential schools (Miller 1996; Ing 2001). A mental health worker, who encountered and documented child abuse as she was dealing with clinical presentations of addiction and family dysfunction in a community in British Columbia in 1987, exposed the enormity of the criminal legacy of the residential schools experience in the courts of British Columbia (Aboriginal Healing Foundation, 3–4, online). The exposure of mass post-traumatic symptoms in the Aboriginal population of Canada became even more evident through the Royal Commission on Aboriginal People (1996) and would become known as "The Residential School Syndrome" (Brasfield 2001, online).

Almost twenty years after the 1987 study, we have begun to understand the insidious nature of the assimilationist project legislated by successive Canadian governments and policies actively supported by churches that targeted Aboriginal children through the residential school mandate (RCAP, online). While not all who participated in the project as individuals may have contributed personally to the abuses (Clifton, online), the positions they held in the institutions as administrators, supervisors, teachers, and staff all contributed to perpetuate a system of cultural genocide by and through the policies of the Government of Canada and with the aid of mainstream churches.

The colonizing process, intended to assimilate Aboriginal people, seems to have had almost the opposite effect in that it created an "apartheid system" that no magic wand or act of legislation, such as the federal government's 1969 White Paper, could rescind (Brasfield 2001, online). The "apartheid system" of the Indian Act (Henderson, online) does not just concern the creation of physical reserves, but also the creation of psychic reserves in the hearts and minds of tens of thousands of Aboriginal people. Children who experienced residential schools as "frightening, intrusive and alien" would respond to school attendance with "fear, helplessness, passivity, and expressed or unexpressed anger" (Brasfield 2001, online). For these children, education and learning was compromised by over-arousal, reactivity, and general distress.

For many, such experiences were generalized as feelings of hyper-vigilance and the inability to concentrate, especially in non-First Nations social settings, resulting in wakefulness, irritability, anger, and an exaggerated startle response (Brasfield 2001, online). To remedy the unbearable psychological trauma resulting from time spent in residential schools, many Aboriginal people have chosen to "self-medicate" with drugs, alcohol, and other destructive diversions in an attempt to quiet internal demons.

Until the late 1980s the trauma of residential schools was probably the best-kept secret in the First Nations communities—communities with very high rates of alcoholism, incarceration, suicide, and family violence and breakdown (Cooper 1995, 209). For the newly developing First Nations tribal authorities such dysfunction created administrative problems and consequently, tribal authorities began to question how community dysfunction was related to the oppression of the colonial agenda. From 1992 to 1994 the Nuu-chah-nulth Tribal Council (NTC) conducted a study to ascertain how its members were impacted by their residential schools experiences (Nuu-chah-nulth Tribal Council 1996; Read 1995). The results were stark and startling. Of the ninety-six individuals interviewed, up to 85 percent indicated that they had suffered some form of abuse (physical, sexual, emotional, spiritual). More than half indicated that they felt they needed some sort of healing process to move beyond these effects and be able to function more normally (Nuu-chah-nulth Tribal Council 1996, 201). The facts of systematic abuse were similar to those identified by Chrisjohn, Young, and Maraun (1997) and the Royal Commission (RCAP, online). With these results in hand, the NTC moved to develop a de-colonizing strategy to address the dysfunction within its membership as part of the process of community and nation building.

Nuu-chah-nulth Tribal Council Strategy

The de-colonizing of Aboriginal bodies and minds requires a strong de-colonizing methodology (Smith 1999) and a cultural revitalization. Decolonization demands a reformation of First Nations institutions and life-worlds that permit reclamation of self-government in response to federal and provincial programming and policy. One such response to the devolution of social and health services was the evolution of tribal councils in the early 1970s, made up of linguistically and geographically related peoples, or First Nations, in Canada. One such tribal council began as the West Coast District Council in the shadow of the Alberni Residential School on the Tseshaht Reserve in Port Alberni, British Columbia, which evolved into the Nuu-chah-nulth Tribal Council. As a result of political action and agreements to devolve service delivery by the Department of Indian and Northern Affairs and Medical Services Branch of Health Canada, the NTC began to grow as an Aboriginal service delivery organization (Read 1995). A gradual shift of service delivery to tribal councils was a first step, and subsequently Alternative Funding Arrangements (AFA) were instituted that required the provision of minimum prescribed services and audit requirements for five-year terms (Read 1995, 311). This arrangement permitted programs to be delivered in more appropriate and culturally sensitive ways. The process was incremental, with audits, annual reports, and multi-year service plans in place as safeguards for the process. In 1988 the Nuu-chah-nulth Health Board began operation after years of negotiations. The province also participated with NTC by delegating responsibility for Child Welfare to the Usma Nuu-chah-nulth Family and Child Services Program (Read 1995, 311). The increased autonomy of the tribal council was a cause for pride and permitted community members to become knowledgeable and skilled in the financial and program management of their social and human service delivery.

Within these tribal organizations cultural revitalization elicited latent cultural strategies of self-governance. In British Columbia, such cultural strategies were amplified through the modern-day treaty process beginning in the early 1980s. The modern-day treaty process (Indian and Northern Affairs Canada, online) required that the Nuu-chah-nulth traditional governance structures of chieftainships be reconstituted. Without the chieftainships and their traditions of *Hahuuthi*,[1] the claims to lands, resources, and Aboriginal rights based in the Constitution made no sense: the minute details of chiefs and lineages of each First Nation in the Nuu-chah-nulth Tribal Council needed to be known in order to articulate treaty claims. Historical governance mechanisms and roles were evoked and resurrected in the treaty process, which breathed life into the outlawed and consequently half-forgotten life-worlds of First Nations cultural knowledge and expression. The process elicited histories, stories, songs, dances, symbolism, architecture, protocols, rituals, governance structures (*Hahuuthi*), genealogies, territorial boundaries, as well as potlatch activities, whaling traditions, Indigenous technologies, medicines, and environmental knowledge (e.g., E. R. Atleo 2004, M. R. Atleo 2001, M. R. Atleo 2006, online) to buttress the claims of Nuu-chah-nulth-aht. So long hidden, the Huupakwanum Tupaat or Treasures of the Nuu-chah-nulth Chiefs were made manifest as a demonstration of authority of nationhood and self-determination in a celebration of "the beauty and complexity of Nuu-chah-nulth culture" (Hoover 2000, 3). The life-world of Nuu-chah-nulth people came into public view.

Ahousaht First Nation

At the community level, another response to decolonization was the development of the Ahousaht Holistic Society in the remote and rugged wilderness of Clayoquot Sound in the territory of the Nuu-chah-nulth (formerly called Nootka), a Wakashan-speaking people. The development of the Holistic Society was a unique initiative by the community of Ahousaht. The initiative was an opportunity to build capacity through a praxis that was informed by engagement with social and health services mandated by the government, while simultaneously based in an Indigenous value system that ties these people to their own territory and history. It was a unique initiative because it permitted Ahousaht people to decide on the weight of the Indigenous values in the context of the government-mandated practice. Satisfying mandated, government-funded practice through culturally and locally valued expression was a first step to self-management of the social and health services in Ahousaht.

The Ahousaht First Nation is an amalgamation of several Kelsmaht and Ahousaht lineages that inhabit much of the central and northern part of Clayoquot Sound on the West Coast of Vancouver Island in British Columbia,

Canada. Three primary hereditary chiefs and an assortment of lineage heads from the territories make up the core of the traditional governance system. Ahousaht is the largest of the fourteen First Nations that make up the Nuu-chah-nulth Tribal Council. The main village of the Ahousaht people is located at Maaqtuusiis on Flores Island fifteen miles, as the crow flies, north of Tofino. The First Nation has twenty-nine small reserves scattered around the Sound and treaty claims for a large part of the territory (Government of British Columbia, online). The remote village of Ahousaht is populated by just less than half of its registered membership of approximately 1800 people. Access to the village from Tofino, where the nearest highway starts, is by boat or plane. Many members live "away from home" in the urban centres of Vancouver Island, the Lower Mainland and Seattle, Washington.

The Ahousaht Band Council, which operates under the Indian Act, manages more than two hundred housing units, a mini mall, a co-op grocery store, a marine ways where fishing boats can be repaired, woodlots, shellfish harvesting licenses, and other sea food enterprises. The Ahousaht Band is one of the four First Nations of the geographic Central Region of the fourteen First Nations that make up the Nuu-chah-nulth Tribal Council. As a member of the Central Region, Ahousaht is party to a funding arrangement, the Interim Measures Agreement (IMA). The IMA is a type of cash advance in the treaty process whereby the Government of British Columbia has provided funding for local economic development such as tourism and small businesses. The fund is monitored by the Central Region Board, which is made up of representatives of the local First Nations as well as local non-Aboriginal membership (Iisaak Forest Resources, online). The Ahousaht Band Council has been involved in joint ventures with forest companies such as Interfor and McMillan & Bloedel to expand value-added and sustainable development in the forestry sector according to the spirit of the Scientific Panel Report on the Clayoquot Sound (Iisaak Forest Resources, online).

Ahousaht First Nations Fisheries manages the enhancement programs in the territory by clearing and restocking salmon streams. An eco-tourism initiative by the women of Ahousaht, "Walk the Wild," in partnership with the West Coast Wilderness Committee (Jones 1996, online), has brought much interest and business from as far away as Europe and Asia. The Ahousaht Geographic Identification System (GIS) training, sponsored by Ecotrust Canada (2006), provides up-to-date research support and documentation for treaty negotiations as well as other current mapping and research requirements.

The community has been on the hydro and telephone grid since the mid-1980s, when it was a thriving fishing and logging community. A community school that now serves almost 300 students opened its doors with 150 students in 1986. The First Native Elementary-Secondary School is now an important institution that offers understanding of mainstream society and hope for the youth through education (August "Construction," online). First Nations administrative staff, teachers, and teachers aides from the community are the mainstay of the school. North Island College delivers on-site access to college-level programming via an instructor and broadband Internet access (August "Meandering," online). Two gyms provide the youth with opportunities to play basketball for most of the year and host visiting teams from around the province. Organized social and athletic activities for youth play an important role in making this island community agreeable to the rapidly expanding population of young people.

Ahousaht Holistic Society

The Ahousaht Holistic Society today stands proudly in the middle of the Maaqtusiis village site on Flores Island as an organization developed to meet community service needs in an evolving Canadian Aboriginal self-government process. Twenty years ago the idea of integrated, holistic community service programming centred on child welfare was a cultural vision.

This vision of an integrated village-based service centre was articulated by Pat Little, who served on the elected council. He was charged by the Ahousaht First Nation with examining the repatriation of children removed by the Ministry of Social Services of the Province of British Columbia since the 1952 amendments to the Indian Act (Henderson, online). The 1952 amendments to the Indian Act gave provinces jurisdiction over the welfare of First Nations children and ultimately resulted in the "60's Scoop" in which more than 11,000

First Nations children were adopted mainly by non-Aboriginal parents, who social workers believed could provide better lives than their natural parents (Aboriginal and Indigenous Social Work, online; Armitage 1999, 61–77). By the mid-1980s, these children were a concern of communities who were trying to rebuild their families and relationships.

Pat Little was well experienced in the management of educational programs for First Nations children. As a child, Little had attended Christie Residential School on nearby Meares Island. The Christie School was run by priests of the Order of Mary Immaculate. He was himself an administrator, working closely with the federal funding agency, Department of Indian Affairs and Northern Development, at two Catholic church-run residential schools, St. Mary's in Mission, B.C. and the New Christie School near Tofino. The closing of New Christie in 1983 brought Pat Little closer to home, so that he eventually was able to bring some of the social capital in administration he had gathered during his career back into the community development framework in Ahousaht.

Devolution of Social and Health Services

The vision of integrated social and health services were very much a part of the yearning for self-government in the community, a yearning that harkened back to the cultural integration of institutions, identity, and relationships. Health services were usually provided by the Medical Services Branch of Health Canada, and doctors and nurses would visit the community several times a week to hold clinics. In addition, there was a local community member trained by Medical Services to provide first-aid, hygiene, and prevention education and act as a liaison for medical needs of the community.

The Community Health Representative (CHR) was the point person for health programming. In the mid-1960s, CHRS were trained to bring basic hygiene and health promotion to First Nations communities across Canada. The CHR model follows the tradition of lay health providers in under-serviced areas internationally, such as the "barefoot doctors" of the Chinese Cultural Revolution (Keane/Nielsen/Dower, online). In time, the role of the CHR had evolved to include drug and alcohol addictions counselling, first-aid, triage, midwifery, personal counselling, help with medical travel documentation, and infant checkups (McCulla, online).

Little's dream of integrated services allowed him to participate with the development of USMA (Precious Ones), a program of child welfare services of the Nuu-chah-nulth Tribal Council. The development of a Nuu-chah-nulth child and family service program began with research in the 1970s and continued through the hiring of a consultant in 1985 with funding from the Department of Indian and Northern Affairs in order to develop an agreement with the provincial and federal governments. A process began involving meetings, negotiations, and workshops to educate the community and the leadership about the duties of child and family services, and of issues of child abuse and neglect. The Nuu-chah-nulth First Nations needed to understand the law that the USMA workers would be enforcing. A program manager was hired and a person from the Ministry of Child and Family Services was seconded by the province to assist in the details of the preparation for the transfer. After a three-year process the child welfare program, including child protection, was delegated to USMA in 1987 (Read 1995, 311). This was the first step in bringing holistic, culturally appropriate, and legally legitimate child and family services to the Nuu-chah-nulth communities of the West Coast.

Moreover, these measures initiated the process of rebuilding the life-world of Nuu-chah-nulth families a little at a time. Pat Little participated to try to make the transition real and meaningful and he began by hiring an individual to trace the lineages of Ahousaht families. The family trees provided data about the missing children that had been lost to the child welfare and residential school system and could identify some of the Precious Ones, facilitating a search that could bring them home. This project was remarkable because Pat Little contracted an industrial engineer to develop actual trees that, in one case, consisted of a forty-five-foot roll of blueprint paper that charted the various relationships in one extended family over six generations.

Pat's vision of a society that could provide integrated services within the community grew. He struck a board and incorporated the Ahousaht Holistic Society in 1990. As with the USMA program development, the board hired a consultant who proceeded to write a counselling program to train counsellors for the community. Funded by Employment Canada for workers on unemployment, its sought to train a cadre of counsellors that could work in the community as a team to provide support for the community health worker in her role as addictions counsellor and family support worker. By 1994 the counselling program was running and several Ahousaht members had graduated. Sadly, Pat's health was failing and he succumbed to liver failure and passed away the same year.[2]

To maintain the momentum after Pat's passing, the board sought the assistance of Bruce Gunn, the United Church minister serving Ahousaht at the time. Gunn, who was secretary-treasurer of the AHS, wrote some successful proposals to secure program funding and keep the society viable. In 1995, the board hired me, a community member living away from home, because I had a graduate degree in family science that could provide legitimacy in the position. Funded by grants from the federal government for health services and the provincial government for family violence services, the articulation of the Ahousaht Holistic Society as an organization began. The mandate was to build an organization by merging and managing programs that would provide social and health services to serve the community in a more integrated and culturally respectful manner. The board had an informal agreement with the band council to consolidate the social programs in the community. The Native justice worker, drug and alcohol counsellor, and the family support worker who worked with the USMA social workers from NTC were relocated from the band office and other venues around the community to a central location, the old health clinic, under the auspices of the Ahousaht Holistic Centre.

Within six months of my arrival the workers had been installed in the new location. The first order of business was to identify funding opportunities, and so proposals were written. The second order of business was to build a multidisciplinary team that could begin to meet the challenge of community care and transforming standard programs into culturally sensitive and valued services. We began to cultivate a team ethos with morning talking circles. The Native justice worker ran one of the cornerstone programs, funded by the provincial government. This person ran an anger-management program for probationers, as well as diversion programming for individuals that provided alternative sentences to reduce the likelihood of recidivism. By the fall, we had secured a small health grant from the provincial government to provide suicide prevention as well as drug and alcohol cessation support, as well as a major smoking cessation grant from Health Canada that provided secure funding for eighteen months. The Ahousaht Holistic Centre (AHC) was open for business with a range of services and programs by the fall of 1995.

Community Social and Health Services: Building a Paraprofessional Team

Central to the development of the AHC was the forging of a strong, multi-program team that could strategize holistically about how to deliver services and provide programming for the community as a whole. The mandate of the Ahousaht Holistic Centre Board was to provide programming that met funding standards and reflected the cultural life-world of the community but, more particularly, supported individuals and their families in overcoming their addictions. The team relied on program funding and a cadre of para-professional workers from the community who could provide vertically and horizontally integrated programming. The initial team consisted of a family support worker that worked with USMA social workers, a drug and alcohol counsellor that counselled clients and referred them to treatment centres, a Native justice worker who had probationers as clients, a child and youth worker that worked with the school, and myself as a program coordinator and manager to develop proposals for funding, set budgets, coordinate programs and liase with community and external organizations.

The family support worker had been in the counsellor-training program sponsored by the Ahousaht Holistic Society and she was a natural corner-stone for team development. The key to holistic strategizing lay in effective communication and division of labour within the team. The old health clinic featured a kitchen, which provided the setting for morning briefings about the upcoming day and debriefings about what had happened the previous night, and the kitchen table became the gathering place for personal and team development through mutual sharing. It was the site where we could work through issues that affected one or all of us and come to consensus on plans of action. The kitchen was not incidentally also a welcoming place for clients to enter a new form of service delivery.

The activity of the Native justice worker provides an example of vertically integrated programming. The Native justice worker had a background in criminology and legal assistance and received some task-specific training opportunities through the ministry that funded the program. She accompanied clients to court dates, mediated their relationship with the probation officers in Port Alberni, supervised their probation and documented community service hours. The worker delivered weekly anger-management sessions mandated for clients using curricula from the ministry, which she adapted to the local culture and standards. She was instrumental in investigating the potential utility of sentencing circles in which community members dealt with offenders after sentencing to restore social relationships. A community consultative committee was struck to work with her to explore the potential of alternative sentencing arrangements and work on the development of bylaws for the band council. The justice worker provided a valuable, local remedy for individuals involved with the criminal justice system that reduced the barriers to that interface. It was at this time that Ahousaht became part of a Tri-Partite Agreement with the provincial and federal government by which a Royal Canadian Mounted Police (RCMP) station was established in the community. Subsequently, the Native justice worker and the RCMP could cooperate to provide greater security for the community and better services for the clients.

The smoking cessation funding that was received from Health Canada under their Tobacco Demand Reduction Program provides an interesting example of vertical and horizontal service delivery. This grant was an opportunity to deliver addiction education and health promotion events, workshops, contests, and programming for eighteen months in a culturally sensitive as well as a community compatible manner. These initiatives were synchronized with other events and activities held in the community and provided by outside agencies. The AHC participated with the band council, the school, the RCMP, the churches and the college in a monthly planning session to coordinate community activities that assured timing and staging of events that were convenient and productive. Because we had funding we could also source other funding and in that period a lay counsellor was hired for the Prenatal Nutrition Program, and a family violence worker and a tobacco reduction worker were also hired. Additionally residential school workers, social workers, nurses, suicide prevention workers, and other social service resources from NTC visited the community regularly to provide services. The Ahousaht Holistic Centre team provided a means of managing service delivery in the community in a way that served the needs of individuals in the context of community social and cultural life-world (M. R. Atleo 1996).

The Challenge of Continuing Community Care: Conclusions

Building community service programming from the bottom up, as in this process of institutional decolonization, brings with it challenges that are to be expected in what Read (1995) has called the "dialectic of culture." Standard programs are contracted out through proposal processes and then delivered in communities that require the content to be translated into local community and cultural terms. The Ahousaht Holistic Society is an attempt to deliver meaningful and effective social and health programming in a remote and rural community for which standard programming, based in mainstream Canadian culture, does not make local sense. The AHS, serviced by local paraprofessionals, permits programs to be interpreted into local and cultural mores to better meet the need of individuals and families. By virtue of their lived experience, local people have a feel for the timing of scheduling and the type of services that would be amenable to the community and can thus provide more effective service. Integrated service delivery can be more time and cost effective. The AHS provides opportunities for employment for individuals who have begun to train in social and health services and who are willing to engage with further training and personal development. The community is empowered by witnessing its own members deliver services in the village and to other communities. Young people in the community have working role models in the social and health services that allow them to aspire to education in these fields. The team spirit of the AHC workers provides a mutual support that is emotional and instrumental, allowing them to work more effectively. With the lack of educational programs that provide front-line worker training specifically designed for Aboriginal social service workers, on-the-job experience and workshops were a front-line approach to meet the need for worker education. The institution of the AHS creates an ownership of service delivery for Ahousaht that is public and organized in a way that makes it recognizable and true to contemporary Ahousaht culture.

Colonization has taken its toll on the First Nations community, but initiatives such as the Ahousaht Holistic Society and Centre is an example of how decolonization can be achieved (and colonization de-constructed) from the inside out. The process of decolonization is painstakingly slow. Colonization has developed over hundreds of years and will not be quickly reversed. The decolonization process requires a lifetime of deconstruction of colonized habits of the mind, attitudes of the heart, and physical behaviours as well as a reclaiming of Indigenous spirit. It happens moment by moment, emotion by emotion, idea by idea, and relationship by relationship.

As First Nations take on the responsibility for the delivery of social and health programming, it provides an opportunity to understand the assumptions and the strategic agenda of the governance process. Once a part of the process, First Nations can negotiate change in its underlying assumptions and strategic direction. Participation permits First Nations to negotiate change in actions that do not reflect First Nations values. Participating in program evaluation permits First Nations to document what works and why as a means of providing feedback for the next program initiative. By being party to governance processes, the workers and board of directors of the Ahousaht Holistic Society have begun to see many of the hidden, strategic agendas of governance. In the cross-cultural interaction between Canadian professionals and First Nations people, the pathologising by Canadian professionals of First Nations people, their behaviours and attitudes, and their way of thinking and being has been the norm. As evolving partners in the process of social and health services development and delivery, such pathologising becomes inappropriate. Indeed, such expectations become reprehensible. First Nations people of Canada, such as the Ahousahts of Maaqtusiis, are equal to the task of becoming full participants in providing meaningful services for their communities and are, in fact, eager to embrace ways to express their values in partnership with federal and provincial social and health programming.

Endnotes

1 *Hahuuthi* (also spelled *Ha hoo thee*) is a Nuu-chah-nulth concept of ownership and management by which hereditary chiefs or eldest-born lineage males were stewards of cultural, physical, social, economic, and human resources of a specific territory centred on watersheds, fishing banks or other hunting grounds. *Hahuuthi* was the whole complex concept, examples of which may be an ancient song that is an oral history about a specific river, a dance that documents a specific event, an ancestor name that is used to remember a tradition, a game which suggests skills attributable to the lineage, a salmon river, a beach, a mountain, and the rights and obligations that are associated with such holdings in relation to the people of the lineage and those who are related.

2 Bruce Gunn, the United Church minister to Ahousaht, was a participant in the development of the Ahousaht Holistic Society and treasurer during my tenure there from 1994 to 1996. Gunn provided some of the details of the development of the society in a telephone conversation I had with him on January 7, 2006.

Bibliography

Armitage, Andrew. (1999). "Comparing Aboriginal Policies: The Colonial Legacy." In *Aboriginal Self Government in Canada*, ed. John H. Hylton. Saskatoon, SK: Purich Publishing, 61–77.

Atleo, Eugene Richard. (2004). *Tsawalk: A Nuu-chah-nulth Worldview.* Vancouver, BC: University of British Columbia Press.

Atleo, Marlene Renate. (1996). *Final Report: Narrative Report to the Board of the Ahousaht Holistic Society, June 28, 1996.* Ahousaht, BC: Ahousaht Holistic Society.

———. (2001). *Learning Models in the Umeek Narratives: Identifying an Educational*

Framework Through Storywork with First Nations Elders. Ph.D. dissertation, University of British Columbia.

Cooper, Mary. (1995). "Aboriginal Suicide Rates: Indicators of Needy Communities." *A Persistent Spirit: Towards Understanding Aboriginal Health in British Columbia*, eds. Peter H. Stepenson, Susan J. Elliot, Leslie T. Foster, and Jill Harris. Canadian Western Geographic Series. Vol. 31. Victoria, BC: University of Victoria, 205–222.

Hoover, Alan, ed. (2000). *Nuu-chah-nulth Voices, Histories, Objects and Journeys.* Victoria, BC: Royal British Columbia Museum.

Ing, Rosalyn. (2001). *Dealing with Shame and Unresolved Trauma: Residential School and Its Impact on the 2nd and 3rd Generation Adults.* Ph.D. dissertation, University of British Columbia.

Kelm, Mary Ellen. (1999). *Colonizing Bodies: Aboriginal Health and Healing in British Columbia, 1900–50.* Vancouver, BC: University of British Columbia Press.

Miller, James R. (1996). *Shingwauk's Vision: A History of Native Residential Schools.* Toronto, ON: University of Toronto Press.

Morse, Brandford W. (1999). "The Inherent Right of Aboriginal Governance." In *Aboriginal Self Government in Canada*, ed. John H. Hylton. Saskatoon, SK: Purich Publishing, 16–44.

Nuu-chah-nulth Tribal Council. (1996). *Indian Residential Schools: The Nuu-Chah-Nulth Experience. Report of the Nuu-chah-nulth Tribal Council Indian Residential School Study, 1992–1994.* Port Alberni, BC: Nuu-chah-nulth Tribal Council.

Read, Simon. (1995). "Issues in Health Management Promoting First Nations Wellness in Times of Change." In *A Persistent Spirit: Towards Understanding Aboriginal Health in British Columbia*, 297–330.

Smith, Linda Tuhiwa. (1999). *Decolonizing Methodologies: Research and Indigenous Peoples.* London: Zed Books.

Internet Sources

Aboriginal and Indigenous Social Work. "The 60's Scoop." http://www.aboriginalsocialwork.ca/special_topics/60s_scoop/index.htm [consulted January 25, 2006].

Aboriginal Healing Foundation. "Reclaiming Connections: Understanding Residential School Trauma among Aboriginal People." http://www.ahf.ca/assets/pdf/english/healing&trauma.pdf [consulted January 25, 2006].

Ahousaht First Nation. "Treaty Offer." http://www.nuuchahnulth.org/tribal-council/treaty/central/Ahousaht.html [consulted January 7, 2006].

Atleo, Marlene Renate. (2006, October 9). "The Ancient Nuu-chah-nulth Strategy of Hahuulthi: Education for Indigenous Cultural Survivance." In *The International Journal of Environmental, Cultural, Economic and Social Sustainability, 2:1,* 153–162 http://ijs.cgpublisher.com/product/pub.41/prod.114 [consulted October 29, 2006].

August, Denise. "Construction on Ahousaht's New High School May Start in 2006." *Hashilthsa.* http://72.14.207.104/search?q=cache:7ZI3ww2m-w0J:www.nuuchahnulth.org/tribal-council/hashilthsa/Oct605.pdf+new+school+%2B+greg+louie+%2B+wiwchar&hl=en [consulted January 7, 2006].

August, Denise. (2006). "Meandering through Maaqtusiis." *Hashilthsa.* http://72.14.207.104/search?q=cache:7ZI3ww2m-w0J:www.nuuchahnulth.org/tribal-council/hashilthsa/Oct605.pdf+new+school+%2B+greg+louie+%2B+wiwchar&hl=en [consulted January 7, 2006].

Brasfield, Charles R. (March 2001). "Residential School Syndrome." *BC Medical Journal. 43:2,* 78–81. http://www.bcma.org/public/bc_medical_journal/BCMJ/2001/march_2001/ResidentialSchoolSyndrome.asp [consulted January 25, 2006].

Chrisjohn, Roland, Sherri Young, and Michael Maraun. (1997). *The Circle Game: Shadows and Substance in the Indian Residential School Experience in Canada.* Penticton, BC: Theytus Books, 87. http://www.treaty7.org/document/circle/circle5.htm [consulted January 25, 2006].

Clayoquot Biosphere Trust. "A Political Space: Reading the Global through Clayoquot Sound." http://www.clayoquotbiosphere.org/ [consulted January 7, 2006].

Clifton, Rodney. "Residential Schools Story More Complicated: All School, Church Employees Shouldn't Be Tainted, Made to Pay for Others' Action." Frontier Centre for Public Policy. http://www.fcpp.org/main/publication_detail.php?PubID=568 [consulted January 25, 2006].

Ecotrust Canada. "Aboriginal Mapping Network." http://www.ecotrustcan.org/amn.shtml [consulted January 25, 2006].

Foxcroft, Deborah. "USMA Nuu-chah-nulth Family and Child Services (Cherished Ones, Precious Ones – The Children)." *A First Nations Model for Child Welfare and Community Collaboration, 4th Annual National Child Welfare Symposium Community Collaboration and Differential Response March 20, 2003.* Banff, AB. http://www.cecw-cepb.ca/DocsEng/

BanffFoxcroft.pdf [consulted January 7, 2006].

Friends of Clayoquot Sound. "What Is Clayoquot Sound?" http://www.focs.ca/clayoquot/index.asp [consulted January 7, 2006].

Government of British Columbia. "Nuu-chah-nulth Framework Agreement." http://www.bctreaty.net/nations_3/agreements/nuuchah_frmwrk.pdf [consulted January 7, 2006].

Henderson, William. (1985). "The Indian Act." R.S.C., c. I-5 (Annotated). http://www.bloorstreet.com/200block/sindact.htm [consulted January 25, 2006].

Iisaak Forest Resources: Central Region Board. http://www.iisaak.com/crb.html [consulted January 7, 2006].

Indian and Northern Affairs Canada. "Fact Sheet: Treaty Negotiations." http://www.ainc-inac.gc.ca/pr/info/trn_e.html [consulted January 25, 2006].

Jones, Susan. (1996, Summer). "Ahousaht Wild Side Heritage Trail." *Wilderness Committee Educational Report, 15:12.* http://www.wildernesscommittee.org/campaigns/rainforest/island/clayoquot/reports/Vol15No12/ahousaht [consulted January 25, 2006].

Keane, Dennis, Christine Nielsen, and Catherine Dower. "Community Health Workers and Promoters in California." http://72.14.207.104/search?q=cache:4BAHIBouCbUJ:www.futurehealth.ucsf.edu/pdf_files/Final_English_101104.pdf+community+health+representatives+%2B+barefoot+doctors&hl=en [consulted January 20, 2006].

McCulla, Karen. "A Comparative Review of Community Health Representatives' Scope of Practice in International Indigenous Communities." http://www.niichro.com/2004/pdf/international-chr-study.pdf [consulted January 25, 2006].

Nuu-chah-nulth Tribal Council. "Nuu-chah-nulth Tribal Council Vision and Mission." http://nuuchahnulth.org/tribal-council/welcome.html [consulted January 7, 2006]

The Royal Commission on Aboriginal People. Vol. 1, part 1, chapter 6. http://www.ainc-inac.gc.ca/ch/rcap/sg/cg6_e.pdf [consulted January 25, 2006].

Falko Brede

The Commission on the Future of Health Care in Canada: A Case Study of Aboriginal Health[1]

Introduction

Since the beginning of the 1980s, Canadian lawmakers have come under increasing pressure to reform the country's national health-care system. Because many Canadians greatly value their medicare system, it has been very difficult for them to agree on a way of instituting structural reforms. As such, in 2001 the federal government appointed Roy Romanow to head the Commission on the Future of Health Care in Canada (hereafter CFHCC). Romanow was asked to study the medicare system and recommend ways in which it could be improved.

In his final report, issued in 2002, Romanow, among other things, addressed the health status of Aboriginal people in Canada (First Nations, Métis and Inuit peoples). His recommendations, and their implications for Aboriginal people in Canada, are the subject of this paper. I will argue that Romanow's proposals were neglected by all levels of government because Aboriginal people, on the whole, did not embrace his concept of Aboriginal

Health Partnerships. Indeed, since the tabling of this report, no structural changes to health care, as it relates to Aboriginal People, have taken place.

In order to understand why Romanow made the recommendations that he did, it is first necessary to highlight the particular health issues and problems that face Aboriginal-Canadians. Then, after having analysed the reform proposals of the CFHCC, I will discuss what has happened since Romanow tabled his report and why most of the recommendations relating to Aboriginal health have not (yet) been implemented. In the final section, I will argue that the reform proposals of the CFHCC failed to attract sufficient support, because there was no *agent of change* who demanded an implementation of the recommendations; moreover, the concept of the Aboriginal Health Partnerships, although very innovative, was not sufficiently rooted in the existing system of health service provision for Aboriginal peoples.

The Status of Aboriginal Health in Canada

The average life expectancy of Aboriginal peoples in Canada has improved significantly in the past fifty years. Nevertheless, significant disparities still do exist: in 2000, the average life expectancy for Canadian males was 7.4 years higher than that of the Status Indian male population; for women, it was 5.2 years higher than that of the Status Indian female population (CFHCC 2002, 218). The severity of the problems in the provision of health services to Aboriginal peoples in Canada was repeatedly stressed by reports of advisory bodies in the recent past. For example, in 1996 the Royal Commission on Aboriginal Peoples proposed a broad agenda for structural changes in the provision of health services for Aboriginal Peoples (RCAP 1996).

One of the biggest health problems in Aboriginal communities is diabetes. Among First Nations and Métis, the prevalence of diabetes is three to five times the national average. These groups also have diabetes complications more often and at an earlier age compared to the national average (CFHCC 2002, 220). Since diabetes is a chronic disease, this is a long-term problem that requires a long-term solution. First Nations also face tuberculosis rates ten times higher than that of other Canadians (Health Canada 1999, 3). Socio-economic factors like poor housing standards and homelessness contribute to the comparatively high rate of new tuberculosis infections. Other risk factors are HIV, substance abuse (including alcoholism) and diabetes (Health Canada 1999, 46).

A huge and growing health problem among Aboriginal people is HIV/AIDS. While the annual number of new HIV cases in Canada has levelled off, the number of HIV cases among Aboriginal people has increased steadily over the last decade. Citizens of Aboriginal descent make up around 3 percent of the total population in Canada, but in 2002, 250 to 450 Aboriginal people were newly infected with HIV (6 to 12 percent of all new HIV cases in Canada). Therefore, one can speak of an HIV epidemic among Aboriginal people in Canada (Public Health Agency of Canada 2004, 4). There are several reasons why the number of new HIV cases among Aboriginal Canadians is rising. For example, Aboriginal people are over-represented in high-risk groups, such as injecting drug users. As well, the high mobility of Aboriginal people between urban and rural areas leads to an "export" of the disease from cities to remote communities (Health Canada 2003, 39).

Another problem is that most studies analyzing Aboriginal health issues concentrate on peoples living on-reserve, but Aboriginal people who are living off-reserve also suffer from a poor health status (Tjepkema 2002). According to Chief Dwight Dorey (National Chief of the Congress of Aboriginal Peoples), "a culture of despair" may be contributing to those health problems:

> In some ways, Aboriginal peoples off-reserve are in the worst of all possible positions—we carry the unhealthy legacy of Aboriginal policies and dysfunctional backgrounds, without the support and encouragement of an Aboriginal community around us. (Chief Dorey quoted in Sibbald 2002, 912)

According to Statistics Canada, almost half of the Aboriginal people living off-reserve suffer from chronic diseases like high blood pressure and arthritis (Tjepkema 2002, 75). The fact that most of the government programs to combat (for example) diabetes are directed to Aboriginal people living on-reserve, contributes to the differences in the health status of Aboriginal people living on- and off-reserve.

In an article in the *Journal of Aboriginal Health*, Terry L. Mitchell and Dawn T. Maracle point out that post-traumatic stress can be considered a significant factor contributing to the disparities in health status between Aboriginal and non-Aboriginal Canadians:

> Post-traumatic stress arises from external trauma and terrifying experiences that break a person's sense of predictability, vulnerability, and control. Aboriginal Peoples' experiences of contact and cultural domination may reasonably be viewed as a loss of predictability and control and increases in vulnerability .... The impact of PTSD [post-traumatic stress disorder] affects the mind, emotions, body, and behaviour. Mentally, people who are traumatized may develop negative beliefs about themselves and their world. Emotionally, they may experience cycles of denial and anxiety. Physically, they can experience sleep disturbance, heightened sensitivity and anxiety, nightmares, and flashbacks. Behaviourally, they may avoid certain situations, isolate themselves socially, drink, and become increasingly aggressive. (Mitchell/Maracle 2005, 15–16)

Therefore, one can identify two interrelated factors that contribute to the poor health status of Aboriginal people: on the one hand, the social determinants of health (living conditions like poor housing and lack of running water, bad financial situations, lack of employment, and poverty) lead to poorer health outcomes among Aboriginals. On the other hand, the current funding structures and the organization of the health service provision make it almost impossible to develop an integrated approach to improve the health status of Aboriginal peoples.

These health problems will become more pressing because the number of seniors of Aboriginal descent will increase significantly in the coming decades. It is estimated that the number of seniors in Aboriginal communities will triple from 1996 to 2016 (CFHCC 2002, 219). These seniors will need not only additional health services but also special care services like palliative and long-term care. Therefore, a new integrated approach to tackle the deficits in the health service provision for Aboriginal communities is needed.

The Financing of Aboriginal Health Services

The jurisdiction for financing and providing health services for Aboriginal peoples is not clearly assigned to one level of government in the British North America Act of 1867, the Constitution Act of 1982, or any other official document (Waldram/Herring/Young 2004, 141–176). Therefore, a range of federal, provincial and territorial programs and services for Aboriginal communities do exist. According to the Constitution Act of 1982, the provincial governments are responsible for regulating health services and insurances. The federal government only has the jurisdiction to provide direct funding for health services, for example, to the Royal Canadian Mounted Police, to military personnel and to inmates of federal prisons.

But the details of federal responsibility to create and maintain health services for Aboriginal people are still a point of debate. Organizations like the National Aboriginal Health Organization (hereafter NAHO) hold the view that health services are a treaty right. Contrary to this position, the federal government has stated repeatedly that it considers the federal responsibility for those health services to be voluntary and—according to the 1974 "Policy of the Federal Government concerning Indian Health Services"—not a treaty right of Aboriginal people (Health Canada, "History of Providing," online).

Currently, provincial governments are paying for all medically necessary health services through their tax-financed health insurance plans (medicare). The federal government only pays for health services for First Nations and Inuit living on-reserve and for medically necessary health-related goods and services through the Non-Insured Health Benefits Program (hereafter NIHBP). Aboriginal people living off-reserve receive their health services through the provincial health programs (Leeson 2002, 8). The NIHBP was created as part of the 1979 Federal Indian Health Policy (Waldram/Herring/Young 2004, 184–187). The NIHBP covers all services that are not insured through other (federal, provincial, or territorial) health insurance programs. The three most important elements of this program are medical transportation, dental care, and pharmaceuticals. Prevention and health education are not part of this program. However, the federal government has set up additional prevention programs (e.g., drug and alcohol abuse-prevention programs).

In order to support Aboriginal self-government, some responsibilities for managing and delivering health services have been transferred from the federal level to local communities as part of the 1989 Health Transfer Policy, which was based on the 1979 Indian Health Policy (Lavoie 2004, 11). But the Auditor General has criticized this transfer of responsibilities because Aboriginal communities are not accountable to Parliament for how they use those funds (CFHCC 2002, 214; auditor general of Canada 2000). Therefore, a transfer of responsibilities, is not a quick fix that can be used to solve the current problems in the provision of health services for Aboriginal people. There is another problem in relation to the transfer of responsibilities: in 1996, roughly five out of ten Aboriginals lived in urban communities (CFHCC 2002, 214). It is almost impossible to transfer responsibilities for the provision of health services to local communities in these urban settings. To summarize, Aboriginal people in Canada at this time have inadequate access to health services, the funding structures and the systems of service delivery are fragmented, and there is a lack of accountability. In addition to this, most of the services provided are inappropriate (Marchildon 2004), as will be discussed next. Thus, the need for a new approach towards Aboriginal health is apparent.

The Reform Proposals of the Romanow Commission

From April 2001 to November 2002, a one-man royal commission, the *Commission on the Future of Health Care in Canada* (also called the *Romanow Commission*) conducted an analysis of Canada's health-care system.

Concerning the state of Aboriginal health services in Canada, the CFHCC concluded in its final report that the existing medicare system was not addressing the specific health needs of Aboriginal peoples (CFHCC 2002, 218). Commissioner Roy Romanow pointed out that the poor health status of Aboriginal people was medicare's greatest failure. Therefore, the commission concluded that the status quo was unacceptable and that structural reforms were needed (CFHCC 2002, 224).

As part of the commission's work, more than one hundred participants were invited to a forum entitled "Dialogue on Aboriginal Health: Sharing our Challenges and our Successes" in Aylmer, Quebec, on June 26, 2002. The forum was organized by the CFHCC in cooperation with NAHO. In three small group discussions, the commission heard presentations from representatives of the Métis, Inuit and First Nations. In a fourth discussion round, urban Aboriginal health issues were analyzed. The afternoon plenary session of the forum was broadcast live on the Cable Public Affairs Channel (CPAC), and viewers had the possibility to call in and comment on the discussions. Since some of the people who had been invited to the forum were unable to travel to Aylmer, there were also seven video submissions. Romanow later pointed out that those consultations made it obvious to him that comprehensive, structural reforms in the area of Aboriginal health were needed (Romanow 2004, 3).

In his final report, "Building on Values," Romanow called for a "more active participation of Aboriginal peoples, communities and organizations in deciding what services are delivered and how" (CFHCC 2002, 214). Thus, Romanow discussed three alternative reform proposals:

1. A continuation of the current practice of negotiations between the federal government and Aboriginal communities for a transfer of funds and responsibilities for health services;
2. Tying the problems concerning the provision of health services to larger issues of self-government, as suggested by the Royal Commission on Aboriginal Peoples;
3. An integration of Aboriginal health services into the provincial health systems. (224)

Each proposal had certain deficiencies, which were discussed in the final report (224). Because none of the aforementioned alternatives seemed sufficient to tackle the huge problems in Aboriginal health policy-making, Romanow suggested a fourth approach.

The central element of Romanow's reform proposals was the new instrument of Aboriginal Health Partnerships (AHPs). These AHPs would become the new basis upon which health services would be provided for Aboriginal peoples. Romanow recommended a two-step approach. First, the currently fragmented funding would be pooled. Then, the AHPs would be created as a new way of providing health services for Aboriginal people and would be financed by redirecting the money currently used to finance a variety of programs in the area of Aboriginal health. Romanow stressed that Aboriginal peoples would have to have a direct input into the design and the details of how health services were to be provided (211).

The Aboriginal Health Partnerships Proposal

In November 2004, the executive director of the Romanow Commission described AHPs in a presentation as being "Aboriginal Health Maintenance Organizations (HMOs)" (Marchildon 2004). HMOs are a form of health insurance organization offering a range of health services to the insured group for a monthly fee.

The AHPs recommended by Romanow were to be funded through consolidated "Aboriginal Health Funds," which were to be created by pooling the financial resources of the federal, provincial and territorial governments currently used for Aboriginal health services. Romanow pointed out that those funds would also include money that is currently transferred to Aboriginal organizations for the provision of health services.

According to the report of the CFHCC, the AHPs could work in the following fashion:

1. A group of physicians who specialized in Aboriginal health would set-up an AHP. A local Aboriginal community could also set-up an AHP;

2. People would have to sign up to be served by the AHP. Usually, non-Aboriginal people would be able to sign up, as well;
3. The AHP would receive funds from the "Aboriginal Health Funds" based on the number of people who signed up;
4. The AHP would use those funds to organize the delivery of health services. It would be accountable for the utilization of the funds that it received. In order to increase transparency and accountability, the administration of the AHPs would—based upon a clear mandate—have to inform the people who signed up on how the AHP was performing. (CFHCC 2002, 227–228)

Theoretically, the AHPs would be a non-profit community corporation with a board of directors and they would represent the institutions who funded and who set up the AHP. In this context, it is very important to stress that it would be vital for the success of an AHP that Aboriginal health professionals take part in the AHPs. In some areas or communities, the existing self-government structures could be used to create an AHP, since it would be possible to transform existing programs to work within the new AHP framework.

Romanow set out three guiding principles for the AHPs:

1. The AHPs should be designed to take a holistic approach to health with a strong focus on prevention;
2. The health services must be adapted to the realities of the Aboriginal communities;
3. The AHPs should reflect the specific (health) needs of the communities they serve. (227)

According to these principles, there would not be one model AHP, but several different forms of AHPs adapted to the specific needs of Aboriginal peoples in different settings. This corresponds with the fact that there would not be one central authority organizing the funding and the delivery of health services. Hence, one can describe the AHP proposal as a bottom-up approach towards a structural reform of Aboriginal health services.

But what would be the advantages of an AHP compared to the current structures? First of all, the reform of the financing of Aboriginal health services, which would be a necessary precondition, would lead to a pooling of the currently fragmented funding. As a result, accountability would be increased and the financial basis for Aboriginal health would be stabilized. AHPs would be a flexible instrument because they could be tailored to the different health needs of different communities and regions. The proposal also recognized the central role Aboriginal people must play in the design and the implementation of health programs. When comparing these elements of the AHP proposal with the existing system, which is funded through a variety of channels and in which direct input of Aboriginal people into how health services are provided is not secured, the advantages of the Romanow proposal become obvious.

In the past, the federal government has reduced its fiscal transfers to the provinces in order to achieve a balanced budget (Broschek/Schultze 2004, 26). Those cuts can be masked much more easily when there are several funding sources and programs. A consolidated budget for AHPs would instead provide stable funding and therefore long-term prospects for the improvement of health services for Aboriginal peoples in Canada. Another advantage of the AHP approach is that the instrument can be adapted to the health needs of Aboriginal people living on-reserve and off-reserve. For example, an AHP could be set up to serve the specific needs of Aboriginal people living in the Toronto area or in remote regions of Nunavut. Finally, a very important advantage of the AHP approach compared to the current health service system would be its strong focus on prevention. Prevention would—according to Romanow—be a key element in any AHP. Currently, preventive measures and programs are not closely linked to the provision of health services because of the fragmentation of these services.

Reactions

When the Romanow report was tabled, most commentators focused their attention on what the CFHCC recommended in relation to the federal-provincial agreements on who should pay what share of the total cost of health care services. The recommendations for reforming Aboriginal health services were largely ignored by the media. In a documentation of the print media coverage (fifty-three newspaper articles) of the presentation of the Romanow report, the term "Aboriginal" can be found only five times in three articles (Canadian Health Coalition 2002, online). None of the articles mentioned "First Nations," "Métis," or "Inuit."

Romanow had tried to develop a new framework for the provision of Aboriginal health services in close cooperation with the organizations of Aboriginal peoples. But the reaction of NAHO towards the recommendations of the Romanow report was very cautious. The executive director for NAHO, Richard Jock, commented on the AHP proposal:

> While the elements of this proposal need to be more fully explored, the case for a change in approach, one which is based upon value of real partnership with Aboriginal people is long overdue. Involvement of Aboriginal Peoples in further discussing potential implementation of this recommendation will be a critical and an essential ingredient to an effective federal / provincial / territorial response to the Commission's report. (NAHO *Romanow Commission's Report* 2002)

In its "Briefing Note," NAHO did acknowledge that the partnership proposal might help to improve the provision of health services at the community level:

> The creation of such partnerships could provide a mechanism by which federal, provincial, territorial, and as appropriate Aboriginal health resources would be consolidated and potentially used more strategically to address health needs at the community level. (NAHO "Briefing Note" 2002, online)

In contrast to the cautious assessment by NAHO, the criticism of the Romanow proposals by the Assembly of Manitoba Chiefs was much more straightforward:

> Romanow's recommendation that all available funding sources for Aboriginal health should be pooled into one consolidated fund in order to finance the establishment of Aboriginal Health Partnerships will not work for the vision of health for First Nations in Manitoba. Our vision for a First Nations health care system in Manitoba is to have an entity that is fully operational in terms of direct control over funding, administration and delivery of health services whether they live on-reserve or off-reserve. This cannot be accomplished through partnering with other Aboriginal groups or the Province of Manitoba. We have a special relationship with the Crown based on treaties and we will not risk our treaty rights through any process that diminishes this relationship. (Assembly of Manitoba Chiefs 2002)

The Métis National Council also openly criticized the Romanow report, because it developed a pan-Aboriginal solution and did not address the specific health needs of the Métis people: "We were very clear in our presentation to the commission that we need Métis solutions to Métis health issues, it doesn't look like we were heard" (Harley Desjarlais qtd. in Métis National Council 2002, online).

Representatives of the Nunavut Inuit also criticized the report because it did not address the unique circumstances of the Nunavut Inuit (Bell "Arctic leaders" 2002, online). But it was acknowledged that the report called for improvements of health services in remote and rural regions. A month before the final Romanow report was tabled, the president of Inuit Tapiriit Kanatami, Jose Kusugak, had already criticized the work of the commission:

> The health-care system you are reviewing barely exists in the Arctic. It is so far removed from our needs and our reality that as I read the commission's interim report I often felt as though I was reading about a different country .... There is a great gap in the quality of health care between North and South, and it is visible in two areas: firstly, the lack of basic programs and services for northern Canadians, and secondly,

the absence of Inuit input when health policy is made. (Kusugak qtd. in Bell "ITK president" 2002, online)

According to Kusugak, many Inuit "feel powerless and intimidated" by the existing health care system since they have no input into the design and provision of health services (Kusugak qtd. in Bell "ITK president" 2002, online).

In an article in the *Canadian Journal on Public Health,* Melanie MacKinnon criticized the Romanow Commission because "its recommendations were specific to health care providers and delivery models and did not address the social and spiritual determinants of health, which are fundamental to a First Nations holistic approach" (MacKinnon 2005, S15). To summarize: the basic premises of Romanow, that more money was needed to address the poor health status of Aboriginal peoples in Canada and that Aboriginal peoples must play a central role in developing and providing health services, were welcomed by all the Aboriginal organizations. However, the AHP proposal was considered to threaten the (existing) self-government structures and the self-determination of Aboriginal peoples in this policy area. Considering these reactions to the report, there were few incentives for the federal government to act on the recommendations developed by the CFHCC concerning Aboriginal health.

Government Reaction to the Romanow Recommendations

After Romanow had tabled his report, the federal government initiated two first ministers conferences to discuss the reform of Canada's health care system. One day before Prime Minister Paul Martin met with the first ministers of the provinces and territories at a first ministers Conference on 14 September 2004, he met with representatives from Aboriginal organizations. The first ministers and the representatives from Aboriginal organizations agreed on an "Action Plan" to improve the health status of Aboriginal peoples in Canada. The federal government pledged to spend CA$700 million on Aboriginal health and to start three different projects to achieve improvements in the delivery of health services for the Aboriginal population. According to Prime Minister Paul Martin, these funds would help "close the gap" between the health status of Aboriginal people and other Canadians (Dunfield 2004, online).

The first project was the creation of a new "Aboriginal Health Transition Fund." The provincial and territorial governments will use additional funds (CA$200 million) transferred by the federal government to address the specific health needs of Aboriginal people. Since the percentage of Aboriginal people in the overall Canadian population is increasing, the first ministers also decided to start an "Aboriginal Health Human Resources Initiative." The goal of this initiative is to increase awareness among doctors and other health professionals of the specific mental, spiritual, and social elements related to Aboriginal health.

Health scientists have emphasized repeatedly that a functioning patient-physician communication is a very important factor for good health outcomes. But when physicians and other health professionals are unable to take account of the holistic view of Aboriginal people towards health and health problems, this inevitably leads to poorer health outcomes. Presently there are a mere 12 practicing Aboriginal physicians in Ontario; but, according to estimates, more than 350 are needed (Ehman 2004, 1028). In 1996, the Royal Commission on Aboriginal Peoples concluded that all governments should work together and commit themselves "to train 10,000 Aboriginal professionals over a ten-year period in health and social services" (RCAP 1996, 269). Therefore, one goal of this new initiative is to increase the number of members from Aboriginal communities who are choosing to become health professionals. In total, the federal government has pledged to spend CA$100 million over a period of five years to train Aboriginal health professionals.

The Government of Canada announced that it would start a range of new programs focusing on health promotion and disease prevention (Health Canada, "Improving" 2004, online) to address some of the health problems mentioned earlier (e.g. diabetes, child and mental health). The federal government pledged to direct CA$400 million to improve the situation in those critical areas. This result of the meeting between the prime minister and representatives from the Aboriginal organizations was considered by the latter to be a promising start towards significantly improving the health status of Aboriginal peoples in Canada (Dolha 2004, online). Not only did the federal government promise to increase the funding levels for Aboriginal health services, Prime Minister Paul Martin also acknowledged that the organizations of Aboriginal peoples must play an increased role in the management and the delivery of health services.

But even though the federal government showed its commitment to improving Aboriginal health, it failed to announce structural reforms to how Aboriginal health problems are being addressed and to how these health services are funded. Instead, the government(s) decided to set up limited, small-scale programs to address specific health problems. It is unlikely that these new programs are going to significantly improve the overall health of Aboriginal peoples, because the underlying structures of how health services are provided are not going to change; the fragmentation of service delivery remains one of the biggest problems in the provision of Aboriginal health services.

The Failure of the Romanow Proposal

More than three years have passed since Romanow presented his report to the Canadian public. Apart from the initiatives undertaken by the Martin government in 2004, no Aboriginal health policy reforms have taken place. The AHPs would have been a new and flexible instrument to provide health services to Aboriginal people in Canada; yet the proposal failed to attract significant support from the political actors and the organizations of Aboriginal people. In fact, the reactions of the Aboriginal organizations to the recommendations contained in the Romanow report stood in stark contrast to the positive overall assessment of the work of the commission by the Canadian public (EKOS Research Associates 2002, online).

There are several reasons why the AHP proposal failed to attract support. Marchildon pointed out the following examples:

1. The recommendations were complex and therefore difficult to understand and to explain;
2. None of the actors currently involved in financing and providing health services would be able to realize quick wins from a structural

change along the lines recommended by Romanow;

3. The AHP proposal was a challenge to the agendas of all federal / provincial / territorial / Aboriginal governments and organizations;
4. Since no model projects existed, the idea of Aboriginal Health Maintenance Organizations was, perhaps, "too foreign" to Canadians. (Marchildon 2004)

The fact that the recommendations challenged the short-term agendas of all levels of government made a structural reform of Aboriginal health services along the lines developed by Romanow and his commission unlikely. The federal, provincial and territorial governments currently all have some influence on certain elements of the provision of health services for Aboriginal people. In some areas, Aboriginal organizations also play a significant role in the provision of health services. The AHP proposal challenged the interests of most of these actors. Had the recommendation been implemented, most of them would have lost their influence in the area of Aboriginal health policy-making. This would have meant that federal, provincial and territorial leaders would have lost the chance to gather electoral support among Aboriginal people by referring to what their governments were doing to improve Aboriginal health. Instead of quick wins, the AHP proposal would have meant long-term losses in their influence on Aboriginal health policies. Aboriginal organizations would experience lost funds, their past funds being pooled and distributed to the new AHPs.

Even though the federal government is currently financing the health services of First Nations living on-reserve and certain other health services through the NIHBP, most of the decisions in relation to Aboriginal health services take place on the local or regional level. Nevertheless, for the introduction of AHPs, a reform of the funding of Aboriginal health services was—according to the Romanow report—an essential precondition. From a systemic viewpoint, such a reform of the overarching funding structures did make sense. But since this reform of the funding agreements was a prerequisite of the introduction of the AHPs, this made it much harder to implement the recommendations of the CFHCC. Structural reforms of funding agreements are always difficult to achieve, especially when there are several groups of actors on different levels with different interest constellations.

This precondition also made it almost impossible to develop regional models because the aforementioned (national) reform was needed to finance the AHPs. Moreover, no model project existed on which the recommendations of the CFHCC were based or at least referring to. In the 1960s, the Royal Commission on Health Services was successful in advocating a tax-financed and publicly administrated health-care system because the commission was able to build on the experience and the success of the Saskatchewan medicare model and to develop reform proposals accordingly (Naylor 1986, 191–234). This made it much more difficult for critics to question the functioning of the model the commission was proposing. In contrast to this, the CFHCC was not able to refer to a model AHP as proof of the viability of this new instrument.

The fact that the commission recommended one instrument to tackle all the health problems in Aboriginal communities made it easier to criticize the model on the grounds that it did not address the specific health needs of different groups of Aboriginal people. Another important factor that decreased the attractiveness of the AHP proposal was the complexity of the recommendations. This made it more difficult to present the concept of AHPs in the media. The fact that HMOs do not exist in the Canadian medicare system added to the difficulty of gathering support for the commission's proposal.

Some critics said that the AHP proposal and indeed the whole discussion of Aboriginal health issues in the final report of the commission were over-generalizing (MacKinnon 2005, S15). This criticism is correct when keeping in mind that the health problems affecting First Nations, Métis and Inuit communities (and the social context factors) differ. But the Romanow Commission was not an advisory body dealing only with Aboriginal health issues. The importance of a structural reform of Aboriginal health policies was emphasized in the report and generalizations were necessary to focus the attention of the federal government—who had initiated the commission—on the underlying, institutional (funding) problems in the provision of Aboriginal health services.

Outlook

The health problems of Aboriginal people in Canada are well known and a variety of reform proposals have been put forward. But it remains to be seen whether the actors involved in the funding and the provision of Aboriginal health services can overcome the existing obstacles in order to implement a structural reform of Aboriginal health financing and service provision. In order to improve the health status of Aboriginal people in Canada, several issues must be addressed:

1. More funds should be used to improve the poor health status of Aboriginal people (for example new prevention programs);
2. A new infrastructure for the provision of health services must be set up. This structure must be designed to take account of the social values and spiritual aspects of Aboriginal health. Integrated service models like the AHPs are a promising instrument to achieve this goal;
3. The political actors must develop a concerted approach to improve the social determinants of health. Aboriginal people in Canada need improved housing, better education and possibilities for economic development (to fight unemployment). In the long run, only socio-economic improvements can lead to an enhancement of the health status of Aboriginal people in Canada;
4. Canada needs more Aboriginal health physicians.

Certainly, some of these problems have been addressed by programs initiated by the federal, provincial and territorial governments. But there is nevertheless a need for a more integrated approach towards Aboriginal health issues. Concerning the work of political advisory bodies, the recommendations of the Romanow Commission dealing with Aboriginal health reveal that in order for a recommendation to be considered, there needs to be an *agent of change* demanding an implementation of the recommendation. Neither NAHO nor any other Aboriginal organization strongly advocated an implementation of the Romanow recommendations on the national level. Hence, the federal, provincial and territorial governments could ignore these recommendations without fear of negative reactions from the media, interest groups, or the general public.

But it may still be too early to assess the success of the Romanow Commission. The CFHCC built on the work of the Federal Royal Commission on Health Services. This commission was chaired by Supreme Court Justice Emmett Hall and presented its final report in 1964. It its report, the Commission recommended the creation of a pan-Canadian, publicly funded health-care system (Naylor 1986, 191–234). But it took the political actors in Canada more than seven years to set up a medicare program according to the recommendations of the Hall Commission in every province. It remains to be seen whether the political actors in Canada are again able to come together and initiate a structural reform, this time of the structures of Aboriginal health services. This would be a necessary first step towards a new and integrated approach towards Aboriginal health.

The Romanow Commission emphasized the current health problems of Aboriginal people in Canada, and it was able to put the topic of Aboriginal health on the agenda of the federal government. This success was emphasized by the "Special Meeting" between the representatives from Aboriginal organizations and the prime minister on September 13, 2004. The meeting was a promising move towards reforming Aboriginal health policies, even though reforms of the underlying funding and service structures were not initiated. On the provincial level, the setting up of a "Romanow Joint Working Group" in Manitoba (MacKinnon 2005, S15) is a first step towards reforming Aboriginal health policy based on some of the recommendations of the Romanow Commission; it is, however, unlikely that the AHP instrument will ever be introduced. With his report, Roy Romanow opened a "window of opportunity" that could change the way in which health services are provided for Aboriginal people in Canada. Romanow emphasized the need for a new, holistic approach towards Aboriginal health, and he made it clear that both funding mechanisms and service provision must be reformed. Now it is up to the Aboriginal organizations and all levels of government to improve the health of Aboriginal peoples in Canada.

Endnotes

1 I would like to thank Kelly Steeves for her support in preparing the English version of this text.

Bibliography

Assembly of Manitoba Chiefs. (2002). "A Distinct Approach Designed by First Nations for First Nations." Press release, December 6, 2002.

Auditor General of Canada. (2000). "Health Canada – First Nations Health: Follow-up." *Report of the Auditor General of Canada*. Ottawa, ON: Office of the Auditor General.

Boychuk, Gerard W. (2002). "Federal Spending in Health: Why Here, Why Now?" In *How Ottawa Spends 2002–2003: The Security Aftermath and National Priorities*, ed. G. Bruce Doern. Don Mills, ON: Oxford University Press, 121–136.

Boyer, Yvonne. (2004). "First Nations, Métis, and Inuit Health Care: The Crown's Fiduciary Obligation." Discussion paper series in *Aboriginal Health: Legal Issues, 2*. National Aboriginal Health Organization.

Broschek, Jörg, and Rainer-Olaf Schultze. (2004). "Föderalismus und Integration: Konzeptionen, Reformen, und Reformwirkungen von Trudeau bis Chrétien." *Zeitschrift für Kanada-Studien, 44:1*, 7–32.

Commission on the Future of Health Care in Canada (CFHCC). (2002). *Building on Values*. Saskatoon, SK.

Ehman, Amy Jo. (2004). "Lack of Aboriginal Health Professionals a 'Huge Issue.'" *Canadian Medical Association Journal, 171:9*, 1028.

Flood, Colleen M. (2002). "The Anatomy of Medicare." *Canadian Health Law and Policy*, eds. Jocelyn Downie, Timothy Caulfield, and Colleen M. Flood. 2nd ed. Markham, ON: Butterworths, 1–54.

Hackett, Paul. (2005, January–February). "From Past to Present: Understanding First Nations Health Patterns in a Historical Context." *Canadian Journal of Public Health, 96, Suppl. 1*, S17–S21.

Health Canada. *Tuberculosis in First Nations Communities, 1999*. Ottawa, ON: 1999.

———. (2003). "HIV/AIDS among Aboriginal Persons in Canada: A Continuing Concern." *HIV/AIDS Epi Updates April 2003*. Ottawa, ON, 35–40.

Jackman, Martha. (2000). "Constitutional Jurisdiction over Health in Canada." *Health Law Journal, 95:8*, 95–117.

Lavoie, Josée G. (2004). "Governed by Contracts: The Development of Indigenous Primary Health Services in Canada, Australia, and New Zealand." *Journal of Aboriginal Health, 1:1*, 6–24.

Leeson, Howard. (2002). "Constitutional Jurisdiction over Health and Health Care Services in Canada." Discussion paper no. 12. *Commission on the Future of Health Care in Canada.* Saskatoon, SK.

MacKinnon, Melanie. (2005, January–February). "A First Nations Voice in the Present Creates Healing in the Future." *Canadian Journal of Public Health, 96*, S13–S16.

Marchildon, Gregory P. (2004). "Romanow & Aboriginal Health: Is Transformative Change Likely?" Guest Lecture. Department of Public Health Services. University of Toronto, November 24, 2004.

Mitchell, Terry L., and Dawn T. Maracle. (2005, March). "Healing the Generations: Post Traumatic Stress and the Health Status of Aboriginal Populations in Canada." *Journal of Aboriginal Health, 2:1*, 14–23.

National Aboriginal Health Organization (NAHO). (2002). *Romanow Commission's Report on the Future of Health Care in Canada*. Press release, 29 November 2002.

Naylor, C. David. (1986). *Private Practice, Public Payment. Canadian Medicine and the Politics of Health Insurance 1911–1966.* Kingston, ON: McGill-Queen's University Press.

Public Health Agency of Canada. (2004, December). "Understanding the HIV/AIDS Epidemic among Aboriginal Peoples in Canada: The Community at a Glance." *HIV/AIDS Epi Notes.*

Romanow, Roy. (2004). "Moving Forward on Aboriginal Health, Notes for Opening Remarks." *Six Nations Vision 2020 Symposium*, 28 September 2004.

Royal Commission on Aboriginal Peoples. (1996). "Gathering Strength." In *Report of the Royal Commission on Aboriginal Peoples.* Vol. 3. Ottawa, ON: Canada Communications Group, 1996.

Sibbald, Barbara. (2002). "Off-reserve Aboriginal people face daunting health problems: StatsCan." *Canadian Medical Association Journal, 167:8*, 912.

Tjepkema, Michael. (2002). "The Health of the Off-Reserve Aboriginal Population." In *How Healthy are Canadians? 2002 Annual Report*, ed. Statistics Canada. Supplement to vol. 13. Ottawa, ON, 73–88.

Waldram, James B., D. Ann Herring, and T. Kue Young. (2004). *Aboriginal Health in Canada. Historical, Cultural, and Epidemiological Perspectives.* Toronto, ON: University of Toronto Press.

Internet Sources

Bell, Jim. (2002, December 6). "Arctic Leaders embrace Romanow Report." *Nunatsiaq News.* http://www.nunatsiaq.com/archives/nunavut021206/news/nunavut/21206_04.html [consulted January 25, 2006].

Bell, Jim. (2002, April 5). "ITK President Blasts Inuit Health-care Standards." *Nunatsiaq News.* http://www.nunatsiaq.com/archives/nunavut020405/news/nunavut/20405_1.html [consulted February 4, 2006].

Canadian Health Coalition. "Romanow Media: November 28–December 4, 2002." http://www.healthcoalition.ca/romanow-media.pdf [consulted Feburary 1, 2006].

Dolha, Lloyd. (2004, Fall). "Aboriginal Leaders Meet with Ministers on Health Care." *First Nations Drum.* http://www.firstnationsdrum.com/Fall%202004/PoliHealth.htm [consulted January 25, 2006].

Dunfield, Allison. (2004, September 13). "PM Announces $700-million for Native Health." *The Globe and Mail Update.* http://www.theglobeandmail.com/servlet/story/RTGAM.20040913.wabori0913/BNStory/Front/ [consulted January 25, 2006].

EKOS Research Associates. (2002, December 6). "EKOS/CBC/Toronto Star/La Presse Poll: The Romanow Report." http://www.ekos.com/media/default.asp [consulted July 31, 2005].

Health Canada. "History of Providing Health Services to First Nations and Inuit People." First Nations and Inuit Health Branch. http://www.hc-sc.gc.ca/fnihb/history.htm [consulted July 31, 2005].

Health Canada. (2004, September 14). "Improving Aboriginal Health: First Ministers' and Aboriginal Leaders' Meeting." News release. http://www.hc-sc.gc.ca/ahc-asc/media/nr-cp/2004/2004_leaders-dirigents_e.html [consulted July 31, 2005].

Métis National Council. (2002, November 22). "Romanow Report on Health Care Offers Very Little for Metis People." Press release. http://www.metisnation.ca/press/nov29-02.html [consulted July 31, 2005].

National Aboriginal Health Organization (NAHO). (2002, November 29). "Briefing Note: Release of Report by the Commission on the Future of Health Care in Canada." http://www.naho.ca/english/pdf/ BN047.pdf [consulted Feburary 4, 2006].

Mansell Griffin and Antino Spanjer

The Nisga'a Common Bowl in Tradition and Politics

In the year 1887, a delegation of Nisga'a travelled by canoe and steamboat to Victoria in order to discuss their land question with the governor of British Columbia. The length of that journey must have seemed immense to the Nisga'a back then, but it was nothing compared to the time they would need in order to get an answer to that question. In 1913 they brought it before His Majesty's Privy Council in London, but it was not until 2000 that they finally achieved what no other First Nation in a Canadian province had achieved before: they were given the rights to about a tenth of their traditional lands (Raunet 1996, 79–80, 136–137). You may ask how the Nisga'a Nation accomplished all this? What made them so exceptional, exceptional in a way that a First Nation of approximately five thousand people from Northwestern British Columbia became a subject of interest in the newspapers around the world? The answer to this question fills about two hundred pages. It is the official document that now grants the Nisga'a Nation the exclusive rights to their land: the Nisga'a Treaty.

Because of this treaty, the Nisga'a Nation received media attention that still is unprecedented in Aboriginal Canada. Because of this treaty, a referendum on the treaty process in British Columbia was held in 2002—a referendum that almost split the province. In fact, this treaty can be called a landmark victory for Aboriginal Canada. Some people disagree, but it clearly is a landmark and, taking the current political situation into account, it will probably remain the most significant and comprehensive treaty within the Canadian provinces for a long time. Fact is at least that "British Columbia has yet to sign a final treaty with the almost two hundred aboriginal nations involved in the land-claims negotiations that began more than ten years ago." If the minister responsible for treaties, Tom Christensen, is only "cautiously optimistic" that "modern treaties are within reach in British Columbia," it is probably wise that he "wouldn't make a time prediction" (Meissner 2006, 2).

The Source of Success

How did the Nisga'a Nation manage to get to such a comprehensive treaty—a treaty that gave them their own government, in a province that has a history of being the most backward in Canada regarding Aboriginal issues?[1] One could argue that it is because of the persistence of the Nisga'a Nation. The answer is a function of the persistence of the Nisga'a Nation. It is not without reason that Daniel Raunet gave the title *Without Surrender, Without Consent* to his book about the Nisga'a Nation—recommended to anyone who is interested in the history of a successful land claim, and in the history of a remarkable First Nation.

As the title of Raunet's book suggests, it is, centrally, persistence that helped the Nisga'a Nation. They fought more than one hundred years to get their treaty. But there is more to it than just persistence. Especially nowadays, you need to be clever to achieve your goals. It is political manoeuvring and public relations that make the difference. Both are skills that the Nisga'a leaders, during the decades of negotiations, became masters of. The journalist Alex Rose, who worked for the Nisga'a Nation for many years, put it like this: "The Nisga'a are not exactly manipulators, but are very skilled at getting their message out."[2] He is right about this. Without clever public relations, the Nisga'a Nation may never have achieved their treaty, especially in a time when some people criticized it to be a third order of government, and claimed it to be unconstitutional.

With this background and within the preceding context, we will now take a closer look at the Nisga'a concept of the Common Bowl, a concept that the Nisga'a Nation promoted all through their campaign for a treaty. It is a concept which states that all Nisga'a lands and resources are common property, and it forms the basis of modern Nisga'a administration. Indeed the idea of sharing, fundamental to this concept, was always part of Nisga'a culture. In fact, the concept of *sayt k'il'hl wo'osihl Nisga'a* (One Nisga'a Bowl or Nisga'a Common Bowl) has been around since time immemorial. Evidence of this can be found in a number of traditional Nisga'a laws and practices (see below).[3]

However, there is also no doubt that the interpretation of the Common Bowl concept by the Nisga'a Nation has changed over time. Today it is different from what it was three hundred years ago, due to changes in the Nisga'a way of life, which, of course, also meant changes for political purposes. And in this regard the Nisga'a Treaty played a significant role. The outward reception of the Common Bowl also began to take up speed very quickly, and it sold well to liberal British Columbians at a time when the Nisga'a Nation needed all the support it could get. This marks the "high tide" of the outward reception of this concept. But what we want to focus on here is a deeper understanding of the roots of this concept and the background of its significance to the present.

The Dynamics of Tradition

In order to understand the roots of the Common Bowl, it is necessary that we first find out if common property was indeed commonly practised in West Coast cultures in northern British Columbia. In 1967 the Calder case came before the British Columbia Supreme Court. In it the Nisga'a Nation claimed that the title to their land had never been extinguished and they asked the court to issue a declaration that testified this. In British Columbia this claim was rejected and the Supreme Court of Canada in Ottawa, in a unanimous decision, upheld the decision that the Nisga'a boundaries at the time of White settlement in the 19th century were territorial and not proprietary. Although not a clear victory for the Nisga'a Nation, six out of seven judges were of the opinion that Nisga'a territory existed at the time of contact and that British law at that time recognized Nisga'a title. This convinced the Canadian government to resume treaty negotiations with First Nations in 1973 after a fifty-year intermission (Rose 2000, 89–91).

The famous anthropologist Willson Duff testified in the Calder case that it was a characteristic of the West Coast culture of northern British Columbia that certain parts of the territory of an Indigenous group were used as common property, as opposed to other parts that were set aside for particular families and their more or less exclusive use. An example of the former characteristic would be forest areas that were used to obtain logs and timber for houses, canoes, totem poles and other objects made out of wood. The latter would be beaches or parts of beaches where the shellfish were gathered. In some cases these could be reserved for the use of one family and its members (Supreme Court of Canada 1968, 112–117).

If we take a closer look at this statement, we see that it both explains and contradicts the Common Bowl concept at the same time. It states that some parts—or to be more precise—some functions of the land clearly belonged to certain families. This contradicts a concept which would be solely based on communal use of land and resources, but on the other hand, certain resources and parts of the land were indeed common property in Nisga'a society. During their campaign for a treaty, the Nisga'a Nation had to stress both parts of their culture. In order to prove possession of the land, the individual land rights of the chiefs were of great significance (Duff's statement in the Calder case reaffirmed this). On the other hand, the communal nature of the Nisga'a Nation's concept of possession was also essential. Internally it gave strength to stand together in their quest for justice and, approaching the end of the negotiation of their treaty, it also made it easier for them to cope with the fact that only about 10 percent of the traditional territory were to become Nisga'a Lands (which meant that a significant number of chiefs would have less rights to their land than others).[4] Externally the Common Bowl philosophy was a part of Nisga'a culture that most non-Aboriginal people who read the newspapers and followed the campaign liked to hear about because it corresponded with their picture of First Nations as gentle peoples. The impact and importance of the latter should not be underestimated, because with all the newspaper articles and with so many columnists arguing for or against the treaty, public opinion became more and more important during the negotiations of the Nisga'a Treaty.

Before we examine historical examples of the Common Bowl philosophy taking shape, it is essential to get a better understanding of the concept of "family" among the members of the Nisga'a Nation, because it applies to a completely different cultural concept in Nisga'a culture than in Western culture. A good place to start, perhaps, is with the Nisga'a kinship system. The Nisga'a word for "mother" (*nox*) means not only the "woman that birthed me" but all of her "sisters." A member of the Nisga'a Nation therefore has many mothers. Similarly, their word for "father" means not only "my dad" but also all of his "brothers." A member of the Nisga'a Nation has therefore not only many mothers but also many fathers. Even the closest family therefore becomes a matter of complicated family trees, often not easy to understand for outsiders. Respectively the Nisga'a word for "brother" includes not only "my birth mother's sons" but also all of "my mothers' sons," and the Nisga'a word for "sister" includes not only "my birth mother's daughters" but also all of "my mothers' daughters." Remembering the Nisga'a definition of "mother" therefore is essential. This can become a long list, but understanding that the birth mother has many sisters (who live dispersed all over the Nisga'a territory) is essential in the upbringing of a Nisga'a child. At a very early age the children understand that "sister" and "brother" means that they have a great many brothers and sisters all over the Nisga'a Nation.

It is important to note that the list of family members, while longer than the usual two brothers and sisters of the nuclear family today, is significantly shorter than it would have been two hundred years ago. After the various epidemics and plagues that beset not only the Nisga'a but people up and down and across the Americas, there were as few as 10 percent of the Nisga'a people remaining. In some cases families became extinct or were reduced to a single woman to continue the bloodline (the Nisga'a are a matrilineal society), which meant that families before the epidemics were significantly larger than today, so that the word for "family-owned" gets a different meaning when referring to pre-contact, because the network behind it was much bigger then.

Another distinction needs to be made here, since the word for family (*wilnaatahl*) is often interchanged with the Nisga'a word for house (*wilp*) as whole families lived in a single building—these were necessarily quite large and have been called "longhouses" by anthropologists. A large family that needed to build additional longhouses would be called a *huwilp* (*huwilp* being plural for *wilp*). The *wilp* was the body that owned specific parcels of land, and it was the chief, or *sim'oogit,* that managed the territory, or *ango'oskw,* for the benefit of the family. If a chief needed to expand from a single *wilp* to a *huwilp,* he would delegate parts of the *ango'oskw* to each of his brothers or nephews, who would then head his own *wilp* within his *huwilp*. From this explanation it already becomes clear that a family-owned territory in historical times in the Nisga'a context, although still family-owned, was much closer to what Western cultures would have called common property.

In line with this we also have to keep in mind that there are perhaps as many as sixty *wilp* or *huwilp,* but only four clans, or *pdeek̲*. Every house (or *wilp*) belongs to the *Lax̲gibuu,* the *Lax̲sgiik,* the *Ganada,* or the *Giskhaast* (Wolf, Eagle, Raven, and Killerwhale clans) and people across clans are considered family. The relationships between houses in the same *pdeek̲,* or clan, increased tremendously after the epidemics, as some houses became very small and so were "taken in" by other families. Similarly, even while some houses remained apart from and distinct from other families in the same clan, they continue, even today, to work closely together to "lighten the load," so to speak, at public functions such as the various Nisga'a feasts.

There is also traditional Nisga'a law that gives evidence for the long-time existence of the Common Bowl concept. On this matter *Ayuuk̲hl Nisga'a* (the Nisga'a traditional law) regulates property sharing between spouses for the benefit of the children of that marriage. Moreover, the husband is granted access to the territories of his wife's family—permission lasting for the life of their marriage. Similarly, children of a marriage have permission to access the territories of their father's family, as long as he is alive.

Furthermore there are historical examples of the Common Bowl philosophy taking shape. The starting point here would be Nisga'a identity. While it is clear that there has been fighting and even wars between families within the Nisga'a Nation, it is also clear that there has always been a Nisga'a identity. Examples of the Nisga'a coming together as a single entity may be found in wars between a Nisga'a group and an outside group. Recognizing the importance of the Nisga'a faction winning, the Nisga'a families would assist to ensure that possession of the valley remained with the Nisga'a. An example is found in the so-called wealth war with the Tsimshian, initiated by Legaic (a famously wealthy Tsimshian chief during the fur trade era). Legaic started a wealth war (a war that is won by the chief who destroys the most wealth). He made the challenge from his canoe and began to throw copper shields into the river—challenging the Nisga'a chief to do the same or be shamed. The Nisga'a chief followed suit. Other chiefs assisted him as Legaic continued and continued. Eventually someone noticed that Legaic was cheating. He had the coppers tied together and someone was pulling them back up the other end of the canoe. When the Nisga'a found out, Legaic was embarrassed and left. The message of the story is that the Nisga'a put their common identity above the individual identity of each chief and forgot about private property when it came to matters that regarded them as a nation (Barbeau et al., 1987, 103-105).

In more recent history, notwithstanding the account of the 1890 meeting of the Nisga'a Land Committee stated below, and consistent with the approach taken by the Nisga'a ancestors in times of war, is where the origins of the contemporary philosophy of the Common Bowl are to be found. The venue was the tenth meeting of the Nisga'a Tribal Council in Gitwinksihlkw (then called Canyon City) in 1964. At that meeting, a Nisga'a elder came forward in a wheelchair and asked the young men how much longer they were going to wait. He said that they had their arrows and that the time was right to test "the White man's justice." He then put about five hundred dollars on the table, which were all his savings, and challenged all present to do the same. They would go to court to fight for Nisga'a title and they would fight together for a common bowl—putting aside the differences of whose territory was where (there are differences between families even today), and agreed that regardless of whose territory it was, it was a Nisga'a territory nonetheless. The story goes that one at a time each chief then got up and put his territory into the bowl, agreeing to fight together (Brody 1991, 46–50).

Figure 3.1 *Nisga'a Canoe Launching*, 2001. Courtesy of Antino Spanjer. © A. Spanjer

With respect to Nisga'a territory being seen as a "bowl," it is clear that this concept has been around for a long time as well. The Nass Valley can be seen—both physically and conceptually—as a bowl. It is a food bowl out of which the family eats. This symbolism is strong and is a vital part of Nisga'a traditions. Its use in customs and ceremonies is demonstrated in Figure 3.1, where a Nisga'a woman holds a wooden bowl with beautiful carvings symbolizing the Nisga'a Common Bowl. The solemn carrying of a wooden bowl is not only common for the launching of carved canoes, but it is also found at other official Nisga'a ceremonies.

An oral example of this, by one of the Nisga'a neighbours—the Tlingit—tells the story of how the Nass came to be named the Nass River (the Nisga'a name for the river is *Lisims*). According to a book about British Columbian place names, the river came to be called the Nass when early fur traders or explorers asked what they thought were the locals what the name of the river was (in fact they were Tlingit entering the Nass estuary to come trading with the Nisga'a further up river). The Tlingit answered *ewen nass* (food bowl) and the name has stuck ever since (Walbran 1991, 351–352).

So the Nisga'a always organized themselves according to a concept that is partly based on common property. But from what we have, it is also clear that strong family groups dominated Nisga'a society in a system of *wilp* and *huwilp*. Each Nisga'a chief had a certain section of land and rights to particular resources in particular areas, in order to maintain his or her family. There is no doubt then that the Common Bowl concept was integral to Nisga'a culture, but the fact that the Nisga'a—as their neighbours—had, and still have, a hereditary chief system in place, means that there were clear distinctions in the areas allotted to and claimed by the chiefs. This situation has changed and, since the Nisga'a Treaty is in place the Common Bowl can be seen as the *ango'oskw* of the Nisga'a Nation *huwilp*. All Nisga'a land will forever remain under the jurisdiction of the Nisga'a Nation (Nisga'a Nation et al. 2000, 60).[5]

This shows that there has been a change in the concept and philosophy of the Common Bowl due to the treaty that the Nisga'a now have. The Common Bowl, quite naturally—for the above named reasons—has been strengthened as a part of Nisga'a culture and identity. This process of changing and accepting the new role of the Common Bowl was culturally an internal process, but it also affected the outward reception of the Nisga'a Nation, and as much as this process was internal and original, the Nisga'a also did not fail to realize its external value for their treaty process. On this matter, similarities to the discussion about the utilization of environmental protection as a political "tool" by Indigenous and traditional peoples spring to mind.

Environmental concerns are not relatively minor "political" issues to traditional societies but in fact are critical life-and-death matters, and only within the last decades have they become a forefront matter for Indigenous peoples. The nuance is that Indigenous people, in most cases, may have been living according to those principles in former times, but at a much more unconscious, undocumented level, and not in its so-called purest form. In this regard the positive outward reception of appearing as a environmentally-concerned group of people may have triggered a certain emphasis of this quality in order to have a stronger political standing (Duenckmann/Sandner 2003, 90).

Clearly the question behind this discussion—be it legitimate or not—is whether the promoted concept was really part of the culture that is now promoting it. In a way we already answered this for the Nisga'a, because we have shown that the Common Bowl concept is, and was, an integral part of their tradition. But this still leaves us with the difficult task to determine what tradition means and whether a universal understanding of it can and should be applied.

Coming from a European background, Anthony Giddens teaches us in *The Consequences of Modernity* that tradition derives its truth from being anchored within the rituals of a group of people. But traditions are not static and are continually being reinvented (as the Nisga'a Common Bowl concept is). Each generation interprets its traditions. But even if traditions are institutions that are matters of change, one of their essential features is that they are not matters of conscious reflection. They are not within reach of any argument for change outside of a traditional nature (Giddens 1990, 37). The question is what conscious reflection really means in this regard. As Florian Duenckmann and Verena Sandner point out in their article on political ecology, conscious reflection of traditions is to be found on ecological matters in Indigenous societies (Duenckmann/Sandner 2003, 88).[6] This would then mean to reflect about a tradition or part of your culture, and make a conscious decision about the significance and role this part of your culture should have from there on. When the Nisga'a elder in his wheelchair came forward and put his money into the "bowl," as described above, he clearly acted out of emotional reasons and was far from reflecting consciously on the interpretation of the Common Bowl concept.

It is not the purpose of this paper to clarify whether the ecological "movement" in the Aboriginal world has been a conscious decision or not. There may be cases where it was and there may be cases where it was not, but it is clear that the Common Bowl concept was not a conscious decision in Giddens' sense. It is, and will be, a tradition that is interpreted. As a side effect, it also became a tradition presented to the outside world. That the presentation was clever and well organized does not take away from the originality and authenticity of the idea itself, and so the concept can be said to never have been an argument for change outside of its traditional nature.

However, we should also not forget that Giddens writes from a "tradition" of Western philosophy. The Nisga'a never came up with such an abstract definition of tradition. For them tradition is defined in their *Ayuuk̲hl Nisga'a,* a complicated body of traditional knowledge which holds their true laws and which serves as a source of guidance for younger generations of Nisga'a. It is an ancient code of customs, which was passed on from one generation to the next, and only recently has it been written down in eight volumes. Tom G. Svensson writes,

> A dominant feature of the *Ayuuk̲hl* is the 'Common Bowl Philosophy,' an expressive metaphor for the ideal of sharing. This fundamental conception was presented to the outside world as early as 1890 by the Nisga'a Land Committee, and has recurred in Nisga'a political articulation ever since. It was frequently referred to in the *Calder* case, and was part of the ideology underlying basic claims during negotiations. For instance, in 1989 the Annual Convention of the Nisga'a Tribal Council adopted as a guiding principle in the continuing negotiations the ancient 'Common Bowl Philosophy'. The reason was to emphasize the collective nature of the Nisga'a Land Question together with the idea of sharing. The metaphor illustrates the notion that the entire Nass Valley should be viewed as a common bowl, the environmental resources within which are to be shared by everyone, *sayutk´ihl wo´osihl* [*sic: sayt k´il'hl wo´osihl*] *Nisga'a*. (2002, 18)

The Common Bowl concept, therefore, is a historical reality with a lot of significance and weight for the Nisga'a Nation. It has undergone a lot of changes , and although it might have been a concept that was less spoken of in former times, because there was less need back then for political discourse, it still is an active and original part of Nisga'a culture and not one that is just spoken of. That the Nisga'a Nation realized the political value of this concept is no contradiction but rather a component of the pragmatic side of Nisga'a culture. It was a significant stepping stone on their way to self-reliance. It helped them win their treaty. This kind of pragmatism could also help other First Nations who will unfortunately, but quite likely, only get back a small percentage of their traditional lands. So it is highly reasonable that they should also crystallize the reality of traditional concepts, to retrieve and divide their lands on a culturally fair basis for everybody. These concepts of course do not have to be a "common bowl." They can look very different but they should be anchored culturally.

Tradition Goes Politics

For the Nisga'a Nation, the Common Bowl concept is much more essential than it was. This is because under the terms of the treaty, the Nisga'a Nation owns Nisga'a Lands in unencumbered "fee simple title." Although most of Nisga'a lands remains in public ownership, specific parcels of land were granted in fee simple title, by Nisga'a Lisims government to Nisga'a village governments. The reason that the four Nisga'a villages have the rights to their own lands, regardless of the population size of each village, which varies from a few hundred in Kincolith to 1,200 km in New Aiyansh, is to be found in the political decision that initiated the Nisga'a Treaty: the first Nisga'a Land Committee in 1890. Back then, four people of each village met, decided, and agreed that this equal share for each village would be their concept to promote (Raunet 1996, 136–138). This concept was carried on by the Nisga'a Tribal Council and thereby found its way into the Nisga'a Treaty.

From what has been said, therefore, the Nisga'a Common Bowl concept can be described as traditional concept that has been strengthened in recent history, because it has been tied to the fact that Nisga'a society had to react to the wrongs that colonial Canada inflicted upon it. It is a tradition that "had to go politics." It was culture translated into an answer to settlers and land commissioners, to negotiators, and finally, also to public opinion. From Giddens' point of view it might have been reflected upon too much, but in Nisga'a philosophy it is tradition in its purest form, because people have been living according to it every day. In fact, they still live it when they go fishing as a nation on special opening days, but they also live it when they have traditional ceremonies with a wooden bowl being carried at the head of a procession.

Endnotes

1 Raunet states that even when British Columbia joined Canada in 1871, it did not end its tough policy on the Indians, despite many complaints from the federal side that was responsible for Aboriginal issues. British Columbia refused to allow the Indians eighty acres of land per family as reserve lands, which was standard in the rest of the dominion they insisted on ten. In 1874

the issue became a crisis, because the Province of British Columbia passed its first land act without any provision for the creation of reserves. The Dominion used its right to interfere, but was, by 1876, more and more willing to compromise and did not insist any longer that reserves of a certain size were to be established. It left the issue to the joint Reserves Allotment Commission, whose chairman was Gilbert Sproat, an admirer of Governor Douglas (Raunet 1996, 77).

2 The quote is taken from an interview conducted with Alex Rose, August 18, 2001.

3 All parts of this article that refer to Nisga'a customs and traditions, which are not quoted otherwise, have been the result of a very fruitful exchange with Mansell Griffin, a member of the Nisga'a Nation, to whom I extend my cordial thanks.

4 This is because some chiefs have territory within the 10 percent of traditional Nisga'a land that is now governed by Nisga'a Lisims government, and some have territory outside of this 10 percent.

5 Under the authority of the *Nisga'a Land Act* (an *Act* enacted by *Wilp Si'Ayuukhl Nisga'a*), the executive of Nisga'a lisims Government may make dispositions of Nisga'a Lands. Whatever disposition is made—for example, grant in fee simple title or permit of occupation—the property remains Nisga'a lands under the authority of the Nisga'a Nation ("Nisga'a Lisims Government," online).

6 This, of course, is a "movement" that is not restricted to modern day Indigenous societies. It is much more a global phenomenon that includes Western societies as well, although it might be noticed more easily within Indigenous societies because they are seen as being more traditional.

Bibliography

Barbeau, Marius, William Beynon, John J. Cove and George F. Macdonald. Tsimshian narratives II: Trade and warfare, vol. II, Mercury series, Directorate paper no.3, Ottawa, Canadian Museum of Civilization, 1987, 243 p. (Posthumous publication).

Brody, Hugh. (1991). *Time Immemorial.* Toronto, ON: Tamarack Productions.

Duenckmann, Florian, and Verena Sandner. (2003). "Naturschutz und autochthone Bevölkerung: Betrachtungen aus Sicht der Politischenökologie." *Geographische Zeitschrift, 91:2*, 75–94.

Giddens, Anthony. (1990). *The Consequences of Modernity.* Palo Alto, CA: Stanford

University Press.

Nisga'a Nation, Province of British Columbia, and Canada. (2000). *Nisga'a Final Agreement.* Ottawa, ON.

Raunet, Daniel. (1996). *Without Surrender, Without Consent: A History of the Nisga'a Land Claims.* Vancouver, BC: Douglas & McIntyre.

Rose, Alex. (2000). *Spirit Dance at Meziadin: Chief Joseph Gosnell and the Nisga'a Treaty.* Madeira Park, BC: Harbour Publishing.

Spanjer, Antino. (2003). "First Nations im Westen Kanadas – zwischen Tradition und Moderne." *Geographische Rundschau, 55:9,* 53–60.

Supreme Court of Canada. (1967, September 27). *Calder et al. v. Attorny-General of British Columbia.* Case on appeal, statement of claim, 112–117.

Svensson, Tom G. (2002). "Indigenous Rights and Customary Law Discourse: Comparing the Nisga'a and the Sámi." *Journal of Legal Pluralism, 57,* 1–35.

Walbran, John T. (1991). *British Columbia Coast Names.* Vancouver, BC: Douglas & McIntyre.

Internet Sources

Meissner, Dirk. (2006, March 7). "Fraser Canyon Aboriginals Reach Treaty Agreement." *Canadian Press.* http://www.canada.com/calgaryherald/news/story.html?id=878a1c78-5c49-43d6-b568-f0bb18ce0a20&k=19945 [consulted March 22, 2006].

Nisga'a Lisims Government. http:// www.nisgaalisims.ca [consulted January 3, 2005].

EDUCATION

Tricia Logan

Métis Scholarship in the 21st Century: Life on the Periphery

Introduction

Métis voices are gaining momentum in the area of Aboriginal research. Trends in research are increasingly inclusive of Métis-specific, community-based work, providing Métis communities with research benefits they were not accustomed to. For over a century, research on Métis often delivered more harm than good to Métis communities. The colonizer's voice dominated Métis research, especially in the areas of history, anthropology and socio-political analysis. The research reflected little of the community-level Métis voice, and a Eurocentric bias quite often affected research outcomes (Dorion/Prefontaine 2001, 13).

As Aboriginal and post-modern research emerged in the late 20th century, Aboriginal people began to be active participants in research rather than objects of research (Brown/Strega 2005, 7). As the body of Aboriginal research increases, individual groups of Aboriginal people, First Nations, Inuit, and Métis will begin to make their individual views heard. In being heard, their communities will be served by both mainstream and Aboriginal methodologies in dynamic ways. Mainstream Canadian researchers are increasingly more willing to incorporate Aboriginal methods and views into their research in order to better serve the needs of those communities (Brown/Strega 2005, 98). At the same time, Aboriginal researchers are steadily adapting and creating their own methods that extend to places beyond the reach of long relied upon mainstream methods. One key aspect of Aboriginal research that extends beyond mainstream is the promotion of distinctions between First Nations, Métis and Inuit research.

Métis research has benefitted from the Aboriginal break from mainstream methods. The Métis voice has greater chances to affect changes for Métis by using progressive research methods, flexibility, and creativity in methodological formation. A research method separate from both mainstream and Aboriginal methods, taking into account Métis history and culture, is needed. There are considerations that need to be made by Métis researchers that are unique from other Aboriginal groups and take the dynamic nature of Métis communities into their frame of understanding.

Canada's West is the heartland to one of the most unique ethnic groups in the world. Métis of Canada created a nation and an identity from the earliest roots of colonial meetings between Canada's Aboriginal peoples and two distinct fur trade companies, the British Hudson's Bay Company and the French North West Company. The biology of 'mixed-blood' and of being an interracial person is a mere detail when compared with the numerous social, cultural and political influences that create ethnic identities for Métis. Métis cannot be separated from the British and French empires; relationships with the British and French colonizers comprised Métis identity. Métis look at colonization in many different ways; they are conscious of this relationship with the colonizer(s) and, in turn, reject it, accept it or are forcibly confined to it (Dorion/Prefontaine 2001, 26–27). Regional distinctions are also key influences on Métis identity. A Métis community's location in proximity to Roman Catholic or Protestant churches, non-Aboriginal communities and rural or urban centres has influenced values and social structures for Métis. Although there may be infinite variables that impact Métis identity, there are consistent values that create union in Métis nationhood. Loyalty to an agenda of Aboriginal-based rights, dedication to celebrations of culture through music, art and dance, regional-based identification and histories of economic, social and political hardships are common values that exist despite regional variables. Distinctions between Métis communities, such as spiritual or religious connections, location, and language, can be quite vast, but they can also provide important indicators to researchers who seek context for approaching Métis communities for study. Métis are First Peoples of Canada, recognized as Aboriginal people in the Canadian Constitution, and are a unique Indigenous group. Métis are not eager to be judged, in any measure, by their connections to First Nations communities or non-Aboriginal communities, and they consider studies of their lives best suited to a context kept true to Métis distinctiveness (Dorion/Prefontaine 2001, 36).

This is the challenge. What is a research paradigm that stays true to Métis? Métis-specific research should be tailored to view Métis lives through a Métis lens. An author or researcher may or may not have originated from a Métis community, but they can still, with care and respect, gain an understanding of Métis community dynamics. These dynamics are often complex when viewed by a "visitor," but realities of Métis life on a community level will provide uncompromising context for detailed research—a new era of Aboriginal study has emerged where all Aboriginal people are no longer objects of research; rather, they are authors of it (Brown/Strega 2005, 7).

Mainstream academic studies that focus on Indigenous people in general rarely mention Métis specifically. Métis are under-represented in literature and research. In *Resources for Métis Researchers,* Lawrence Barkwell states,

> This compendium reveals that Métis issues such as residential schools, health, justice, economic development, natural resources and human services such as child welfare are under-represented in the literature and in some cases references are almost non-existent. Compared to the body of literature and research which makes reference to these issues for First Nations and the Inuit, the Métis have been truly ignored and neglected. (Barkwell, et al. 1999, 1)

Often arbitrarily joined with First Nations and Inuit, Métis have fallen victim to forms of homogenization. Although being labelled under the same broad stroke of "Indigenous" may ease the Native Studies student's time, it glazes over the unique aspects of Métis culture and their place in the greater scheme of Indigenous life. Often left to be the "other" Aboriginal people, Métis are compared and contrasted under other people's contexts rather than their own.

Métis are aware of where their place is; however, negotiating the dominant understanding of this place is an obstacle. Métis have attempted to adjust to the current era of Aboriginal rights and responsibilities by working to continually define themselves. At times, it seems as if there could be a thousand different definitions for Métis, Métis identity, and ways of thinking about who Métis are. It is just as important to reflect on what Métis are not. Some Métis prefer to self-define by process of elimination rather than in any other way. For instance, Métis are not non-status Indians. Métis are not defined by biology or blood quantum. However, defining Métis by their relations to First Nations communities fragments Métis identity and contributes to lateral violence and infighting (Battiste/Henderson 2000, 37).

Government actions have placed limits on Métis identity by forcing definitions for this identity. Métis are forced to find their place under government limitations. In doing so, Métis do not always fight the cause of the limitations, but instead they fight each other. The reserve system in Canada, illegal administration of scrip (Ens 1996) in the late 1800s, the Indian Act, Bill C-31, education systems and other various government-initiated policies have turned Métis against one another. Jealousy, blaming, infighting, malicious gossip, and petty arguments have engulfed entire Métis communities. Government tactics, such as using blood quantum or ties to one specific cultural trait as a measurement of "Métis-ness," further work to fragment Métis communities.

Life on the Periphery

Métis have spent their lives on the periphery and they are relegated to a position as the "other" Aboriginal people (Ashcroft et al. 1995, 169). A lack of Métis research inevitably reflects a scarcity of Métis researchers. For a non-Aboriginal researcher conducting research on Métis, an understanding has to be reached that they will be accessing information from the centre to the margins. Extending one's lens to include the margins and view life of the "other" may have limits, but with a paucity of Métis research within the conceivable grasp of mainstream academia, a shallow view of who Métis are has been formulated; we need to extend the lens (Brown/Strega, 68).

Without engaging with Métis communities, historical studies about Métis can be biased. In terms of written histories and historically-based studies, Métis have a disproportionate voice. History written about Métis often falls into a classic Western model, and as a result, the most well-known Métis histories circulating through mainstream academia are written by the victors. Early texts were written in favour of colonial governments, and claimed that the Métis were "lazy" and lost the land allotted to them by their own fault (Barkwell in Barkwell et al. 2001, 468). Histories of the Métis are dominated by interpretations and reinterpretations of military battles of the old North West, of prominent figures like Louis Riel and Gabriel Dumont and of Canada's first "treasonous" rebels (Dorion/Prefontaine 2001, 14).

After 1885 Métis were forced out of their homes, on to road allowances, and out of comprehensive written histories. As soon as Métis lives became less about the buffalo hunt and "rebellious" actions and became more about mothers feeding their children during the Depression on road allowances, Métis became less visible in mainstream Canadian historiography. Non-Aboriginal writers, historians and anthropologists were the dominant voice before 1975. After 1975 Métis writers Bruce Sealey and Antoine Lussier wrote about "The Forgotten People," the real Métis, in one of the first social histories written by Métis for Métis. Sealey and Lussier extended their history of Métis beyond the popular mainstream stories of Riel and Dumont and interpreted stories of other Métis into written history (Sealey/Lussier 1975, 3).

In mainstream educational systems there is often a place for Aboriginal people, but far less often a place for Métis. Métis are too frequently forgotten about, under-researched, and always under-represented. In a new era, when public understanding about Aboriginal issues is at an all-time high,

Métis occupy an interesting position. For instance, efforts to decolonize and eliminate stereotypes have started to dominate research involving Indigenous populations; you can now see the tide beginning to turn. Care and caution are exercised at every level of Indigenous research. Research methods and protocols in mainstream institutions are created to serve Indigenous interests in increasing capacities. Research processes are delicate and political, placing Indigenous knowledge into a mainstream framework. Terms, referencing styles and writing methods must be chosen carefully. The improper use of terms has the potential to offend and will detract credibility from the researcher and research.

I personally find myself torn between studying Métis Studies within the discipline of Native Studies. With all the taboos, political implications, and intricacies of decolonization to navigate, I wonder if I am doing my best for Métis in Native Studies. A considerable amount of time is spent by academics in defining what their discipline is. Decolonization often is the prime focus in those discussions. A point that is re-iterated through those discussions is that Indigenous voices need to dominate (Smith 1999, 28). It seems to me that there is little agreement on how those voices should be represented. All of the readings and discussions always seem to lead me back to the same place. If this knowledge is being examined by mainstream academia, should the methods come before the topic? If the empire cannot be extracted from Métis, should we blindly research in written forms only as an excuse for not fully exploring Métis methods?

Knowledge Is Power

Métis-specific information or academic study is in high demand; it is rare and often hard to find, even today. Métis organizations fight for it and hoard it. If knowledge is power, Métis are in a position to be grateful for what they can get their hands on. Whether stemming from forced colonization that leads to lateral violence or infighting, Métis recognize the value of Métis research and end up fighting for it. In Métis organizations, I have been part of a system where I have been given specific instructions not to share information. In turn, information was withheld from me for the very same reasons. Keep in mind this was not political or confidential information: it was part of the public record and historical material valuable to all Métis. Knowledge is power and lateral violence becomes quite evident again as Métis groups fight for this power.

Another Other?

The colonizers distinguish themselves from Indigenous people. By using preconceived concepts of primitivism, the colonizer always works under a binary and hierarchical system (Ashcroft et al. 1995, 169). The system creates a divide between the "self," the colonizer, and the "other," the colonized. Research about Aboriginal people has been dominated by the "self's" voice as a self-proclaimed expert on the "other" (Ashcroft et al. 1995, 37). It has only been through recent developments in decolonization research that the dominant self, the Euro-Canadian self, has been able to shift its view of the Aboriginal other. This lens has opened up and has created an entirely new view of how Aboriginal or Indigenous knowledge can be used. It is a lens that emerged from decolonization but is now used widely in Aboriginal communities. It has even allowed some marginalized groups like Métis to focus on their own worldview separate from a larger whole.

But have Aboriginal people begun to "other" themselves through this lens? There is an undeniable relationship between the "self" and the "other." Each works to define their counterpart. The colonizer "others" the colonized by excluding, marginalizing and steadily comparing itself to the "other"—the Aboriginal People of Canada (Ashcroft et al. 1995, 173).

Consider the case of Métis. As the "other" Aboriginal people, Métis have been highly excluded by both the colonizers and by the Aboriginal majority, First Nations. Métis take pride in having a language, culture and customs separate from First Nations. That pride was born, in part, because of a historic connection that Métis have to exclusion, marginalization and comparison. Left to live on road allowances, in makeshift shantytowns, Métis were swindled out of their land (Shore/Barkwell 1997, 75). It is a common Métis trait to be resilient, innovative and entrepreneurial. In the 21st century, Métis have taken a huge step, by using the legal system to fight for their position as the "other" Aboriginal people. For a century, Euro-Canada made efforts to extract Métis from federal and provincial responsibility. In some respects, exclusion, marginalization and negative comparisons of Métis in Canada were quite severe. Some of the exclusion faced by Métis could be compared to forced removal, such as the case of Saint Madeleine, Manitoba (Zelig/Zelig 1987, 4), where Métis homes were burned and an entire community was destroyed in order to force them from their town and make room for Euro-Canadian farmland. In acts of systemic malicious ignorance, Métis were forcibly cast aside by dominant Canada, by movements that favoured European settlement in Canada's West (Shore 2001, 77).

Attempts by the Canadian federal government to provide for First Nations were carried out in a manner that the government thought was adequate, and possibly even fair. Attempting to adhere to treaties was Canada's way of acknowledging that the land they now reside upon was once solely First Nations land. Canadians imagined that they were responsible or accountable to First Nations and their attempts to address this responsibility, however weak, were still carried out with some (if minimal) recognition of their title to some lands (Friesen/Friesen 2004, 26).

Even in 2006, the federal government was unwilling to do the same for Métis and to acknowledge that their land was unlawfully taken from them as well. Métis were forced off their land by the dominant Euro-Canadians and were excluded from the safety of their homeland. Métis did not feel safe in the homes they had made in the Northwest for over one hundred years. As settlers moved west, Métis were forced to move farther west and north (Sprague/Frye 1983, 27). Efforts like the reserve system, treaties, and mandatory attendance at residential schools were all used to address Canada's "Indian Problem" (Milloy 1999, 7). In order to see this clearly, one must visualize the deplorable conditions of First Nations reserves, conditions that continue even today. First Nations were forcibly confined to the reserves on a pass system for years, living in Fourth World conditions. Métis communities lined the roads leading up to and bordering these reserves; their road allowance communities were literally situated on the periphery (Shore/Barkwell 1997, 77).

If reserves are a physical manifestation of the "other" brought about by the colonizer, then there is no doubt that the people denied membership in the "other" became the "other other." In addition, these communities bordered non-Aboriginal communities where settlers lived in towns, occupying land that was once well-populated by Métis. Métis would answer these situations by identifying with whichever community would benefit them. Road allowances have become an important symbol of the marginalization of Métis. They represent a physical manifestation of "othering." Not only are Métis excluded from the community geographically, but they are also cut out socially, politically and economically. Poverty, food insecurity and government-funded benefits are all damaging impacts that were often underscored by systemic racism against Métis. Living for the most part in "have-not" areas of Canada's rural West and North, Métis were often left with few options to address their needs. Being and becoming Métis on the margins embraced the post-colonial paradox of the "other," the endless struggle to improve life on the margins. "Marginal groups do not necessarily endorse the notion of a fixed centre .... The marginal therefore indicates a positionality that is best defined in terms of limitations of a subject's access to power" (Ashcroft et al. 1995, 135).

Métis are proud of their margins. Métis life flourished, and their resilience on the margins created pride in their nations. If identifying with the visible "other," First Nations, was beneficial to them, then they did so with pride. It also takes pride to associate oneself with the non-Aboriginal community. Living one's life as a lie, denying one's identity, language and people in order to identify with another culture (in some cases as French, Ukrainian, Russian, or British) in order to provide a better life for your family, escape persecution and racial discrimination, is a classic Métis tactic and should not be considered anything less than Métis pride. Adopting the characteristics of the "centre" was a conscious and intentional move to advance Métis interests. The Government of Canada created an atmosphere that caused some Métis to suffer for their identity. Courage was a key to opposing that atmosphere and embracing life on the margins. Even though the political climate is changing in Canada, Métis still adopt these tactics with their relations to the centre.

MÉTIS SCHOLARSHIP

Métis scholars are marginalized by their proximal location to both the pan-Aboriginal and mainstream centres. Métis scholarship faces two spheres of power. Modern Métis are not only working constantly to "define" their limitations according to the dominant centre, but they also face another front. Métis are currently forced to compete against other Aboriginal groups for funding and research. Dominant mainstream funders support the popular pan-Aboriginal models and leave the Métis, First Nations, and Inuit to function under their parameters (Lamouche 2002, 4). First Nations are a dominant voice in Aboriginal research and therefore create an academic criss-crossing of centres. Métis are dually marginalized.

It may be easy to transpose Métis research into one of the popular Indigenous methods in order to suit the needs of Métis; however, the question lingers of whether or not their needs will be met. In the same way that Métis communities worked with their margins in the past, scholars today have been asked to do the same. Without necessarily adopting the centre, finding a "space inbetween" to create their own methods leaves Métis in a unique situation.

In many cases, Métis communities benefit from using similar methods to those of First Nations. Some Métis have lived their lives in communities that border First Nations communities, and often present tobacco to Elders, participate in smudging, or conduct their interviews entirely in a First Nations language. In other cases, however, Métis values encompass a different range of commonly accepted values that are most often associated with First Nations. Sometimes the values they use are mostly associated with Métis. Often presentation of a gift that is not necessarily tobacco or medicine related, such as a gift of tea, a blanket, or food, is used more readily in some situations. Approaching Métis Elders often depends on the regional differences, the researcher's connection to the Elder, and community standards on approaching

Elders. This may be a Métis method or the beginning steps of one. Identifying if one should or should not expand their methodological thinking in research to encompass Métis-specific values is possibly a study in itself.

Conclusion

Consideration for a research subject's gender, culture, religion, mental capacity, and social structure are paramount in 21st-century research. Métis researchers often do not have the luxury of conducting research with predetermined protocols that their Indigenous counterparts have. Borrowing protocols from others often replaces the creation of their own, and Métis accept their position on academic margins and adopt methods from both centres. The benefits of doing so may, however, favour the researcher and not the researched. The voice of Métis is like no other. It is a voice that encompasses a margin and a life created to work on the margins, not inside them. A margin is not a barrier for Métis: it is their way of being. A margin is a starting point for academic questioning and it runs infinitely with Métis researchers. Accepting, rejecting, or being forcibly confined to the margins is a choice all Métis make.

Bibliography

Ashcroft, Bill, Gareth Griffiths, and Helen Tiffin, eds. (1995). *The Post-Colonial Studies Reader*. London: Routledge.

Battiste, Marie, and James Youngblood Henderson. (2000). *Protecting Indigenous Knowledge and Heritage*. Saskatoon, SK: Purich.

Barkwell, Lawrence, Leah Dorion, and Darren Prefontaine. (1999). *Resources for Métis Researchers*. Winnipeg, MB: Louis Riel Institute.

Barkwell, Lawrence, Leah Dorion, and Darren Prefontaine, eds. *(2001). Métis Legacy*. Winnipeg, MB: Pemmican.

Brown, Leslie, and Susan Strega. (2005). *Research as Resistance*. Victoria, BC: Canadian Scholars Press.

Dickason, Olive P. (1985). "One Nation in the Northeast to 'New Nation' in the Northwest: A look at the emergence of the metis." In *The New Peoples, Being and Becoming Métis in*

North America, eds. Jacqueline Peterson and Jennifer Brown. Winnipeg, MB: University of Manitoba.

Dorion, Leah, and Darren Prefontaine. (2001). "Deconstructing Métis Historiography: Giving Voice to Métis People." In *Métis Legacy*, eds. Lawrence Barkwell, Leah Dorion, and Darren Prefontaine. Winnipeg, MB: Pemmican, 13–36.

Friesen, John, and Virginia Lyons Friesen. (2004). *We Are Included: The Métis People of Canada Realize Riel's Vision*. Calgary, AB: Delselig Enterprises.

Ens, Gerhard. (1996). "Métis Scrip." In *The Recognition of Aboriginal Rights*, eds. S. Corrigan and J. Sawchuk. Brandon, MB: Bearpaw.

Lamouche, James. (2002). *Environmental Scan of Métis Health Information, Initiatives and Programs*. Ottawa, ON: National Aboriginal Health Organization.

Milloy, John S. (1999). *A National Crime*. Winnipeg, MB: University of Manitoba Press.

Sealey, Bruce, and Antoine Lussier. (1975). *The Métis: Canada's Forgotten People*. Winnipeg, MB: Pemmican.

Shore, Fred. (2001). "The Emergence of the Métis Nation in Manitoba." In *Métis Legacy*, eds. Lawrence Barkwell, Leah Dorion, and Darren Prefontaine. Winnipeg, MB: Pemmican, 71–78.

Shore, Fred and Lawrence Barkwell. (1997). *Past Reflects the Present, The Métis Elders Conference*. Winnipeg, MB: MMF.

Smith, Linda Tuhiwai. (1999). *Decolonizing Methodologies: Research and Indigenous Peoples*. London: Zed Books.

Sprague, D. N., and R. P. Frye. (1983). *The Genealogy of the First Métis Nation*. Winnipeg, MB: Pemmican.

Verges, Francoise. (1999). *Monsters and Revolutionaries: Colonial Family Romance and Metissage*. Durham, NC: Duke University Press.

Zelig, Ken, and Victoria Zelig. (1987). *Ste. Madeleine: Community without a Town*. Winnipeg, MB: Pemmican.

Barbara Walberg

Responding to the Needs of Post-Secondary Aboriginal Education: The Development of the Indigenous Leadership and Community Development Program

Aboriginal peoples[1] in Canada are presently engaged in a process of decolonization, in the restructuring of their societies through self-government and in the reaffirmation of their knowledge and worldview within the discourse of mainstream society. Central to this project is the need to reform the formal post-secondary education system in a way that will address these goals and aspirations. This reform must contemplate the possibility of a two-way exchange of knowledge, whereby Indigenous knowledge[2] and more traditional Western knowledge are integrated to create a new paradigm of learning with relevance to both worldviews. It must also address the needs for critical examination of the central questions of where we are and where we are going in this post-colonial, post-modern, and global world. An analysis and case study of the grounds-up development of a new degree level program in Indigenous Leadership and Community Development demonstrates the considerations necessary in order to meet these challenges.

BACKGROUND

Participation by Aboriginal peoples in formal post-secondary education in Canada before 1970 was almost negligible. Joanne Archibald and Sheena Selkirk-Bowman suggest that this was a result of poor outcomes from years of residential schools, public education that did not meet the needs of Aboriginal children, and the legacy of legislative barriers, which discouraged Aboriginal peoples from pursuing higher education (1995, 161). Since that time, there have been many efforts to improve outcomes for adult learners in post-secondary institutions. Aboriginal institutions have been created; universities and colleges have attempted to address policies, curriculum and pedagogy in an effort to meet the needs of Aboriginal students and the aspirations of Aboriginal society. Yet, in spite of the structural, policy, curriculum and other improvements, the Royal Commission on Aboriginal Peoples (RCAP) reported in 1996 that the post-secondary system was still not adequately meeting the needs of Aboriginal learners (Ministry of Supply and Services Canada 1996, 434). More recent census data confirms that there is a serious gap in completion of post-secondary education between Aboriginal and other Canadians. As of 2001, only 41 percent of First Nations had completed high school compared to 68 percent of other Canadians. Completion of post-secondary education rates show a similar disparity, with 24 percent completion by Aboriginal Canadians compared to 41 percent completion by other Canadians (Indian and Northern Affairs Canada 2001, online).

While the reasons for these figures are quite complex, recent critiques have focused on three main issues: the need to structure education for Aboriginal peoples in a way that will contribute to their existing project of decolonization, the need to recognize and integrate Indigenous knowledge and world views into the curricula, and the more fundamental need to replace the existing Eurocentric philosophy of education with an approach that educates for change and empowerment.

In the winter of 2002 a group of faculty and staff from Negahneewin College of Indigenous Studies, at Confederation College of Applied Arts and Technology in Thunder Bay, and community members from First Nations in

Northwestern Ontario, began a collaborative journey to design a degree-level program in Indigenous Leadership. This program would address the need for a meaningful and relevant post-secondary program for Aboriginal people as well as the aforementioned concerns.

Decolonizing Education

The impact of colonialism on Aboriginal peoples in the past has been well documented. What is less recognized is the legacy of colonial practices that still remain within the institutions of education in this post-colonial era. Marie Battiste describes the challenges which exist, suggesting that "Post-colonialism is not only about the criticism and deconstruction of colonialism and domination but also about the reconstruction and transformation, operating as a form of liberation from colonial imposition" (Battiste 2004, 1, online). She goes on to acknowledge that this will require the construction of "new relations, new frames of thinking and educational processes ... that engage each of us to rethink our present work and research" (Battiste 2004, 1, online). The *Report of the Royal Commission on Aboriginal Peoples* echoes this call for a new approach as it calls upon Canadian academic institutions to "decolonize their traditional presumptions, curricula, research and teaching practices in order to live up to their obligations, mission statement and alleged priorities for Aboriginal peoples" (Ministry of Supply and Services Canada 1996, 454).

Paulo Freire's study of dispossessed peoples in Brazil sheds some light on what might be needed in education to aid in the decolonizing process. In *Pedagogy of the Oppressed,* Freire sets out a theory and pedagogy for working with people recovering from oppression. Freire believes that education must begin with a process called *conscientização,* in which people develop a "critical consciousness" of the social, political, and economic forces that shape their lives and expose "the myths created and developed in the old order." He notes that "as long as the oppressed remain unaware of the causes of their condition, they fatalistically 'accept' their exploitation" (Freire 1970, 64). However, once they become conscious of the real history and forces that have contributed to their present situation, they will be able to see that it is possible for them to take action and create change.

Our own awareness and critical consciousness of these forces led us in our discussions as we explored the best way to address the Canadian legacy of colonialism. It was important that the program was future focused, finding ways to create opportunities for personal and community growth and development. It was also important to acknowledge and address the fact that colonialism has two partners: the oppressed and the oppressor. The program would have to reconcile the need for decolonization as it relates to a redefinition of the relationship between Aboriginal and Canadian society.

The Inclusion of Indigenous Knowledge

In the search for a creative vision of leadership that does not recreate the dominance and oppression of colonialism, Aboriginal peoples need only to examine their own traditions and rich cultural systems, world views, values, and structures. Although many of these traditions were repressed and discouraged under the colonial government policies, much of the knowledge still remains in the minds and hearts of Aboriginal peoples, communities and elders. Battiste explains, "Aboriginal epistemology is found in the theories, philosophies, histories, ceremony and stories as ways of knowing. Aboriginal pedagogy is found in talking or sharing circles, meditation, prayer, ceremonies or storytelling as ways of knowing and learning. The distinctive features ... are learning by observation and doing, learning through authentic experiences and individualized instruction and learning through enjoyment" (2002, 18). This way of knowing is also "inherently tied to the land" and is "both empirical (based on experience) and normative (based on social values). It embraces both the circumstances that people find themselves in and their beliefs about those circumstances" (Battiste 2002, 7).

The working group was conscious of the past failure of post-secondary institutions to fully integrate these principles of Indigenous knowledge and pedagogy in a comprehensive way. As Cathy Richardson and Natasha Blanchet-Cohen suggest, while there have been some attempts to improve the relevance of education to Aboriginal students at the post-secondary level, these efforts have often been limited to "added on" approaches that do little more than "dress up pre-existing methods and curricula to make them appear more culturally appropriate for Aboriginal people" (Richardson/Blanchet-Cohen 2000, 170).

The decision to embed the curriculum with the Indigenous philosophical framework[3] by fully integrating Indigenous authors, scholars, and knowledge from all traditions was considered by the working group to be integral to the program. While exploring the nature of the ideal graduate, it became apparent to the Aboriginal members of the group that the characteristics could be captured by principles which were common to their experience as Aboriginal peoples. Thus the principles of responsibility, reciprocity, relationship, reflection, and realization were chosen as the lens through which all the content of the program would be framed. We felt that in addition to making the knowledge relevant to the Aboriginal students, this would also provide a necessary breadth of perspective and quality of knowledge that could benefit all students interested in social change and the exploration of creative models of leadership.

It was also recognized that for this process of change and integration in education to work effectively, it had to be grounded in consultation and input from Aboriginal peoples in the community. This was part of the requirements set out by Aboriginal peoples since the release of Indian Control of Indian Education in 1973. Marie Battiste, Linda Bell and L. E. Findlay call this process of involvement "animation" and suggest that, "Animation recognizes that Aboriginal education requires a process of participation, consultation, collaboration, consensus building, participatory research and sharing led by Aboriginal people and grounded in Indigenous knowledge rather than the (neo) colonial command economy that imposes programs, courses and information generated in the university by academics and administrators to 'assist' Aboriginal students" (2002, 86). As a result, community consultation was the next step in the process of development. A series of focus groups and consultations were set up across Northwestern Ontario to flush out the ideas, opinions and details about what was important to leadership. These consultations brought back the perspectives of elders, community members and leaders, which were then integrated into the program. To a large extent, the consultations confirmed our work to that point by defining the need for leadership education based on critical consciousness, integration of Indigenous knowledge, relationship to the land, and the finding of common ground.

A New Theoretical and Pedagogical Approach

Research concerning the existing post-secondary system's lack of success in meeting the needs of Aboriginal students has recently focused on the philosophical foundation of the institutions which deliver higher learning. Battiste suggests that without an examination of the very foundation and goals of these institutions, there can be little meaningful change for Aboriginal students. She explains, "Much literature in the last decade has focused on the importance of diverse cultural methodologies to support ... and address the needs of Aboriginal students. The studies however do not examine the culture of the schools themselves to see ... what or whom the curriculum or pedagogy represses, excludes or disqualifies" (2002, 16).

At the post-secondary level, educational philosophy has been primarily represented by either the liberal or progressive theories of education. Sue Scott explains that "the aim of a liberal education is to discipline or exercise the mind through the study of absolutes, often articulated in the form of principles" (1998, 181). These principles were originally based on the premise that "Eurocentric knowledge represents the neutral and necessary story for all of us" (Battiste/Bell/Findlay 2002, 83). This belief has excluded and denigrated Indigenous and other knowledge systems and does not represent an appropriate foundation for education that is relevant to the expressed needs of Aboriginal peoples. In addition, much of Canadian post-secondary education is seen as "an important mechanism of socialization, social control and political legitimization" (Burns 1998, 2). As a result, it does not adequately allow for critique or inquiry of the status quo, which is a necessary process for the examination of dominant structures which have resulted in marginalization through colonialism (Hampton 1998, 37).

In response to such critiques, the RCAP recommended that institutions implement a different theoretical framework to meet this need. The theoretical framework that was suggested involved the theory of transformative learning: "Excellent study and practice in education have emerged from other parts of the world where people have also experienced colonialism or racial oppression. This form of education includes transformative education, popular education and critical pedagogy, which acknowledge that the educational process is one of unequal power relationships" (Ministry of Supply and Services Canada 1996, 483). The Negahneewin working group also recognized that there was a need to find a new approach to education. We had all experienced the high dropout rate of our students. We had long given up on traditional textbook curriculum which ignored Aboriginal perspectives or presented little or no meaningful alternative to Eurocentric knowledge. We wanted an approach that would be different, that would be relevant, and that would provide a framework for addressing meaningful change and transformation not only for communities, but also for individuals.

The development of an appropriate pedagogy that embraces transformative learning emerges from the work of both Paulo Freire and Jack Mezirow. The methods, which these theorists define as central to tranformatory pedagogy, include grounding the curriculum in the lived experiences of the students and engaging students in a process of critical reflection through the use of dialogue or "rational discourse" (Cranton 1998, 192). Freire's work goes one step further in suggesting that the outcome of this process be linked to "praxis," which is the continuous cycle of "action-reflection-action."

Freire also firmly rejects the traditional "banking approach" to education, where teachers as experts "deposit" knowledge to students who are presumed to know nothing. He advocates an approach where learning is focused on the themes that emerge from the lives and problems faced by the students, suggesting that such "problem-posing" education "takes the people's historicity as their starting point" (Freire 1970, 84) and that this allows people to "develop their own powers to perceive critically the way that they exist in the world with which and in which they find themselves: they come to see the world not as a static reality, but as a reality in process of transformation" (83). Similarly, Mezirow suggests, "It is the learner's experience that is the starting point and the subject matter for transformative learning.... Experience is seen as socially constructed, so that it can be deconstructed and acted upon. It is this experience that provides the grist for critical reflection" (Mezirow qtd. in Taylor 1998, 8).

Transformative learning theory and pedagogy provides the exact focus and methodology that captured our goals for leadership education. It offers a philosophy that acknowledges the need for educating to take action to create change which embraces the project that Aboriginal peoples are engaged in at this moment in history. Shedding the personal, social, economic, and political legacy of colonialism requires a careful critique of the forces that have led to the present situation and the relationship of Aboriginal people to mainstream society. The struggle for self-government will necessitate an analysis of the prescribed behaviours of internalized colonialism as well as the ability to find ways to create meaningful structures that do not recreate the domination and oppression of the system that they are leaving behind. Critical reflection and dialogue will be necessary in the exploration of how to integrate Indigenous knowledge in a substantive way, while at the same time coexisting in a world shaped by a dominant Eurocentric world view. Personal healing must also be addressed through personal development and self-awareness if leaders are to be able to withstand the conflicting forces within their communities. Our own belief about the outcome for our students in this new program echoes the words of Eber Hampton, who suggests that "the graduates of our schools must not only be able to survive in a white dominated society, they must contribute to the change of that society" (1998, 41).

Case Study and Analysis

The resulting Indigenous Leadership and Community Development Degree of Applied Learning was developed to create "agents of change who are able to negotiate the diverse demands of Indigenous and other communities in the context of the global society of the 21st century."[4] An analysis of its development, content, and pedagogy illustrates how well it meets the need discussed in this paper. It provides a new model for Aboriginal post-secondary education that addresses the complex needs of decolonization, the meaningful integration of Indigenous knowledge, and the transformative framework necessary to prepare individuals to lead Aboriginal communities into the future.[5]

In the process of developing this degree, the group was fully committed to consultation and involvement with Aboriginal peoples and communities. This is acknowledged in the submission to the Ontario Postsecondary Education Quality Assessment Board (OPEQAB)[6], which states, "A major contributor to the distinctiveness is the grassroots origin of the program. In the process of researching and outlining the initial stages, Negahneewin relied upon informal conversations, community visits, key informant interviews, surveys and focus groups with many community representatives" (Negahneewin College of Indigenous Studies 2002). As previously discussed by Battiste, this process of "animation" is seen an important starting place for the development of meaningful and respectful Aboriginal education. The degree program also evolved through critical reflection, dialogue and cooperation between individuals with diverse backgrounds, thus providing a "grounds up" approach to both content and pedagogy, which was based on many accumulated years of experience in education and community work with Aboriginal students. In this way, the development has modelled the approach and philosophy that is intended to be used with the students.

The interdisciplinary theoretical courses clearly fulfill the need identified by Freire of conscientization, or the understanding of historic, social, political, and economic forces that contribute to ongoing power imbalances and oppression, which are the lingering remnants of colonialism. "Major areas of inquiry include political and social theory, process skills, mediation, facilitation and negotiations, cultural diversity and evolving legal and political frameworks." It is clear from the language used by the program's designers—"outline and critique social and political ideas from various intellectual traditions" and "there will be a critical analysis of the ecological, political and cultural impact of globalization including the displacement of Indigenous groups and dispossession of traditional lands"—that these topics will be addressed through an analytical lens intended to move students towards a critical perception of the world, which will help them identify the socially constructed nature of marginalization and poverty.

The philosophical foundation,[7] based on Indigenous principles of responsibility, reciprocity, relationship, realization and reflection, grounds each of the courses in meaningful engagement of Indigenous knowledge. Cultural identity based on relationship to the land informs much of the content. The submission notes that "particular attention will be paid to the varied approaches by which Indigenous communities maintain their cultural identity while endeavouring to create social and economic sustainability" and suggests that the goal is to "create globally aware leaders whose competencies are grounded in a relationship to the land."

At the same time, its curriculum embraces both Indigenous and Western knowledge in the search for creative new solutions for a future that speaks to the humanity of all. In section 10.2, the submission proposes that "the cross cultural dimension of the program encompasses something more than the standard cultural comparisons: the organization into topics within the courses places diverse content side by side for the purpose of establishing breadth in the student rather than creating an apprehension of difference." This focus on finding "common ground" ensures that the structures and visions created for the future are truly life giving. Issues of power and a focus on changing patterns of oppression are addressed throughout the curriculum and are found in particular in courses such as Community Consensus Building and Negotiation Strategies, which suggest in their descriptions that "personal, structural, organizational and other kinds of power will inform the discussion."

Self-transformation, as described by Mezirow, is evident in the acknowledgement of the centrality of self-development and identity grounded leadership as critical themes and objectives. The submission suggests that "themes of personal self growth through self knowledge, an awareness of healing strategies and the fostering of individual and community identity is as integral to the program as the study of economics." This is reinforced by a variety of courses that centre on self-reflection, in the belief that "self reflection is absolutely pivotal to the development of sound leadership ability and … to becoming a fully developed thinker." In this, the program appears to be recognizing that healing from colonialism means addressing the formation and development of identity through self-knowledge.

A unique feature of this degree is a subset of courses (one per semester) known as "Negahneewin Courses." These leadership courses are seen as the "core community skills" for the degree. They provide the opportunity for students to engage in reflective dialogue about the difficult circumstances of their life world such as abuse of power, lateral violence, racism, and other aspects of internalized colonialism. The description of the course, Negahneewin: Community Healing and Self Reliance, illustrates the commitment to learning through dialogue rather than didactic means as the basic pedagogy for these specific courses. It suggests that "dialogue is necessary to facilitate understanding of these issues. The goal is to encourage critical thought and identify issues, sometimes painful and taboo, which are distorting the concept of healing and preventing communities from moving forward. This can take place only through careful thought and dialogue."

The "Negahneewin Courses" also incorporate other needs of Aboriginal pedagogy through the emphasis in many of the courses on experiential, active learning. Negahneewin: Leadership, Self and Identity, for example, indicates that "this course is intended to be experiential rather than didactic" and another course, called Negahneewin: Bridging Communities, suggests that the learning will be "fully applied in that learners will essentially be doing community work for credit." These diverse pedagogical approaches to learning allow for accommodating the many possible learning styles of students while at the same time exposing them to the wide range of possibilities in which knowledge can be explored.

The incremental introduction and use of problem-based learning encompasses many of the principles of transformative pedagogy through its use of problem-posing, real-life situations that allow for knowledge construction by the students. The emphasis on moving students away from dependence on the "teacher as expert" and towards collaborative group problem solving can be seen as a genuine step towards "praxis" as discussed by Freire.[8] In the classroom this provides opportunities to try out ideas and demonstrate leadership skills in a safe and nurturing environment, as well as to build confidence before moving out into the community. This emphasis on taking action is reinforced in the submission, which indicates that "throughout the program, there are expectations that learners will gradually become independent, self directed individuals who by the final semester are not so much studying community development as participating in it and practicing it as internalized experience."

Praxis is further reinforced and demonstrated through the two summer co-op placements, where students will be required to carry out and evaluate their ability to become active initiators of change in community-based projects. The notion of praxis as a relationship between conscious critical reflection and action is implied by the description of the co-op placement, which states, "Learners will engage in self reflection around their learning experiences and co-op placement. In the course of this self reflection they will be asked to identify situations where bridging difference is essential to progress and to assess positive and negative outcomes."

The co-op experience is further intended to solidify the Indigenous philosophy, skills and knowledge gained throughout the program and to provide opportunities for meaningful demonstration of the ability to create positive change in communities. The submission suggests that "there will be a clear expectation that the learners will be able to actualize their theoretical learning and propose, develop and implement a mutually agreed upon community-based project that reflects the depth of their understanding about community development in terms of responsibility, reciprocity, realization, and self reflection."

Finally, the focus on cross-cultural dialogue, diversity and building bridges will allow for the creation of a vision whereby Aboriginal people can consider becoming agents of change in larger society, by offering the learning from their own experiences as models for a more just, equitable and sustainable world. In keeping with the beliefs of Freire that oppression must not be a simple exchange of power in which those who have been oppressed take on the role of oppressor, the program is intended to model and demonstrate a different vision of leadership, community development, and change.

Conclusion

This program began from a need expressed by communities for a better education that would address the future aspirations of Aboriginal peoples in this post-colonial, postmodern world. It is a journey, however, which is not exclusive to Aboriginal peoples. All Canadians, and in fact most of the world, are increasingly coming to terms with the end of colonialism and the need to explore other ways of moving forward in the future which are more inclusive, equitable, and sustainable. On this journey, others will be taking a similar path to find new ways to combine diverse worldviews, and to create opportunities to creatively explore different ways to solve the problems and issues that are created by the rapid pace of change in the world. For this reason, the model of education that has evolved in the creation of this program should be viewed not only as appropriate for Aboriginal education, but appropriate education for all people who are seeking to find ways to create a new vision for the future.

Endnotes

1 Aboriginal, First Nations, Native, and Anishanabek are all common terms used to describe first inhabitants in a land. In this document, the term "Aboriginal" is recognized as the most common Canadian term when discussing the people. However, the term "Indigenous" is also used when discussing the broader scope of international work of First People in pedagogy, philosophy, and knowledge systems.

2 Indigenous knowledge is described by Marie Battiste as "the complex set of technologies developed and sustained by Indigenous civilizations" (2002, 2). The word "Indigenous" is used in this document to reflect the ideas, pedagogy, and philosophies that might encompass these international perspectives. In this program it is not limited to one tribal perspective.

3 The "Indigenous framework" also draws on worldwide Indigenous traditions and writings to explore the multidisciplinary subject matter of leadership and community development.

4 Negahneewin College of Indigenous Studies. "Indigenous Leadership and Community Development" web page at http://www.confederationc.on.ca/ilcd/calendar/. The case study quotes from this website.

5 Information regarding the program content is taken from the course calendar found at www.confederatonc.on.ca/ilcd/calendar and from the submission of the "Indigenous Leadership and Community Development (BAHS)" proposal by Negahneewin College of Indigenous Studies to the Ontario Postsecondary Education Quality Assessment Board. There are no page numbers in the submission.

6 The Ontario Postsecondary Education Quality Assessment Board is responsible for accrediting new programs in the province of Ontario.

7 Compare with appendix A for Indigenous framework as envisioned by the Negahneewin Working Group.

8 "Praxis" is the term used by Freire to explain the conscious cycle of action and reflection that is involved in the creation of change. It is this ability to reflect on the past and then use this reflection *to take action* that Freire suggests is critical to the ability of those who are oppressed to transform their future (Freire 1970, 85–98).

9 Taken from, Negahneewin College of Indigenous Studies "Indigenous Leadership and Community Development (BAHS)" submission by Negahneewin College of Indigenous Studies to the Ontario Postsecondary Education Quality Assessment Board, May 2002.

Bibliography

Archibald, Joanne, and Sheena Selkirk-Bowman. (1995). "First Nation's Postsecondary Education: A Review." *Canadian Journal of Native Education, 21:1*, 161–191.

Battiste, Marie. (1995). *First Nations Education in Canada: The Circle Unfolds.* Vancouver, BC: UBC Press.

———. (2000). "Maintaining Aboriginal Identity, Language, and Culture." In *Reclaiming Indigenous Voice and Vision*, ed. Marie Battiste. Vancouver, BC: UBC Press, 192–208.

———. (2002). *Indigenous Knowledge and Pedagogy in First Nation's Education: A Literature Review with Recommendations.* Prepared for the National Working Group on Education. Ottawa, ON: Ministry of Indian and Northern Affairs Canada.

Battiste, Marie, Linda Bell, and L. E. Findlay. (2002). "Decolonizing Education in Canadian Universities: An Interdisciplinary, International Indigenous Research Project." *Journal of*

Native Education, 26:2, 82–95.

Burns, George. (1998). *Towards a Redefinition of Formal and Informal Learning: Education and the Aboriginal People.* Toronto, ON: Ontario Institute for Education of the University of Toronto.

Cranton, Patricia. (1998). "Transformative Learning: Individual Growth and Development through Critical Reflection." In *Learning for Life*, eds. Sue Scott, Bruce Spencer, and Alan Thomas. Toronto, ON: Thompson Educational Publishing, 188–199.

Freire, Paulo. (2003). *Pedagogy of the Oppressed.* 30th ed. New York: Continuum.

Haig-Brown, Celia. (1998). "Taking Control: Contradictions and First Nation's Adult Education." In *First Nations Education in Canada: The Circle Unfolds*, eds. Marie Battiste and Jean Barman. Vancouver, BC: UBC Press, 260–288.

Hampton, Eber. (1998). "Towards a redefinition of Indian Education." In *First Nations Education in Canada: The Circle Unfolds*, 10–45.

Ministry of Supply and Services Canada. (1996). *The Report of the Royal Commission on Aboriginal Peoples.* Ottawa, ON: Canada Communications Group Publishing.

Negahneewin College of Indigenous Studies. (2002). *Indigenous Leadership and Community Development (Bachelor of Applied Human Services; BAHS).* Submission to the Ontario Postsecondary Education Quality Assessment Board. Toronto, ON: Government of Ontario.

Richardson, Cathy, and Natasha Blanchet-Cohen. (2000). "Postsecondary Education Programs for Aboriginal Peoples: Achievements and Issues." *Canadian Journal of Native Education, 24:2*, 169–185.

Scott, Sue. (1998). "An Overview of Transformation Theory in Education." In *Learning for Life*, eds. Sue Scott, Bruce Spencer, and Gordon Selman. Toronto, ON: Thompson, 178–188.

———. (1998). "Philosophies in Action." *Learning for Life*, 98–107.

Taylor, Edward W. (1998). "The Theory and Practice of Transformative Learning: A Critical Review." In *Adult Career and Vocational Education.* Columbus, OH: Center on Education and Training for Employment.

Internet Sources

Battiste, Marie. (2004). "Animating Sites of Postcolonial Education: Indigenous Knowledge and the Humanities." CSSE Plenary Address, Manitoba. http://www.usask.ca/education/people/battistem/csse/battiste.htm [consulted December 6, 2004].

Confederation College of Applied Arts and Technology. (2004). "Program Calendar 2004–2005." Thunder Bay, ON. http://www.confederationc.on.ca/calendar [consulted December 4, 2004].

Indian and Northern Affairs Canada. (2001). "Post-Secondary Education and Labour Market Outcomes Canada." http://www.ainc-inac.gc.ca/pr/ra/pse/01/pt1-1_e.html#psea [consulted December 4, 2004].

Negahneewin College of Indigenous Studies. "Indigenous Leadership and Community Development." http://www.confederationc.on.ca/ilcd/calendar [consulted December 3, 2004].

Appendix A: The Indigenous Framework of Curriculum as Envisioned by the Negahneewin Working Group

Figure 2.1 Indigenous leadership and community development: The ideal graduate

Responsibility
- Analytical – understanding political structures
- Responsible for self, family, community
- Progressive thinker, sustainability, advanced
- Decision maker, ethical, dynamic, innovative
- Process oriented

Realization
- Action/change – advocacy
- Committed to change
- Can follow policy, history, information, models of governance
- Innovative, transformative
- Planning
- Committed to empowerment
- Healthy infrastructure

Reflection
- Self – personal development
- Fun in work
- Independent, articulate
- Passionate, confident
- Aware
- Open to change
- Focus
- Reflection – action
- Philosophical
- Overcoming victimization

Relationship
- Collaborative – creating dialogue
- Healthy organizations, collaborative
- Negotiation, team player, trustworthy
- Flexible, common ground,
- Respect for difference

Reciprocity
- Context – political theory
- Globalization
- Aboriginal principles
- Informed
- Work ethic, reliable, dependable, supportive, respectful
- Values clearly understood, economic development

Appendix B: The 'Negahneewin Courses'[9]

These course descriptions are provided to illustrate a sample of the Negahneewin Courses that are offered in each semester. They demonstrate the integration of Indigenous knowledge and the relevant and didactic learning methodology discussed in the article.

Semester One – Negahneewin: Leadership, Self and Identity

This course will provide learners with the theoretical and practical foundations from which to explore the concepts of selfhood and identity as essential to leadership. Learners will discuss the formation of identity within the nexus of culture, with particular attention to the Indigenous awareness of the land as essential to self knowledge. Models of selfhood presented will contrast the individual with the self-in-relationship and will be framed by a multidisciplinary discussion of personality development and self reflection.

Delivery: Seminar

The course is intended to be experiential rather than didactic. While there will be required readings which will be discussed, at least half of the course will be delivered in historical or cultural settings including the outdoor environment ...

Semester Two – Negahneewin: Leadership in Contemporary Communities

This ... course will introduce learners to principles of leadership, grounded in an Indigenous framework, as reflected in traditional practices and customary laws. Learners will identify a range of Indigenous leaders, discussing and comparing the differing leadership styles demonstrated in Indigenous and non-Indigenous communities. Key themes will be the recognition of strengths, conflicts, and challenges to contemporary Indigenous leadership and the distinction between formal and informal models of leadership.

Delivery: Seminar/Discussion

Learners require an opportunity to digest and integrate their readings, to relate content concerning traditional ways into contemporary scenarios. This involves a process of discussion and group interaction combined with reflection and writing.

Semester Three – Negahneewin: Community Healing and Self Reliance

This course will explore the concept of healing as a journey into self reliance at both personal and community levels. Learners will discuss the practice of healing in Indigenous communities and identify the challenges and barriers to creating balance, drawing upon specific examples of community healing strategies. The discussion will explore definitions of healing which are based on Indigenous understanding of personal responsibility grounded in relational thinking and will provide learners with opportunities to engage in empowering forms of healing activities.

Delivery: Seminars and Guest Speakers

Dialogue is necessary to facilitate an understanding of these issues. The purpose of the course is not however therapeutic. The goal is to encourage critical thought and identify issues, sometimes painful or taboo issues, which are distorting the concept of healing and preventing communities from moving forward. This can only happen through frank and careful dialogue.

The remaining Negahneewin Courses (edited descriptions) include:

Semester Four – Negahneewin: Writing Power

This course offers a forum of discussion and expression whereby learners will further develop their voice through self-reflection .... Topics will include a discussion of the deconstruction of the objective voice in written discourse and the affirmation of subjective experience.

Semester Five – Negahneewin: Accountability Frameworks

This course will discuss a range of approaches to practicing responsibility as underlying accountability to self and community. It will explore the problem of accountability from various perspectives such as the personal, the political, organizational and fiscal. Learners will be required to identify the ethical demands of these different frameworks, and to discuss them in the context of accountability challenges as presently observed in communities.

Semester Six – Negahneewin: Community Advocacy and Mobilization

The purpose of this course is to prepare learners to strategize effectively for various types of community action. Learners will engage in discussion of the meaning of advocacy, the challenges of ethical advocacy and will practice listening and speaking skills to transform ideas into action.

Semester Seven – Negahneewin: Ethical Administration

In this course learners will explore ethics as the underpinning of administrative process. The exploration will be framed by Indigenous values and the challenges of applying these values within administrative structures. Assignments will provide an opportunity to incorporate this understanding with creative and problem solving skills to suggest new approaches.

Semester Eight – Negahneewin: Reciprocity in Practice

This course will require learners to address the application of reciprocity or "giving back." A key area of discussion will be the meaning of reciprocity with reference to Indigenous intellectual property, and how to protect a sense of community ownership in the products of development initiatives.

Semester Eight – Negahneewin: Bridging Communities

Learners will engage in self reflection around their learning experiences and in particular their co-op placements .... Learners will be expected to articulate the importance of bridging differences between communities whether cultural, organizational, and personal or problem-based.

IMAGINING AND IMAGING THE "INDIAN"

Geneviève Susemihl

The Imaginary Indian in German Children's Non-Fiction Literature

The stereotypical image of Native people among German children and young adults is that of the Plains Indian. The Indian is a mounted warrior and buffalo hunter, who rides through the endless prairies, wearing war paint and a headdress, dwells in a tipi, and sits around the campfire in a dignified manner, smoking a peace pipe. Even small children have a firm picture of an Indian and instantly recognize the stylized mounted chief in fringed buckskin as Karl May's "Winnetou" and the Indian girl with long black hair as Pocahontas. This essay explores the images of North American Native people in German children's non-fiction literature and examines how these limited and partly distorted perceptions of Native people affect young people. After looking at the general image German children and young adults have of Native people, I will discuss samples of children's non-fiction literature that contain stereotypical representations of Native people.

The Image of the Indian in the World of Children

Generally, children's perceptions of Native people are formed by a variety of sources, including teachers, parents, museum displays, food packages, advertisements, toys, and books. German children learn from these sources that Native people always wear feathered headdresses, frequently brandish tomahawks, and live in tipis. These images play a crucial role in distorting their attitudes toward Native people, since, according to Kenneth Clark,

> ... children's attitudes toward [Native people] are determined chiefly not by contact with [Native people], but by contact with the prevailing attitudes towards [Native people]. It is not the [Native person], but the idea of the [Native person] that influences children. (Clark qtd. in Moore/Hirschfelder 1981, 8)

By being continuously exposed to the stereotyped images of Native people in books, television programs, movies, and toys, all of which are reinforced by the societal discourse, young children internalize these images; eventually they develop attitudes toward Native people that are unrealistic and incorrect, but that will remain with them throughout adulthood.

A recent sample survey I conducted with seventy-six university students[1] between the ages of nineteen and thirty-two confirmed that the romanticized "Plains Indian" remains the predominant German stereotypical Indian among young adults in Germany. The vast majority of students associated Native people with "hunting buffalo with bow and arrow" (82 percent); "living in tipis in the prairies" (81 percent); "unfair suffering" (71 percent); "adventure" (68 percent); "stories at the camp fire" (61 percent) and "brave warriors, riding on horseback" (60 percent). The typical "Indian" is also identified as having "long, black hair" (97 percent); is "friendly and civilized" (52 percent), as well as "brave, courageous and heroic" (51 percent). More than half of the students further associated Indians with the fictional characters "Winnetou" and "Old Shatterhand"[2] (64 percent), and only about a third of them with "agriculture and farming" (32 percent), "dwellings made out of adobe, grass or earth" (36 percent), and "democracy" (11 percent). The best-known Native leaders among the participants of the survey are Sitting Bull (34 percent), Geronimo (8 percent) and the fictional Winnetou (8 percent). While about a fifth of the students believe that Winnetou really existed, about half of the students take Pocahontas for a fictional character. The best known nations are Winnetou's Apaches (63 percent), Sitting Bull's Sioux (62 percent), and the Iroquois (25 percent). The students predominantly claim that their knowledge about Native people comes from *Winnetou* films (81 percent) and other feature films (75 percent), novels by Karl May (69 percent), television documentaries (62 percent), non-fiction (54 percent), and fiction books (50 percent). Less than half of them learned about Native people at school, from the Internet, museums, relatives, or trips to North America.

This survey shows that today, approximately twenty-five years after Hartmut Lutz's study on *"Indianer" und "Native Americans"* (1985), the picture has not fundamentally changed. The stereotype of Native people in the world of German children and young people is that of the Indian of the past, wearing traditional clothing and engaged in traditional activities. This can also be confirmed by an empirical study of the existing stereotypical image of Native people in Germany conducted by Sebastian Krebes in 2002, in which 179 German junior high and high school students between the ages of twelve and twenty participated (appendix A). Comparing his results with the survey conducted by Hartmut Lutz in 1977–78, Krebes observed that the students' answers in both surveys were rather homogeneous, and that the two surveys found similar stereotypes, presenting the same standardizing and idealizing features. The children in the 1977–78 study merely seemed to know more names of actual people and chiefs, which might indicate a generally greater interest in Native people in the late 1970s in Germany. Today, with the hype of Harry Potter and other fantasy literature, Indians seem to have been pushed aside from their former privileged place in young people's literature; instead of "noble Indians," clever witches and other fantastic creatures have conquered the imaginations of children.

Krebes noted, however, differences in two significant fields: firstly, in the characterizing of "Indians"; and secondly, in the sources of children's knowledge. He claims that today we find far more positive than negative characteristics and argues further that,

> The visual media such as television and especially Karl May movies ... seem to play a dominant role when it comes to creating and transporting images of the Native Americans, whereas the print media including

> May's novels have only marginal impact on the participants' attitudes towards the North American Indians. (Krebes 2002, 99)

Indeed, in Krebes survey we find a strong influence of the tremendously popular German film *Der Schuh des Manitu* (*The Shoe of Manitu*, 2001), a parody of other films that deal with Native people, such as *Winnetou* (1963), and their stereotypical clichés. However, because the film only humorously challenges the themes, it maintains and encourages the use of the existing stereotypes. Characters from *Der Schuh des Manitu*, such as "Listiger Lurch" (third place), "Abahachi" (fifth place), and "Winnetouch" (eighth place) reached top positions in the list of prominent chiefs among the high school students. Before the movie came out these results would have been impossible (Krebes 2002, 37). Krebes' findings are confirmed by the survey in 2003–04, in which only half of the students claim to have gained their knowledge from print media.

Although the results of Krebes' survey suggest that German children and teenagers predominantly acquire their knowledge about Native people from movies and television, they are still very much influenced by children's books that reinforce existing stereotypes. During the past two centuries, the German publishing industry has produced hundreds of children's books about Native people, and generations of German children have grown up reading adventure stories about stalwart, crafty "redskins," biographies of the "great chiefs," or books about the "real" life of the "Indians." Karl May, for instance, has had a tremendous influence on the creation of the imaginary "German Indian." In most cases, literature merely reflects images projected by non-Indian writers, and "the reality, past and present, has often been lost in the shuffle" (Dorris in Hirschfelder/Molin/Wakim 1999, ix). Many of these books, therefore, frequently transmit stereotypes and inaccurate information about Native people, "thus preventing children from developing a realistic picture of past and contemporary Native life" (Hirschfelder 1999, 139).[3]

In a study of the imaginary Indian in the world of German children, I analyzed thirty-five titles of children's non-fiction books available in German book stores and libraries in 2005.[4] Besides skimming books *about* Native people, I also surveyed books that dealt with themes that were, more or less, unrelated to Native people, such as alphabet books or books with instructions for handicrafts or children's parties. In order to examine the context in which stereotyping occurs, I analyzed the books in terms of historical accuracy (past and present), cultural and geographic accuracy, and ethnic and gender awareness, with an emphasis on texts and visual images. While the general quality of these books seems to have changed within the past three decades, there are still many shortcomings. During the 1970s and 1980s many non-fiction books—"cheap productions, flooding the market on the tide of Indianthusiasm, carelessly put together and badly illustrated," as Lutz observed (Lutz 2002, 42)—emphasized the exotic, in which

> the actual presentation is often so racist that it thoroughly confirms existing stereotypes, even those of the bloodthirsty or animal-like savages. Culturally amorphous but eurocentrically idealized Indians frequently serve as vehicles to transport petty bourgeois attitudes about the importance of cleanliness and order and about gender roles. (Lutz 2002, 41)

Today, open racism is almost non-existent and many books are written and illustrated with a great love for accuracy. Native people are, however, still predominantly presented as people of the past, not as contemporaries. And while most books try to distinguish between cultural groups, some books still combine elements of entirely different Native groups. Finally, we find among the non-fiction books many "how to" books, instructing children how to become "Indians" themselves. Older books especially, that are still available in libraries, books in translation, and books for young children continue to spread racist stereotypical images, as Lutz noted in 1981 (Lutz, 248). Arlene Hirschfelder, who has analyzed toys that "convey incorrect and often offensive" images of Native people, has identified categories such as the "Indians-of-the-Past," the "Indians-as-a-Mixture," and the "Indians-as-Occupation-or-Role" (Hirschfelder 1999, 141). Applying these categories, I will, in the following analysis of German children's non-fiction books, discuss specific examples of

(1) exhibiting Native people in a past vs. a contemporary setting; (2) generalizing Native culture vs. paying attention to cultural diversity; and (3) treating "Indian" as a role versus presenting his/her ethnic identity.

Representations in the Past and the Contemporary

As the above presented surveys have shown, German children and young adults have romanticized, and even false ideas, about who Native people are and how they live, behave, and dress. Many children are fascinated by traditional Native cultures and see Native people as a people of the past. Authors, illustrators, and publishers contribute to this notion not only by portraying them in the past, but also by juxtaposing Native people of the past with contemporary non-Native cultures.

Of the thirty-five books I analyzed in this study, eighteen include no reference to the contemporary life of Native people at all. Books for the very young and books with a theme unrelated to Native people often take place in an unidentified "sometime" and "somewhere." Though often demonstrating the distinct Native cultures in the historical past in great detail, some books sampled in this survey are not written to enlighten the reader about actual historical events. More than half of the twenty-six books describing the culture of the people are either not concerned with Native history at all or recognize key events in history only. There are books that go into more detail about Native history; however, they simplify or even falsify it. In fact, many books "tend to construct myths which obscure rather than expose imperial conquest and internal colonialism," following the "complacent nineteenth-century European American projection that Native Americans were a 'dying race.' They perpetuate the view ... that fate condemned Indians to extinction" (Lutz 2002, 35). Their culture, apparently, survived only in museums. Lutz has labelled these myths the "myth of the dying race" and the "myth of a culture gone forever" (Lutz 1981, 256–57). "As a result," Lutz continues, "Native American history is constructed as inevitably 'tragic,' and Native Americans as peoples are projected as beings of the past, not as contemporaries" (Lutz 2002, 35).[5]

A rather unpleasant example of this "myth of a dying race" category is Jean Marcellin and Jean Robert Masson's 1995 book, *Die großen Indianerhäuptlinge: Cochise, Geronimo, Crazy Horse, Sitting Bull* (*The Great Indian Chiefs: Cochise, Geronimo, Crazy Horse, Sitting Bull,* 1994), which recounts the heroic lives of the "great chiefs" and indicates that there were no other great Native leaders throughout history. Native people are pictured dancing in ceremonies, hunting buffalo, dying heroically, either shot by "bluecoats"[6] or falling off their horses. Quotes from Forrest Carter help romanticize the picture of a *rancheria,* where Geronimo was dwelling before he fought his last stand. The back cover states,

> The crucial battles between the tribes and the 'blue coats' as well as the life of the Indians, their customs and rituals, their ways of thinking and their bitter fight against the intruders are shown in this book with many illustrations and an informative text. The end of the great chiefs stands also exemplary for the dusk of the Indian people on their way to reservations. (Marcellin/Masson, back cover; translation G. S.)[7]

In this sense, there seems to be no tomorrow; life in reservations thus means the end of traditional "Indian" life.

Marion Wood's 1998 book, *Die Welt der Indianer Nordamerikas* (*The World of Native Americans,* 1997), takes the reader on a "fascinating journey through the world of Native Americans," showing in "colourful, detailed pictures the world of the native inhabitants of North America as it was before it was destroyed forever by the white conquerors" (Wood 1998, back cover; translation G. S.).[8] Again, there is no indication of contemporary life in the book. The "tragic disappearance of Native culture" is also pictured in books for the very young, as in Ute Fuhr und Raoul Sautai's *Die Indianer* (*The Indians,* 1995): "With the building of the railroad, cities and ranches, the old America of the Indians has forever disappeared" (Fuhr 1995; translation G. S.).[9]

In children's fiction, which was not the principle object of the study,[10] the past is even more dominant, as can be seen in Renate Jacob's *Indianergeschichten* (*Indian Stories,* 2002), a collection of short stories about white children (called

Max, Nina, and Niklas) playing "Indian" at home and school, and Native children (named Beautiful Flower and Warwuk) playing in the prairies or the woods in the historical past. Whereas all stories deal with problems of friendship, competitiveness among children, or the relationship between children and adults, the stories of the white children are set in the present, while the "Indian stories" are played out in an indefinite pre-contact time. By juxtaposing "Indian" past and mainstream contemporary culture, the young reader may have the impression that Native people no longer exist, and it is, therefore, acceptable and even necessary to revive Native culture and "play Indian."

In seventeen of the analyzed titles the contemporary life of Native people is mentioned; in seven books, however, only very little space is dedicated to it. In many of these books there are either no visual images or only small images of modern Native life illustrating the text. Often, these photographs and drawings are of Native people dressed in traditional Plains regalia, dancing at powwows. While these images indicate that traditional ceremonies are still being performed today and have thus "survived" into modern times, they are at the same time perpetuating the romantic stereotype of Plains Indians, as there are no other illustrations representing contemporary Native life.

Angela Weinhold's *Bei den Indianern* (*With Indians*, 2002) is a typical example. The book tries to answer various questions concerning Native people. Only on the last page is the question asked: "Are there still Indians today?" The text explains that there are two million Native Americans living in the United States today, of whom "one third lives on reservations far away from big cities," where,

> [l]ife is not easy ... finding work is difficult for the Indians, and many are often poor. Dependent on social welfare, many drink too much alcohol. Slowly their situation is improving. Children attend the reservation schools and study English, as well as their own language. In the big cities Indians work as craftsmen, doctors, lawyers, actors, and in many other jobs. Their children live like white children. (Weinhold 2002, 16; translation G. S.)[11]

While the text states that Plains Indians do not live in tipis anymore, a picture shows a car in front of a tipi. The text further informs us about the original and modern character of powwows. And while the pictures show Native children and adults dressed in traditional powwow outfits, there is no picture of a "modern Indian" in modern clothing—possibly because Weinhold considers it difficult to draw a child dressed in modern clothing and indicate at the same time that she is Native. Thus, except for the car/tipi picture and a very small image of a reservation road sign at the top of the page, there is nothing on that page or in the book that supports the text and provides the reader a visual image of Native life today.

The same is the case with Philippe Jacquin's *So lebten sie zur Zeit der Indianer: Die spannende Geschichte der Ureinwohner Amerikas* (*How People Lived During the Times of the Indians: The Exciting History of the Indigenous People of America*, 1994)—a book about the historical past, written in the present tense. The text is meant to educate young readers about past and present traditions but fails; even though social and cultural conditions of various cultures are described and illustrated very colourfully and in detail, only three of sixty-eight pages are reserved for facts about the present. Three contemporary photographs illustrate the text: a picture of houses on a reservation, a portrait of Native people in traditional Plains regalia marching in a parade, and an image of the protests at Wounded Knee in 1973. It is explained that "today the Native Americans are in an inner conflict between tradition and revolt.... Their tragic fate makes it necessary that they obtain a place within the America of the Whites that is worthy of their culture and history" (Jacquin 1994, 67–68; translation G. S.)[12]; one wonders if Jacquin refers to a museum in describing this "worthy place."

David Murdoch's *Indianer*: *Wie die Bewohner Nordamerikas wirklich lebten. Von den Pueblovölkern im Südwesten bis zu den Jägern des Nordens* (*North American Indian*, 1995) claims to be a "non-fiction picture book of the new generation." By examining photographs and reading short texts, according to the back cover, children get to know how many tribes "really lived." However, only one chapter, two pages in length, is dedicated to contemporary Native people. It shows photographs of a Mohawk construction worker, a helmet painted by a Native artist, an unidentified powwow dancer in traditional Plains regalia, a group of Apaches dancing a ritual dance, a Navajo woman baking bread in a traditional oven, a Native person working in a casino, Ojibwa children at a powwow in traditional dresses, and a group of Native people sitting in a meeting. The captions of the different photographs seem to label images of the "modern Indian": "boldness," "modern art," "old ceremonies," "keeping the old traditions," "gambling," "powwow," "education," and "together against injustice."

A pleasant reading is Karin von Welck's *Bisonjäger und Mäusefreunde* (*Buffalo Hunters and Mice Friends*, 1982). In her well-written and detailed text, Welck writes about the life of the various cultural groups, clearly differentiating between the past and present. Yet, the text is sometimes confusing and misleading. Reading about the conditions at the Flambeau Lake reservation school in Wisconsin, where children are taught in their mothe tongue instead of in English, the reader might think that all Native children learn the language and history of their people, which is still not the case. Furthermore, by putting the words in the "old and wise" Inuit's mouth that it is "too bad" that young people do not want to go hunting "as their fathers did" anymore (von Welck 1982, 41), the author gives the young reader the impression that modern development is wrong and a loss for the Inuit, verifying the "myth of the culture gone forever."

Native cultures were and are extremely diversified and can not be typified by the outdated and inaccurate "Indian-of-the-Past" image so often used in non-fiction children's literature. Moreover, the misrepresentation of contemporary life in children's non-fiction literature runs the risk of conveying a stereotypical picture of Native people. When questioned about the present realities of Native people, the participants of Krebes' study differentiated between three alternatives:

> Many assume that there are hardly any Natives left and that they will soon disappear. Others favour the idea of acculturation; they are convinced that the Native Americans have given up their traditional lives in order to integrate themselves into the white mainstream society.

> Finally, a third group believes that most Natives fight hard to protect their traditional values and lifestyles and therefore they try to retreat from the white mainstream society. Although it seems as if German children know very little about the life of Native Americans in the 21st century, there are certain details that appear to be well known to many students. Apparently issues such as alcoholism and unemployment are understood to be typical features of the life of the majority of modern Native Americans and hence there is certainly a great danger of creating new and unfair stereotypes. (Krebes 2002, 99)

Indeed, when writing about the present, authors have to be careful not to fall once again into stereotyping. Images of depressed, alcohol-addicted "Indians" on reservations or rich casino-owners, relieving non-Natives of a handful of dollars, are quite common, as the following statements of university students in the 2003–04 survey illustrate:

> They live on reservations and little by little their traditions are forgotten. Since they are also genetically not used to a modest life, many are overweight due to fast food etc. Many are also alcoholics. Often they are excluded by others and hardly get work. (Female student, 21 years)[13]

> Poor dogs, those living on reservations. Getting drunk and fighting for their daily survival is their daily bread. They hardly find work and if they do, the white man exploits them. They fight for every piece of land that the white man has stolen from them. (Male student, 22 years)[14]

> Indians in reservations are financially well off, because Uncle Sam runs casinos for them. Nevertheless they are not well-liked. Some day old deeds should be forgotten, considering the stealing of land and so on. (Male student, 25 years)[15]

In reality there are roughly 3.5 million Native people living in Canada and the USA today, and many cultures and traditions of Native peoples have remained or have been rediscovered and are being practiced. This should be reason enough for children's books to go further than just mentioning contemporary Native life as a side remark. In addition, children's books should critically explain and expose stereotypical images and the intentions behind their use, as Hauke Kock does in *Der Wilde Westen* (*The Wild West*, 1996). Setting historical incidents in context, Kock explains that already in the 19th century the transfiguration and marketing of the "Wild West", its legends often diverging from historical truth. In her book published in 1998, *Indianer in Nordamerika* (*Native Americans*, 1997), Fiona MacDonald gives a specific example for selling the imaginary "Indian" and appropriating their image for commercial reasons: "With this eye-catcher—an Indian warrior with a headdress made of eagle feathers—a restaurant and a shopping centre is advertised" (MacDonald, 22; translation G. S.).[16] If Native people are not represented in a contemporary context, they remain "pitiful museum pieces" (Lutz 2002, 36) and only little information will be provided about their present existence.

Generalization versus Cultural Diversity

Although the Plains Indians seem to be the only "real Indians" for German children, they are still very often part of a puzzle including pieces of various Native cultural groups. Generalizing and mixing are most often, but not exclusively, visible in books for the very young and books that are unrelated to Native themes. Many of the sampled books use the generic term "Indian" when referring to a unique people. Seven of the thirty-five sampled books in this survey describe an unspecified "Indian" stereotypical culture, seven books are concerned with one specific Native culture, and twenty titles introduce the reader to different Native cultures. Most often Plains culture is described, followed by the Northwest Coast, Pueblo and Eastern Woodlands groups.

Many of the non-fiction books that claim to give the answers to all questions concerning Native people frequently use the term "Indian" when referring to a specific people or cultural group only. While Marilis Lunkenbein in her book *Indianer* (Indians, 1995) refers to various cultural groups using the generic

"Indian," Ruth Thomson writes in her 1992 book *Indianer: Wie sie lebten. Mit Anleitungen zum Spielen und Basteln* (*Indians of the Plains [Craft Topics]*, 1991) about Plains people without ever specifically naming them, thus generalizing and oversimplifying reality. The back cover of Falk Scheithauer and Stefan Hulbe's *Die Indianer* (*The Indians*, 1996) finally claims that with "the example of Little Cloud [a ten-year old Plains Indian], children get to know the way of life and history of the different Native people." (Scheithauer/Hulbe, back cover; translation G. S.).[17] One wonders how that is actually possible. Except for a brief introduction to other Native cultural groups, the young reader finds very little reference to other people and their past and present lifestyle.

A very insensitive, inaccurate, and even racist reading in this category is the book *Zehn kleine Indianer* (*Ten Little Indians*, 1995) tells the story of ten little "Indians," one disappearing or dying after the other. While running away from a buffalo "with loud screaming and whining," one climbs up a tree, but he becomes prey to the buffalo anyway. Others spend their days lazily in their wigwam instead of bravely hunting buffalo, fall into their own traps or off their canoes and drown, get carried away by a moose or an eagle, suffocate from the smoke of a peace pipe, or get carried away by a storm, clinging tightly to their tipi. The remaining two "Indians" visit a "squaw," and while one is "gallant and clever and quickly makes her his wife," the other one "sees red and dies shortly afterwards." The couple lives happily ever after and soon has ten new little "Indians" that are pictured sitting around a campfire, telling stories.

The "Indians" are drawn childlike, with puffy faces, red cheeks and big smiles, yet seem to be ageless. They are obviously Plains Indians, wearing moccasins, colourful buckskin leggings, headbands, feathers in their braided hair, and necklaces. The woman wears a long, kimono-like dress and flowers in her long black hair. However, the colourful book also features buffalos, tipis, tomahawks, pipes, wide grasslands, canyons and steep mountains, as well as coniferous and deciduous forests, rivers, moose, eagles, totem poles, painted pottery, and fibre baskets, thus combining elements from the cultures and landscapes of the Plains, the Northwest Coast and Southwest Native groups. Like the tipi, the totem pole with its column of carved animals and birds, has become a visual symbol for all Native people, despite the fact that totems were only displayed in villages along the Pacific Northwest Coast. What is more, Plains people did not weave baskets or make clay receptacles, but used buffalo hide containers to hold food or other items. With the use of terms such as "redskins" or "squaws," the language in the book is clearly derogatory.

It is possible for a picture book to show accurate Plains culture; this is proven in Klaus Bliesner's *Mein Indianerdorf* (*My Indian Village*, 1995), which also features a Plains Indian village. Bliesner, unlike other authors, does not combine elements from various Native cultures. Men, women and children are portrayed performing daily activities. Women are shown drying meat, setting up a tipi, carrying their babies, and preparing food. Children are shown playing and refining their skills with a bow and arrows. The men of the village are depicted hunting buffalo, riding on horseback, dancing in a ceremony, and greeting a friendly white trader arriving in a canoe. Even though contact with non-Native settlers is made and the West is settled—in the background a stagecoach is passing with full speed through "Indian" territory—there are almost no signs of white civilization within the village. While showing concern for cultural differences that exist in dress, housing and customs, Bliesner paints an idealized picture of the "Indian" community enjoying an almost uninterrupted harmonious lifestyle, which excludes forthcoming problems.

Generalizing and mixing of cultures can especially be found in books whose theme and contents are not necessarily related to Native people, such as instruction books or alphabet books. In Günther Kälberer's *Komm, bau mit mir!* (*Let's Build Something!*, 1999), a book for creative parents, teachers and children, instructions are given for building the dwellings of various people; the text briefly informs the reader about different people's dwellings, such as wigwams, igloos, chickees, and pueblos. In the photographs of the models, however, cultural elements are mixed and plastic Plains Indians are, for example, set in front of a stone dome-shaped house with totem poles in the background, while the text states that this style of houses was built and inhabited by people in Italy (Kälberer 1999, 103). In alphabet books the generic (Plains) "Indian" is so frequently found under the letter "I" that Robert

B. Moore and Arlene Hirschfelder wonder if "there is a lack of other words beginning with that letter" (Moore/Hirschfelder 1981, 16). On the "I"-page in Nathalie Belineau and Silvia Löttrich's *Das Alphabet* [*The Alphabet*, 2001] the little "Indian" Ivo paddles to his girl friend Ida, who is stranded on an island together with three hedgehogs.[18] The children have braided hair, and wear feathers, moccasins, and buckskin. While all other settings in the book are distinctly recognizable and children can relate to the scenes at a lake, a school, or a costume party, the island where Ivo and Ida play, which features a palm tree and hedgehogs, is entirely unrealistic.

The majority of the analyzed books, however, give an overview of different Native cultures and present a cultural diversity, partly using the different cultural groups as structuring device for their books, giving each cultural group a separate chapter (for example, MacDonald and Wood). Cultural diversity and landscapes, including flora and fauna, are presented in text and pictures. Most books, though, explain cultural diversity with the help of material culture, and do not go into detail explaining different beliefs or world views. In their book *Indianer und ihre Welt,* published in Germany in 1996 (*North American Indians,* 1995), Andrew Haslam and Alexandra Parsons, for instance, give instructions for building models of dwellings and various Native objects, illustrating their pages with photographs and short references to history. That it is possible to create awareness for cultural differences and historical progress even among very young children is demonstrated in Fuhr and Sautai's *Die Indianer* (*The Indians,* 1995), in which transparent pages illustrate changes to landscapes and settlements very vividly.

The widespread notion that all "Indians" are alike has allowed authors, illustrators, and publishers to pick and choose Native cultural elements, particularly tipis and totems, as though they are all pieces of the same puzzle. Being frequently exposed to this mixture of "Indian" cultures, children are not able to differentiate between different people and their cultures. Authors and illustrators should, therefore, refrain from amalgamating Native people into one large "Indian tribe," but develop concern for cultural differences that exist in dress, housing, customs, decorations, and beliefs; this can be found only in a few children's books at present.

"Indians" as Roles

A third characteristic of Indian imagery in books and toys that Hirschfelder has identified is "the treatment of Native Americans as an occupation or role rather than as an ethnic identity" (Hirschfelder 1999, 158). For many children, "playing Indian" is just like playing fireman, police man, knight, or pirate; many books help with the game by giving instructions for playing the role: how to dress, speak, and, finally, become an "Indian."

"Playing Indian" is a favourite pastime, especially at children's parties, and there are countless books instructing parents, teachers, and children how to have a real "Indian party." Adelheit Utters-Adam's *Kinderfeste* (*Children's Parties*, 1996), for example, introduces "great ideas for each month of the year," and while other parties are celebrated under the motto of winter, circus, or pirates, Winnetou's "Indian party" takes place in May. The author is quite aware of the fact that when children think of Indians, they think of certain objects and Indian skills, such as moving noiselessly through the woods or reading tracks, and she uses these images for activities and games like "Hunting Buffalos" or "Enemy Tribes" (Utters-Adam 1996, 43).

Hajo Blank's *Ich bin ein Indianer* (*I Am an Indian*, 2000) is, as the back cover states, "compulsory reading for all those who want to become Indians." In this book children learn, so the back cover continues, "how Indians play, communicate, behave, fight and make up again" (Blank 2000, back cover; translation G. S.).[19] Children can read about the clothing of Native people and that "squaws" typically wear long dresses over their leggings. We are told that "Indians" are not named Andre or Kevin but have rather special names such as Little Red Feather, Great Heart, Busy Ant, and Whispering Grass. We learn about character traits of "Indians": They are helpful, patient, brave, smart, skilful, strong, merciful and just—"like Winnetou, chief of the Apaches" (Blank 2000, 10). The text further states,

> Indians are free as the clouds and the birds in the sky. Property means little to them. Therefore, they share with their friends and take care of them when they need help. They respect all plants and animals and live

> together in harmony with them. ... They fight so that our wonderful world is not polluted and thoughtlessly destroyed. (Blank 2000, 10; translation G. S.)[20]

Children learn how they can become chief, and how "Indians" communicate with each other, using sign language, smoke signals or mirror reflections. Authors of children's books seem to be especially fascinated with the sign language of Native people. In fact, so many children's non-fiction books list specific signs for children to practice that it seems to be the only means of communication among Native people. Hartmut Lutz's survey confirms the stereotypical image of "wild" Native people who are not able to speak a civilized language, but rather use monosyllabic expressions such as "hugh," "squaw," and "manitu" (Lutz 1985). It is therefore important to explain to the young reader that Native people spoke different languages and possess a rich oral culture; books by Nicolas Grenier, Jacquin, and MacDonald are good examples.

Jörg Sommer's enormously popular book *Oxmox ox Mollox: Kinder spielen Indianer* (*Oxmox ox Mollox: Children Are Playing Indians*, 1992) aims at giving teachers and educators ideas for playing history with children, providing suggestions for games, arts and crafts, dances, recipes, and other activities. Collecting his practical experience from "Indian workshops" that Sommer organized with German children, the author/educator designed concepts for an "Indian birthday party" or an "Indian weekend." His experience shows that "from nobody else can children learn as intensely what social and ecological behaviour means as from Indians" (Sommer 1992, 126).[21] The book is a collection of activities that are supposed to teach ethnic principles and basic attitudes to children, in, for example, such fields as environmental protection. By not including any visual images of contemporary Native people and by depicting them in an infinite past through using only short references to the present situation of Native people in the text, Sommer reinforces the image of the nature-loving, primitive "Indian."

Marion Zerbst and Werner Waldmann's *Tipi, Mokassin und Powwow: Das bunte Indianer-Spiel- und Sachbuch* (*Tipi, Moccasin and Powwow: The Colourful*

Indian Play and Non-Fiction Book, 1999) is a similar "journey to Indian country," albeit in contemporary times. Children are given ideas for designing and making various Native items, preparing food, and are called upon to organize their own powwow. All photographs in the book, however, are contemporary, depicting Native people in modern clothing as well as traditional regalia, living in trailers on reservations, and participating in powwows, thus giving the Native a present identity.

Treating "the Indian" as a role or occupation seems to be common practice in the world of German children, and the ethnic identity of Native people often plays only a minor role when constructing a picture of them. But one can not become an "Indian" by dressing up in a feathered headdress, fringed buckskin, and moccasins, as Hirschfelder emphasizes: "Having children dress up and play Indians encourages them to think Native Americans are nothing more than a playtime activity rather than an identity that is often fraught with economic deprivation, discrimination, gross injustice, and powerlessness" (Hirschfelder 1999, 159). Authors and illustrators must therefore make children aware that to be Native is a state of being, an ethnic identity, and that it is not necessary to revive Native culture in order to keep it alive, but that Native people keep alive their traditions themselves.

Suggestions and Guidelines

Children's books are not merely entertainment; they are part of a society's culture and reflect the shared values and ideas of that society, while at the same time reinforcing and perpetuating existing images and stereotypes. No single illustration or story is enough to create stereotypes in children's minds. But when many books contain these images, and the general culture reinforces them to such a degree that there is a cumulative effect, as Moore and Hirschfelder argue (1981, 7), false and negative perceptions about ethnic groups or minorities are the result. What is more, children are not equipped to make value judgments concerning the merit of the books they are reading. They do not stop to consider whether the books are discriminatory, racist, or sexist. They absorb the content of them with little reflexive thought. "This is because children have limited cognitive skills and have not mastered the ability to evaluate information," Hirschfelder explains, but "simply believe what they see. And what they see quite often are toys [and books] that convey derogatory and false images of Native Americans" (Hirschfelder 1999, 141).

Most of the books analyzed in this sample portray Native people as people of another culture and ethnicity, Karl May's clichés still influencing many of them. As long as Forrest Carter, James F. Cooper, and Karl May are recommended as further readings (as in Thomson) the image of romanticized "Plains Indians" will continue into the future. Only very few of the sampled books question and criticize the "imaginary Indian." Rainer Crummenerl and Peter Klauke give a very detailed and diverse picture of modern-day Native people in their *Das große Arena-Buch der Indianer* (*The Big Arena-Book of Indians*, 1996), including photographs of a modern sweat lodge; by presenting a portrait of Irving Powless Junior, a "modern chief of the Onondaga" (Crummenerl/Klauke 1996, 55); and by describing and strictly rejecting the stereotypical image in the text. They explain that today, after "decades of poverty, addiction and apathy," the Native world is fighting against disadvantages and discrimination and is searching for the roots to foster traditions.

In the world of German children, an image of Native people is being created that "conceals Native American lifestyles and thoughts from the understanding" of our children (Berkhofer 1979, 195). Emma LaRoque's demand for "defeathering the Indian" is therefore still highly relevant. Toy manufacturers, authors and illustrators must learn to portray Native people without relying on feathers and tipis. Instead of exhibiting the "Indian" in the past, or generalizing and treating the "Indian" as a role, accurate representations of diverse Native cultures must appear in children's books, toys, and films. Illustrations must be drawn with knowledgeable respect and accuracy. Instead of using the generic term "Indians," the names of the respective people must be used when referring to one people only. Peoples' origins must be identified and their lifestyle must be portrayed accurately, both as they existed in the past and as they have evolved to the present. Native people must be placed in a contemporary world, and it must be explained that they deal with contemporary problems that our children can relate to. Furthermore, parents and teachers must become aware of their role in facilitating or preventing the development of prejudices, not just questioning the image but naming it and making children aware of it. In this way they will help counteract the misconceptions about Native people that constantly confront children outside of the classroom.

Finally, extensive empirical studies concerning the influence of racist literature for children and young adults on children, teenagers and young adults must be undertaken, as the problems of stereotyping are not limited to the construction of the image of Native people. Images of other ethnic and social groups are constructed in similar ways, manifesting the "otherness" of those groups in society.[22] A lack of responsibility in the publishing industry may thus lead to damaged self-concepts among children of minority groups and also reinforce those stereotypes which eventually turn children into racist adults. "Protecting children from racism [therefore] is every bit as important as insuring that they avoid playing with electrical sockets," as Michael Dorris points out. "Poison is poison, and ingrained oppressive cultural attitudes are at least as hard to antidote, once implanted, as ingrained oppressive cleaning fluids" (Dorris qtd. in Hirschfelder 1999, 167). The images and stereotypes, however, are not eternally fixed in our society. Instead, we have the ability and the means to change the meanings of images by employing new ways of looking and interpreting them. Only then our children will be able to learn to read and interpret those images in a different way than the generations before them.

Notes

1 The survey was conducted by Sebastian Krebes and Geneviève Susemihl at the English Department of the University of Rostock in 2003 and 2004.

2 The author Karl May (1842–1912), whose *Winnetou* series was published in Germany between 1876 and 1910, has been most influential in shaping the German image of the "Indian." In his novels the white protagonist "Old Shatterhand" rides through the prairies in the company of his noble Native friend "Winnetou," both fighting for law and order and for the victory of white civilization.

3 For the historical and literary background of the images of Indians in German children's

literature, see Hartmut Lutz' *"Indianer" and "Native Americans"* (1985).

4 The study was conducted from March to May, 2005, in children's libraries and book stores in Rostock, Germany.

5 The concept of the "vanishing Indian" can be related to Darwin's theory of the survival of the fittest, Christian conversion zeal, and the concept of manifest destiny. In the 19th century Native people were seen as vanishing physically from disease and genocide, vanishing culturally as a result of colonialism and assimilation, and vanishing geographically from land due to displacement, imperialism, and "progress." The belief that Native people are a "dying race," condemned by fate, not only persisted but also spread throughout American culture, and the concept of the "vanishing Indian" appeared in science, literature, art, popular culture, and federal policy. Artists, photographers, and writers thus attempted to immortalize the "Indians" before they vanished completely. Today many writers and illustrators still follow the projection that Native people are a "vanishing race." For more information, see Robert F. Berkhofer's *The White Man's Indian: Images of the American Indian from Columbus to the Present* (1978), Brian W. Dippie's *The Vanishing American: White Attitudes and U.S. Indian Policy* (1982), and Daniel Francis' *The Imaginary Indian: The Images of the Indian in Canadian Culture* (1992).

6 The term "bluecoats" refers to the American army during the so-called Indian Wars.

7 "Die entscheidenden Schlachten zwischen den Stämmen und den 'Blauröcken' ebenso wie das Leben der Indianer, ihre Sitten und Riten, ihre Denkweise und ihr erbitterter Kampf gegen die Eindringlinge werden in diesem Buch mit vielen Illustrationen und informativem Text verdeutlicht. Das Ende der großen Häuptlinge steht auch exemplarisch für die Abenddämmerung des indianischen Volkes auf dem Weg in die Reservate" (Marcellin/Masson 1995, back cover).

8 "Dieses Buch zeigt in farbenprächtigen, detailgenauen Bildern die Welt der Ureinwohner Nordamerikas—wie sie war, bevor sie von den weißen Eroberern für immer zerstört wurde" (Wood 1998, back cover).

9 "Mit dem Bau der Eisenbahnlinien, Städten und Ranches ist das alte Amerika der Indianer für immer verschwunden" (Fuhr 1995).

10 For a discussion of fiction for German children, see Hartmut Lutz' *"Indianer" und "Native Americans"* (1985).

11 "Das Leben in der Reservation fernab von den großen Städten ist nicht leicht. Die Indianer haben es schwer, Arbeit zu finden und sind oft arm. Auf staatliche Unterstützung angewiesen, trinken sie zuviel Alkohol. Nur langsam verbessert sich ihre Situation. Die Kinder besuchen Reservationsschulen und lernen neben Englisch auch wieder ihre eigene Sprache. In den

großen Städten arbeiten Indianer in verschiedenen Berufen: sie sind Handwerker, Ärzte, Rechtsanwälte, Filmschauspieler und vieles mehr. Ihre Kinder leben wie die weißen Kinder auch" (Weinhold 2002, 16).

12 "Heute befinden sich die Indianer in einem inneren Zwiespalt zwischen Tradition und Revolte .... Ihr tragisches Schicksal macht es erforderlich, dass sie im Amerika der Weißen einen ihrer Kultur und ihrer Geschichte würdigen Platz erhalten" (Jacquin 1994, 67-68).

13 "Sie leben in Reservaten und nach und nach geraten ihre Bräuche in Vergessenheit. Da sie auch von der Genetik her das sittsame Leben nicht gewohnt sind, sind viele übergewichtig durch Fast Food etc. Viele sind auch Alkoholiker. Sie werden von anderen oftmals ausgegrenzt und bekommen schwer Arbeit" (Studentin, 21 Jahre, 2004).

14 "Arme Hunde, die in Reservaten leben. Sich betrinken und um ihr tägliches Überleben kämpfen ist ihr täglich Brot. Sie finden kaum Arbeit und wenn, nutzt der weiße Mann sie aus. Sie kämpfen um jedes Stück Land, das der weiße Mann ihnen geraubt hat" (Student, 22 Jahre, 2004).

15 "Indianer in Reservaten stehen finanziell sehr gut da, weil Uncle Sam für sie Casinos betreibt. Trotzdem sind sie nicht sehr beliebt. Irgendwann sollten vergangene Taten vergessen werden, von wegen Landraub und so" (Student, 25 Jahre, 2004).

16 "Mit diesem Blickfang – einem indianischen Krieger mit Kopfschmuck aus Adlerfedern – wird für ein Lokal und ein Einkaufszentrum geworben" (MacDonald 1998, 22, caption).

17 "Was spielt der Indianerjunge 'Kleine' Wolke am Liebsten? Und wann darf er zum ersten Mal mit auf die Jagd gehen? Am Beispiel von 'Kleiner Wolke' lernen Kinder die Lebensweisen und Geschichten der verschiedenen Indianervölker kennen" (Scheithauer/Hulbe 1998, back cover).

18 The German word for hedgehog is 'Igel.'

19 "In diesem Buch erfahrt ihr, wie Indianer spielen, sich verständigen, sich benehmen, sich streiten und wieder versöhnen – eine Pflichtlektüre für alle, die Indianer werden wollen!" (Blank 2000, back cover).

20 "Indianer sind frei wie die Wolken und die Vögel am Himmel. Besitz bedeutet ihnen wenig. Deshalb teilen sie mit ihren Freunden und kümmern sich um sie, wenn sie Hilfe benötigen. Sie achten die Pflanzen und Tiere und leben mit ihnen im Einklang. ... Sie verehren die Erde und wissen, dass sie allen, den Pflanzen, den Tieren und den Menschen, gleichermaßen gehört. Sie kämpfen dafür, dass unsere wunderschöne Welt nicht verschmutzt oder leichfertig zerstört wird" (Blank 2000, 10).

21 "Kinder [können] von niemandem so eindinglich lernen ... was soziales und ökologisches Verhalten bedeutet, wie von den Indianern" (Sommer 1992, 126).

22 Numerous monographs and articles on the representation of ethnic and gender groups have been published in Germany within the past few decades, of which I randomly want to mention the following: Kodjo Attikpoe. (2003). *Von der Stereotypisierung zur Wahrnehmung des "Anderen": Zum Bild der Schwarzafrikaner in neueren deutschsprachigen Kinder- und Jugendbüchern, 1980–1999.* (*Stereotyping to the Perception of the "Other": The Picture of Black Africans in Newer German Children's and Youth Books*). Frankfurt: Lang; Claudia Häfner. (1987). *Geschlechterrollenstereotype im Kinderbuch: Das Verständnis der Mutter- und Vaterrolle in zeitgenössischen "Aufklärungsbüchern" für Vorschulkinder.* (*Stereotypes of Gender Roles in Children's Books: The Understanding of the Roles of the Mother and Father in Contemporary Educational Books for Children in Preschool*). Frankfurt: Lang.; Gottfried Mergner and Ansgar Häfner, eds. (1985). *Der Afrikaner im deutschen Kinder- und Jugendbuch: Untersuchungen zur rassistischen Stereotypenbildung im deutschen Kinder- und Jugendbuch von der Aufklärung bis zum Nationalsozialismus.* (*The African in German Children's and Youth Books: Studies on the Development of Racist Stereotypes in German Children's and Youth Books from the Enlightenment to National Socialism*). Hamburg: Ergebnisse Verlag.

Bibliography

Primary Literature

Belineau, Nathalie, and Silvia Löttrich. (2001). *Das Alphabet: Dein erstes buntes Wörterbuch,* Illus. Sylvie Michelet. Saarbrücken: Fleurus Verlag.

Blank, Hajo. (2000). *Ich bin ein Indianer.* Moses Kleine Hosentaschen-Bibliothek, 18. Kempen: moses Kinderbuchverlag.

Bliesener, Klaus. (2001). *Mein Indianerdorf.* Ravensburg: Ravensburger Buchverlag.

Crummenerl, Rainer, and Peter Klauke. (1996). *Das große Arena-Buch der Indianer.* Würzburg: Arena-Verlag.

Fuhr, Ute, and Raoul Sautai. (1995). *Die Indianer.* Mannheim: Meyers Lexikonverlag.

Grenier, Nicolas, and Donald Grant. (1986). *Auf der Spur der Indianer.* Ravensburg: Ravensburger Buchverlag.

Haslam, Andrew, and Alexandra Parsons. (1996). *Indianer und ihre Welt: Entdeckt und Nachgebaut.* Nürnberg: Tessloff Verlag.

Hirschfelder, Arlene. (2001). *Die Geschichte der Indianer Nordamerikas*, trans. Margot Wilhelmi. Hildesheim: Paletti/Gerstenberg Verlag.

Jacob, Renate, and Rooobert [*sic*] Bayer. (2002). *Indianergeschichten*. Reihe: Schmöckerbären. Bindlach: Gondolino, Gondrom Verlag, 2002.

Jacquin, Philippe, and François Davot. (1994). *So lebten sie zur Zeit der Indianer: Die spannende Geschichte der Ureinwohner Amerikas*, trans. Sabine Göhrmann. Nuremberg: Tesseloff Verlag.

Kälberer, Günther. (1999). *Komm, bau mit mir! 50 tolle Sachen zum Bauen und Basteln mit Kindern ab 8 Jahren*. Niedernhausen/Ts.: Falken Verlag.

Kock, Hauke. (1996). *Der Wilde Westen*. Hamburg: Carlsen Verlag.

Lunkenbein, Marilis, and Andreas Piel. (1995). *Indianer: Mein erstes Frage- und Antwortbuch*. Bindlach: Loewe Verlag.

MacDonald, Fiona. (1998). *Indianer in Nordamerika*, trans. Gisela Klemt. Münster: Coppenrath Verlag.

Marcellin, Jean, and Jean Robert Masson. (1995). *Die großen Indianerhäuptlinge: Cochise, Geronimo, Crazy Horse, Sitting Bull*. Erlangen: Boje Verlag Erlangen, 1995.

Murdoch, David, Stanley A. Freed, and Lynton Gardiner. (1995). *Indianer: Wie die Bewohner Nordamerikas wirklich lebten. Von den Pueblovölkern im Südwesten bis zu den Jägern des Nordens*. Reihe Sehen. Staunen. Wissen. Hildesheim: Gerstenberg Verlag.

Nußbaum, Margret, and Ulla Häusler. (2002). *Heut' feiern wir ein Fest: Schöne Kindergarten-Feste für das ganze Jahr*. Freiburg: Christophorus Verlag, 2002.

Planche, Bernard, and Donald Grant. (1985). *Eskimos: Leben im ewigen Eis*. Ravensburg: Ravensburger Buchverlag Otto Maier, 1985.

Purin, Sergio. (1989). *Die Urvölker Amerikas: Von Alaska bis Feuerland. Geschichte der Menschheit*. Illus. François Davot. Stuttgart: Union Verlag.

Rieupeyrout, Jean-Louis, and Jose Maria Miralles. (1980). *So lebten sie zur Zeit des Wilden Westens*. Hamburg: Tessloff Verlag.

Scheithauer, Falk, and Stefan Hulbe. (1996). *Die Indianer: Das will ich wissen*. Würzburg: Arena Verlag.

Seiler, Signe. (2002). *Indianer: Ein Was ist Was-Buch*. Illus. Jörn Henning and Frank Kliemt. Nürnberg: Tessloff Verlag.

Sommer, Jörg. (1998). *Oxmox ox Mollox:* Kinder spielen Indianer. Münster: Ökotopia Verlag, 1992.

Stuart, Gene S. (1977). *Drei kleine Indianer: Bücher für junge Entdecker*, trans. Christian Feest.

Wien: Breitschopf, National Geographic Society.

Sutton, Felix. (1964). *Der Kampf um den Wilden Westen: Ein Was ist Was-Buch.* Illus. Leonard Vosburgh. Nürnberg: Tessloff-Verlag.

---. (1985). *Indianer: Ein Was ist Was-Buch,* trans. Doris Biester. Illus. Leonard Vosburgh.1969. Nürnberg: Tessloff Verlag.

Thiel, Hans Peter, and Marcus Würmli. (1995). *Die Indianer.* Reihe: Entdecke deine Welt. Gütersloh: Bertelsmann Lexikon Verlag.

Thomson, Ruth. (1992). *Indianer: Wie sie lebten. Mit Anleitungen zum Spielen & Basteln,* trans. Luzia Czernich. Illus. Chris Price. München: F. Schneider Verlag.

Utters-Adam, Adelheit. (1996). *Kinderfeste: Tolle Ideen für jeden Monat des Jahres.* München: Mosaik Verlag.

von Welck, Karin. (1982). *Bisonjäger und Mäusefreunde. Wie die Indianer in Nordamerika früher lebten und wie es ihnen heute geht.* Ravensburg: Otto Maier Ravensburg.

Weinhold, Angela. (2002). *Bei den Indianern: Wieso? Weshalb? Warum?* Ravensburg: Ravensburger Buchverlag.

Wolfrum, Christine, Susanne Bräunig, and Harald Vorbrugg. (1996). *Indianer: Alles klar.* Ravensburg: Ravensburger Buchverlag.

Wood, Marion. (1998). *Die Welt der Indianer Nordamerikas,* trans. Jochen Schürmann. Hamburg: Carlsen.

(1995). *Zehn kleine Indianer.* Nürnberg: Sebald Kinderbücher.

Zerbst, Marion, and Werner Waldmann. (1999). *Tipi, Mokassin und Powwow. Das bunte Indianer-Spiel- und Sachbuch.* Kinderbuchverlag Luzern.

Secondary Literature

Berkhofer, Robert F., Jr. (1979). *The White Man's Indian: Images of the American Indian from Columbus to the Present.* New York: Vintage Books.

Byler, Mary Gloyne. (1973). *American Indian Authors for Young Readers: A Selected Bibliography.* New York: Association on American Indian Affairs.

Dippie, Brian W. (1982). The Vanishing American: White Attitudes and U.S. Indian Policy. Middletown, CT: Wesleyan University Press.

Ewers, John C. (1999). "The Emergence of the Plains Indian as the Symbol of the North American Indian." In *American Indian Stereotypes in the World of Children: A Reader and*

Bibliography, eds. Arlene Hirschfelder, Paulette Fairbanks Molin, and Yvonne Wakim. 2nd ed. Lanham, MD: Scarecrow Press, 11–23.

Francis, Daniel. (1992). *The Imaginary Indian: The Image of the Indian in Canadian Culture.* Vancouver, BC: Arsenal Pulp Press Ltd.

Hirschfelder, Arlene, Paulette Fairbanks Molin, and Yvonne Wakim, eds. (1999). *American Indian Stereotypes in the World of Children: A Reader and Bibliography.* 2nd ed. Lanham, MD: Scarecrow Press.

Hirschfelder, Arlene. (1999). "Toys with Indian Imagery." In *American Indian Stereotypes in the World of Children: A Reader and Bibliography*, 139–169.

Krebes, Sebastian. (2002). "Zum Bild des nordamerikanischen Indianers im Deutschland des 21. Jahrhunderts: Versuch einer empirischen Analyse vorherrschender Stereotypen und Untersuchungen ihres realhistorischen Ursprungs." State examination thesis. Rostock: University of Rostock.

LaRoque, Emma. (1975). *Defeathering the Indian.* Agincourt, ON: The Books Society of Canada.

Lutz, Hartmut. (1981). "Der edle Wilde auf dem Kriegspfad. Indianerbilder für die deutsche Jugend." In *Das Gift der frühen Jahre: Rassismus in der Jugendliteratur*, eds. Regula Renschler and Roy Preiswerk. Basel: Lenos Verlag/Z-Verlag, 235–278.

———. (1985). *"Indianer" und "Native Americans": Zur sozial- und literaturhistorischen Vermittlung eines Stereotyps.* Hildesheim: Olms Verlag.

———. (2002). "Images of Indians in German Children's Books." In *Approaches: Essays in Native North American Studies and Literatures*, ed. Hartmut Lutz. Augsburg: Wißner Verlag, 13–47.

Moore, Robert B., and Arlene Hirschfelder. (1981). "Feathers, Tomahawks and Tipis: A Study of Stereotyped 'Indian' Imagery in Children's Picture Books." In *Unlearning "Indian" Stereotypes: A Teaching Unit for Elementary Teachers and Children's Librarians.* Council for Interracial Books for Children, 5–23.

Appendix A: Study of the Image of Native people in Germany

The study was originally conducted in German, and this questionnaire translated by Geneviève Susemihl.

Fragebogen zum Bild des nordamerikanischen Indianers im Deutschland des 21. Jahrhunderts (lokale Betrachtung)

1. Welchem Geschlecht gehörst Du an?

   Junge ☐ Mädchen ☐

2. Wie alt bist Du? ☐☐

3. Welchen Beruf hat Deine Mutter / bzw. welchen hatte sie zuletzt?

4. Welchen Beruf hat Dein Vater / bzw. welchen hatte er zuletzt?

5. Wie viele Bücher gibt es bei Euch zu Hause (keine Zeitungen, Zeitschriften oder Schulbücher)?

   0–10 ☐ 11–50 ☐ 51–100 ☐ 101–500 ☐ mehr als 500 ☐

6. Woran denkst Du bei dem Wort "Indianer"?

	fa sehr	eher ja	teils-teils	eher nein	nein gar nicht
Tapfere Krieger auf Pferden	☐	☐	☐	☐	☐
Büffeljagd mit Pfeil und Bogen	☐	☐	☐	☐	☐
Büffeljagd mit Gewehren	☐	☐	☐	☐	☐
Landwirtschaft, Ackerbau	☐	☐	☐	☐	☐

Kämpfe mit den Europäern	☐	☐	☐	☐	☐
Geschichten am Lagerfeuer	☐	☐	☐	☐	☐
Winnetou und Old Shatterhand	☐	☐	☐	☐	☐
Lange schwarze Haare und Federn	☐	☐	☐	☐	☐
Zelte und Tipis auf der Prärie	☐	☐	☐	☐	☐
Indianer skalpieren Weiße	☐	☐	☐	☐	☐
Weiße skalpieren Indianer	☐	☐	☐	☐	☐
Ungerechtes Leiden der Indianer	☐	☐	☐	☐	☐
Demokratie	☐	☐	☐	☐	☐
Abenteuer	☐	☐	☐	☐	☐
Lehmhäuser, Gras- und Erdhütten	☐	☐	☐	☐	☐

7. Wie würdest Du die Indianer Nordamerikas beschreiben/charakterisieren, die dort lebten, als die ersten Europäer nach Amerika kamen?

	fa sehr	eher ja	teils-teils	eher nein	nein gar nicht
Tapfer, mutig, heldenhaft	☐	☐	☐	☐	☐
Hinterhältig, verräterisch	☐	☐	☐	☐	☐
Grausam und kriegerisch	☐	☐	☐	☐	☐
Wild, primitiv und unzivilisiert	☐	☐	☐	☐	☐
Friedlich und zivilisiert	☐	☐	☐	☐	☐

8. War es für Dich schwer, den Indianern in Frage 7 Charaktereigenschaften zuzuordnen?

Ja ☐ Nein ☐

9. Woran mag es liegen, dass die Zuordnung von Charaktereigenschaften nicht immer einfach ist – vor allem im Falle der Indianer?

10. Welcher der folgenden Aussagen zur Herkunft der Indianer würdest Du zustimmen? Kreuze nur eine Antwort an!

Die Indianer kamen vor über zehntausend Jahren aus Asien über eine Landbrückenach Amerika und besiedelten den Kontinent (Beringstraße). ☐

Die Indianer kamen bereits vor den Wikingern aus Europa nach Amerika. ☐

Die Indianer haben sich in Amerika vom Affen zum Menschen entwickelt. Sie haben also schon von Anfang an dort gelebt. ☐

Die Herkunft der Indianer ist vollkommen ungeklärt. ☐

Die Herkunft der Indianer mag geklärt sein, aber ich kenne die Antwort nicht. ☐

11. Nenne die Namen von Häuptlingen.

1. ______________________

2. ______________________

3. ______________________

4. ______________________

12. Nenne die Namen von Indianerstämmen.

1. ______________________

2. ______________________

3. ______________________

4. ______________________

13. Sind die folgenden Personen und Gruppen für Dich wirklich, erfunden oder unbekannt?

	wirklich	erfunden	unbekannt
Pocahontas	☐	☐	☐
Old Shatterhand	☐	☐	☐
Geronimo	☐	☐	☐
Sitting Bull	☐	☐	☐
Winnetou	☐	☐	☐
Buffalo Bill	☐	☐	☐
Apachen	☐	☐	☐
Sioux	☐	☐	☐
Irokesen	☐	☐	☐

14. Wo hast Du schon viel über Indianer gehört, gelesen oder gesehen?

	sehr viel	viel	mäßig viel	wenig	nichts/ sehr wenig
Sachbücher	☐	☐	☐	☐	☐
Romane Karl Mays	☐	☐	☐	☐	☐
Andere Romane	☐	☐	☐	☐	☐
Reportagen im Fernsehen	☐	☐	☐	☐	☐
Winnetou-Filme (Karl May)	☐	☐	☐	☐	☐
Amerikanische Western	☐	☐	☐	☐	☐
Andere Spielfilme	☐	☐	☐	☐	☐
Urlaub in Amerika	☐	☐	☐	☐	☐
Besuch in Museen	☐	☐	☐	☐	☐
Karl May Festspiele	☐	☐	☐	☐	☐
Internet	☐	☐	☐	☐	☐
Eltern	☐	☐	☐	☐	☐

Großeltern	☐	☐	☐	☐	☐
Schule	☐	☐	☐	☐	☐

15. Was weißt Du über das heutige Leben der Indianer in den USA?
    Antworte bitte auf der
    Rückseite!

Vielen Dank für die Mitarbeit!!!

Questionnaire Concerning the Image of the North American Indian in Germany in the 21st Century (Local Study)

1. What gender are you?
   Male ☐ Female ☐

2. How old are you? ☐☐

3. What is you mother's occupation? / What job did she last work in?

4. What is your father's occupation? / What job did he last work in?

5. How many books does your family have at home (except newspapers, magazines, or text books for school)?

   0–10 ☐ 11–50 ☐ 51–100 ☐ 101–500 ☐ more than 500 ☐

6. What do you think of when you hear the term "Indian"?

	Yes, strongly	Yes, a little	Some-what	No, a little	No, not at all
Courageous warriors on horseback	☐	☐	☐	☐	☐
Hunting buffalo with bow and arrow	☐	☐	☐	☐	☐
Hunting buffalo with guns	☐	☐	☐	☐	☐
Agriculture, farming	☐	☐	☐	☐	☐
Fights with the Europeans	☐	☐	☐	☐	☐
Stories at the campfire	☐	☐	☐	☐	☐
Winnetou and Old Shatterhand	☐	☐	☐	☐	☐
Long black hair and feathers	☐	☐	☐	☐	☐

Tents and tipis on the prairie	☐	☐	☐	☐	☐
Indians scalp whites	☐	☐	☐	☐	☐
Whites scalp Indians	☐	☐	☐	☐	☐
Unjust suffering of the Indians	☐	☐	☐	☐	☐
Democracy	☐	☐	☐	☐	☐
Adventure	☐	☐	☐	☐	☐
Adobe houses, huts of grass and earth	☐	☐	☐	☐	☐

7. How would you describe/ characterize the Indians of North America who lived there when the first Europeans came to America?

	Yes, strongly	Yes, a little	Some-what	No, a little	No, not at all
Brave, courageous, heroic	☐	☐	☐	☐	☐
Deceitful, treacherous	☐	☐	☐	☐	☐
Cruel and hostile	☐	☐	☐	☐	☐
Wild, primitive and uncivilized	☐	☐	☐	☐	☐
Peaceful and civilized	☐	☐	☐	☐	☐

8. Was it difficult for you to assign character traits to the Native Americans in question 7?

   Yes ☐ No ☐

9. Why do you think is it difficult to assign character traits—especially in the case of the Native Americans?

10. Which of the following statements about the origin of North American Indians would you support? Mark only one answer!

The Indians came from Asia to America over a land bridge more than ten thousand years ago and settled the continent (Bering Strait).	☐
The Indians came before the Vikings from Europe to America.	☐
The Indians have developed from ape to human in America. They therefore lived there from the beginning.	☐
The origins of the Indians are not clarified yet.	☐
The origins of the Indians might be clarified, but I do not know the answer.	☐

11. Name the Native American chiefs that you know.

1. ____________________

2. ____________________

3. ____________________

4. ____________________

12. Name the Native American tribes that you know.

1. ____________________

2. ____________________

3. ____________________

4. ____________________

13. Are the following individuals and groups real, fictitious or unknown to you?

	Real	Fictitious	Unknown
Pocahontas	☐	☐	☐
Old Shatterhand	☐	☐	☐
Geronimo	☐	☐	☐
Sitting Bull	☐	☐	☐
Winnetou	☐	☐	☐
Buffalo Bill	☐	☐	☐

Apaches	☐	☐	☐
Sioux	☐	☐	☐
Iroquois	☐	☐	☐

14. Where have you heard, read or seen much about Native Americans?

	Very	Much	Neutral	A little much	Not at all
Non-fiction literature	☐	☐	☐	☐	☐
Karl May fiction	☐	☐	☐	☐	☐
Other fiction	☐	☐	☐	☐	☐
Documentaries on TV	☐	☐	☐	☐	☐
Winnetou films (Karl May)	☐	☐	☐	☐	☐
American Westerns	☐	☐	☐	☐	☐
Other films	☐	☐	☐	☐	☐
Holidays in America	☐	☐	☐	☐	☐
Visits to museums	☐	☐	☐	☐	☐
Karl May Festival	☐	☐	☐	☐	☐
Internet	☐	☐	☐	☐	☐
Parents	☐	☐	☐	☐	☐
Grandparents	☐	☐	☐	☐	☐
School	☐	☐	☐	☐	☐

15. What do you know about the life of Native Americans in America today? Please answer on the back of this sheet!

Thank you for your participation!!!

Siobhán N. Smith

The Art of Exclusion: The Status of Aboriginal Art in the McMichael Canadian Art Collection[1]

Introduction

> The exclusion of the arts of Native peoples implies that the artistic and cultural contributions to Canadian history by Canada's First Nations are non-existent.
> —Martin 1991, 19

Since 1927, with the National Gallery of Canada's colonialist exhibition titled *Exhibition of Canadian West Coast Art, Native and Modern*, Canadian public art galleries have been grappling (often unsuccessfully) with how Aboriginal and Euro-Canadian artworks should come together to define Canadian art.[2] In spite of more than two decades of effort by Aboriginal artists and curators to create change, Aboriginal art in Canada still occupies a peripheral place in mainstream Canadian art histories and galleries.

During the 1980s, Canada's public museums and galleries came under scrutiny for their unwillingness to include Aboriginal art into their definitions of Canadian art. By the 1990s, amidst the political upheaval of the rejection of the Meech Lake Accord, the armed standoff in Oka, Quebec, and the protests against the celebration of Columbus Day, various Aboriginal groups, including the Society of Canadian Artists of Native Ancestry, demanded policy changes to Canadian museums and galleries (Martin 2002a, 50). Specific requests for change were outlined in three major reports: in 1991, Lee-Ann Martin's *The Politics of Inclusion and Exclusion: Contemporary Native Art and Public Art Museums in Canada*; in 1992, the Task Force on Museums and First Peoples' *Turning the Page: Forging New Partnerships Between Museums and First Peoples*; and in 1996, "Gathering Strength," volume three of the *Report of the Royal Commission on Aboriginal Peoples*. The recommendations of these three reports focused attention on four major issues affecting Aboriginal communities' interactions with museums: interpretation, access, representation, and repatriation.

Due to the release of these three reports, many major public museums and arts-funding agencies in Canada have instituted changes to their collecting, exhibiting, funding, and hiring practices in order to be more inclusive of Aboriginal Canadians. Changes have ranged from the introduction of the Canada Council for the Arts' Aboriginal-focused grant programs to specific policies for the repatriation of cultural objects and human remains in museum collections. Both the National Gallery of Canada and the Art Gallery of Ontario have made changes to their permanent collection installations of Canadian historical art to "explore the complex relationships among First Nations and the French and British settler societies" (Art Gallery of Ontario, online). Despite these changes, the place of Aboriginal art within the histories of Canadian art is still not certain or secure. One art gallery that has been attempting to incorporate Aboriginal art into the history of Canadian art since the 1960s is the McMichael Canadian Art Collection, a public art gallery located in Kleinburg, Ontario.

Between the 1980s and 1990s, the McMichael Canadian Art Collection (MCAC) was progressive in implementing inclusive collecting and exhibiting policies and practices.[3] Amendments to its mandate in the 1980s officially incorporated Aboriginal art into its definition of "Canadian cultural heritage," so that between 1982 and 2000, the board of the MCAC could collect "works of art created by Indian, Inuit and Métis artists" (*McMichael Canadian Art Collection Act* 1989). However, on November 2, 2000, Bill 112, An Act to amend the McMichael Canadian Art Collection Act, became law, and among the amendments was the erasure of any reference to Aboriginal art in the gallery's collecting mandate. The legislation had been tabled at the request of gallery co-founder Robert McMichael, and was fuelled by his desire to regain control of the public gallery's collecting practices. At that time, it was suggested that this statute had finally put an end to "one of the country's longest-running artistic fights," that is, an end to the fight between gallery co-founder Robert McMichael and the board of directors of the MCAC for control over the gallery's collecting practices (Procuta 2000, A1). In the explanatory note of Bill 112, it is stated that the Bill would recognize Robert McMichael's claim that "the focus of the collection has changed over time" and that it was therefore necessary to "return the collection to, and then maintain it in, the spirit of its original focus" (*Bill 112* 2000). In defence of the necessity for Bill 112, Robert McMichael argued that the MCAC collection had strayed from *his* original intent for the gallery, which, he claimed, had been to focus the collection around the works of the Group of Seven painters and a select few of their contemporaries (Legislative Assembly of Ontario 2000, 1740). However, I will illustrate in this essay that it was not the collection that changed over time, but rather Robert McMichael's version of what had been the original intent of the collection.

This study represents the first intensive review and analysis of the impact that legislative changes to the McMichael Act have had on the MCAC's mandate. Through an analysis of the history of the MCAC's legislated collecting policies and practices, I will examine the changes to the legal status of Aboriginal art in the MCAC mandate. I will argue that the removal of references to Aboriginal art in the MCAC's mandate, via Bill 112 in 2000, was an act, unwitting perhaps, of cultural racism[4] on the part of the Ontario Provincial Government, and that to leave the legislation as it stands would be to accept the government-imposed erasure of Aboriginal art from the once inclusive collecting mandate of the MCAC.

General History of the MCAC and Its Collection

The McMichael Canadian Art Collection (MCAC) was created by a donation from husband and wife, Robert and Signe McMichael, to the Province of Ontario in 1965, and named to honour their generosity.[5] The gallery began as the private home of the McMichaels, and this house, along with the fourteen-acre property and 187 artworks, were officially opened to the public in July 1966.[6] The original 1965 mandate of the MCAC appointed Robert McMichael as the director and allowed the gallery to collect works of art "reflecting the cultural heritage of Canada," such as those created by Tom Thomson, Emily Carr, David Milne, the Group of Seven—arguably Canada's most well-known landscape painters—and "other artists ... who have made contributions to the development of Canadian art" (*Agreement* 1965, para. 13). Under Robert McMichael's direction, the gallery collected artworks by the ten named artists, as well as First Nations and Inuit art.

The MCAC was the first, and today is one of the few, public art galleries to collect and exhibit exclusively the art of Canada. This was a unique model of collecting and exhibiting at a time when no other major public art gallery in Canada was committed to collecting both Euro-Canadian and Aboriginal artworks.[7] Robert McMichael's personal commitment to the collection of Aboriginal art was clear from the MCAC's beginning. As he recounts in his autobiography, McMichael's obsession with collecting Aboriginal art ("collecting fever") came about after a trip to Vancouver in 1957 (McMichael 1986, 91). It was on this trip that he and Signe met Haida artist Bill Reid and purchased their first Aboriginal artwork—a black raven mask carved by Kwakiutl artist Dick Price (94). Collection records indicate that in the sixteen years that McMichael was director of the MCAC (1965–81) approximately 2500 works were acquired, of which 1060 works, or 42 percent, were by Aboriginal artists (MCAC, *Collection Statistics* 1989).

Although Robert McMichael would later claim otherwise, it was clear, even to the public, that by 1970 the MCAC did not represent solely the works of the Group of Seven and Tom Thomson. In a 1970 *Globe and Mail* article,

Kay Kritzwiser highlighted the fact that more than half of the MCAC's artworks were created by artists other than the Group of Seven. In highlighting the importance of Aboriginal art to the MCAC, Kritzwiser stated, "McMichael feels that the beautiful collection and property which he and his wife gave to the province of Ontario should also be synonymous with early Indian culture" (Kritzwiser 1970, 23). She went on to quote Robert McMichael as stating, "We'd like to have more West Coast Indian work and better Eskimo sculpture" (23). In a 1974 article titled "Gallery Not Just for 'Seven,'" Lenore Crawford noted that "less than 50 percent of the McMichael Conservation Collection of more than 1,000 works are by the Group of Seven" (Crawford 1974, 49). She went on to describe the key points of a speech that Robert McMichael had given to the London Art Gallery Association. According to Crawford, McMichael described the MCAC as containing "Indian and Eskimo art and the works of Tom Thomson, David Milne and Emily Carr. Also, the gallery maintains one room for transient exhibitions by Canadian artists of today" (49). Crawford also quoted McMichael as stating that he hoped "the board of directors and others responsible for the permanent collection *never will put on blinkers and decide that good Canadian art stops at a certain period*" (49; emphasis added). In other words, McMichael's original intention was for the collection to develop and change over time. Along with McMichael's personal support via his collecting practices, the importance of First Nations art and culture was literally built into the MCAC; the section of the gallery referred to as the Western Canada Gallery contains a forty-foot-long cedar bench and red cedar arches in a doorway, both of which depict First Nations imagery carved by Kwakiutl artist Douglas Cranmer.

Throughout the 1990s, the gallery actively collected contemporary Aboriginal art, and at least thirteen exhibitions of contemporary First Nations and Inuit art were held during these years. In 1994, the MCAC hired Lynn A. Hill as a First Nations curator-in-residence—three years before the Canada Council had even established their Aboriginal Curator Residency Program. It is significant that the MCAC was collecting and exhibiting *contemporary* as well as historical Aboriginal art, because in the report published by the Task Force on Museums and First Peoples, the importance of including contemporary works in a museum context was highlighted:

> The role of First Peoples in Canadian history should be stressed. This approach should replace the stereotyped exhibitions that depict First Peoples as dying, primitive and inferior cultures, or as cultures isolated from Canada's history, in "pre-history" galleries. The linkage between Aboriginal heritage and the present circumstances of First Peoples should also be represented; in fact, museums should become forums for discussions of relevant contemporary issues ... In addition to First Peoples' access to existing ethnographic collections within museums, there was also discussion of the lack of representation of contemporary Aboriginal art in public art galleries. It was agreed that Canadian art museums should be encouraged to work with artists of First Nations ancestry to enhance their collections and exhibition programming in this area. (Assembly of First Nations 1992, appendix A)

Now, after forty years of collecting, the MCAC has grown from the original 187 artworks to almost 6,000, and it remains a distinctive institution by collecting exclusively *Canadian* works and exhibiting both Aboriginal and Euro-Canadian works.

Legal History of the MCAC Mandate and Collection

> The Crown shall, with the advice and assistance of Robert McMichael and Signe McMichael, establish, develop and maintain in perpetuity at Tapawingo a collection of art reflecting the cultural heritage of Canada ... comprised of paintings by Tom Thomson, Emily Carr, David Milne, A. Y. Jackson, Lawren Harris, A. J. Casson, Frederick Varley, Arthur Lismer, J. H. MacDonald, Franklin Carmichael, and other artists, as designated by the advisory committee, who have made contributions to the development of Canadian art. (*Agreement* 1965, para. 13)

Paragraph 13 of the original 1965 agreement named ten artists of primary significance to the collection, but it also left open the possibility of adding more artists' names. In fact, the precedent for this collection being more than ten core artists was set even before the 1965 agreement had been signed. In a letter to Premier John P. Robarts dated July 5, 1965, Robert McMichael stated that along with the Tom Thomson shack, land, buildings, and artworks, he and his wife Signe also intended to deed to the province their "collection of wood carvings, Eskimo stone carvings, West Coast Indian Mask and Totem Pole" (McMichael 1965).

Despite the inclusion of these Aboriginal carvings in the original donation, it soon became clear that there were serious limitations to the original 1965 Agreement, particularly since it did not actually allow for the purchase of more works by Aboriginal artists. In 1968, Robert McMichael wanted to purchase "four Eskimo carvings" for the collection, but it was pointed out to the Hon. James A. C. Auld, then minister of tourism and information, that the 1965 Agreement "does not appear to provide for the purchase of Eskimo carvings."[8] Furthermore, S. J. Wychowanec, then director of the Legal Services Branch of the Department of Revenue, stated that "if it is the intention of all the parties to the agreement to expand the scope of the Collection, then I think it would be advisable for the Crown and the McMichaels to amend the 1965 agreement to provide for this" (Wychowanec, 1969). Therefore, on September 30, 1969, Premier Robarts, Robert McMichael and Signe McMichael signed a letter stating, "As the second paragraph of the preamble to the Agreement indicates, the Collection has always included not only paintings but also drawings, sculpture and artefacts. Accordingly, notwithstanding any apparent implication to the contrary in the Agreement, the Province has always contemplated that the Collection may be augmented through the acquisition, by donation or purchase, of works of a similar nature reflective of the cultural heritage of Canada" (Robarts et al., 1969). With the official approval of Robarts, the MCAC was able to collect and accept donations of any artworks deemed to represent "the cultural heritage of Canada." However, in spite of the apparent problems with the wording of the original Agreement, the same language would be used for the revised mandate in 2000.

Between 1966 and 1971, the MCAC experienced a massive increase in attendance rates along with growth in the number of artworks; this expansion led to the decision to make the MCAC a Crown corporation (a corporation wholly owned, directly or indirectly, by the government in lieu of the Crown). This was accomplished through the passing of Bill 216, An Act to establish the McMichael Canadian Collection, on November 23, 1972.[9] As amendments were made to the MCAC mandate, Robert McMichael was affected on a very personal level. It is clear in McMichael's own writing that he was unable to separate himself from the MCAC after he and Signe donated the gallery to the Province of Ontario. In 1981, the board of directors proposed to request amendments to the 1972 act, in order to "confirm that the powers of the Board of the Directors are governed only by that Act [of 1972] and are not limited by the Agreement [of 1965]" (McMichael 1986, 399). McMichael found the board's decision to override the restrictions of the original 1965 agreement to be "humiliating—it was devastating—a sickening end to all our hopes and a mockery of the terms of our gift in 1965" (399). Similar sentiments were revealed again years later when Robert McMichael sued the gallery.

In 1981, due to serious management concerns on the part of the MCAC, the board of directors asked Robert McMichael to resign as director and to assume the new position of "Founder, Director-Emeritus" (*McMichael v. Ontario* 1997, para. 91). The following year, more legal amendments were made to the McMichael Canadian Art Collection Act. These amendments not only created the new position of director-emeritus for Robert McMichael, but also changed the mandate to recognize the importance of the Aboriginal art holdings of the MCAC collection. After the passing of the 1982 Bill 175, An Act to amend the McMichael Canadian Collection Act, the collecting mandate of the MCAC read as follows:

> The focus of the collection is the art work and objects created by,
> (a) Tom Thomson, Emily Carr, David Milne, A. Y. Jackson, Lawren Harris, A. J. Casson, Frederick Varley, Arthur Lismer, J. H. MacDonald, Franklin Carmichael,
> (b) the indigenous peoples of Canada, and other artists who have made

> contributions to the development of Canadian art and whose art work and objects will be consistent with the general character of the collection. (*McMichael Canadian Collection Amendment Act,* 1982, c.3.)

For the first time, the act specified in statute format, that the focus of the collection was not only the Group of Seven and three of their contemporaries alone, but also the artwork of Aboriginal Canadians. While the primary goal of the amendments made to McMichael Canadian Collection Act in 1982 was to ensure proper management of the MCAC now that Robert McMichael was no longer director, the significance of the change to the "nature of the collection" cannot be overlooked. For the first time since the MCAC had been open to the public, the gallery's mandate was amended to include the legal recognition of Aboriginal works of art, which by this time, represented nearly half of the collection. The changes made to the McMichael Canadian Art Collection Act should be seen in light of the changes being made in the overall operations of the MCAC, and within the larger context of social, political, and legal changes in Canadian society at the time. Three items of particular significance to the MCAC occurred at this time. Firstly, in 1981 the board of the MCAC adopted the code of ethics for museum professionals of the Canadian Museums Association (Legislative Assembly of Ontario 1982, 2100). Secondly, on November 17, 1981, news of the draft of Bill 175, An Act to amend the McMichael Canadian Collection Act, shared the *Globe and Mail*'s front-page headlines with an article on the fight for the entrenchment of Aboriginal rights into the proposed Canadian Charter of Rights. Finally, on April 17, 1982, the Canadian Charter of Rights and Freedoms came into effect, and just a few days later, amendments to the McMichael Act passed in the Ontario Legislature.

In 1989, Bill 209, An Act to revise the McMichael Canadian Collection Act, was enacted and further clarified the types of objects that comprised the collecting mandate, and the importance of Aboriginal art was once again reinforced in the MCAC collection. Where the 1982 act stated very generally that the MCAC's collection could include artworks by "the indigenous peoples of Canada," (*McMichael Canadian Collection Amendment Act* 1982, c.3, para.7) after Bill 209 (1989), the nature of the MCAC collection was stated as follows: "The focus of the collection is the works of art created by Indian, Inuit and Métis artists, the artists of the Group of Seven and their contemporaries and other artists who have made or make a contribution to the development of Canadian Art" (*McMichael Canadian Collection Act* 1989, c.44, para.8). Further to the changes made to the mandate, the 1989 amendments allowed for the Board of the MCAC to nearly double in size: from nine trustees to seventeen. While Signe and Robert McMichael were still guaranteed their position on the board, they were now vastly outnumbered when it came time to vote on new acquisitions. It was Robert McMichael's frustration with his loss of control over the art acquisitions process that would eventually lead to the lawsuit *McMichael v. Ontario*, 1996.

After resigning as director in 1981, Robert McMichael did not agree with many of the acquisition choices of the board of the MCAC; they had been collecting and exhibiting contemporary artworks that did not appeal to his personal aesthetic tastes. McMichael was so displeased that in 1996 he sued the gallery, a Crown Corporation, for breach of trust. Despite his own earlier interest in Aboriginal art and contemporary art of the 1970s and 1980s, in 1996, Robert McMichael challenged the MCAC's acquisition of works by artists other than the Group of Seven painters and their contemporaries. In his affidavit from the 1996 court case, McMichael took particular aim at John McEwen's 1991 sculptural installation piece *Babylon*, and Plains Cree artist Gerald McMaster's 1989 sculpture *Bases Stolen from the Cleveland Indians and a Captured Yankee* (fig. 7.1)—an artwork that Robert McMichael himself had approved for acquisition in 1990.[10] The trial judge, Justice Peter Grossi, agreed with Robert McMichael that the contemporary works in question were inappropriate for the MCAC collection, and in his ruling stated that "these works, no doubt, have significant artistic merit but, in my view, they bear no relationship to the original character of the Collection" (*McMichael v. Ontario* 1996, para. 20). Although Justice Grossi agreed with Robert McMichael's accusation, McMichael's victory was short lived. In 1997 the Crown appealed Justice Grossi's decision and the Ontario Court of Appeal reversed the trial court's judgment. Despite this legal defeat, Robert McMichael remained determined to regain control of the collecting powers of the MCAC. In 1998, McMichael filed an application for leave to appeal to the Supreme Court of Canada, but this application was later dismissed. With no further opportunities to overturn the lower court's decision, Robert McMichael and his supporters, most notably writer Pierre Berton, enlisted the help of the Ontario Conservative Party.

Despite the fact that Canada's public art museums are supposed to operate at arms-length from the government, Robert McMichael managed to convince the Honourable Helen Johns, then Ontario's minister of citizenship, culture, and recreation, to have the First Reading of Bill 112, An Act to amend the McMichael Canadian Art Collection Act, introduced in Parliament on June 22, 2000.[11] While it became increasingly clear to members of the Ontario Provincial Government that there were serious flaws with the proposed legislation, Bill 112 passed third reading by a fifty-one to thirty-five vote on November 1, 2000. Under the new legislation, Robert and Signe McMichael were made lifetime members of the Art Advisory Committee to ensure that no future board of directors could reduce their influence on acquisitions. The government also recognized the importance of maintaining reference to the ten key artists as stated in the original 1965 mandate, as well as maintaining a clause that allows for the collecting of "other artists." However, the government removed the reference to Aboriginal artworks in the MCAC mandate, sending the message that Euro-Canadian artists were more worthy of specific legal reference.

In the months leading up to the new legislation, criticisms of the proposed changes came from numerous respected members of the Canadian artistic and museum professional community; however, the Conservative Party in power largely overlooked the concerns voiced regarding the effect that the new legislation might have on First Nations and Inuit artworks in the collection. Issues of discriminatory practice, ethics, and bad museology were raised in Professor Gaile McGregor's lengthy memo addressed to the trustees, officers and "friends" of the MCAC in 2000. McGregor went so far as to suggest that the legislation was "vulnerable to a constitutional challenge under section 15 of the charter, as interpreted in light of section 27, the multicultural clause" (McGregor 2000, 1). During the subcommittee hearings in the Ontario legislature, numerous members of Toronto's museum community voiced their opinions on the proposed legislation. Michael Burns, former chairman of the board of directors for the MCAC stated, "The legislation does not allow us to maintain First Nations, Inuit or Métis art, as the 1989 act did. It's a strange thing that a government would act in this way. Why must the mandate change? Because one person changed his mind? ... The elimination of First Nations, Inuit and Métis art is a grave mistake" (Legislative Assembly of Ontario 2000, 1650). Similarly, Jamie Cameron who spoke on behalf of the Society of Inuit Art Collectors, stated, "We regard the omission of any mention of the art of indigenous peoples as a glaring omission in this piece of legislation ... the failure to specifically protect the art of indigenous peoples under section 8 is detrimental to the leadership and the forward energy the McMichael has shown in educating the public about the art of the indigenous peoples" (1640).

Ignoring the warnings of respected members of the Canadian museum community and the Board of the MCAC, the Ontario Provincial Government rewrote the MCAC mandate and removed all references to Aboriginal art. Not only was the legislation an affront to the arm's-length relationship ordinarily held between cultural institutions and government, but it also undermined the gallery's accomplishments in its previous collecting policies and exhibition practices. And so, after years of legal battles, the personal wishes of Robert McMichael were entrenched into the legislation governing the publicly owned MCAC. Not only did this act of the Ontario Provincial Government set an alarming precedent regarding the control of public museums, but it also instantiated cultural racism by eliminating the references to Aboriginal art from the definition of Canadian cultural heritage in the MCAC mandate.

Contemporary Issues

In the years when the board of directors of the MCAC was still legally allowed to focus its collecting activities on contemporary, rather than historical art, they were able to foster a greater understanding of the current artistic practices of Aboriginal people in Canada. Many of the artworks collected were "charged with social and political influences that questioned past injustices" (MCAC, "Contemporary First Nations" 2001). Just before the passing of the 2000 legislation, First Nations curator Richard William Hill wrote an article for the Canadian art magazine *FUSE* to voice his concern over the threat posed by Bill 112 on contemporary First Nations artworks: "The status of First Nations art is especially bizarre. I'm sure the McMichaels will be happy to keep their Norval Morrisseau paintings, which they see as innocuous enough, but they don't want more explicitly contemporary works by First Nations artists" (Hill 2000, 56). Hill's forewarning has now become reality. Although Robert McMichael passed away in November of 2003, his personal distaste for particular works of contemporary art continues to have an impact on the gallery, as evidenced in the narrow focus of exhibition and collecting practices of the MCAC since the new legislation passed—no artworks by Aboriginal Canadians have been collected, and many of the politically-interested and challenging works in the MCAC's collection were removed from display. In a scathing 2003 review of the MCAC's ongoing exhibition series, *Sense of Place,* Toronto-based art critic Sarah Milroy wrote, "The gallery has been stymied by the stubbornness of its founding donor, Robert McMichael ... Attempts to gracefully loosen the grand vizier's grip of steel have come to naught, with the province appointing successive waves of like-minded souls to the board to defend the rough-hewn ramparts from the encroachments of contemporaneity. No sticky incursions of race will be welcomed in this Mighty Whitey chapel of Canadiana" (Milroy 2003).

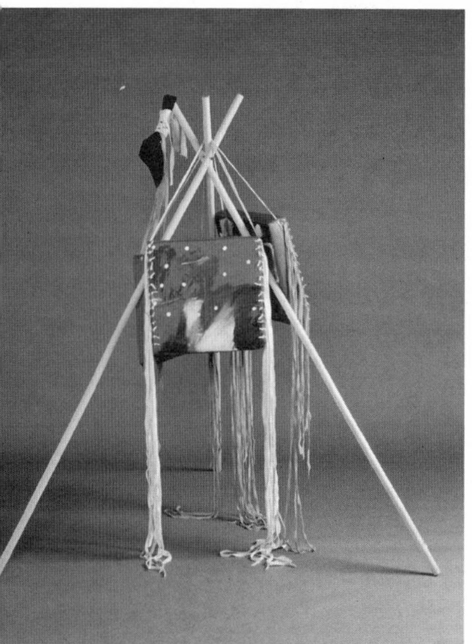

Figure 7.1 Gerald McMaster, *Bases Stolen from the Cleveland Indians and a Captured Yankee*, 1989. Courtesy of McMichael Canadian Art Collection. © Gerald McMaster. Photo © McMichael Canadian Art Collection

Figure 7.2 Gerald McMaster, *Trick or Treaty*, 1990. Courtesy of McMichael Canadian Art Collection. © Gerald McMaster. Photo © McMichael Canadian Art Collection

Works no longer on display at the MCAC include those by Plains Cree artist Gerald McMaster. McMaster's artwork combines irony and humour to create biting social commentary, and as such, his art is especially significant as an addition to a Canadian art gallery because of its ability to challenge cultural stereotypes. In a work much criticized by Robert McMichael—the 1989 sculpture *Bases Stolen from the Cleveland Indians and a Captured Yankee* (fig. 7.1)—McMaster addresses the appropriation of First Nations' names and images by major league baseball teams (Canadian Heritage, online). By juxtaposing Plains Cree symbols with actual baseball equipment, McMaster re-presents the *all-American* sport from a First Nations perspective.

In his 1990 painting *Trick or Treaty* (fig. 7.2), also part of the MCAC's collection, McMaster once again uses humour to raise awareness of political issues. *Trick or Treaty* is a satirical look at historical treaty agreements, and pictured in clown makeup is Canada's first prime minister, Sir John A. Macdonald. The title of the work and accompanying text, "Have I got an act for you," refers to Macdonald's "trickery" in the treaty agreements between Aboriginal people and the Canadian government (MCAC, "Gerald" 1997, online).

As well, the outdoor sculptural installation *Lichen* (fig. 7.3), created in 1998 by Nimpkish/Kwakiutl artist Mary Anne Barkhouse and Ojibway artist Michael Belmore, was removed from the MCAC property in 2002 and sent to the Woodland Cultural Centre in Brantford, Ontario, where it remains on long-term loan. *Lichen*, originally installed at the MCAC in 1999, consists of a bus shelter surrounded by bronze-cast wolves. On a panel inside the bus shelter, where advertising would normally be displayed, there is a backlit black and white image of a raven perched on a bare tree trunk. *Lichen* highlights the ways in which human development has transformed life in Canada and encourages

Figure 7.3 Mary Anne Barkhouse and Michael Belmore, *Lichen*, 1998. Courtesy of McMichael Canadian Art Collection. © Mary Anne Barkhouse and Michael Belmore. Photo © Mary Anne Barkhouse and Michael Belmore

the viewer to consider the effects of human encroachment into wilderness. Removing these artworks from view at the MCAC silences the important social and political commentary that they represent within the context of a Canadian institution.

In 2004, an attempt was made to temporarily reintroduce contemporary Aboriginal perspectives into the MCAC Gallery. From August 27–28, 2004, Kent Monkman, an artist of Swampy Cree and mixed English and Irish descent, was one of four First Nations artists in residence at the MCAC. Monkman's artworks—including performance, painting, and film—often explore themes of colonial conquest in order to insert an all-too-often marginalized Aboriginal voice into the WASP-dominated history of art in Canada. In a performance that was inspired by his own disappointment with the MCAC's removal of *Lichen*, Monkman dressed as "Miss Chief Share Eagle Testicle" in an elaborate feather headdress, platform shoes, and a sequined loin cloth (patterned after a Hudson's Bay Blanket), and rode atop a white horse through the wooded grounds of the MCAC (fig. 7.4).

Also on display during Monkman's residency at the MCAC were a series of his watercolours from 2001. In these paintings, Monkman took aim at the "sacred cows" of Canadian landscape painting: the Group of Seven (Whyte 2005, C8). Each watercolour depicted a "Cowboy and Indian" duo engaged in a somewhat ambiguous sexual encounter against the backdrop of a canonical Group of Seven-esque landscape. There could not be a more appropriate location than the MCAC—advertised as the "Spiritual Home of the Group of Seven"—to begin to deconstruct the iconic status of these Euro-Canadian male painters. However, the opportunities for such interventions to take place at the MCAC are few since Aboriginal art and artists are no longer recognized in its mandate. The legislation, as it stands today, represents a government-imposed erasure of Aboriginal Canadian art from the history of Canadian cultural heritage written in the collecting policy of the MCAC. By removing explicit references to Aboriginal works of art in the MCAC's mandate in 2000, the Ontario Provincial Government acted unethically, and this act instantiated cultural racism.

Conclusion

> We must combat the colonial legacy that has maintained the exclusion of Aboriginal art histories and Aboriginal contemporary art in mainstream art galleries in Canada into the twenty-first century. (Martin 2002b, 239)

In 1998, Carol Tator, Frances Henry, and Winston Mattis, the editors of *Challenging Racism in the Arts,* illustrated the connection between cultural racism and the role of cultural institutions in Canadian society: "We contend that racial exclusion is reinforced by the dominant culture, which controls marginalized groups' access to and participation in the arts. Mainstream cultural institutions and cultural 'authorities' have the power to render invisible and inaudible the images, stories, and voices of ethno-racial minority communities, their artists, and their activists" (Tator et al. 1998, 6). It is especially important to recognize and dismantle cultural racism in our "mainstream cultural institutions" because they play an important role in the production, support, display and definition of national identities. Further to this, the director of the University of Alaska Museum, Aldona Jonaitis, has argued that the status of Aboriginal artworks within a museum is particularly important because of the authority that a museum holds: "Museums create knowledge

Figure 7.4 Kent Monkman as "Miss Chief Share Eagle Testicle," 2004. Courtesy of Kent Monkman. © Kent Monkman. Photo © Jody Shapiro

by addressing those concepts deemed as relevant and omitting other concepts. Because museums represent a significant level of cultural authority, their vision of information is particularly powerful" (Jonaitis 2002, 19).

Therefore, it is not surprising that many Canadian museums' collecting and exhibiting practices have been called into question for their limited view of what constitutes "Canadian Art." For example, in 1993, art historian Anne Whitelaw critiqued the National Gallery's presentation of the history of Canadian art in its Euro-focused Canadian galleries. Whitelaw stated, "[T]he belief that the Canadian art galleries' trajectory of works, from the 17th century through to the Group of Seven (Canada's self-proclaimed national painters), and culminating in the abstraction of the Automatistes and the Painters Eleven, represents the heritage of all Canadians exemplifies the assumptions underlying Canadian identity" (Whitelaw 1995, 39–40). Since the mid-1990s, most major public museums in Ontario have changed their collecting, exhibiting, and hiring practices in order to be more inclusive of Aboriginal Canadians. With a substantial collection of Aboriginal artworks, the MCAC has the potential to allow Aboriginal Canadian voices to be heard within a museum context and contribute to the revision of Canadian art, culture, and national identity. However, the legislated mandate (2000) of the MCAC has taken a step backwards and excluded all references to Aboriginal art.

Along with recognizing and dismantling cultural racism in general, the importance of including specific reference to Aboriginal art into any definition of Canadian art, and into any gallery's collection of Canadian art, cannot be ignored. To date, very few books published on the history of Canadian art have seriously considered the contributions of Aboriginal artists. There was, and in many cases still is, a prevailing narrative of Canada having two founding nations, Britain and France, as evidenced in the canonical texts on Canadian art history.[12] This Eurocentric narrative is reflected in the current collecting mandate of the MCAC, and it places Aboriginal peoples in Canada in an ambiguous position in Canada's myth-making and national identity. Just as published texts give readers a sense of the scope (or lack thereof) of Canadian art history, so too do the collections and exhibitions in Canadian public art galleries. Institutions such as the MCAC, the Art Gallery of Ontario, and the National Gallery of Canada, with their commitment to collect Canadian artworks and their status as cultural authorities, are central in the construction of Canadian art history and culture. It is therefore pertinent that these institutions move beyond Eurocentric definitions of "Canadian Art," which are too often reflected in their collecting and exhibiting practices. Canadian cultural institutions have the capacity, as Trudy Nicks, senior curator of Anthropology at the Royal Ontario Museum has stated, "to contribute to new directions in art history and, ideally, to expand understanding on the part of visitors who encounter [their] exhibitions" (Nicks 2002, 158).

Many museums in Canada and around the world are finally making changes towards inclusivity. Along with individual institutions, larger international organizations such as the International Council of Museums (ICOM) have taken steps to encourage and recognize cultural diversity. ICOM's annual International Museum Day, founded in 1977, promotes the roles which museums play in affecting social change with the message that "museums are an important means of cultural exchange, enrichment of cultures and development of mutual understanding, cooperation and peace among people" (ICOM, online). In May 2005, the theme for International Museum Day was "Museums Bridging Cultures" and with this, the ICOM was able to raise public awareness of cultural issues in museums as well as "pay tribute to cultural diversity and to encourage museums in their role of spanning various ethnic, religious, and national divides" (ICOM, online). Given its collection and its history, the MCAC has the potential to act as a "cultural bridge."

Similarly to the 1980s, when the Ontario Provincial Government decided it was time to include legal recognition of Aboriginal works in the MCAC's collecting mandate, it is today, once again, time for amendments to be made to the McMichael Canadian Art Collection Act so that references to Aboriginal art can be rewritten into the mandate. Through a revised mandate that contains specific reference to Aboriginal art, the MCAC could once again become a model cultural institution for those interested in enhancing our understanding of Canadian art and cultural heritage. However, the current status of Aboriginal art at the MCAC reflects what Martin has termed "soft inclusion," whereby token and temporary projects involving Aboriginal artists allow the gallery to maintain the illusion of inclusivity without any real commitment on the part of the institution (Martin 1991, 25). In describing "soft inclusion," Martin has stated, "Periodic or 'soft' inclusion ... absolves the institution from a long-term commitment to the serious treatment of works by Native artists" (25). Thus, while the *temporary* display of works by an Aboriginal artist might occur on the grounds of the MCAC, as was the case with Monkman's three-day residency, the gallery is not making any long-term commitments in relation to Aboriginal art. Further complicating this matter is the lack of legal backing for the MCAC to acquire Aboriginal works of art. Amendments to the MCAC mandate were required in 1969, in 1982, and again in 1989, to specifically permit the gallery to collect Aboriginal works of art; now all such references have been categorically removed. As such, any attempts to acquire Aboriginal art for the MCAC's permanent collection could arguably be considered *ultra vires*, that is, beyond its legal authority. The exclusion of Aboriginal art from the mandate divests the MCAC of its ability to make a sustained commitment to the art and culture of Aboriginal Canadians. With amendments to the McMichael Canadian Art Collection Amendment Act, 2000, the MCAC would once again have the capacity to build bridges between Aboriginal and non-Aboriginal Canadians and help to expand understandings of Canadian art and culture.

Afterword

The research for this article was financially supported by the Canada Graduate Scholarships Program of the Social Sciences and Humanities Research Council of Canada (SSHRC). In June 2005, a version of this paper was presented to Joan Murray, interim executive director and CEO of the McMichael Canadian Art Collection. Shortly thereafter, the MCAC announced that they would host an exhibition of photographs by Iroquois/Onondaga artist Jeff Thomas. *Jeff Thomas: Portraits from the Dancing Grounds* was on display between December 10, 2005, and March 19, 2006, and was the first major exhibition of contemporary First Nations art at the MCAC since 1998. As well, in November 2005 the MCAC launched its redesigned website.[13] In a section of its website titled "The Collection—Overview," the MCAC has added "Contemporary" to its previous three collecting categories of "Group of Seven," "First Nations," and "Inuit" art. Although the newly redesigned website suggests otherwise, it is only the Group of Seven artists, not First Nations or Inuit artists, who are recognized in the current legislated mandate (MCAC, "The Collection").

Endnotes

1 In this paper I have used the terms "exclusion" and "inclusion" as they are defined in the anthology *Challenging Racism in the Arts: Case Studies of Controversy and Conflict*, 1998. Editors Tator, Henry, and Mattis define exclusion as "the state of group disempowerment, degradation, and disenfranchisement maintained by systemic barriers and supported by an implicit ideology of ethnic and racial superiority" (Tator et. al. 1998, 274). The term inclusiveness is defined as "exist[ing] when disadvantaged communities and designated group members share power and decision-making at all levels in projects, programs, and institutions" (275).

2 I use the term "Aboriginal" as provided by Indian and Northern Affairs Canada: "the term 'Aboriginal people' generally applies to First Nations, Inuit and Métis" (DIAND, online). Terms such as "Eskimo" and "Indian" may be used in this paper in two contexts: firstly, where such terms are used in quotations from other sources; secondly, where "Indian" or "Eskimo" is the term used in legislation or policy and hence in discussions concerning such legislation or policy (for example, the Indian Act).

3 Between 1965 and 1972 the gallery was legally known as "The McMichael Conservation Collection of Art." In 1972, as a Crown corporation, the name was changed to the "McMichael Canadian Collection." With the passing of Bill 209 (1989), the gallery became known as the "McMichael Canadian Art Collection d'art canadien," which it remains today. I will refer to the gallery by the abbreviation "MCAC."

4 The tem "cultural racism" is borrowed from the anthology *Challenging Racism in the Arts: Case Studies of Controversy and Conflict*, 1998. Editors Tator, Henry, and Mattis see cultural racism as one of four elements of racism, the other three being individual racism, institutional racism, and systemic/structural racism (Tator et. al. 1998, 276). Tator, Henry, and Mattis argue that it is important to recognize cultural racism as a fundamental aspect of racism, because

"it includes ideas that are deeply embedded in the value system of society—as a part of the invisible network of beliefs, attitudes, and assumptions that define the cultural value system of society" (Tator 1998, 22).

5 The MCAC is an agency of the government of Ontario under the Ministry of Culture. The gallery receives financial assistance from various levels of government as well as corporate donations, donations from private individuals, and gifts-in-kind.

6 It should be noted that some references to the original donation incorrectly state that there were 194 works donated. This error was made due to the fact that one of the works, *Ontario Scenes* (1958–60), a drawing by A. J. Casson, was incorrectly listed as being eight separate drawings when in fact it is eight small sketches on one piece of paper.

7 Until the 1970s, only anthropologically-based museums and the Department of Indian and Northern Affairs Canada were serious institutional collectors of First Nations and Inuit cultural objects.

8 John P. Robarts, Robert McMichael, and Signe McMichael. Letter. 30 September 1969. Archives of Ontario, Toronto.

9 For further discussion of the terms of the 1972 *Act*, see A. J. McClean, "McMichael v. Ontario – One Man's Obsession," esp. 497-498.

10 *Babylon* was removed from the MCAC grounds and sent on long-term loan to the McLaren Art Centre in Barrie, Ontario. For Robert McMichael's full explanation of which artworks he did not approve of, see *Affidavit* of Robert McMichael sworn 12 February 1996, in the matter of *McMichael v. Ontario*, para. 53-54. See also *McMichael v. Ontario* 154 D.L.R. (4th) 50 (Ont. C.A. 1997), para. 99.

11 For a discussion of the close relationship Robert and Signe McMichael shared with the Conservative Party see Kenneth R. Cavalier, "Case Notes: One Premier's Obsession?" 2002.

12 See William Colgate's *Canadian Art: Its Origins and Development* (1943), Graham McInnes' *Canadian Art* (1950), Russell Harper's *Painting in Canada: A History* (1966), and Dennis Reid's *A Concise History of Canadian Painting* (1988), none of which recognize the contributions of First Nations or Inuit artists to the history of Canadian art. Newton MacTavish's *The Fine Arts in Canada* (1925) does recognize that Aboriginal people in Canada made art, however, he refers to Aboriginal peoples in past tense and his brief discussion is racist in tone and does not actually describe any artists or artworks in particular.

13 http://www.mcmichael.com.

BIBLIOGRAPHY

Agreement. (1965, November 18). "The Crown," "The McMichaels," and "the M.T.R.C.A."

Assembly of First Nations. Task Force on Museums and First Peoples. (1992). *Turning the Page: Forging New Partnerships between Museums and First Peoples.* Ottawa, ON: The Canadian Museums Association.

Bill 112, An Act to amend the McMichael Canadian Art Collection Act. (2000, November 1).

Bill 112, An Act to amend the McMichael Canadian Art Collection Act. (2000). 1st session, 37th Parliament, SO.

Bill 175, An Act to amend the McMichael Canadian Collection Act. (1982).

Bill 209, An Act to revise the McMichael Canadian Collection Act. (1989).

Bill 216, An Act to establish the McMichael Canadian Collection. (1972, November 23).

Cavalier, Kenneth R. (2002). "Case Notes: One Premier's Obsession? The McMichael Legislation in Ontario." *International Journal of Cultural Property, 11:1*, 65–79.

Colgate, William. (1943). *Canadian Art: Its Origins and Development.* Toronto, ON: Ryerson University Press.

Crawford, Lenore. (1974, May 30). "Gallery not just for 'Seven.'" *London Free Press*, 49.

Harper, Russell. (1966). *Painting in Canada: A History.* Toronto, ON: University of Toronto Press.

Hill, Richard William. (2000). "Indian Givers: The McMichaels' Revenge on Contemporary Art." *FUSE, 23:2*, 55–56.

Jonaitis, Aldona. (2002). "First Nations and Art Museums." *On Aboriginal Representation in the Gallery*, eds. Lynda Jessup and Shannon Bagg. Hull, QC: Canadian Museum of Civilization, 17–26.

Kritzwiser, Kay. (1970, August 22). "A Collection moves beyond Its Group of Seven image." *Globe and Mail*, 23.

Legislative Assembly of Ontario. (1982, April 6). *Hansard Transcripts.*

MacTavish, Newton. (1925). *The Fine Arts in Canada.* Toronto, ON: Macmillan.

Martin, Lee-Ann. (1989). "Canadian Indian Art." In *The McMichael Canadian Art Collection: Twenty-fifth Anniversary Edition, 1965-1990*, eds. Jean Blodgett et al. Kleinburg, ON: McMichael Canadian Art Collection, 161–173.

———. (1991). *The Politics of Inclusion and Exclusion: Contemporary Native Art and Public*

Art Museums in Canada. Ottawa, ON: Canada Council.

———. (2002a). "An/Other One: Aboriginal Art, Curators, and Art Museums." In *The Edge of Everything: Reflections on Curatorial Practice,* ed. Catherine Thomas. Banff, AB: Banff Centre, 49–56.

———. (2002b). "Negotiating Space for Aboriginal Art." In *On Aboriginal Representation in the Gallery*. Hull, QC: Canadian Museum of Civilization, 239–246.

McClean, A. J. (1998). "*McMichael v. Ontario*: One Man's Obsession." *International Journal of Cultural Property, 7:2,* 496–511.

McGregor, Gaile. (2000, July 18). "Some Comments on the Possible Legal Ramifications of Bill 112." In *Memorandum to the Trustees, Officers, and Friends of McMichael Gallery*. Kleinburg, ON: McMichael Canadian Art Collection Archives.

McInnes, Graham. (1950). *Canadian Art*. Toronto, ON: Macmillan.

McMichael Canadian Collection Act. (1972). SO, c.134.

McMichael Canadian Art Collection Act. (1990). RSO, c. M.4.

McMichael Canadian Art Collection Amendment Act, 2000. (2000). SO, c. 21.

McMichael Canadian Art Collection. *Annual Report: 1990–91*. (1991). Kleinburg, ON: McMichael Canadian Art Collection.

McMichael Canadian Art Collection. *Annual Report: 1999–00*. (2000). Kleinburg, ON: McMichael Canadian Art Collection.

McMichael Canadian Art Collection. (1989, December 12). *Collection Statistics*. Kleinburg, ON: McMichael Canadian Art Collection Archives.

McMichael Canadian Art Collection. (2002, June 13). *Creative Strategy*. Unpublished. Kleinburg, ON: McMichael Canadian Art Collection Archives.

McMichael Canadian Art Collection. (2000, July 7). *Founder's Choices*. Kleinburg, ON: McMichael Canadian Art Collection Archives.

McMichael Canadian Collection Act, 1989. (1989). SO, c.44.

McMichael Canadian Collection Act. (1972). SO, c.134.

McMichael Canadian Collection Amendment Act, 1982. (1982). SO, c.3.

McMichael Conservation Collection of Art. (1972). *Report*. Toronto, ON.

McMichael v. Ontario, 141 D.L.R. (4th) 169, 1996 GD.

McMichael v. Ontario, 154 D.L.R. (4th) 50, 1997 CA.

McMichael, Robert. (1986). *One Man's Obsession*. Scarborough, ON: Prentice-Hall.

McMichael, Robert. (1965, July 5). Letter to Hon. John Robarts. Toronto, ON: Archives of Ontario.

Milroy, Sarah. (2003, July 25). "New Ideas Need Not Apply." *Globe and Mail.* R5.

Nicks, Trudy. (2002). "Expanded Visions: Collaborative Approaches to Exhibiting First Nations Histories and Artistic Traditions." In *On Aboriginal Representation in the Gallery.* Hull, QC: Canadian Museum of Civilization, 149–162.

Procuta, Egle. (2000, June 23). "Group of Seven Bill Aims to End Long Art War." *Globe and Mail.* A1, A6.

Reid, Dennis. (1988). *A Concise History of Canadian Painting.* Toronto, ON: Oxford UP.

Robarts, John P., Robert McMichael, and Signe McMichael. (1969, September 30). Letter. Toronto, ON: Archives of Ontario.

Spence, G. H. (1968, December 11). Letter to Hon. James A. C. Auld. Toronto, ON: Archives of Ontario.

Tator, Carol, Frances Henry, and Winston Mattis. (1998). *Challenging Racism in the Arts: Case Studies of Controversy and Conflict.* Toronto, ON: University of Toronto Press.

Whitelaw, Anne. (1995). "Land Spirit Power: First Nations Cultural Production and Canadian Nationhood." *International Journal of Canadian Studies, 12,* 31–49.

Whyte, Murray. (2005, June 12). "Dare We Reinterpret the Group of Seven?" *Toronto Star.* C 8.

Wychowanec, S. J. (1969, August 7). Letter to J. K. Reynolds. Toronto, ON: Archives of Ontario.

Internet Sources

Art Gallery of Ontario. "Permanent Collection." http://www.ago.net/info/collection/collection.cfm?collection_id=4 [consulted November 15, 2004].

Canada. Department of Indian and Northern Development. "Words First: An Evolving Terminology Relating to Aboriginal Peoples in Canada." http://ainc-inac.gc.ca/pr/pub/wf/index_e.html [consulted July 19, 2004].

Canadian Heritage. "Significant Treasures: McMichael Canadian Art Collection." http://www.cffm-fcam.ca/Significant_Treasures/English/sigtresprov.html [consulted July 19, 2004].

International Council of Museums. http://icom.museum/imd.html [consulted March 11, 2005].

Legislative Assembly of Ontario. (October 16, 2000). *Hansard transcripts.* http://www.ontla.on.ca/hansard/house_debates/37_parl/session1/L089A.htm [consulted November 23, 2004].

Legislative Assembly of Ontario. (October 18, 2000). *Hansard transcripts.* http://www.ontla.on.ca/hansard/house_debates/37_parl/session1/L091A.htm [consulted November 23, 2004].

McMichael Canadian Art Collection. "Contemporary First Nations Art at the McMichael." http://www.mcmichael.com/web1/our_collection/first_nation_art.shtml [consulted July 19, 2004].

McMichael Canadian Art Collection. "The Collection: Overview." http://www.mcmichael.com/collection/ [consulted November 15, 2005].

McMichael Canadian Art Collection. "Gerald McMaster." http://www.mcmichael.com/mcmaster.htm [consulted November 15, 2005].

McMichael Canadian Art Collection. "What's the McMichael?" http://www.mcmichael.com/kidsarea/what/index.shtml [consulted June 4, 2005].

Canada. Royal Commission on Aboriginal Peoples. "Gathering Strength." Vol.3. http://www.ainc-inac.gc.ca/ch/rcap/sg/si1_e.html#Volume%203 [consulted January 26, 2005].

Appendix A: Chronology of Collection

1951	Robert and Signe McMichael purchase their property in Kleinburg, Ontario, just north of Toronto.
1954	The McMichaels move into the cabin built on their Kleinburg property.
1955	The McMichaels purchase the painting *Montreal River* by Lawren Harris.
1956	The McMichaels purchase their first Inuit carving.
1962	The McMichaels acquire the shack behind the Studio Building that Tom Thomson had once occupied, move it to their property, and set about restoring it.
1965	The McMichaels donate their property, home, and collection of art and artifacts to the Province of Ontario.
July 8, 1966	Official opening of the McMichael Conservation Collection of Art.
May 1967	First publication of the *McMichael Conservation Collection of Art,* a catalogue of the collection with an introduction by Paul Duval. Images of 251 artworks were reproduced in the catalogue.
October 7, 1980	Robert McMichael agrees to resign as director of the MCAC in favour of a new appointment as founder director-emeritus.

July 1, 1981	Michael Bell is appointed to the position of director and CEO of the MCAC.
1986	Publication of the book *One Man's Obsession* by Robert McMichael, Scarborough, ON: Prentice-Hall Canada.
June 30, 1986	Michael Bell resigns from the position of director and CEO of the MCAC.
September 1986	Barbara Tyler is appointed to the position of director and CEO of the MCAC.
1991	John McEwen's sculpture *Babylon and the Tower of Babel* is installed along the driveway leading into the MCAC.
1996	*McMichael v. Ontario*.
1996	Justice Peter Grossi of the Ontario Court's General Division agrees that the gallery's original 1965 mandate should not change.
1997	Justice Grossi's decision is overturned on appeal.
1998	Leave to appeal dismissed by the Supreme Court of Canada
March 2000	After thirteen years, Barbara Tyler retires from the position of executive director and CEO of the MCAC.
March 9, 2000	Vincent J. Varga is named executive director and CEO of the MCAC.

November 2, 2000	Royal Assent of Bill 112, An Act to amend the McMichael Canadian Art Collection Act.
2001	John McEwen's sculpture *Babylon and the Tower of Babel* is removed from the grounds of the MCAC and placed on long-term loan at the MacLaren Art Centre.
2002	Mary Anne Barkhouse and Michael Belmore's sculpture *Lichen* is removed from the grounds of the MCAC and placed on long-term loan at the Woodland Cultural Centre.
November 18, 2003	Robert McMichael dies at age 82.
November 26, 2004	Vincent J. Varga resigns from the position of executive director and CEO of the MCAC. Joan Murray is named as interim executive director and CEO.

Appendix B: Legislative Timeline

November 18, 1965	Agreement signed between the McMichaels and the Province of Ontario.
November 18, 1965	Deed of gift signed by Robert Laidlaw to the Province of Ontario.
September 30, 1969	Amendment to the 1965 agreement. In order to address the confusion in regards to the (in)ability of the Collection to acquire Inuit sculpture, a letter was written by the former premier of Ontario John Robarts and co-signed by Signe and Robert McMichael stating that "the Collection may be augmented through the acquisition, by donation or purchase, of works of a similar nature reflective of the cultural heritage of Canada."
November 30, 1972	Royal Assent of Bill 216, the creation of the McMichael Canadian Art Collection Act designating the Collection a Crown corporation.
April 23, 1982	Royal Assent of Bill 175, an Act to Revise the McMichael Canadian Collection Act.
July 13, 1989	Royal Assent of Bill 209, an Act to Revise the McMichael Canadian Collection Act.
1996	*McMichael v. Ontario*: Judge Grossi sides with the McMichaels and agrees that the gallery's original 1965 mandate should not change.

1997	Judge Grossi's decision is overturned on appeal.
1998	Leave to appeal dismissed by the Supreme Court of Canada.
2000	The Ontario government passes legislation (Bill 112) to restore the gallery to the McMichaels' original vision.
June 22, 2000	First Reading of Bill 112, An Act to amend the McMichael Canadian Art Collection Act.
October 4, 2000	Second Reading of Bill 112, An Act to amend the McMichael Canadian Art Collection Act.
October 16, 2000	Subcommittee Report on the McMichael Canadian Art Collection Act. Presenters who supported the proposed legislation: Pierre Berton, Dr. Robert Salter, Paul Duval, John MacEachern, Mary McArthur, Robert McMichael, George McLean. Presenters opposed to the proposed legislation: Joyce Zemans, Ontario Association of Art Galleries; Paul Reinhardt, Kleinburg Business Improvement Association; Janet Brooke, Canadian Museums Association; Mary Mastin, Marie Lalonde and Barry Lord, Ontario Museum Association; Pat Fairhead; Virginia MacDonnell.
October 18, 2000	Second day of the Subcommittee Report on the McMichael Canadian Art Collection Act.

	Presenters who supported the proposed legislation: Geoffrey Zimmerman, Fred Burford, Lucy Kristan, Ken Danby, Doug Wright.
	Presenters opposed to the proposed legislation: Vincent Tovell; Paul Thompson, West Toronto Art Newspaper; Jane Martin, Canadian Artists' Representation Ontario; Jamie Cameron, Society of Inuit Art Collectors; Michael Burns; David Braley; Jean Eadie; Margaret McBurney; Kate Davis, Canadian Art Museum Directors Organization; Ron Bolt, Royal Canadian Academy of Arts.
October 25, 2000	Final day of the Subcommittee Report on the McMichael Canadian Art Collection Act.
	Presenters who supported the proposed legislation: Rudy Bies, Lynn Bevan.
	Presenters opposed to the proposed legislation: Joy Cohnstaedt; Elizabeth Gilbert, Canadian Society of Painters in Watercolour; John McEwen; Don Lake; John Challinor, Compaq Canada; David Silcox.
November 1, 2000	Third Reading of Bill 112, An Act to amend the McMichael Canadian Art Collection Act.
November 2, 2000	Royal Assent of Bill 112, An Act to amend the McMichael Canadian Art Collection Act.

Appendix C: MCAC Mandates In Comparison

1. Excerpt from agreement. "The Crown," "The McMichaels," and "the M.T.R.C.A." (November 18, 1965):

   > 13. The Crown shall, with the advice and assistance of Robert McMichael and Signe McMichael, establish, develop and maintain in perpetuity at Tapawingo a collection of art reflecting the cultural heritage of Canada; the said collection shall be known as the "McMichael Conservation Collection of Art" (hereinafter called "the Collection"), and shall be comprised of paintings by Tom Thomson, Emily Carr, David Milne, A. Y. Jackson, Lawren Harris, A. J. Casson, Frederick Varley, Arthur Lismer, J. H. MacDonald, Franklin Carmichael, and other artists, as designated by the advisory committee, who have made contributions to the development of Canadian art.

2. Excerpt from 1969 amendment to the agreement, made by Hon. John P. Robarts:

   > As the second paragraph of the preamble to the Agreement indicates, the Collection has always included not only paintings but also drawings, sculpture and artifacts. Accordingly, notwithstanding any apparent implication to the contrary in the Agreement, the Province has always contemplated that the Collection may be augmented through the acquisition, by donation or purchase, of works of a similar nature reflective of the cultural heritage of Canada.[8]

3. Excerpt from Bill 216, An Act to establish the McMichael Canadian Collection (1972, Royal Assent April 2, 1972):

Explanatory Note

The Bill establishes a non-share capital corporation, to be known as The McMichael Canadian Collection, to operate the McMichael Art Gallery.

The constitution of the Board of Trustees of the Corporation is set out, together with the powers and duties of the Board, and other related matters.

Provision is made for the guarantee by Ontario of loans to the Board for the purpose of carrying out its objects.

6. The objects of the Corporation are,

to hold, manage, control, maintain, exhibit, display, develop and stimulate interest in the collection for the benefit of the public;

to hold and preserve the lands described in the Schedule as a permanent site for a public gallery and related facilities for the collection;

to maintain and operate the gallery mentioned in clause b; and

to hold, manage, control, maintain, preserve, administer and develop the lands of the Corporation in conjunction with the operation of the gallery and for the benefit of the public.

7. The Board shall ensure that the art works and objects acquired from time to time as part of the collection are not inconsistent with the general character of the collection at the time of such acquisition.

4. Excerpt from Bill 175, An Act to amend the McMichael Canadian Collection Act (1982, Royal Assent April 23, 1982):

Explanatory Notes

Section 1. Section 7 of the *Act* is re-enacted to ensure that the Board continues to maintain the present character of the collection.

...

Section 7 of the *McMichael Canadian Collection Act*, being chapter 259 of the Revised statutes of Ontario, 1980, is repealed and the following substituted therefore:
7. The Board shall ensure that the focus of the collection is the art work and objects created by,
(a) Tom Thomson, Emily Carr, David Milne, A. Y. Jackson, Lawren Harris, A. J. Casson, Frederick Varley, Arthur Lismer, J. H. MacDonald, Franklin Carmichael,
(b) the indigenous peoples of Canada,
and other artists who have made contributions to the development of Canadian art and whose art work and objects will be consistent with the general character of the collection.

5. Excerpt from Bill 209, An Act to revise the McMichael Canadian Collection Act (1989, Royal Assent July 13, 1989)

Explanatory Note
The main provisions of the Bill are as follows:
To provide an English name and a French name for the corporation.
To increase the number of members of the Board.
To clarify the financial and administrative arrangements of the Board.
To clarify the objects and the collection mandate of the corporation
...
7.—(1) The objects of the Corporation are,
(a) to acquire art works, objects and documentary material for the collection;
(b) to preserve and exhibit the collection;
(c) to conduct research on and provide documentation for the collection;
(d) to stimulate interest in the collection;

(e) to conduct activities in order to enhance and complement the collection;
(f) to hold, maintain and use the land described in the Schedule to the *McMichael Canadian Collection Act,* being chapter 259 of the Revised Statutes of Ontario, 1980, as a permanent site for a public gallery and related facilities for the collection.
...
8. The Board shall ensure that the focus of the collection is the works of art created by Indian, Inuit and Métis artists, the artists of the Group of Seven and their contemporaries and other artists who have made or make a contribution to the development of Canadian Art.

6. Excerpt from Bill 112, An Act to amend the McMichael Canadian Art Collection Act (2000, Royal Assent November 2, 2000)

Explanatory Note
The Bill amends the *McMichael Canadian Art Collection Act* as follows:
1. The Bill recognizes the gift of the McMichael Canadian Art Collection in 1965 and the original vision of Robert and Signe McMichael for the collection. The Bill also recognizes that the focus of the collection has changed over time and that it is appropriate to return the collection to, and then maintain it in, the spirit of its original focus. (Section 2 of the Bill)
2. The composition of the Board of Trustees of the McMichael Canadian Art Collection is altered. Under the alterations, a new section 3.1 is added to the *Act* to emphasize that Robert McMichael and Signe McMichael are life members of the Board. If either of them is unwilling or unable to continue as a trustee, then provision is made for the McMichaels to appoint substitutes during their lifetimes. (Section 3 of the Bill)
3. The Board's powers to make by-laws and establish committees

and its power to appoint or remove the director are made subject to the Minister's approval until the day three years following Royal Assent to this Bill (or until such time as the collection conforms to section 8 of the *Act*, whichever is later). The Board is also limited in that its committees may be composed only of trustees, employees and volunteers of the Corporation. (Sections 4 and 6 of the Bill)

4. The Board is required to establish an art advisory committee. Initially the committee will consist of Robert McMichael and Signe McMichael, the chair and vice-chair of the Board and a trustee chosen by the Board from amongst the trustees appointed by the Lieutenant Governor in Council. The art advisory committee will make recommendations to the Board with respect to the acquisition and disposal of art works, objects and related documentary material. The art advisory committee is also empowered to designate the artists who have made contributions to the development of Canadian art. (Section 5 of the Bill)

5. The nature of the collection is redefined. The collection is to reflect the cultural heritage of Canada and to be comprised of art works, objects and related documentary material created by or about Tom Thomson, Emily Carr, David Milne, A. Y. Jackson, Lawren Harris, A. J. Casson, Frederick Varley, Arthur Lismer, J. H. MacDonald and Franklin Carmichael and those artists designated by the art advisory committee as having made contributions to the development of Canadian art. (Section 7 of the Bill)

6. The definition of "Minister" is updated. (Section 1 of the Bill)

...

The purpose of this *Act*, as amended in 2000, is to recognize the following:

1. In 1965, Robert and Signe McMichael gave the people of Ontario their collection of Canadian art, their home, and 14 acres of surrounding lands.

2. The art collection, now known as the McMichael Canadian Art

Collection, was to display distinctively Canadian art reflecting the cultural heritage of Canada and the images and the spirit of the nation, focusing on those artists known as the Group of Seven and their contemporaries.
3. Robert and Signe McMichael had a vision that the gallery and the art collection that it housed would continue to retain the spirit that they had originally created by remaining true to its focus on those artists who had celebrated the nation's beauty in a uniquely Canadian way.
4. The focus of the collection has changed over time.
5. It is appropriate to return the collection to, and then maintain it in, the spirit of its original focus.
6. There should be an appropriate corporate structure to administer the collection.
7. There should be an art advisory committee to advise on matters related to the composition and display of the collection.
8. Robert and Signe McMichael should continue to have significant roles in matters related to the collection
...
7. Section 8 of the *Act* is repealed and the following substituted:
Nature of collection
8. The Board shall ensure that the collection reflects the cultural heritage of Canada and is comprised of art works and objects and related documentary material created by or about,
(a) Tom Thomson, Emily Carr, David Milne, A. Y. Jackson, Lawren Harris, A. J. Casson, Frederick Varley, Arthur Lismer, J. H. MacDonald and Franklin Carmichael, and
(b) other artists who have been designated by the art advisory committee under clause 4.1 (2) (e) for their contributions to the development of Canadian art.

LITERATURE

Nancy Grimm

"Decolonizing the Mind": Drew Hayden Taylor's Play with the Semantics of Irony in *Only Drunks and Children Tell the Truth*

Charting the Territory

Approaches toward Native (Canadian) texts often ask the ones accessing these texts to become conscious of their own cultural background. Broadly speaking, as a European, or German for that matter, one is ultimately influenced by Western concepts of thinking. These concepts, often "hampered by the irrational and stifling legacies of colonialism and eurocentrism" (Lutz 2002, 1), thus have an enormous impact on approaches to Native Canadian texts. While one's approaches, especially to fictional texts, are channelled by Western literary theory and criticism, one may also encounter a certain notion of diffidence when venturing to explore Native Canadian texts as discourses from a culture that may contemplate non-Western, and therefore inherently unfamiliar, ideological and philosophical perspectives. This insecurity already starts on a terminological level. Is one to abide by the politically correct and government-consented term "Aboriginal Peoples of Canada" and thereby disregard the formerly endorsed term "First Nations," or should one speak of "Native Canadians" and thereby adapt US-American terminology?

Whatever the decision may be, it soon becomes evident that all of these terms are inherently insufficient—as are our theoretical and often Eurocentric approaches to and analyses of texts written by Native Canadian authors. While the former terminology overrides the existences of different Aboriginal cultures subsumed under one single and, above all, generalizing term, the latter often fails to address and correctly understand the literary as well as the cultural merits of Native Canadian literatures:

> The more overt protest books of the 1970s often combined their sharp analyses of society with wit, humour, poetry, history, anthropology, and/or personal reflections. Authors turned to the facts of biography to humanize the much dehumanized "Indian." Instead of being read as new genres, they were attacked as biased and parochial. Few bookstores, libraries, or professors knew what to do with Native writing that crossed or integrated well-defined genres, styles, or schools. (LaRocque 1990, xviii)

This being said, it is a structural and analytical prerequisite of this paper to approach the Native (Canadian) play analyzed therein in a self-reflexive manner, thereby always being aware of my own cultural background and inherent predispositions. However, knowing that any solution with regard to terminology—however self-reflexive—will turn out to be deficient, I have tried to refrain from using generalizing terms, instead addressing the respective Aboriginal culture(s) whenever possible and implied by the text discussed. As for information and statements made in a general manner and thus generally pertaining to all Aboriginal cultures of North America, I have chosen to use the term "Native (Canadian)." As for the use of the term "Indian" (in apostrophes), it is exclusively used in passages that discuss existing stereotypes about "the Indian" as a creation of the Western imagination.

Against the background of the aforementioned need for cultural awareness when approaching Native Canadian literary genres, this article will initially be concerned with a brief introduction to Native Canadian drama, thereby also contextualising the playwright Drew Hayden Taylor. Secondly, a section on the discussed play's capacity to "decolonize the mind" will consider salient theoretical assumptions in the postcolonial debate about decolonization. With selected (con)textual information thus established, the paper will move on to demarcate the semantics and functions of irony in Taylor's *Only Drunks and Children Tell the Truth* (1998) as this contribution's central concern. Finally, a conclusive passage will again delineate and summarize the main argument.

(CON)TEXT: DREW HAYDEN TAYLOR AND NATIVE CANADIAN DRAMA

Native (Canadian) authors are publishing in a variety of genres, ranging from the oral tradition and adaptations of allegedly Western genres such as poetry and autobiography to both short and long prose narratives. However, it is the dramatic genre that has brought Native Canadian authors to national recognition (Lutz 2002, 124–125) not only in Canada but also beyond Canadian borders. While with the production of texts of their own—whether fictional or non-fictional— "Native authors are speaking out against the misuses of their cultural heritage by non-Natives who claim varying degrees of authority and initiation" (Lutz 1991, 4), it is imperative to accentuate that "contemporary Native writing moves beyond the mere imitation or reproduction of a European, or mainstream North American literary style" (Schorcht 2003, 5). What is generally described as a process in which "Native authors translate the genre conventions of Native oral tradition into written forms, developing Native perspectives on North American literature and history" (5) is also true for the dramatic genre, which, with its inherent verbal qualities and structures of performance art, bears a resemblance to the characteristics of the oral tradition and may be considered its continuation (Lutz 2002, 125).

Therefore it is the dramatic genre that, by its adaptation to the needs and desires of Native authors, carries on the oral tradition in dramatic texts that are both "substantially Native and substantially Western" (Ruppert 1995, 9). However, the objectives of an oral tradition that has been adapted to the dramatic genre always remain within a definition of the oral tradition that Hartmut Lutz, in an interview with Maria Campbell, has expressed as follows: "The way I understand the oral tradition is that it tells people who they are, and where they are headed, where they come from. If you read about it, or if storytellers are asked, that is more or less what it seems to come down to: the oral tradition tells people who they are, gives them identity" (Lutz 1991, 56). Drew Hayden Taylor, while focusing in particular on the inherent relation between storytelling and humour, voices a similar account of the oral tradition or storytelling:

> I grew up in a world of humor and storytelling. Theatre is the next logical progression in storytelling. It's just going from telling stories around a campfire to telling stories around a stage. Like storytelling, theatre has the ability to take the audience on a journey, using your voice, your body, and your imagination .... So it became obvious to me that theatre became the number one form of expression in those early years. It's something most Native people are familiar with—telling a story. Like a joke or any story, theatre has a beginning, a middle, an end. And you set up confrontation resolution. (Taylor, online)

As a playwright who draws upon storytelling, Drew Hayden Taylor writes in the tradition of such renowned playwrights as Tomson Highway and David Daniel Moses. The former, with his uniquely composed plays *The Rez Sisters: A Play in Two Acts* (1986) and *Dry Lips Oughta Move to Kapuskasing* (1989), has established a tradition of playwriting which, although it is "firmly rooted in Native life" (Lutz 2002, 124), appeals to both Native and non-Native readers, critics and researchers. Highway takes into account "the complexities of a world in which tragedy and burlesque, the sacred and the profane, Native sharing and economic greed, birth and cancer, professional hockey and sacred traditions exist simultaneously" (124) and dramatist Daniel David Moses played an important part in the Native Theatre Renaissance that emerged in the mid- and late 1980s.

Drew Hayden Taylor is Ojibwa/Caucasian, or, as he likes to put it, "My standard joke is I'm half Ojibwa, half Caucasian, so that makes me an 'occasion'" (Taylor, online). Taylor has published in a variety of genres: in the genres of prose and drama, there is his short story collection *The Fearless Warrior*

(1998) and the investigational play *alterNatives* (2000). A best-of collection of columns published by Taylor in the *Peterborough Examiner, Windspeaker,* and *The Prairie Dog* was published under the title *Funny, You Don't Look Like One: Observations of a Blue-Eyed Ojibway* (1996). Further contributions by Taylor include the mystery drama *The Strange Case of Bunny Weequod* (1999), the documentary films *Circle of All Nations* (1999) and *Redskins, Tricksters and Puppy Stew* (2000), as well as his most recent projects *400 Kilometres* (2005) and *Me Funny* (2006), a collection of stories by Native (Canadian) people. Taylor is also recognized for the two one-act plays, *Toronto at Dreamer's Rock* and *Education Is Our Right* (both 1990), the farcical comedy *The Bootlegger Blues* (1991) and its sequels *The Baby Blues* (1999) and *The Buz'Gem Blues* (2002). While other dramatic work by Taylor includes the two one-act plays *The Boy in the Treehouse* and *Girl Who Loved Her Horses* (both 2000), it is with *Someday* (1993) and its sequel *Only Drunks and Children Tell the Truth* that Taylor's works become explicitly defined—an astute combination of the tragically dramatic, the insanely farcical, and the hilariously witty.

Taylor's interest in venturing into the world of humour is closely related to the process of "decolonizing the Western mind," which, particularly for the ones on the receiving end of texts like Taylor's, is "a process, never ending and always providing new and often unpleasant surprises and insights for those embarked on it" (Lutz 2002, 1). For Taylor, "decolonizing the Western mind" is ever more crucial as certain misperceptions about Native Canadians still persist: "If you watch the dominant media and pop culture, we are often only portrayed as being about land claims, blockades, or substance abuse .... I wanted to represent ... that we weren't all oppressed depressors" (Taylor, online).

Text: The Relevance of Taylor's Play for a "Decolonization of the Mind"

Only Drunks and Children Tell the Truth initially chronicles the fate of Janice Wirth, who, according to her own declaration, "was taken into custody by the

Children's Aid Society in 1955 in the false belief that her mother ... was not maintaining a proper and adequate home environment for the infant" (*Only Drunks and Children Tell the Truth*; hereafter ODCTT, 97). This excerpt from the play makes reference to the so-called scoop-up, an institutionalized and, above all, assimilative and paternalistic policy instituted by the Canadian government in which Native (Canadian) children were taken away from their birthparents and placed in foster care (most often) with Euro-Canadian families. With the implementation of these policies, Canadian authorities anticipated that Native (Canadian) cultural roots would be cut off and made inaccessible. Against this political background Taylor delineates the soul-searching journey of Janice, who, in spite of having experienced a success story in Euro-Canadian culture as a lawyer, falls into a double bind when the death of her Ojibwa birthmother compels the self-sufficient Torontonian to return to her Ojibwa roots. Certain that her biological mother was accountable for her having been placed in foster care, Janice's firm positioning within Euro-Canadian culture starts to disintegrate when she realizes that it has been the Euro-Canadian society that has betrayed her, with their policies of assimilation and appropriation.

It is interesting to note Taylor's opinion when, in his introduction to *Only Drunks and Children Tell the Truth*, he recollects, "This play has been called a clash of wills, of cultures, of philosophies ...." (ODCTT, 12). In her foreword to the play, Lee Maracle notes,

> Characters like those in *Only Drunks and Children Tell the Truth* can be found on any reserve; the sage, in the form of the not-so-old Tonto, full of understated humour; the clown Rodney; the modern woman with strong historical roots, Barb; and her sister, the not-quite-as-likely Grace [Janice], the lawyer. This play is subtly layered: the conflict between Western values and Native values played out through the sisters, free of the usual didactic preaching; the conflict between Western ideology and Native wisdom, played out through the interaction between Tonto and Grace [Janice]; and within each are the very specific conflicts

> that go on within the members of a family which has been torn apart through no fault of its own—the internal conflict of those besieged by external forces and dis-membered. (Maracle 1998, 7)

As an approach toward an individual and family history, *Only Drunks and Children Tell the Truth* tries to subtly rectify stereotypical perceptions of Native (Canadians) by drawing primarily on *their* voice, *their* intellect, and *their* approach to negotiating the clash between non-Native and, in this instance, Ojibwa culture. A text such as this supports the widely held attitude—relating of course to postcolonial discourses—that Native (Canadian) people did not "'need to read books written by white people about [their] people that show [them] as being oppressed, and poor, and colonized ... since [they] will tell [their] own story'" (Maria Campbell in Lutz 1991, 60). This line of argument corresponds to Gayatri Chakravorty Spivak's distinction between derisory representations and adequate portrayals of what she calls the "subaltern" in her renowned essay "Can the Subaltern Speak?" (1988). Spivak criticizes individuals of a macro-culture or dominant ideological regime who speak for the needs and desires of individuals from a micro-culture, since it ultimately denies the ones spoken for the opportunity to escape their object-position in order to enter that of an articulate subject. Thriving on the chasm between the colonizing elite and colonized peoples, the established power-relations facilitate a misconstruction of what is generally perceived as the inferior "Other."

Taylor's play illustrates these power-relations by depicting salient problems within intercultural discourses. In doing so, he takes a critical approach toward policies of the Euro-Canadian macro-culture, which, during the past two centuries, have been characterized by assimilative practices. Wlad Godzich captures the mindset at the root of these policies in his introduction to Michel de Certeau's *Heterologies: Discourse on the Other* (2000): "Western thought ... has always thematized the other as a threat to be reduced, as a potential same-to-be, a yet-not-same ... for it is ideologically inconceivable that there should exist an otherness of the same ontological status as the same, without there being immediately mounted an effort at its appropriation" (Godzich 2000, xiii). Taylor's play seriously challenges these attempts at assimilation, and the Wabungs as a dis-membered family are proof of the serious repercussions that are a result of these policies. As such, the play aims at "re-membering" family and kin, thereby reconciling the many facets of cross-cultural identities.

Only Drunks and Children Tell the Truth reflects upon the struggle to reclaim a complex notion of "native-ness" on three internally interconnected levels: First, it thrives on the importance of retracing individual histories within a cross-cultural dialogue. Second, it reflects upon the history of foreign control and paternalism, as well as the processes of assimilation and appropriation. Third, it depicts the problematic search for coherent Native (Canadian) identities after the impact of Euro-Canadian attempts to "civilize," Christianize, and assimilate these very identities. However, far from being solely immersed in recreating the past and nurturing resentment, multi-faceted and progressive approaches such as Taylor's distance Native (Canadian) people from the object/victim-position that has been prevailing for too long. The increase of self-assertion amongst Native Canadian people has encouraged a request for balanced and culturally-sensitive histories—histories that not only tell the story of colonization and suffering, but that also refer to the realities, joys, and sorrows of present-day Native (Canadian) life. However, one major objective has remained salient in contemporary, especially post-1990, Native (Canadian) texts: to reassess cultural identities that had been co-opted by the discourses of the macro-culture, resulting in a master-narrated epic about the "Indian Other" that thrives on stereotypical and ultimately destructive images. Such an objective, in conjunction with an adaptation of (post)modern Western concepts of narration, makes Native (Canadian) literature most productive as translator, mediator, and interpreter of Native (Canadian) traditions that insist on the link between past, present, and future.

(Sub)text: The Semantics of Irony in *Only Drunks and Children Tell the Truth*

Texts such as *Only Drunks and Children Tell the Truth* strive to revise power-relations in that they attempt to provide their Native (Canadian) audience with the status of the superior and the knowing, while the non-Native reader is often not only left at the margins of the text, but also openly attacked and sometimes even vilified—a position that the formerly objectified "Indian Other" had previously been assigned. To illustrate this claim, one may consider the following example from the play, which stages a conversation between the protagonists Tonto and Janice:

> TONTO: Rodney's cool for a brother. A little too book smart though .... He once spent an hour making a comparison of ... the colonization of North America based on two sci-fi books: *The Martian Chronicles* and *Cat's Cradle*. That guy needs to spend a little more time on this planet. He needs to know tradition.
>
> JANICE: And you can teach him this tradition?
>
> TONTO: I listen to the Elders. It's all really obvious. The trouble with Rodney is he thinks like a white person. His heart's Native but that brain of his needs a good tan.
>
> JANICE: Why do you say that?
>
> TONTO: There! Boom! You just said the magic word. The whole difference between Native people and White people can be summed up in that one, single three-letter word. "Why?" White people are so preoccupied with why everything works. Why was the universe created? Why is the sky blue? Why do dogs drool when you ring a bell? "Why" is their altar of worship. (*ODCTT*, 58)

This textual approach ultimately marginalizes mainstream culture and renders Native (Canadian) culture the focus of attention. What is more, however, it is not only non-Native (Canadian) culture that is disparaged. The mocking tone of the utterance "that brain of his needs a good tan" is directed at Rodney, a member of the Native in-group who, due to his often clownish and careless behaviour (which, of course, plays on Trickster-like qualities), needs to be taught Native tradition.

To a degree, some Native (Canadian) authors embrace the current post-modern freedom of inherent contradictions and dialogic interplay embodied in Trickster-figures that are able to take on different shapes and sexes, being clown and hero at the same time. In *Only Drunks and Children Tell the Truth* one may assert that the dialogic interplay between Tonto and Rodney in their relation to the two female protagonists, Janice and her sister Barb, makes it possible for the quartet to "subvert and delegitimise monologic 'white discourse' and to 'decolonise the mind' of a future generation (both white and non-white)" (Jannetta 2000, 101). In this subversion of the dominant ideological discourse, Taylor "employ[s] aspects of Native American ontology and epistemology without violating their multifaceted and pluralistic components of identity ... thereby destabilizing clear-cut boundaries and establishing a third space beyond binary oppositions" (101). It is this third space that gives rise to a "hybrid moment of political change" (Bhabha 1994, 28), whose capacities Homi K. Bhabha asserts as follows: "The transformational value of change lies in the re-articulation, or translation, of elements that are *neither the One ... nor the Other ... but something else besides,* which contests the terms and territories of both" (28).

In spite of still being interested in some didactical purposes (which, however, seem rather subordinate), texts such as Taylor's play also appreciate the creative facets of literature. Not only is the diversity of topics enriched, but also the use of literary devices, of which irony—ranging from the humorous to the transgressive—is what this essay focuses on. In the post-modern age, the concept of truth seems to have been utterly debunked; an apodictic and absolute notion of "truth" may no longer exist. Taylor adapts a concept of narration advocating that, as Linda Hutcheon describes, "to re-write or to re-present the past in fiction and in history is, in both cases, to open it up to the present, to prevent it from being conclusive and teleological" (Hutcheon 1992, 110). A means to achieve this objective is irony, with its subtle strategies of defiance and non-compliance. Northrop Frye once captured the diversity and slipperiness of the ironic mode with the following equation: "Hence satire is irony which is structurally close to the comic: the comic struggle of two societies, one normal and the other absurd, is reflected in its double focus of morality and fantasy .... Two things, then, are essential to satire; one is wit or humor founded on fantasy or a sense of the grotesque or absurd, the other is an object of attack" (Frye 1957, 224). Although the dividing line between the many facets of irony is often difficult to draw in this play, it is crucial to consider the use of the various functions of irony, each of them serving a different purpose, thus adding to its diversity. For my discussion of the functions of irony in *Only Drunks and Children Tell the Truth,* I have relied on Hutcheon's study *Irony's Edge: The Theory and Politics of Irony* (1995). I will introduce five different facets of irony in an attempt to answer the following question(s): do Native (Canadian) authors employ the semantics of irony merely to entertain by creating laughter; do they use it as a conscious means of attack; or is it employed as something else entirely?

The Humorous Face of Irony

The dialogue between one culture and another thrives on the interplay of differences between Native and non-Native approaches toward meaning and identity within a specific cultural system. Native (Canadian) culture is different from mainstream Canadian culture in many respects and Taylor is fond of advancing these differences. He takes advantage of a clash of cultural attitudes in that he stages an often ironic exchange of stereotypes, whereby he exposes their unacceptable simplification. One facet of the ironic mode is the humorous, which features prominently throughout the play. Moderate humour may put an audience at ease, especially a non-Native audience. Free of the anxiety that often disturbs cross-cultural discourses, these audiences may be enabled to put their preconceptions into a new and revised perspective. To support this, one may consider this example from the play:

JANICE: Do you come to *Toronto* often?

BARB: As Rodney says, "It's a nice place to visit but I wouldn't want to put a *land claim* on it." (*ODCTT*, 28; emphasis added)

At this stage the teasingly humorous mode of irony is employed both to refer to historical crimes committed by the settler culture and, above all, to invert history. Taylor, following the example of, among others, Tomson Highway, "satirizes Toronto's assumed hegemonic importance and centrality in Canada" (Horne 1999, 136). This inversion or distortion of the "grand narrative" of Western history then evolves into a vehicle of revision and truth-telling from a Native point of view. Equally important, the humorous facet of irony is a salient means of distancing Native cultures from false empathy, which may be generated in members of the macro-culture: "Humor—cognate with 'humus,' or soil, and 'human,' or person—implies a personality at ease and grounded in its own identity. The term assumes a perspective on things, as it were, one that enjoys flexibility" (Lincoln 1993, 32).

Demystifying Perceptions

Taylor's play also features a facet of irony that demystifies stereotypical perceptions of Native cultures that have invaded the Western mind through the extensive portrayal of estheticized images of grace, dignity, and nobility embodied by "the Indian" in media discourses and popular culture in general:

JANICE: I seem to remember *canoes and buckskin*. I don't remember why though.

BARB: Couldn't have been me then. Never had a buckskin dress in my life. And I hate canoeing, my legs cramp.

JANICE: I wonder if that's why I bought that *white fur coat* of mine, my heritage coming through.

BARB: Doubt it. You're the only Indian I know who has one. (*ODCTT*, 99; emphasis added)

Reminiscent of instances of non-Natives engaging in ongoing practices of "playing Indian" as, for example, in U.S.-American sports culture and its "Indian" chiefs, warriors and braves facilitated as team names or mascots, Janice has essentially internalized stereotypical and simplistic images of the "the Indian"; these images are erroneously defined by buckskin dresses, canoeing, and fur coats that preferably—to Janice—are white. Elizabeth Bird has described the subconscious relation of these images of "the Indian" to the changing attitudes of the Western mind: "Thus the 'noble savage' has been with us for generations, along with his alter ego, the 'ignoble savage.' With the ebb and flow of cultural images of who *we* are, so the image of the Indian changes—now becoming everything we fear, in the person of the marauding, hellish savage, then becoming everything we envy, in the person of the peaceful, mystical, spiritual guardian of the land..." (Bird 1996, 3). In partly reproducing the romanticized images of "the Indian," it might be argued that the character of Janice has fallen victim to what Dee Horne has described as colonial mimicry:

> The process of colonial mimicry involves a disavowal of one's American Indian culture. This leads to a conflict between one's values and those of one's American Indian community. To wit, the colonial mimic desires to become like settler's, which often necessitates becoming unlike American Indians. The consequence of settler disavowal for assimilated colonial mimics is that they encounter a double bind; they become

> alienated not only from their American Indian culture and themselves but also from settler society. (Horne 1999, 116–117)

To counter colonial mimicry, demystifying irony is employed to expose these stereotypes as "distorted reflections of our own fears, fancies, and wistful longings ... reminders of a history that we would prefer not to remember and confusing our fantasies with real-life demands" (Bordewich 1996, 17–18). As such it not only decries stereotypical images that have prevented culturally-sensitive portrayals of "native-ness" from emerging, but also subsequently allows for Native (Canadian) cultures to escape cultural appropriation. However, there is a flaw in Horne's definition of the process of colonial mimicry, as it implies that there is a continuum of "native-ness" along which one can plot oneself. This line of argument suggests that there exists a notion of "cultural authenticity," which, in turn, must immediately prompt the question of what it means for a culture to be "authentic" and whether or not such a hypothesis can really be sustained. Does the character of Janice indeed fall victim to colonial mimicry or should her hybrid identity be considered just as valid? Can she not be both Native and a successful lawyer when one perceives of a concept of culture(s) constantly in flux? In this respect, one should note Taylor's considerations: "Well, it turns out that what is available for Native actresses out there is basically three roles. You're the mother in jeans and plaid shirt, that's unemployed with six kids. You're an alcoholic or you like to play Bingo. Or you're the victim of some sort of physical or sexual abuse .... Here comes the character of Janice, driving a Saab, wearing a white fur coat, and being a successful lawyer" (Taylor, online). Here Taylor asserts that our concept of cultural identity can no longer be static and homogenous, but must inevitably be subject to a process of constant change and transformation. Therefore, Horne's pondering of an impermeable demarcating line between an allegedly homogenous "American Indian culture," on the one hand, and an equally uniform "settler culture," on the other, does not realize the processes of hybridization both within and between these two respective cultures, which are, above all, inherently heterogeneous in themselves.

Complex Readings

In the play the key issue of alcohol abuse is referred to both ironically and tragically. It is handled in a comical manner whenever a sweeping statement about general alcohol abuse by Native (Canadian) people is uttered. As such it tries to confront prevailing stereotypes in a corrective manner:

> JANICE: I thought all Indian men drank.
>
> TONTO: I thought all women could cook.
>
> JANICE: Touché. *Stereotypes* everywhere ...
>
> JANICE: If you don't mind me asking, why don't you drink?
>
> TONTO: My mother died of the stuff. (*ODCTT*, 55; emphasis added)

Such an approach then takes a turn toward gravity when the partial truth of a particular stereotype is exposed in favour of assigning complexity to issues that have formerly been generalized. As such, the tragic and more complex facet of irony is a means of defiance and survival. Kenneth Lincoln explains in his extensive study on *Indi'n Humor*: "Indian humor clarifies the splits between fantasy and fact as it tempers the strain; it strengthens the survivors to witness a difference. The arts of humor—verbal wit, focused complexity, delightful masking, comic inversion, riddling wisdom, structural symmetries—give pleasure beyond pain as they bear witness to survival" (Lincoln 1993, 55).

Subversive Strategies

At another point in the play, the subversive irony that is derived from insiders' jokes aimed at a Native audience—in that their denotation is culture-bound and subject to an insider's knowledge—lampoons non-Native beliefs. Note Taylor's extensive play with the myth of Amelia Earhart, which Western culture seems to be strangely obsessed with and which, in this excerpt from the play, has become part of Native storytelling:

> JANICE: And everybody in the village knows this? I mean about Amelia Earhart.
>
> RODNEY: Yeah, it's not as if it's a secret. Almost every kid from the Reserve has done some essay or project on her in school. After a while the teachers were getting suspicious so we had to make up a story about Indians having a special affinity for her, respecting her because she personifies the feminine presence of the eagle as it flies across Grandmother Moon. One guy even equated her with a legend of "the woman who circled Turtle Island" which he made up during lunch hour.
>
> TONTO: That was me. *White people buy all this kind of stuff.* (ODCTT, 43; emphasis added)

While some may be concerned about the approach that is taken with sacred and traditional Native stories, it serves an interesting purpose with regards to a "decolonization of the Western mind." Merged into one, the male protagonists Rodney and Tonto—the first with an assertive personality, the latter prone to understated humour—personify a reinvented Trickster-figure that employs a subversive mode of mimicry: "Instead of replicating the colonial relationship, subversive mimicry gives a refracted reflection in which colonizers may see images of themselves through the eyes of the colonized. The re-presented image of the colonizer and the colonial relationship has been altered and, in some cases informed by previously denied colonial knowledges and rules of recognition"

(Horne 1999, 14). Subversive mimicry undermines colonial mimicry, which has been encouraged by the settler culture as a means of appropriating the "Other." It is, of course, also part of subversive mimicry that Taylor has chosen to name one of his central characters "Tonto," apparently referring to Tonto in *The Lone Ranger* (1938) as yet... another stereotyped implementation of "the Indian" in U.S. American popular culture here "serving European-American expansionism and law-and-order ideology" (Lutz 2002, 50).

As a counter-discourse against colonial mimicry, subversive mimicry is one means of reconstructing Native Canadian identities as complex and, above all, non-static:

> The point stands: our common past determines connective play. Kinship interconnects comically—perhaps not to 'others,' but comedy makes them the butt, not the audience. We laugh at ourselves to 'play' with common ties. We survive a shared struggle and come together to laugh about it, to joke about what-was and where-we-have-come, even if the humor hurts. It is a kind of personal tribalism that begins with two people, configurates around families, composes itself in extended kin and clan, and ends up defining a culture. (Lincoln 1993, 62–63)

In the context of the history and tradition of Native cultures these multi-faceted approaches give rise to positive and productive methods of growing and renewal against the background of formerly experienced loss. Tricksters like Rodney and Tonto play with the perceptions of the macro-culture by overtly wearing the mask of the colonized:

> Trickster is a mimic without succumbing to colonial mimicry. His/her subversive mimicry is analogous to that of impersonators, who mimic others through exaggeration, caricature, mockery, and satire without being disavowed. In adopting the persona of the target subject, the impersonator creates the illusion that he/she is the target in order to critique the actual target audience, and to translate it through laughter. (Horne 1999, 140)

As such, Tricksters challenge and supersede the simplistic dichotomy of "us versus them" by turning the limited position of the former object into that of the knowing subject: "While it is not possible to become another, it is possible to 'become Other'; settlers may momentarily see themselves as the one now being othered" (Horne 1999, 20). Once this transfer is momentarily realized, it is meant to "challenge cultural norms and boundaries and present an alternative vision in which American Indians are no longer positioned as alter, as colonizers' constructed others" (Horne 1999, 23). Bhabha asserts that "in these instances of social and discursive alienation there is no recognition of master and slave, there is only the matter of the enslaved master, the unmastered slave" (1994, 131).

Transgressive Dynamics

As textual evidence shows, Taylor makes extensive use of the semantics of irony. However, the author is aware of both the constructive as well as destructive effects of irony, which has often been accused of thriving on a *laissez-faire* and hypocritical approach to the signifying system of language. Thomas Mann once outlined a condescending irony which "glances at both sides, which plays slyly and irresponsibly—yet not without benevolence—among opposites, and is in no great haste to take sides and come to decisions" (1947, 173). In addition, irony often carries a destructive function when installed as a detrimental attack on something or somebody—an attack thriving on bitterness and the urge to destroy without attempting to work correctively toward the dominant ideology culture, but merely revealing disapproval and ridicule (Hutcheon 1995, 54). Sometimes, irony seems to be speaking from an elevated and ideologically superior position. In *Only Drunks and Children Tell the Truth*, Taylor deliberately employs irony to prevent any definite notion of "truth" from emerging. On the whole, irony—since in Taylor's play it tends to subtly offend—has the capacity to be transgressive in subversively countering prevailing discourses of the dominant ideological system:

JANICE: ... Quite an interesting man [Tonto]. Has he ever been to university?

BARB: He painted the residence at Trent University one summer but that's about it. That's our Tonto.

JANICE: I bet if he really applied himself ... Rodney too.

BARB: Don't underestimate Rodney. He's taken more university and college courses than there are pearls in your necklace. They're both kind of the same. They just learn what they want to know, then move on.

JANICE: Some would consider that a waste of time and money.

BARB: Not everybody wants to be a lawyer. Some people are happy being who they are.

JANICE: What if who they are is a lawyer.

BARB: Then God help them. Cheers. (ODCTT, 73–74)

Here transgressive irony serves to counter the dominant ideological regime of the macro-culture with a definition of learning and knowledge that is a counter-discourse. Hutcheon captures this notion by asserting that "[f]or those positioned *within* a dominant ideology, such contesting might be seen as abusive or threatening; for those marginalized and working to undo that dominance, it might be *subversive* or *transgressive* in the newer, positive senses that those words have taken on in recent writing about gender, race, class and sexuality" (1995, 52).

Conclusion

Taylor's play is based on versatile approaches towards both Native and non-Native cultures and calls for both sides to question simplistic perceptions of either the Native or the non-Native culture. Thus Taylor has created a dramatic work that refuses to present steadfast opinions and moral positions. The accepted canons of literature, however, prevent Native (Canadian) texts from reaching a wider audience. A "decolonization of the Western mind" may not be achieved as long as literature written *about* Native people features more prominently in school and academic canons than literature written *by* Native people. Taylor, who asserts that "because we have an oral history, we can copy the language much better in terms of writing it up for theatre" (Taylor, online), captures the capacity of Native literatures for mediating between cultures and thus realizes what Mikhail Bakhtin has described as the intricate "process of coming to know one's own language as it is perceived in someone else's language, coming to know one's own belief system in someone else's system" (1981, 365). Literature is a powerful vehicle for the translation and reassertion of culture and ethnicity. Literary expressions have the power to translate 'otherness' into awareness.

Like all culture, Native (Canadian) culture is not static. Native (Canadian) writing, as an expression of Native (Canadian) cultures, likewise, continues to develop. Some writers tell stories in traditional ways, while others write in what one may call an adapted or "Westernized" style. In short, Native (Canadian) literatures entertain and involve audiences in ways other literatures seldom do. The semantics of irony with their many facets are a fundamental part of that uniqueness, for, as Paula Gunn Allen emphasizes, "there is this tradition of humor, of an awful lot of funniness, and then there's this history of death. And when the two combine, you get a power in the work; that is, it moves into another dimension, it makes it transformational" (Gunn Allen in Coltelli 1990, 22). While the semantics of irony constitute a dialogue by exploring differences, they are also a means of working against cultures drifting apart, for irony encourages not only a "decolonization of the Western mind," but may also promote cross-cultural understanding. After all, bridges between cultures may be built on the fundament of laughter.

Bibliography

Bakhtin, Mikhail. (1981). *The Dialogic Imagination: Four Essays by Mikhail Bakhtin*, ed. Michael Holquist. Austin, TX: University of Texas Press.

Bhabha, Homi K. (1994). *The Location of Culture*. London: Routledge.

Bird, Elizabeth, ed. (1996). *Dressing in Feathers: The Construction of the Indian in American Popular Culture*. Oxford: Westview Press.

Bordewich, Fergus M. (1996). *Killing the White Man's Indian: Reinventing Native Americans at the End of the Twentieth Century*. New York: Doubleday.

Campbell, Maria. (1991). "Interview with Hartmut Lutz." In *Contemporary Challenges: Conversations with Canadian Native Authors*, Hartmut Lutz. Saskatoon, SK: Fifth House Publishers, 41–65.

Coltelli, Laura. (1990). *Winged Words: American Indian Writers Speak*. London: University of Utah Press.

Frye, Northrop. (1957). *Anatomy of Criticism*. Princeton, NJ: Princeton University Press.

Godzich, Wlad. (2000). "Introduction." *Heterologies: Discourse on the Other*, trans. Brian Massumi. Theory and History of Literature 17. Minneapolis, MN: University of Minnesota Press, vii–xxi.

Horne, Dee. (1999). *Contemporary American Indian Writing*. American Indian Studies 6. New York: Lang.

Hutcheon, Linda. (1992). *A Poetics of Postmodernism: History, Theory, Fiction*. London and New York: Routledge.

———. (1995). *Irony's Edge: The Theory and Politics of Irony*. London: Routledge.

Jannetta, Armando E. (2001). *Ethnopoetics of the Minority Voice: An Introduction to the Politics of Dialogism and Difference in Métis Literature*. Beiträge zur Kanadistik 10. Augsburg: Wißner.

LaRocque, Emma. (1990). "Preface or Here Are Our Voices—Who Will Hear?" *Writing the Circle: Native Women of Western Canada*, eds. Jeanne Perreault and Sylvia Vance. Edmonton, AB: NeWest, xv–xxx.

Lincoln, Kenneth. (1993). *Indi'n Humor: Bicultural Play in Native America*. New York and Oxford: Oxford University Press.

Lutz, Hartmut. (1991). *Contemporary Challenges: Conversations with Canadian Native Authors*. Saskatoon, SK: Fifth House Publishing.

———. (2002). *Approaches: Essay in Native North American Studies and Literatures*. Augsburg: Wißner.

Mann, Thomas. (1947). "Goethe and Tolstoi." *Essays of Three Decades*, trans. H. T. Lowe-Porter. New York: Knopf.

Maracle, Lee. (1998). "Introduction." *Only Drunks and Children Tell the Truth*. Burnaby, BC: Talonbooks, 7–8.

Ruppert, James. (1995). *Mediation in Contemporary Native American Fiction*. London, OK: University of Oklahoma Press.

Schorcht, Blanca. (2003). *Storied Voices in Native American Texts: Harry Robinson, Thomas King, James Welch and Leslie Marmon Silko*. New York: Routledge.

Spivak, Gayatri Chakravorty. (1988). "Can the Subaltern Speak?" *Marxism and the Interpretation of Culture*, eds. Cary Nelson and Lawrence Grossberg. Chicago, IL: University of Illinois Press, 271–313.

Taylor, Drew H. (1998). *Only Drunks and Children Tell the Truth*. Burnaby, BC: Talonbooks.

Internet Sources

"Aurora Online with Drew Hayden Taylor: An Afternoon with Drew Hayden Taylor, Playwright." Four Season Indigenous Speaker Series for the Centre for World Indigenous Knowledge and Research. *The Aurora Interview Collection Online*. http://aurora.icaap.org/2005Interviews/haydentaylor.html [consulted November 18, 2005].

Eva Gruber

Humorous Restorifications: Rewriting History with Healing Laughter

> There are only *truths* in the plural, and never one Truth; and there is rarely falseness per se, just others' truths.
> —Linda Hutcheon, "Historiographic Metafiction," 76

> "There are no truths, Coyote," I says. "Only stories."
> —Thomas King, *Green Grass, Running Water,* 393

Introduction

In *Truth and Bright Water,* a novel by Cherokee/Greek/German author Thomas King, trickster artist Monroe Swimmer makes a living by restoring old paintings:

> "One day, the Smithsonian called me in to handle a particularly difficult painting. It was a painting of a lake at dawn, and everything was fine except that the paint along the shore had begun to fade, and images that weren't in the original painting were beginning to bleed through ... So I

> worked on the painting until it looked as good as new.... But something went wrong."
>
> "You messed up?"
>
> "The new paint wouldn't hold. Almost as soon as I finished, the images began to bleed through again .... You know what they were?" says Monroe.
>
> "What?"
>
> "Indians," says Monroe. "There was an Indian village on the lake, slowly coming up through the layers of paint. Clear as day." (King 1999a, 130)

Monroe decides to put "the Indians back into the painting" (133) and starts to restore other paintings in like manner, eventually getting himself fired: "I don't think they wanted their Indians restored .... I think they liked their Indians where they couldn't see them" (247). King's metaphorical use of painting in *Truth and Bright Water* in many ways mimics the politics of Western historiography: mainstream North America has indeed tended to blot out or gloss over important aspects of its history, has put its "Indians" where it does not see them—at least not in ways that might discolour its bright self-conceptualization. Yet, especially since the 1990s, Canada's Indigenous "colours" have started to "bleed through," as increasing numbers of Native writers "paint" Native people back into the picture.

This article explores one aspect of this development in particular, namely contemporary Native writers' use of humour in engaging with Euro-Canadian history and historiography. That humour should be a means by which Canada's Native population responds to a past that, in many respects is nothing short of tragic, still comes as a surprise to many readers, although the phenomenon has started to attract wider attention and recognition in recent years.[1] Are genocide, relocation, residential schools, and forced conversion laughing matters? Hardly. Yet undoubtedly humour is a frequent response to past and present oppression and discrimination. As the following discussion will show, this is partly because of humour's ability to retain an essential optimism and its capacity to build a bridge of understanding between Canada's Native and Euro-Canadian population.

Canadian History, Historiography, and Native Humour

It is widely acknowledged that the colonizers, not the victims, write the history. In situations of power imbalance, of conquest and the ensuing domination of a self-appointed centre over a marginalized "other," historiography becomes an instrument of "sense-making," an "apologetic enterprise" (Isernhagen 2001, 169). For the Western nation states that have divided North America between them, it offers a revisionist version of the past that both substantiates current dominance and allows for a positive identification with the country's historical development and the national consciousness built on this collective memory. What implications does this have for Canada's Native people?

Most obviously, knowing and venerating one's history are important factors in the cultural identity formation of a group. Yet Canada has long denied its Native population a dignified history of its own. While Euro-Canadians are taught to take pride in their history,[2] especially regarding the period of exploration and expansion with its fearless adventurers and pioneers, the Indigenous population in most historical accounts is reduced to an obstacle in the way of this development, a hindrance to the spread of civilization over yet another continent. The devastating consequences on Native cultural identity need not be detailed; yet the situation is more complex than that. As Scott Vickers observes, "Indian history since 1492 has been 'written' ... by white authority, [and] ... the author of history also assumes the power of the author of identity and the arbiter of authenticity" (Vickers 1998, 9). In other words, not only does Western historiographic discourse deprive Native people of a self-determined historical identity (often by denying their presence altogether), but, in a hierarchical approach, it also imposes Western academic standards of what counts as history on Indigenous ways of relating the past, distinguishing between "legitimate" history and less "authentic" or "objective" categories, such as myth or folklore. Garnet Raven, the young Ojibway protagonist of Richard Wagamese's novel *Keeper'n Me* (1994), subversively sums up this hierarchical approach when he recollects, "Indians never got mentioned in any of the schoolbooks except for being the guides for the brave explorers busy discovering the country. I could never even figure out how you could discover something when you needed a guide to help to find it. But Indians were always second to the explorers who were creating the *real history* of North America" (Wagamese 1994, 12; emphasis added).

In the course of the postmodern/poststructuralist crisis of representation, this link between specific modes of discourse and hegemonic power structures has been widely explored. Allegedly value-neutral Western historiographic discourses have been exposed as not simply describing a particular set of facts. By defining both what qualifies as history and the interpretive frames within which it is analyzed, historical discourses self-confirmingly perpetuate and reinforce particular ideologies. Truth, as Michel Foucault argues, is never

> outside power .... Truth is a thing of this world; it is produced only by the virtue of multiple forms of constraint. And it induces regular effects of power. Each society has its own regime of truth, its 'general politics' of truth; that is, the types of discourse which it accepts and makes function as true, the mechanisms and instances which enable one to distinguish true and false statements, the means by which each is sanctioned, the techniques and procedures accorded value in the acquisition of truth, the status of those who are charged with saying what is true. (Foucault 1980, 131)

Consequently, history as a discursive formation is self-validating; what appears within its authoritative system of utterances is *made true*. Both history and literature, as Hayden White has pointed out, create narratives of the past, after all. Even history with its alleged focus on "factual" subject matter can never deliver an objective rendering. Depending on the kinds of questions asked (White 1987, 43), the result is a necessarily subjective interpretation of events, characters, and motivations—be it through the value-ruled selection of events to be represented (or left out) as historical "facts," or through the way in which these events are discursively framed and combined to form a meaningful coherence not inherent in the data itself.

As Linda Hutcheon points out, "Both historians and novelists *constitute* their subjects as possible objects of narrative representation ... and they do so by the very structures and language they use to present those subjects" (Hutcheon 1995, 78). Through its very terminology, history may practice nothing short of a legitimation of colonization and genocide, as apparent in expressions such as "discovery" for a brutal conquest or "virgin land" for an already settled continent. In addition to having to cope with the horrible *events* of the past, Native people also feel trapped by a Western academic *discourse* that effectively bolsters Western dominance and excludes Native viewpoints.

In an effort to disrupt these degrading dynamics, many Native writers—evincing a traditional belief in the literally creative/coercive powers of language—use language to "reformulate" the past. They engage in the struggle over representation and thereby quite literally reclaim the authorship of Native history and, ultimately, Native identity. Choctaw/Irish writer and scholar Louis Owens observes, "To Native Americans, the authoritative discourse of European America, that discourse which ... comes with its authority already fused to it and simply demands allegiance, can inspire both trauma and a tricksterish subversion" (Owens 1998, 6). The following discussion will focus on the latter response. As will become apparent, it is through their use of humour that Native writers from Canada protest Eurocentric representations of history, as well as contest and undercut both the distinction between history and story and the discursive practices by which Native people are barred from the former.

Humour as a Weapon-Cum-Snare

Humour directed at the shared Native-Euro-Canadian history in texts by contemporary Native writers from Canada may accomplish various ends, which, for the sake of clarity, will be discussed one at a time, although they are not, by any means, isolated strategies or mutually exclusive. On the whole, humour in relations between Native people and non-Natives tends to play a didactic and to some extent diplomatic role. Nevertheless, there are instances where humour appears to be used in rather *confrontational* ways in order to vent some of the anger and frustration that result from the injustices of colonization. As Vine Deloria says, "Many Indians, of course, believe it would have been better if Plymouth Rock had landed on the Pilgrims than the Pilgrims on Plymouth Rock" (Deloria 1977, 177); and the narrator of King's *Green Grass, Running Water* makes a pun on the initial lines of the Canadian national anthem, "O Canada! Our home and native land," turning them into: "Hosanna da, our home on Natives' land" (King 1994, 270).

Albeit less coarse, the barbed humour in Cree/Métis poet Marilyn Dumont's "Letter to Sir John A. Macdonald" points in the same direction. Not without a certain malicious joy, it addresses the first Prime Minister of Canada, who was the driving force behind the building of a transcontinental railway and thus responsible for the displacement of the Métis:

> Dear John: I'm still here and halfbreed,
> after all these years
> you're dead, funny thing,
> that railway you wanted so badly,
> there was talk a year ago
> of shutting it down,
> the dayliner at least,
> 'from sea to shining sea,'
> and you know, John,
> after all that shuffling us around to suit the settlers,
> we're still here and Metis. (Dumont 1996, 52)

The poem clearly plays on one of the ironies of Canadian history. Euro-Canada's (colonial) self-conceptualization, based as it was on the dichotomy between self and other, left little room for acknowledging Métis existence. Yet obviously Euro-Canada has not managed to marginalize the Métis out of existence. Instead, the railway, one of the declared symbols of Euro-Canadian civilization is under threat of unceremoniously disappearing from the scene, and as the poem shows, the Métis cogently claim their rightful place in Canadian society. In addition to asserting Métis presence and survival, the humour in Dumont's poem intentionally hits Canada where it is most vulnerable. Not only does it deride the reduced importance of the railroad which, in combination with the Royal Mounted Police, provided for Canada's allegedly more "peaceful" settlement when compared to its Southern neighbour's policy, but it also alludes to the way in which this first great accomplishment was supposed to unify the young nation:

> and John, that goddamned railroad never made this a great nation,
> cause the railway shut down
> and this country is still quarreling over unity
> Riel is dead
> but he keeps coming back
> in all the Bill Wilsons yet to speak out of turn or favour
> because you know as well as I
> that we were railroaded
> by some steel tracks that didn't last
> and some settlers who wouldn't settle
> and it's funny we're still here and callin ourselves halfbreed.
> (Dumont 1996, 52)

Dumont gloatingly links the closing down of the railroad to two interconnected issues: first to the continuing qualms over Canada's (lack of) identity and internal dividedness (into East and West, Anglo- and Franco-Canada); and secondly, to historical and contemporary Indigenous influences on Canadian politics, by referring to Louis Riel and Bill Wilson.[3] In its humorous derision of Euro-Canada, the poem forcefully reminds Canadians that, unless they acknowledge the chronological primacy and continued presence of the Indigenous population, they will never overcome their own identity problems. At the same time, it constitutes a celebration of Métis culture by defiantly demonstrating mutual solidarity in coping with a traumatic history and a present that is still difficult. With her use of humour, Dumont provides an integrating impulse for Métis readers, making use of the bonding effects of shared laughter—if at the expense of Euro-Canada. In this explicitly defiant capacity, humour allows Métis and Native people to think of themselves in terms other than, simply, "victim," to regain or maintain their dignity, and imagine themselves as a strong community. Euro-Canadian readers who cannot laugh at themselves might be offended, however, and essentializing divisions may be upheld rather than deconstructed.

As is the case in Dumont's poem, laughter directed at something unpleasant or problematic may also serve as a *distancing* device. In the form of gallows humour, it offers a means of jokingly addressing experiences that are otherwise too painful to confront. Ojibway writer Armand Garnet Ruffo's "Creating a Country" details the settlement of North America from the perspective of Susanna Moodie and Lt. Col. George Armstrong Custer, both prominent heralds of "culture" on the newly discovered continent.

> But the process of creating
> a country took much longer than most ever imagined.
> For there were a myriad unforeseen obstacles
> in this formidable new land. Like mosquitoes and Indians.
> Undaunted, the pioneering spirit persisted.
> (Ruffo 1998, 397)

Ruffo sardonically mocks European rationalizations, which relegated North America's Indigenous population to a less-than-human level in order to justify their marginalization. His sarcastic understatement—likening "Indians" to bothersome insects—comically brings to attention the way in which the discourse of settlement trivialized genocide by portraying the "vanishing Indian" as a 'natural' phenomenon. As Fergus Bordewich sarcastically asks, "It was as if the Indians' disappearance were the result of some force completely beyond the human power to stay, like a tidal wave or a change of season.... Was it really a crime to kill someone whom God, Manifest Destiny, or the law of natural selection had condemned to die anyway? Might it not even have seemed more moral to serve as an instrument of plainly assigned fate?" (Bordewich 1996, 49, 51). The comically subversive mimicry of this line of argument in Ruffo's poem, while not erasing the nightmarish consequences for Native people, at least allows them to distance themselves from the historical horrors of colonization through laughter.

Humour may not be the panacea for all injuries that history has inflicted on Native people, especially when their effects are still being felt; yet it does have a *therapeutic* function and helps people to cope with the consequences of a traumatic past, to exorcize some of the pain, and to recover from tragedy. For instance, Garnet Raven, the above-mentioned protagonist from Wagamese's *Keeper'n Me*, had been taken from his family against their will at a very early age and had been placed in Euro-Canadian foster care in the city (a frequent Department of Indian Affairs policy). When he returns to his family on the reserve as a grown-up, he is initially shocked by the poor living conditions. Yet he explains,

> One of the things I caught onto real quick was the humor. Reason no one minds the welfare so much, or the government's empty promises, or the lack of lots of things, is on accounta they always find some funny way of looking at it. They find a way to laugh about it. Keeper says that it's the way they survived everything and still remained a culture. Lotsa Indian ways changed when the whiteman got here, lotsa people suffered, but they stayed alive on accounta they learned to deal with things by not taking them so damn serious all the time. Go anywhere where there's Indians and chances are you'll find them cracking up laughing over something. (Wagamese 1994, 87)

A similar approach characterizes Kuna-Rappahannock playwright Monique Mojica's *Post-Colonial-Stress-Disorder: A Theatrical Monologue* (first performed in 1997). This text literally builds on the healing capacities of humour in that it frames its full-blown satirical critique of colonial regimes entirely in the discourse of clinical psychology, thereby linking the traumatic effects of dispossession and colonization to a certified mental disorder.[4] This allows soothing laughter to be directed at the effects of Western domination on North America's Indigenous population. The description of "Post-Colonial Traumatic Stress Disorder," a disease first manifesting itself in America "500 and 5 years ago [(i.e., 1492), which] has now reached epidemic proportions" (Mojica 2001, 88), lists the consequences of European colonization as "symptoms." Establishing communication by direct address, the performer comically entices the audience to imaginatively put themselves in Native people's position as they follow this checklist:

> If you are profoundly disoriented by flesh-colored band-aids,
> you may be suffering from Post-Colonial Traumatic
> Stress Disorder.
> If you are allergic to milk, WHITE flour, WHITE sugar and alcohol
> you may be suffering from Post-Colonial Traumatic
> Stress Disorder.
> If you find yourself talking back to Walt Disney movies
> you may be suffering from Post-Colonial Traumatic
> Stress Disorder – or –
> ETHNOSTRESS!!!!!!!!!
>
> (Mojica 2001, 88)

Mojica's look at Western North America from a Native perspective, with its close attention to detail, challenges Eurocentrism, its definition of Western culture and "Whiteness" as "the norm," and its relegation of Native people to the margin. It dislodges a Western audience from its complacent position at the centre and engages in the colonizers' (medical) discourse to elicit humorous self-recognition and reconsideration. With increasing linguistic playfulness, the text draws attention to the degrading practices Native people are subjected to at the hands of the Euro-American/Canadian governmental bureaucracies:

> If you lose your identity and your nationality every time you put
> Your foot across a border,
> "You must produce a tribal band card stating

your blood quantum"
Mmmongrel -g-r-r- ped-i-gree- gree g-r-r-r
"In addition you must produce a letter, on
tribal letterhead,
stating your lineage at least as far
back as your grandparents proving that you are at
least 51% or better Native American." ...
Mmmongrel ... bloodquantum ... gree, gree, ped-i-
gree
G-R-R-R-ROWL.
(Mojica 2001, 88-89)

By using the vocabulary of breeding and simultaneously blurring the sounds of the colonizers' language to resemble the snarl of an aggressive dog, Mojica's text makes visible, or rather audible, the hidden racist aggressiveness underlying these policies. The combination of matter-of-factly quoted regulations with increasingly irrational wordplay acoustically epitomizes the very grotesqueness inherent in these standards (which call to mind the certificates of Aryan descent that people had to produce in Nazi Germany). This allusive muttering may incite laughter, but through comic de-familiarization it also elicits a de-centering and reconsideration of principles, definitions, or policies otherwise accepted as "normal."

The text remains within the (colonizers') jargon of medical language throughout, analyzing the factors instrumental in the historical decimation of Native people and the destruction of Native cultures with sardonic playfulness. It cautions, for instance, that colonization has been "known to kill on contact" (pun intended) through various infectious diseases or

to lead to a long, lingering death from:
Drug addiction, Diabetes, Tuberculosis, Suicide, Family
Violence, In-grown
Toenails and –
"... for Thine is the Kingdom and the Power, and the Glory,

forev..., forev..., forev"
Post-Col-mat... traum stress olonial alone colon- eth-eth
no... no
Disor-Disor.
(Mojica 2001, 89)

Not only do the "In-grown Toenails" comically disrupt the nightmarish catalogue of the previously listed afflictions; their incongruous juxtaposition with the Lord's Prayer constitutes an idiosyncratically tragicomic reminder of how certain Christian denominations participated in the process of colonization. The immense cultural disruption and trauma caused by forced conversion is symbolized within the text by the disruption of linguistic coherence, culminating in a perplexed "Disor-Disor"—evocative of both error and disorientation. The jumbled language fragments, on the one hand, make for the comicality of the performance, and on the other hand, they signal that Native people, caught in mind-numbing repetitions of prayers they could initially not even understand, were forcefully deprived of their own cultural systems, language, and epistemologies. Residential/boarding or mission schools provided a means by which Native children were alienated from their cultures, forbidden to speak their Native language, and forcefully assimilated into a Western, Judeo-Christian mainstream. Mojica's *Post-Colonial Traumatic Stress Disorder* is thus exemplary of the Native "laughter and jokes ... directed at the horrors of history, at the continuing impact of colonization, and at the biting knowledge that living as an exile in one's own land necessitates" (Gunn Allen 1992, 158).

In addition to offering a way to come to terms with incredibly sad episodes in Native-Euro-Canadian history, however, the humour in Mojica's text holds up Western rationalizations for re-inspection. Clearly, the monologue's final repeated beckoning to "De-Colonize your mind" (Mojica 2001, 90) addresses the audience irrespective of racial/ethnic affiliation; it calls upon Native people to see themselves independently of the colonizer's gaze, but it also summons both Native and Western readers to transcend such binary categories as self and other, centre and margin, Euro-American/Canadian and Native, legal and illegitimate, or sacred belief and "pagan superstition" by collapsing them in laughter.

In King's "A Short History of Indians in Canada," readers are in for an even more thoroughly de-familiarizing experience. The text follows the tradition of classical trickster tales in that its humour primarily proves to be *disruptive*—not only of the conventions of realism and causality but also of the expectations arising from its title. A wonderful example of what Dee Horne has called "unsettling literature" (Horne 1999), King's slightly grotesque text requires readers to decode a puzzle that juxtaposes concepts and terminologies from two vastly disparate fields—ornithology and (stereotypical ideas about) Native cultures. The story revolves around Bob, a businessman visiting Toronto for the first time. Unable to sleep, he leaves his hotel and is heading for Bay Street when he sees "a flock of Indians fly into the side of a building. Smack! Smack!" (King 1999b, 62). Bill and Rudy, two birdwatchers/rangers whom Bob encounters, are busy categorizing the stranded "Indians":

> Got a Mohawk, says Bill.
> Whup! Whup!
> Couple of Cree over here, says Rudy.
> Amazing, says Bob. How can you tell?
> By the feathers, says Bill. We got a book...
> Bob looks around. What's this one? He says
> Holy! Says Bill. Holy! Says Rudy.
> Check the book. Just to be sure.
> Flip, flip, flip.
> Navajo!
> Bill and Rudy put their arms around Bob. A Navajo! Don't normally see Navajos this far north.
> (King 1999b, 63)

King's incongruent combination of ornithological categorization and "Indians"—the hilarious idea of "telling Indians by their feathers"—evokes surprised laughter. Yet the story also lures readers into pondering further the underlying connection, an effect that is enhanced by the kind of discourse in which the rangers frame their observations on the "Indians." They tell Bob that he is lucky to witness the spectacle: "A family from Buffalo came through last week and didn't even see an Ojibway" (King 1999b, 64). Further, Bob is informed that Indians are "nomadic" and "migratory," and fly into skyscrapers because "Toronto's in the middle of the flyway .... The lights attract them" (64); and that the rangers' policy is to "bag" the dead ones and "tag" the live ones— "Take them to the shelter. Nurse them back to health. Release them in the wild" (64). Haunting parallels emerge between "wild" birds and "savage Indians," the implication being that Native people are unfit for contemporary urban life, are at home "in the wild," need to be kept under control ("tagged"), and should be patronizingly looked after in order to survive. The notions of identifying "Indians" with a book and viewing them as a spectacle for tourists mocks the detached and reifying approach taken by both Western anthropologists and by the general public in their popular infatuation with "the Indian"; each group reduces Native people to fascinating and slightly exotic objects of study or entertainment.[5]

As A. Roy Eckardt points out, "Humour parades before us its own brand of seeming illogic, yet unless it nurtures some kind of deeper logic it fails to realize itself" (Eckardt 1992, 47). King's brief sketch on the surface seems grotesque and illogical. It develops logic, however, once readers realize the implicit satiric criticism of popular, political, and academic conceptualizations of "the Indian": belonging to the world of natural phenomena, still only an interesting "feathered species" and a nostalgically tinted spectacle to be enjoyed as a remnant of a long-gone past. The story closes on a rather biting note in that it thoroughly ridicules the cliché of the "vanishing Indian," likening it to the discourse on "endangered species." Upon his return to the hotel, Bob is greeted by the doorman's comment: "Not like the old days. The doorman sighs and looks up into the night. In the old days, when they came through, they would black out the entire sky" (King 1999b, 64). Especially in light of its title, King's "A Short History of Indians in Canada" thus eventually emerges as a barbed derision of the way in which Canadians often pride themselves on both a less violent history of settlement and a more liberal contemporary attitude towards "their" Native people in comparison to the United States. By doing so, Canadians tend to hypocritically neglect the fact that, just like their Southern neighbours, they decimated the Indigenous population (only to sentimentally miss it afterwards).

As all of these examples illustrate, humorous approaches to the past in contemporary Native writing from Canada very much depend on the condition of colonization. They illustrate that "laughter is always a *fait social* ... [that] each instance of laughter is inextricably tied up with social and power relations and framed within a social situation" (Pfister 2002, vi). As Manfred Pfister further observes, in societies characterized by a distinction between centre and margin, "the most significant form of laughter can arise from the margins, challenging and subverting the established orthodoxies, authorities and hierarchies" (vi). In view of the Fourth World situation of Native cultures, one might therefore ask whether humour directed at Canadian history is, by definition, a laughing *at* Euro-Canada, or whether it can also constitute a form of laughing *with* non-Native readers. While it often has a cutting edge to it, such humour is at the same time, as Kenneth Lincoln explains, the very means of "ton[ing] insults toward cultural negotiation. We [non-Natives] can laugh at ourselves, ... laughing with natives laughing at us. This generates an intercultural sense of humour" (Lincoln 1993, 101).

Humour in texts by contemporary Native writers from Canada does not gloss over conflict, nor does it downplay the impact of conquest and colonization; yet the pleasure gained from the humour opens up and lures readers into a space in which confrontational issues can be addressed in a manner that does not foreclose further intercultural dialogue.[6] By laughing, non-Native readers are (often unwittingly) tricked into assuming new perspectives, into acknowledging the validity of Native viewpoints, and possibly even into questioning their own. As King explains about his use of comedy,

> I think of myself as a dead serious writer. Comedy is simply my strategy. I don't want to whack somebody over the head, because I don't think it accomplishes much at all. There's a fine line to comedy. You have to

> be funny enough to get them laughing so they really don't feel how hard you hit them. And the best kind of comedy is where you start off laughing and end up crying, because you realize just what is happening halfway through the emotion. If I can accomplish that, then I succeed as a storyteller. (King in Canton 1998, 97)

As a kind of Trojan horse, humour sneaks up on readers unnoticed. It may therefore subvert Western epistemologies and historiographic representation from within and align the readers' empathy and solidarity with Native viewpoints.[7] It can bring to attention aspects of Native-Western history that a Euro-American perspective tends to blot out, allowing precarious topics to be addressed in a *mediational* and playful way that retains a basis for communication. In a discussion of the work of Luiseno performance artist James Luna, Jose Tama offers a fitting assessment of the use of humour as a "weapon-cum-snare" for confronting the skeletons in the Native-Western history closet:

> To entertain is to seduce, and to successfully seduce, trust has to be forged. What better way to create trust than through humour? Stand-up comics know this well, and they can get away with saying almost anything if they are funny because comedy disarms us. As such, the performance artist who strategically uses humour can more easily win over audiences and lure them into listening to more challenging material. Furthermore, laughter can help us confront painful truths that create guilt, and what greater scarlet letter on the American chest is there than the near genocide of the vanquished indigenous people whose voices are almost unheard of as a minority within minorities? (Tama 2001, 17)

Thus, in this sense, just as traditional tricksters have always transgressed established rules and paradigms to make the audience laugh and have incited them to reassess these very rules, contemporary Native writers through their use of humour induce laughter among their audience. They free readers of colonial ignorance or stifling concepts of guilt—either of which prohibits seeing Native people for what they are—and shatter their familiar interpretive patterns so that they may re-evaluate their own perspectives and epistemologies.

Humorous treatments of the past in these texts therefore constitute an opportunity for renegotiation and reassessment—not only of Native-Western history as such but also of the very frames of reference from which a particular representation of history originated and the discursive structures within which it is discussed. This latter characteristic is especially visible in King's short story "Joe the Painter and the Deer Island Massacre" (King 1993, 95–118; see Atwood 1990, Gruber 2005); yet it is also illustrated epigrammatically by his poem "Coyote Sees the Prime Minister":

Coyote went east to see the
PRIME Minister.
I wouldn't make this up.
And the PRIME Minister was so HAPPY
to see Coyote
that he made HIM a member of
cabinet.
Maybe you can HELP us solve the
Indian problem.
Sure, says Coyote,
WHAT's the problem?
(King 1990, 252)

Within a few sentences, the text manages to successfully convey to its readers the powerful workings of discourse, as Coyote trips readers into stumbling over the often heard, yet unchallenged expression "the Indian problem." It reveals the term's implicit shift of blame away from the colonizer and onto Native people, and consequently brings to light how the very language used to discuss Native history and presence in Canada is informed by apologetic and rationalizing colonial agendas. Most astonishingly, it does so not only in a culturally specific but also a very funny and hardly offensive manner. Rather than turning away non-Native readers, King gets them to take a closer look—at the text at hand, but maybe also at their own preconceived notions.

Humorous Restorifications[8]

One of the most effective strategies for generating critical reassessments is engaging with the very practices and conventions of historiographic discourse and amusingly making them transparent. The goal is to show in humorous fashion that history is "never simply history, but always 'history-for,' history written in the interest of some infrascientific aim or vision" (White 1978, 55). Kimberley Blaeser identifies this simultaneously investigative and didactic function in the work of Anishinabe mixed-blood writer Gerald Vizenor. His humorous representations of history, she observes, "work to unmask and disarm history, to expose the hidden agendas of historiography and thereby remove it from the grasp of the political panderers and *return it to the realm of story*" (Blaeser 1996, 85; emphasis added). Such humorous restorifications may be a more promising means of getting an audience to reconsider their understanding of Canadian history than countering mythologically overdetermined and clichéd representations of the past with detailed factual information. Turning the line between the discourses of the real (historiography) and of the imaginary (fiction) into a humorous frontier,[9] Native writers contest and undercut both the distinction between history and story and the practices by which Native people are barred from the former.

Dumont's poem "On the Surface" constitutes such a humorous restorification of history. It literally "return[s Canadian history] to the realm of story," comically highlighting the gaps and distortions in Euro-Canada's historiographic representation:

> Moniyaw[10] are natural
> storytellers, you know?
> There's a story of
> Canada, a good story,
> but a story, nevertheless,

> that Samuel de
> Champlain was one of
> the first humans to set
> foot in this country,
> apparently the Six
> Nations were merely
> extras. You have to give
> them credit, these
> moniyaw, are pretty good storytellers.
> (Dumont 2001, 192)

In Western cultures, "storytelling" is considered entertainment for children, while the term "history" is reserved for academically bolstered accounts of the past. When encountered in non-Western cultures, storytelling is therefore romanticized on the one hand, but on the other hand also belittled and denied any of the authoritative truth value that Western historiography is given. By turning the tables and transforming Canada's history into story, Dumont's text both debunks historiography's self-assumed "natural" authority and defies the Eurocentric assumption that North American history began with the arrival of Europeans.[11]

Yet even if—as has been increasingly the case in recent decades—the historic existence of Native people is explicitly acknowledged, the mode of presentation, as Dumont's poem moves on to show, may implicitly convey the impression that they were both utterly unimportant and a phenomenon of the past:

> I watch a four part history of a famous Canadian
> fortification   and knowing where beginnings usually
> begin I am relieved and somewhat surprised, that this
> time, history begins with Indians; however, this portion
> of the film seems a bit tacked on upon viewing the
> introduction of settlement
> as an Academy Awards premiere   grand music and

> fireworks herald the arrival of settlement *to appear*
> *to star, play the lead, get top billing, have one's name in*
> *lights* "the Indian" portion of the film, however, looks
> like it's been directed by Franz Boas who
> chiselled his own camera
> Stone age and non-threatening half-chewed
> femurs and flint knives matted hair (dreadlocks
> before their time) disappointment on the
> faces of the natives that say, *Ah heck, I wanted to be a star*
> *this time.*
> (Dumont 2001, 192)

The exquisite irony of sentences like "knowing where beginnings usually begin" amusingly exposes the paradoxical aspects of the alleged logic by which Western historiography presents a particular course of events as self-evident. So even with Native history being "tacked on" to the Euro-Canadian past, the angle from which it is viewed remains a safely "non-threatening" ethnographic one—which effectively denies the relevance of continued Indigenous presence. The mirth evoked by the image of a "stone-age-equipped Franz Boas" therefore also implicitly poses the question as to why Native people are customarily restricted to an ethnographic and historicizing frame of reference. The remainder of the text provides some possible explanations, setting forth its satiric attack on the revisionism of certain Canadian historians by using unusual metaphors and similes:

> there is a layered belief covering this idea of 'Canada,' no 'North America'
> and this layer, thinking topsoil so to speak, appears to be known as the history
> of this continent just as Columbus thought, erroneously,
> that this country was India
> however, my colonial experience has been
> that it's as if we lived in a nation that was eternally snow covered

> that we didn't have enough snow shovels
> that we were snowed-in,
> a snow-blower wasn't a luxury
> that we lived in a constant *whiteout*
> a snow job
> where snow-blindness was endemic.
> (Dumont 2001, 193)

Playing on "Whiteness" as the self-set norm with regard to skin colour on the one hand and on Canada's self-conceptualization as the national anthem's "True North strong and free" on the other, the snow imagery with witty effectiveness conveys how the Indigenous presence in Canada is "covered up." Conventional historiography induces an endemic "blindness" or at least clouds the vision towards facets of history other than those represented in Eurocentric accounts. Accordingly, the text refers to the few instances in which Native people successfully claimed their rights as "clear spots," which emerge from underneath this cover— "but they were risky ... all icy patches, black ice / to be plowed and sanded" (Dumont 2001, 193). The humour of Dumont's poem itself brushes away some of the "thinking topsoil" that is Canadian history, clears some of the muting snow masses, and lures readers onto risky patches of playfully imaginative "alterNatives" (Drew Hayden Taylor) to established historical paradigms.

Conclusion

"That 'great narrative of entropy and loss' which is the Euro-American version of Native American history since the 15th century is being revised and rewritten in contemporary Indian literature from an Indian perspective," observes Owens (1992, 22). As has been shown in the examples discussed here, contemporary Native writing from Canada does so with lots of humour, freeing both Native and Euro-Canadian readers from their conventional frames of reference and the corresponding historical paradigms in which Western superiority appears as a given, while Native perspectives are still repressed or relegated to the margin. By engaging with, and humorously subverting, a colonial discourse that, as Dumont's poetry suggests, "covers up" both Native history and continued Indigenous presence, these texts defy the myth of the "vanishing Indian." Instead, they demonstrate how a Eurocentric textualized past still affects the present, since distorting representations of history rob Native people of their cultural identity and rightful position. However, as Blaeser emphasizes, only when Native people "refuse to accept and be determined by the romantic linear history which ends with the tragic death or museumization of Indian people, can they continue to imagine their place in the story of ongoing life .... Because historical stories, imaginative stories, cultural stories work to form our identity, the disarming of history through satiric humour liberates and empowers us in the imagination of our destinies" (Blaeser 1998, 172). Native writers' use of humour in many of its various forms pulls the presumably stable epistemological ground from underneath the readers' feet and opens their minds to a re-evaluation of their underlying cultural assumptions. Shared laughter at Eurocentric versions of history thus exorcizes the pain inflicted by centuries of misrepresentation and helps to envision a more self-determined future for Canada's Native people.

Endnotes

1 See for instance Ojibway playwright Drew Hayden Taylor's NFB documentary *Trickster, Redskins, and Puppy Stew. The Healing Powers of Native Humour* (2000), and Baker's article "An Old Indian Trick Is to Laugh" (1991). Blaeser (1998), Lincoln (1993), and Lowe (1994), among others, address the subject in a Native American context.

2 Tellingly, "the emergence of history [as a discipline] in European thought is coterminous with the rise of modern colonialism, which in its radical othering and violent annexation of the non-European world, found in history a prominent, if not *the* prominent instrument for the control of subject peoples. At base, the myth of a value free, 'scientific' view of the past, the myth of the beauty of order, the myth of the story of history as a simple representation of the continuity of events, authorised nothing less than the construction of world reality" (Ashcroft/Griffiths/Tiffin 1995, 355).

3 Louis Riel was the leader of the Red River Rebellion 1869–70 and the Northwest Rebellion

1885, in which the Métis fought for self-determination and against expropriation and displacement. Bill Wilson is an Indigenous politician and activist from British Columbia.

4 PTSD—Post-Traumatic Stress Disorder—in its most basic definition refers to a psychiatric disorder resulting from the experience or witnessing of life-threatening or extremely distressing events. While originally used with regard to traumatized war veterans, the concept has gained wide currency and is increasingly used to discuss the long-term effects of conquest, colonization, and the ensuing disruption on North America's Native people ("Intergenerational PTSD" or "Post-Colonial Stress Disorder"). *The Tribal College Journal* has dedicated a recent issue (Volume 17:3 Spring 2006) to the topic and includes a detailed "Resource Guide on Historical Trauma and Post-Colonial Stress in American Indian Populations" compiled by Dr. Maria Yellow Horse Brave Heart and Tina Deschenie.

5 As King writes elsewhere, "Somewhere along the line, we ceased being people and somehow became performers in an Aboriginal minstrel show for White North America" (King 2003, 68).

6 See Leslie Silko's observation that "especially [with] areas in justice, loss of land, discrimination, racism, and so on, that there's a way of saying it so people can laugh or smile ... so you can keep their interest, so you can keep talking to them. Oftentimes these things are told in a humorous way" (Silko in Coltelli 1990, 146–147).

7 See James English: "Indeed, a very important feature of the work performed through comic exchange is that even while the transaction intensifies certain lines of difference and antagonism it selectively obscures other such lines, effecting false consensus, overlaying a scene of necessary and ongoing conflict with the illusions of identity (community) and agreement (communication)." English argues that humour "intervene[s] in a particular system, of social relationships .... And this intervention must always entail certain shifts in subjective alignment or identification, momentary adjustments along the axes of hierarchy and solidarity" (English 1994, 14, 16).

8 The neologism "restorification" was coined to combine two major aspects of the process elicited by such texts: 1. the way in which such texts may "return [history] to the realm of *story*" (Blaeser 1996, 85; emphasis added) by emphasizing both forms' shared narrative characteristics; and 2. the way they *restore* history for Native people by highlighting Native presence and importance.

9 See Blaeser (1998). King in his characteristic tongue-in-cheek manner meditates on this distinction between ("factual") history and ("fictional") story in his essay "How I Spent My

Summer Vacation: History, Story, and the Cant of Authenticity" (King 1998).

10 This is the Cree expression for Euro-Canadians/Euro-Americans.

11 As Anishinabe student Charlie in Ruby Slipperjack's play *Snuff Chewing Charlie at University* remarks to himself when looking at his lecture notes from history class: "Canadian history from the first contact to the present. From the first contact of what? It sounds like some kind of disease or something. If it is disease, we know who brought it, don't we?" (Slipperjack 2001, 171).

Bibliography

Ashcroft, Bill, Gareth Griffiths, and Helen Tiffin, eds. (1995). *The Postcolonial Studies Reader.* London: Routledge.

Atwood, Margaret. (1990, Spring/Summer). "A Double-Bladed Knife: Subversive Laughter in Two Stories by Thomas King." *Canadian Literature, 124/125,* 243–253.

Baker, Marie Annharte. (1991, Fall). "An Old Indian Trick Is to Laugh." *Canadian Theatre Review, 68,* 48–49.

Blaeser, Kimberley M. (1996). *Gerald Vizenor: Writing in the Oral Tradition.* Norman, OK: University of Oklahoma Press.

———. (1998). "The New 'Frontier' of Native American Literature: Dis-Arming History with Tribal Humor." In *Native-American Writers,* ed. Harold Bloom. Philadelphia, PA: Chelsea House, 161–173.

Bordewich, Fergus M. (1996). *Killing the White Man's Indian: Reinventing Native Americans at the End of the Twentieth Century.* New York: Doubleday.

Canton, Jeffrey. (1998). "Coyote Lives: Thomas King." *The Power to Bend Spoons: Interviews With Canadian Novelists,* ed. Beverly Daurio. Toronto, ON: Mercury, 90–97.

Coltelli, Laura. (1990). *Winged Words: American Indian Writers Speak.* Lincoln, NE: University of Nebraska Press.

Deloria, Vine. (1977). *Custer Died for Your Sins: An Indian Manifesto.* New York: Macmillan.

Dumont, Marilyn. (1996). *A Really Good Brown Girl.* London, ON: Brick.

———. (2001, Autumn). "On the Surface." *Prairie Fire, 22:3,* 192–193.

Eckardt, A. Roy. (1992). *Sitting in the Earth and Laughing: A Handbook of Humor.* London: Transaction.

English, James F. (1994). *Comic Transactions: Literature, Humor, and the Politics of Community in Twentieth-Century Britain.* Ithaca, NY: Cornell University Press.

Foucault, Michel. *Power/Knowledge.* Brighton: Harvester, 1980.

Gunn Allen, Paula. (1992). *The Sacred Hoop: Recovering the Feminine in American Indian Traditions.* Boston, MA: Beacon.

Gruber, Eva. (2005). "Humour in Contemporary Native Canadian Literature: Reimagining Nativeness." *Zeitschrift für Kanada-Studien, 25:2,* 103–113.

Horne, Dee. (1999). *Contemporary American Indian Writing: Unsettling Literature.* New York: Peter Lang.

Hutcheon, Linda. (1995). "Historiographic Metafiction." In *Metafiction,* ed. Mark Currie. London: Longman, 71–91.

Isernhagen, Hartwig. (2001). "Identity and Exchange: The Representation of 'The Indian' in the Federal Writers Project and in Contemporary Native American Literature." In *Native American Representations: First Encounters, Distorted Images, and Literary Appropriations,* ed. Gretchen Bataille. Lincoln, NE: University of Nebraska Press, 168–195.

King, Thomas. (1990, Spring/Summer). "Coyote Sees the Prime Minister." *Canadian Literature, 124/125,* 252.

———. (1993). *One Good Story, That One.* Toronto, ON: HarperCollins.

———. (1994). *Green Grass, Running Water.* Toronto, ON: HarperPerennial.

———. (1998). "How I Spent My Summer Vacation: History, Story, and the Cant of Authenticity." *Landmarks: A Process Reader,* eds. Roberta Birks, Tomi Eng, and Julie Walchli. Scarborough, ON: Prentice Hall Allyn and Bacon Canada, 248–255.

———. (1999a). *Truth and Bright Water.* New York: Grove Press.

———. (1999b, Summer/Autumn). "A Short History of Indians in Canada." *Canadian Literature, 161/162,* 62–64.

———. (2003). *The Truth About Stories: A Native Narrative.* Minneapolis, MN: University of Minnesota Press.

Lincoln, Kenneth. (1993). *Indi'n Humor: Bicultural Play in Native America.* New York: Oxford University Press.

Lowe, John. (1994). "Coyote's Jokebook: Humor in Native American Literature and Culture." In *Dictionary of Native American Literature,* ed. Andrew Wiget. New York: Garland, 193–205.

Mojica, Monique. (2001, Autumn). "Post-Colonial Traumatic Stress Disorder: A Theatrical Monologue." *Prairie Fire, 22:3,* 88–90.

Owens, Louis. (1992). *Other Destinies: Understanding the American Indian Novel.* Norman, OK: University of Oklahoma Press.

———. (1998). *Mixedblood Messages. Literature, Film, Family, Place.* Norman, OK: University of Oklahoma Press.

Pfister, Manfred. (2002). "Introduction: A History of English Laughter?" In *A History of English Laughter: Laughter from Beowulf to Beckett and Beyond,* ed. Manfred Pfister. Amsterdam: Rodopi, v–x.

Ruffo, Armand Garnet. (1998). "Creating a Country." *An Anthology of Canadian Native Literature in English,* eds. Daniel David Moses and Terry Goldie. Toronto, ON: Oxford University Press, 397–398.

Slipperjack, Ruby. (2001, Autumn). *Snuff Chewing Charlie at University. Prairie Fire, 22:3,* 165–186.

Tama, Jose Torres. (2001, September/October). "Healing with Humor: New American Perspectives from James Luna and Dan Kwong." *Art Papers, 25:5,* 17.

Taylor, Drew Hayden. (2000). *alterNatives.* Burnaby, BC: Talonbooks.

Vickers, Scott B. (1998). *Native American Identities: From Stereotype to Archetype in Art and Literature.* Albuquerque, NM: University of New Mexico Press.

Wagamese, Richard. (1994). *Keeper'n Me.* Toronto, ON: Doubleday Canada.

White, Hayden. (1978). *Tropics of Discourse: Essays in Cultural Criticism.* Baltimore, MD: The Johns Hopkins University Press.

———. (1987). *The Content of the Form: Narrative Discourse and Historical Representation.* Baltimore, MD: The Johns Hopkins University Press.

Filmography

Taylor, Drew Hayden, dir. (2000). *Trickster, Redskins, and Puppy Stew: The Healing Powers of Native Humour.* National Film Board of Canada.

Thomas Rüdell

Modernizing the "Indian": Literary Constructions of the Native in Selected Novels by Thomas King

> Boy, hard to keep track of this world.
> You know, in Germany I told the story about how
> Coyote went over to the west coast to get some fire because he was cold.
> Good thing he went travelling in the olden days before he needed a credit card.
> —Lionel James in *Medicine River,* 172

If we take the reports by European explorers to the present territory of Canada, written in the 16th century, as the beginning of written Canadian Literature, this makes for a literary history of about four centuries, give or take a few years. The Native inhabitants of Canada have always been an integral part of this literary history: it is obvious that they were one of the main objects of the explorers' reports; it is also obvious that the "newly discovered" people quickly became a topic for Canadian poetry and prose, and also for Canadian everyday culture. While these literary constructions of the Native were subject to a few changes over the centuries, it was not before the second half of the 20th century that a fundamental change of the image of the Native in Canadian literature took place. This is due to the fact that during this period more and more Native people began to pursue careers in literature, thus offering a new, mostly contrastive, perspective to the literary constructions of the Native by non-Native authors (Petrone 1990, 136).

One of the most prominent members of the group of contemporary North American Native authors is Thomas King (Cherokee), whose four published novels are not only bestsellers but also highly acclaimed study objects for literature critics and theorists. This article deals with the question of how Thomas King in his works modernizes the literary "Indian." There are two aspects to the "modern Natives" in King's novels and short stories: his protagonists are modern in that they are different from most earlier literary constructions of the Native in Canadian literature, and they are modern in that they have modern, socially accepted lifestyles, which are comparable to those of non-Native people, but still distinct enough.

Due to his biographical background (King's father was Cherokee, his mother is Greek, and he grew up in California; he currently lives and works in Canada and holds Canadian and United States citizenship) King has a strong interest in the "idea of Indianness." As he states in an interview with Jace Weaver, "I don't want people to get the mistaken idea that I'm an 'authentic Indian,' or that they're getting the kind of Indian that they'd like to have .... One of the questions that's important to ask is 'Who is an Indian? How do we get the idea of Indianness?'" (Weaver 1993, 56). Indeed, King has made clear on several occasions that he does not really believe in a concept of "Indianness." In an interview with Jeffrey Canton he has called that a "fluid construct which we make up as we go along" (Canton 1994, 2). In the same interview, King said that, although he is half Cherokee, he identifies more with the Alberta Blackfoot than with the Cherokee, because he lived in a Blackfoot community for about ten years (Canton 1994, 3).

When we look at King's biography, as told in *The Truth about Stories,* there are several instances in which the difference between non-Native expectations of what a ("real") Indian is (or is supposed to be) collide with reality. This makes for amusing anecdotes: the German cook on the tramp steamer on which young Thomas King emigrates to New Zealand who claims to know about "real Indians" because he has read the works of Karl May; the immigration official in New Zealand confusing North American Indians with East Indians, and so on. Finally, King gets a job as a photojournalist in Australia: "I got the job, in part because I was an American and an Indian—the exotic combination being too much for folks to resist" (King 2003, 51). Yet these are more than mere biographical anecdotes—they all play into the question of "real Indians" and, for that matter, "modern Indians." The humorous situations only occur because the cook, the official, and the newspaper staff cannot cope with the idea that there are "real" Indians still around in the 1960s, looking pretty much like everybody else, and applying for modern jobs.

In order to demonstrate the extent to which the literary construction of the Native in King's work has helped to break up stereotypes and indeed to create a new literary image of the Native, I will first survey previous constructions of the Native in Canadian literature from the beginnings to the 20th century. This is followed by an analysis of Thomas King's first and second novels, *Medicine River* and *Green Grass, Running Water*.

Constructions of "the Native" in Canadian Literature

In W. H. New's *Encyclopedia of Literature in Canada* (New 2002), under the keyword "Natives in Literature," N. E. Currie gives an overview of the development of literary constructions of the Native in Canadian literary history. His first examples come from the reports of French explorers, such as Jacques Cartier (1491–1557), and French Jesuit missionaries. While these reports claimed to be close to reality in their description of the newly discovered world and its inhabitants, they were still written from the perspective of Europeans about to take possession of their New World. The same can be said for later reports by English explorers. While some authors, like Alexander Mackenzie and David Thompson, apparently meet the claim of neutrality of their descriptions, Samuel Hearne's *Narrative of a Journey to Prince of Wales' Fort* (1795), "shifts from objective scientific description to figurative language in an account of the 'massacre' of a group of Inuit .... Passive sentence structures deny agency, allowing Hearne to evade responsibility for ... killing a young Inuit woman" (Currie 2002, 800). In short, Hearne tries to de-emphasize his active part in a massacre of a group of Inuit by using passive constructions.

The same lack of neutrality is evident in the *Jesuit Relations,* regular report letters from the Jesuit missionaries in Quebec to their superiors in Rome and Paris, which were started in 1611 and were published from the year 1632 on. Here, the Native people in Quebec are described as enemies of Christianity. They are judged from a European perspective and, of course, they are to be converted. Probably the best-known example from the *Jesuit Relations* is the report about the death of Father Jean de Brébeuf, who was tortured to death in 1649 by the Iroquois. The *Relations* describe Brébeuf as a martyr who stoically and heroically suffers his torture, during which he never stops preaching: "Father de Brébeuf endured like a rock, insensible to fire and flames, which astonished all the blood-thirsty wretches who tormented him. His zeal was so great that he preached continually to these infidels, to try to convert them" (Mealing 1985, 69).

The first change in the literary construction of the Native comes in 1769 with Frances Brooke's *The History of Emily Montague,* the first Canadian novel written in English. Brooke, born in Great Britain, was highly influenced by Jean-Jacques Rousseau's European primitivism and his theory of the "noble savage," which she contrasted with her own experience in Quebec. Ed Rivers, a character from *Emily Montague* describes Native people as children of nature, enjoying "true liberty": "Other nations talk of liberty, they possess it .... They assert and they maintain that independence with a spirit truly noble .... They are not only free as people, but every individual is perfectly so. Lord of himself, at once subject and master, a savage knows no superior" (Brooke 2001, 25–26). Among the several other portrayals of the Native in Canadian literary history are "the blood-thirsty savage" (as featured in John Richardson's *Wacousta,* 1832) and "the proud people doomed to perish" (Duncan Campbell Scott's sonnet "The Onondaga Madonna", 1898). Later authors used the Native as a symbol for Canadian identity (Margaret Atwood in *Surfacing,* 1972) or as "foils, by which white characters understand themselves and their place in the world" (Currie 2002, 801; Laurence 1974).

From the 1970s onward, several thematic studies in Canadian literature have been published, which, among other things, look at literary constructions of the Native. Among the first of these studies is Margaret Atwood's classic *Survival: A Thematic Guide to Canadian Literature* (1972). Central to the work is her famous "victim theory" ("survival" as the central symbol for Canada in CanLit, Canada and its inhabitants as collective victims), in which victims are categorized into four positions:

> Position One: To deny the fact that you are a victim .... Position Two: To acknowledge the fact that you are a victim, but to explain this as an act of fate, the Will of God, the dictates of biology .... the necessity decreed by History, or Economics, or the Unconscious, or any other general powerful idea .... Position Three: To acknowledge the fact that you are a victim but to refuse to accept the assumption that the role is inevitable .... Position Four: To be a creative non-victim. (Atwood 1972, 36)

Native people, in this frame, fall into position two: according to Atwood, the literary native is "the ultimate victim of social oppression and deprivation" (Atwood 1972, 97). This is the final stage of a development; while Native people, in the beginning, are "nature's children, living a jolly carefree life until the advent of the white man" (Atwood 1972, 92), as in Charles Mair's *Tecumseh* (1886) and Joseph Howe's poem "Song of the Micmac" (year unknown), the positive aspect of being close to nature fades with time. Native people are described more and more as cruel beasts, as "instruments of Nature the Monster" (Atwood 1972, 192). Here, Atwood cites E. J. Pratt's long poem "Brébeuf and his Brethren" (1939) as an example. The next step in this development sees the Native as "being doomed," which culminates in the Native people being the ultimate victim. This makes them a "yardstick of suffering, against which the whites can measure theirs and find it lacking" (99). Examples for the yardstick-metaphor are George Ryga's play *The Ecstasy of Rita Joe* and the Tonnerre-family in Margaret Laurence's Manawaka-novels. Atwood sums up,

> So far we have seen Indians used in Canadian literature for two main purposes: as instruments of Nature the Monster, torturing and killing white victims; and as variants themselves of the victim motif. Canadian writers seem to have been less interested in Indians and Eskimoes *per se* than they have been in Indians and Eskimoes as exotic participants in their own favourite game. (Atwood 1972, 102, emphasis original)

Since it takes a victor and a victim to play this "favourite game," the description of the Native is always dependant upon non-Native figures.

In his 1989 study *Fear and Temptation* (partially published in Thomas King's *The Native in Literature,* 1987), Terry Goldie uses terms from the field of semiotics to characterize the literary constructions of the Native: "The indigene is the semiotic pawn on a chessboard under the control of the white signmaker ... within one field of discourse, that of British Imperialism" (Goldie 1987, 70). The Native person cannot influence the way he or she is described in literature. Goldie further defines this "semiotic field of the indigene": "In most literary accounts of the indigene, sex and violence, whether depicted directly or indirectly, are important factors. They are poles of attraction and repulsion, temptation by the dusky maiden and fear of the demonic violence of the fiendish warrior" (70). Goldie's examples include Richardson's *Wacousta,* featuring the "brutal warrior" as well as the "seductive maiden," and Joseph Howe's poem "Acadia," in which Native characters develop from noble savages (before contact) to bloodthirsty barbarians (after arrival of the European settlers). Similar to the reports written by explorers and missionaries, the Native people here are a mere means to an end—to create sympathy for the European settlers.

Another important aspect of literary constructions of the Native that is discussed both by Atwood and by Goldie is the focus on the past when depicting Native people: "The present indigene is deindigenized, no longer valid, so the focus of indigenization must be the 'real' indigenes, the resonances of the past" (Goldie 1989, 168). Goldie's example is taken from Atwood's 1972 novel *Surfacing*, in which the narrator encounters a Native family who remains mere "vague glimpses, with none of the visionary power of the rock paintings which their ancestors left" (Goldie 1989, 168):

> I was remembering the others who used to come .... There was one family left. Every year they would appear on the lake in blueberry season and visit the good places the same way we did, condensing as though from the air, five or six of them in a weatherbeaten canoe: father in the stern, head wizened and cordoned like a dried root .... They would check to see how many blueberries there were, faces neutral and distanced, but when they saw that we were picking they would move on. (Atwood 1992, 122)

The Native family in the narrator's memory, simply called "the others," consists of shadowy figures, barely visible, appearing like a weather phenomenon. They are closely connected to nature and remain distant from the narrator. The rock paintings, on the other hand, drawings of which the narrator's father has left for her, are manifest and concrete: their location is marked on a map, their content has been analyzed by scientists. Although the expert's report sounds patronizing ("reminiscent of the drawings of children,") (146–147), it points out a possible connection to "powerful protective spirits" and "significant or predictive dreams" (146–147). Thus, the rock paintings from the past have a greater influence on the narrator than her Native contemporaries.

Summing up Currie's, Atwood's, and Goldie's findings about the Native in Canadian literature, one can say that Native people have been portrayed as victims (maybe even "the ultimate victim") of social circumstances since the arrival of the European explorers in the 16th century. Originally closely connected to nature, they are forced to change their lifestyle. Since they oppose the Eurocentric idea of progress, they have to be literally "put away," physically as well as psychologically. In order to colonize the land completely, its Native inhabitants have to be converted to the Christian religion. An alternative figure to the Native as obstacle for civilization is the figure of the "noble savage," who is envied by parts of the mainstream society for his way of life, but is seen as doomed at the same time. In any case, Native people in literature function as a measure for White society. Native people are outcasts who live at the edge of society; they are rarely depicted as parts of (mainstream or Native) communities. As King himself points out, "The idea of community and family is not an idea that is often pursued by non-Native writers, who prefer to imagine their Indians as solitary figures poised on the brink of extinction" (King 1990, xiv). In most cases, they are associated with violence, alcoholism, and sexuality. Furthermore, they are associated with a romanticized image of a Native of the past, an image that is highly influenced by earlier literary descriptions.

"You know, be a modern Indian": The Native in the Works of Thomas King

Herb Wylie points out several characteristics of King's work that clearly distinguish his literary construction of the Native from that of other authors, Native and non-Native alike. According to Wylie, King's work reclaims images of Native people from stereotyping by the dominant culture (Wylie 1999, 106), and while doing so reasserts and privileges a Native perspective. Wylie further notes, "King's work quite clearly reflects a consciousness of and a resistance to a long history of Eurocentric misrepresentation" (118).

Percy Walton argues similarly in regard to King's first novel *Medicine River*. She states, "In *Medicine River*, a positive Native presence is generated through its difference from the negative attributes that the native has been made to signify within English-Canadian discourse" (Walton 1990, 78). According to Walton, King's work is "metadiscursive" in that "rather than trying to refer to a 'reality' outside of language it refers to a discourse constructed about the native. It's a discourse about discourse" (Walton 1990, 78). Another very important aspect of King's Native figures, again described by Wylie, is that they are not victims: "While *Green Grass, Running Water* and ... *One Good Story, That One* do foreground the struggles and hardships of being Native in a racist society, they do so in a way that resists depicting Native people as victims and resists defining them exclusively in relation to the dominant culture or according to its expectations" (Wylie 1999, 118). The following are some examples of each of the aforementioned characteristics. The passages quoted are from King's first and second novels, *Medicine River* (*MR*) and *Green Grass, Running Water* (GGRW).

Reclaiming the Image: Will Horse Capture, Harlen Bigbear, and Eli Stands Alone

Will and Harlen, the protagonists of King's first novel, *Medicine River* (1989) are two good examples of King's new way of constructing the literary Native. Walton points out the attack on cliché Indian images in mainstream media discourse, when, in the very beginning of the novel, Harlen imitates a TV Indian by making funny noises:

> 'Hey-Uh. Saw Will Sampson on television. It was a movie about him being a sheriff. That's what he said all the time. Hey-uh. He's a real Indian, too. What do you think?'
>
> I couldn't help it. I started to laugh. 'Harlen', I said, 'it sounds dumb as hell' (*MR*, 10).

Here, the Native perspective represented by Will and Harlen reveals the non-Native cliché: "Metadiscursively, King's representations of natives laugh at the representations of natives in the media, and the text draws a distinction between the two. The constructed native of the past shares little in common with King's representations of the native of the present" (Walton 1990, 81). Will and Harlen differ from the mainstream media image of the Native on several occasions throughout the novel, and they are confronted with the Indian cliché repeatedly. For example, at the hospital Will is mistaken for the father of Louise Heavyman's newborn daughter. Will is asked for a name for the child and answers with a joke about the girl being born in the South Wing of the hospital and maybe they would call her that. The non-Native nurse answers, "'Is that a traditional Indian name?'" (*MR*, 40) and writes it down on the official form.

Another important passage is the one about the funeral of Jake Pretty Weasel, one of Will and Harlen's former team mates from the Medicine River Friendship Centre basketball team. Harlen, being the team coach, delivers the funeral eulogy. Will describes the scene as follows:

> The service was short. The priest wouldn't come because it was a suicide, so January got this fellow she knew from the Mormon Church. Harlen made a little speech about how life was like basketball and how Jake had just fouled out of the game. The Mormon guy came over after and told January how sorry he was about her husband's death, and he told Harlen how much he enjoyed his life-is-like-basketball talk and would it be okay if he used it some time. (MR, 47)

The "official" religion of the dominant culture is not present here—the priest refused because of Jake's suicide. So the widow gets a substitute from the Mormon Church and Harlen uses a metaphor from mainstream sports culture in order to honour a dead friend. Leslie Monkman, in his study *A Native Heritage,* points out that Native religious traditions are not recognized and acknowledged by non-Native writers, citing E. J. Pratt's "Brébeuf and his Brethren" as an example (Monkman 1981, 21). This ignorance of Native religious traditions is being ridiculed in this passage: King has Harlen create an alternative to Euro-Canadian funeral rites, profane as it may be. The little speech given by the coach of the "Medicine River Friendship Centre Warriors"[1] has nothing to do with Blackfoot religious traditions, but it is still much more personal than the "short service" held by a nameless "guy from the Mormon church." Another sting in the flesh of the conventional Native image comes with the request of the Mormon to use the basketball simile in one of his sermons. The "Indian way" found by Harlen becomes a part of Mormon funeral rites; the Native community actively and creatively takes part in Western religion instead of passively enduring it.

Eli Stands Alone, a central figure in King's second novel *Green Grass, Running Water,* is another good example of King's "modern Native." Eli is a retired professor of English Literature who has moved back to rural Alberta from Toronto after his mother's death (similar to Will in *Medicine River*). He lives in his mother's log cabin that is under threat of being torn down to make way for a hydro dam project; Eli blocks the project by getting court injunctions and simply by refusing to give up the cabin. Another retrospective plot line features Eli's relationship with his girlfriend, Karen, who died in a car accident after recovering from cancer. At the end of the novel, Eli dies in the flooding that happens after the Trickster Coyote causes the dam to break. The cabin is also washed away, and what is left of the dam has to be torn down.

Clifford Sifton is the manager of the dam project. His name refers to Sir Clifford Sifton, the minister of the interior and superintendent of Indian affairs of the Laurier government. The historical Clifford Sifton was an aggressive champion of Euro-Canadian settlement, which forced the Native inhabitants of the Canadian Prairies on to reservations (Flick 1999, 150). Eli and Cliff Sifton are in a forced relationship: every morning, Sifton asks Eli officially to grant the title for his log cabin to the provincial government of Alberta. Eli refuses every time. In addition to the official request, interesting dialogues between the two men develop. Clifford, resembling his namesake, asks Eli to give up the cabin in favour of progress. After all, the treaties were not made for "modern Indians" like Eli and his Blackfoot relatives:

> 'Besides, you guys aren't real Indians anyway. I mean, you drive cars, watch television, go to hockey games. Look at you. You're a university professor.'
>
> 'That's my profession. Being Indian isn't a profession.'
>
> 'And you speak as good English as me.'
>
> 'Better,' said Eli. 'And I speak Blackfoot, too. My sister Norma speaks Blackfoot. So do my niece and nephew.'
>
> 'That's what I mean. Latisha runs a restaurant and Lionel sells televisions. Not exactly traditionalists, are they?'

> 'It's not exactly the nineteenth century, either.'
>
> 'Damn it. That's my point. You can't live in the past.' (*GGRW*, 141)

Sifton clearly does not want to grant Native people a modern lifestyle. However, his argument is a contradiction: on the one hand, a "real Indian" can only be "an Indian of the past" as defined by Walton and Goldie—"real Indians" are not university teachers and do not watch hockey. On the other hand, Sifton argues that Eli is living in the past by not giving up his land. These talks between Eli and Clifford Sifton show that there is no such thing as "the Indian" or "the real Indian" in King's fiction; the group of Canadian Native people in the 20th century is far too heterogeneous to make such generalizations.

King portrays Eli as a modern Native man; he has left the reservation to get a degree and a job in Toronto. Initially, Eli has problems accepting his origin and his traditions, and he does not keep in touch with his family once he arrives in Toronto. Until his return to Alberta, Eli's biography does indeed fulfil the stereotype of the assimilated Native. Eli, being a well-educated man, notices this:

> The Indian who couldn't go home. It was a common enough theme in novels and movies. Indian leaves the traditional world of the reserve, goes to the city, and is destroyed. Indian leaves the traditional world of the reserve, is exposed to white culture, and becomes trapped between two worlds. Indian leaves the traditional world of the reserve, gets an education, and is shunned by his tribe (*GGRW*, 286).

But by coming back to Alberta after his mother's death, and by fighting for his mother's land, Eli resists the stereotype in what Arnold E. Davidson calls "an act that subverts the generic White-authored narratives about Natives who leave the reserves never to return again" (Davidson et al. 2003, 139). Eli's evaluation of his situation sounds humble and a little self-deprecating:

> Eli ... looked about the house at what he had become. Ph.D. in literature. Professor emeritus from the University of Toronto. A book on

> William Shakespeare. Another on Francis Bacon. Teacher of the Year. Twice. Indian. In the end he had become what he had always been. An Indian. Not a particularly successful one at that. (*GGRW*, 262)

But behind Eli's understatement lies a great achievement: he has had a career which was successful even by mainstream Canadian standards (he was named teacher of the year, he has published two books on important minds in European intellectual history, his English is better than that of Anglo-Canadian Clifford Sifton), but he still manages to remain "Indian," or rather to "become what he had always been." Furthermore, Eli uses the knowledge he gained in the "White world" to strengthen his position as the "anti-stereotype"; when Sifton says, "'My dam is part of the twentieth century. Your house is part of the nineteenth,'" Eli simply answers: "'Maybe I should look into putting it into the historical register'" (*GGRW*, 141). Although this is surely a tongue-in-cheek statement, it shows that Eli is capable of turning the tables on Sifton: if Sifton does not accept Native traditions, Eli considers the option of making his house part of non-Native (written) history.

Similar to the character Harlen Bigbear in *Medicine River*, Eli stands for the connection between the traditional and the modern: on the one hand, he defends his modern lifestyle and intellectual career in the conversations with his offensively traditional sister Norma:

> 'Nothing wrong with getting away from the reserve.'
> 'We've been here thousands of years.'
> 'Tourist talk, Norma.' (*GGRW*, 287)

On the other hand, Eli stands up for his Native roots whenever he talks to Clifford Sifton. He argues that being Native does not prevent anyone from getting an education: "'That's my profession. Being Indian isn't a profession'" (*GGRW*, 141). Although Eli dies in the end, the family tradition of living in the log cabin is kept alive: Norma begins to rebuild the cabin and announces that she is going to live in it.

The White Girl and the Warrior: Eli's Girlfriend Karen

While Eli is a student at the University of Toronto, he meets Karen. Karen is an Anglo-Canadian student with rich, "progressive" parents. After their initial conversations about literature, she soon becomes Eli's girlfriend. Karen brings Eli books to read, some of which he likes: "Others were not as interesting. 'These are about Indians, Eli. You should read them'" (*GGRW*, 161). The fact that Eli is Native is always a topic in their relationship, and obviously it is also a reason for Karen's interest in him. Her views on his taste in literature, however, are condescending: "Karen liked the idea that he was Indian, and she forgave him, she said, his pedestrian taste in reading, and at the end of the summer ... she and Eli moved in together" (*GGRW*, 163). Eli clearly is a sex object for Karen: "That first night in bed ... Karen rolled on top of Eli, straddled him, and held his arms down by the wrists. 'You know what you are?' she said, moving against him slowly. 'You're my Mystic Warrior.' And she pushed down hard as she said it" (*GGRW*, 164). Davidson et al. note that their relationship is a strategic alliance of some sort: "Eli's desire to pass as White is facilitated by a partnership that validates his choice. Concomitantly, Eli offers Karen access to the culture of the indigenous other, whose ties to the land precede the claims of colonial settlers; through this association, she can play at being Indian" (Davidson et al. 2003, 138). Karen's question "You know what you are?" leaves room for the assumption that young Eli does *not* know what or who he is.

Karen's Eurocentric perspective becomes most obvious when Eli takes her with him to the Sun Dance in order to introduce her to his family. Karen is truly excited about the scenery: "'My God,' she said. 'That's beautiful. It's like it's right out of a movie .... It's like going back in time, Eli. It's incredible.' ... in the sky above a lone bird floated in the morning air. 'Is that an eagle?' asked Karen. 'No, it's a vulture'" (*GGRW*, 203).

After their return to Toronto, Karen remembers only superficial features of the Sun Dance: "'You know what I remember most? ... All those tepees. That's what I remember,'" (*GGRW*, 261) while Eli remembers people: "Aunties, uncles, cousins, in-laws, friends. People he hadn't seen in years. People who greeted him as if he had never left" (*GGRW*, 261). While Karen's attempts to understand Eli and his Native roots might be well-meaning, they are certainly futile: her expectations and imaginations result from books *about* Native people (written by non-Native authors), not from personal experience *with* Native people: "Karen reads the ceremony through her previous knowledge of westerns and commercialized representations of Indian traditions" (Davidson et al. 2003, 138). Although she is living with a Native man, she only sees the stereotype of the "Mystic Warrior." Karen romanticizes Eli's cultural background; her perspective, influenced by Hollywood discourse, does not withstand reality: the bird in the sky is not an eagle, but a vulture. Although she has been Eli's girlfriend for more than two years, she does not recognize contemporary 20th century Native life; for her, the trip to the Sun Dance is a "trip back in time,"[2] or at best it is "like a movie."

Metadiscourse and Misrepresentations: Portland Looking Bear's Short-lived Hollywood Career

One of the most prominent examples of the way in which King attacks "Eurocentric misrepresentations" is certainly the character of Portland Looking Bear in *Green Grass, Running Water.* Portland is a B-movie actor. Two years after his arrival in Hollywood, he starred in most of the cheap Western movies, playing all sorts of minor Native characters. In order to get major roles, he assumes the pseudonym "Iron Eyes Screeching Eagle"[3]—according to his wife "the most absurd name they could imagine" (*GGRW*, 151)—which proves to be a smart career move: "Before the year was out, Portland was playing chiefs. He played Quick Fox ... Chief Jumping Otter ... and Chief Lazy Dog .... He was a Sioux eighteen times, a Cheyenne ten times, a Kiowa six times, an Apache five times, and a Navaho once" (*GGRW*, 151). But his fame fades after a while and Portland goes back to Alberta. Fifteen years later, he attempts a comeback: together with his fifteen-year-old son, Charlie, he moves back to Hollywood. But the comeback fails; Portland and his son have to work as parking valets at Remmington's restaurant, where they have to dress up as Indians (while the waiters wear cowboy outfits); Portland also works as a background dancer at a strip club. He is not offered any more movie parts.

Portland's time in Hollywood is important in several ways: the fact that he gets only minor parts until he changes his name to something more "authentically Indian" is a good example of the unofficial rules that govern Hollywood. Also, the names of the chiefs that Portland portrays are nonsensical. King ridicules the screenplays of Hollywood Westerns, most of them written by authors of European descent; he seems to imply that the authors used a popular practice sentence for first-graders ("The quick brown fox jumps over the lazy dog") for inspiration (Flick 1999, 152). This line only makes sense in form, not in content: it contains all the letters of the alphabet for kids to practice their handwriting. The overemphasis on the superficial that is at work in Hollywood becomes even more prominent with the parts Portland gets: he is a Blackfoot actor playing members of five different nations in forty movies—with not a single Blackfoot among them. Apparently, Indians all look the same to non-Native producers and moviegoers. The Remmington's restaurant and the Four Corners strip club are also examples of Hollywood's superficial view on things: Charlie, while watching his father's performance at the Four Corners notices,

> The woman, tall and good looking, was dressed up as if she were going to park cars at Remmington's .... And then, for no particular reason, she began to rotate her hips ... another man, dressed up in a cowboy outfit, looking for all the world like one of the waiters at Remmington's leaped onto the runway" (*GGRW*, 211–212).

The Native stereotype produced by Hollywood culture is self-referential—it depicts itself. *Green Grass, Running Water* is a metadiscursive text as defined by Walton: the passage in the strip club does not refer to reality outside language, but to Hollywood, which does not refer to reality outside language either (Walton 1990, 78). It could not be more obvious that the "semiotic field of the indigene" as described by Goldie is a see-through construct. And the "Native perspective," taken by the Native minority among the Hollywood actors (see *GGRW*, 182: "Mexicans, Italians, Greeks, along with a few Indians, some Asians, and Whites playing Indians again and again and again") does indeed see through it. Charlie sees the dressed-up strip dancers for what they are, and Portland's wife, Lilian, laughs at the fake nose Portland has to wear in order to look more "Indian" for the camera. Even Portland, who loves Hollywood, has to admit that his background dancing is a "dumb routine" (*GGRW*, 212).

Atwood's Favourite Game and King's Refusal to Play: Will Horse Capture, Latisha Red Dog and George Morningstar

A very important aspect of King's novels is his explicit refusal to depict Native people as victims. As we have seen, victimization is a very prominent feature of literary constructions of the Native in Canadian literature, regardless of the nomenclature chosen to describe it ("ultimate victim," "doomed savage" etc.). Active de-victimization—ascribing another role than that of the victim (within the Atwoodian *victor/victim* relation)—to the literary Native must be seen as an important break with Canadian literary tradition. Because King does not intend to answer the question "which culture is better" (King 1991, 111), this repositioning of *victor* and *victim* takes place in rather harmless contexts. King's victims are not victims in a sense that they are, for example, struck with social disadvantages, drug addictions, sickness or death. But the focus is not on victimizing non-Natives in order to make the victor/victim equation work; it is on the fact that Native people are *not* victims.

For example, in *Medicine River*, Will and Harlen drive back at night from a basketball tournament in Utah and pass the Custer National Monument in Wyoming. When Harlen proposes to stop for a visit, Will's answer is sarcastic: "'You think they let Indians in?' 'Why would they keep us out?'" (*MR*, 107). The visit, however does not happen anyway—Will and Harlen get lost[4] and when they finally make it to the monument, the guard is about to close the gate:

> Harlen came back to the car. 'It's closed for the night, Will.'
>
> 'What?'
>
> 'Young fellow, friendly enough. Told us to come back tomorrow.'
>
> 'We won't be here tomorrow.'
>
> 'I told him that.'
>
> 'Did you tell him that we drove all this way just to see the monument?'
>
> 'I told him that.'
>
> 'Shit.'
>
> 'He said he was sorry.'
>
> 'Did you tell him,' I said, rolling down the window and shouting into the night, 'did you tell him, we're Indians!'
>
> 'I told him that, too, Will. He said he was sorry.'
>
> I got out and stood by the car and imagined I could see that kid hiding in the dark, hunkered down behind the fender of the Bronco, his hands shaking around his rifle, waiting for us to come screaming and whooping and crashing through the gate. (*MR*, 112)

On a surface level of the passage, the two Native men might be seen as being disadvantaged. One might read the passage in a way that the dominant culture keeps them from visiting a historical site that is important for them. On the other hand, this is all just about a missed guided tour and bad timing:

the real reason for the guard to lock up early is neither racism nor ignorance but game seven in the hockey finals. As Will states correctly, "'The Blackfoot didn't fight Custer'" (*MR*, 107). But in Will's fantasy, things work out a little differently: Will and Harlen are the dominant culture here; the young non-Native guard is the victim. The fact that the scene takes place at the foot of the Custer National Monument near Little Big Horn, where the Sioux defeated Custer in a historic battle in 1876, adds to the tongue-in-cheek inversion of victim/victor-roles. The ironic mood of the passage is echoed in the guard's answer "I'm sorry" to Harlen's statement "But we're Indians."

However, the one figure that resists the classic Native victim position in the most obvious way is Latisha Red Dog from *Green Grass, Running Water.* After a nine-year marriage to (non-Native) "no-good" George Morningstar, she finally gets a divorce after George leaves his family before the birth of their third child. Early in the novel, the reader learns that George "used to beat hell out of her" (*GGRW*, 57). Although George's last name sounds like a Native cliché, he is a non-Native citizen of the United States. The figure George Morningstar is obviously modelled after General George Armstrong Custer (Flick 1999, 146–147): "Son of the Morningstar" is the name General Custer got from the Arikara in Dakota. George's appearance (long, blond hair) and the reference to his being born in Ohio and growing up in Michigan are further links to the historical Custer. This resemblance between George Morningstar, wife-beating husband, and George Custer, "famous Indian fighter who has acquired mythic status in American history" (Flick 1999, 149) adds a historic dimension to the incidents of domestic violence: George stands as a metaphor for non-Native violence against Native people. While in the beginning, Latisha is the victim of George's attacks, she emancipates herself and gets a divorce. The most obvious sign of her successful emancipation is the fact that she stops reading George's letters after they are separated.

Towards the end of the novel, George is forced to leave the site of the Sun Dance after he tries to take press photographs of the ceremony. This triggers the final step in Latisha's emancipation process: supported by her family, she commits a successful act of resistance against attempts by the mainstream media to exploit Native culture, while George, for the final time, proves to be a racist when discussing the Sun Dance: "'A bunch of old people and drunks sitting around in tents in the middle of nowhere. Nobody cares about any of this'" (*GGRW*, 386).

Yet the character Latisha Red Dog is used by King in more than one way to attack the cliché of the Native victim: although she is a single mother of three, she is also a hard working, successful businesswoman. This undercuts the "stock image of the alcoholic Native woman on welfare." Her problems, though true to life, are not necessarily and exclusively Native problems; she has to run her own business and organize her family life. The type of business Latisha runs is yet another attack on the victim cliché: she owns the "Dead Dog Café," where (non-Native) tourists are led to believe that they are served dog meat. "'It's a treaty right,' Latisha explained. 'There's nothing wrong with it. It's one of our traditional foods'" (*GGRW*, 132); in reality it is, of course, beef. This is Atwood's *victor/victim* model turned upside down once again: it is the gullible tourists who are the victims of a well organized rip-off-scheme. Like Eli, Latisha also knows her metadiscourse: by explaining to her patrons that it was a treaty right to serve dog stew, by referring to (non-Native) written history, she gives them the proof they want. One might accuse Latisha of selling her culture and traditions to the "White man"—but, as opposed to Portland's engagement at the Four Corners strip joint, it is the Native woman setting the price and the rules of the game. It certainly is no coincidence that Latisha's restaurant bears the name of Thomas King's CBC radio comedy, "The Dead Dog Café Comedy Hour." The feedback from one of the show's listeners (as quoted by King in an interview) describes both the show and the restaurant: "If this is written by Whites, it's not funny at all, but if it's written by Indians then it's hysterical" (Andrews 1999, 174).

The Traditional and the Modern: Summing Up King's Narrative Strategy

The fiction of Thomas King has been instrumental in breaking up dominant stereotypes of the "Indian" in mainstream Canadian literary history. There is no doubt that King has managed to modernize the image of the Native. The most important aspect of this modernization process is the "de-victimization" of King's literary characters. King's Native figures, such as Latisha Red Dog and Eli Stands Alone, are not marginalized victims but rather strong members of modern communities. King modernizes the Native by normalizing the relationship between his Native characters and their non-Native surroundings: most of his characters, as far as their social positions are concerned, do not differ from their non-Native counterparts. Eli, Will, and Latisha are modern Canadian citizens who work in modern, socially accepted, and therefore "normal" professions, which makes them a part of strong communities. This clearly distinguishes King's Native characters from the Eurocentric literary constructions of the Native over the past centuries. King changes the role of Native people from marginalized, exotic, means-to-an-end-figures to characters with agency, without neglecting their distinct Native features. His Native characters differ from non-Natives in their distinct consciousness of their history; this consciousness, however, does not prevent them from leading modern lives, as is shown, among other things, in the dialogues between Eli and Clifford Sifton in *Green Grass, Running Water*.

By pairing up his Native characters with non-Native minor characters (Eli/Karen, Latisha/George etc.), King shows that balancing out traditional and modern lifestyles is only a problem for non-Natives, not for Native people. Conflicts arise from different perceptions of the traditional and the modern: the non-Native characters' expectations of contemporary Native culture are outdated (Clifford Sifton), blurred, and distorted by media discourse (Portland Looking Bear's pseudonym, Karen's view of the Sun Dance) or overtly racist (George Morningstar). In none of these cases are they based on facts. Native characters in *Medicine River* and *Green Grass, Running Water* are the opposite of what non-Native characters believe or want them to be. Thus, on another level, the Native characters are also very different from how they have previously been portrayed in the Canadian literary canon. While the author creates enough opportunities for his non-Native characters to realize this imbalance, they fail or refuse to do so. The reader, however, does see the difference between non-Native (perhaps his/her own) perceptions and modern Native reality and is thus compelled by King to revise his or her own view of the Native.

Endnotes

1 The name of the team, consisting of the opposites "friendship" and "warrior," in itself hints at a multifaceted image of the Native.

2 See Walton: "The Native of the Present Has No Presence" (1990, 81).

3 The pseudonym clearly refers to Hollywood actor Iron Eyes Cody, who, although non-Native by birth (his parents were Italian immigrants), claimed to be of Cherokee and Cree origin. He became most famous for his clichéd rendition of "The Crying Indian" in a 1970s Public Service Announcement on environmental pollution ("Iron Eyes Cody," online).

4 Contrary to the stereotype of the "typical Indian" who is good at finding the way through the wilderness, Will gets lost several times throughout the novel. This mostly happens when Trickster Harlen gives him directions (see *MR*, 138).

Bibliography

Andrews, Jennifer. (1999). "Border Trickery and Dog Bones: A Conversation with Thomas King." *Studies in Canadian Literature, 24:2*, 161–185.

Atwood, Margaret. (1992). *Surfacing*. 1972. London: Bloomsbury.

———. (1972). *Survival: A Thematic Guide to Canadian Literature.* Toronto, ON: House of Anansi Press.

Brooke, Frances. (2001). *The History of Emily Montague*, ed. Laura Moss. Ottawa, ON: The Tecumseh Press Ltd.

Canton, Jeffrey. (1994). "Interview with Thomas King." *Paragraph, 16:1*, 2–6.

Currie, N. E. (2002). "Natives in Literature." In *Encyclopedia of Literature in Canada*, ed. William H. New. Toronto, ON: University of Toronto Press, 800–802.

Davidson, Arnold E., Priscilla L. Walton, and Jennifer Andrews. (2003). *Border Crossings: Thomas King's Cultural Inversions*. Toronto, ON: University of Toronto Press.

Flick, Jane. (1999). "Reading Notes for Thomas King's *Green Grass, Running Water*." *Canadian Literature, 161:162*, 140–172.

Goldie, Terry. (1989). *Fear and Temptation: The Image of the Indigene in Canadian, Australian, and New Zealand Literatures*. Montreal, QC, Kingston, ON: McGill-Queen's University Press.

———. (1987). "Fear and Temptation: Images of Indigenous Peoples in Australian, Canadian, and New Zealand Literature." In *The Native in Literature*, eds. Thomas King et al. Toronto, ON: ECW, 67–79.

Howe, Joseph. (1874). "Acadia." Joseph Howe. In *Poems and Essays*. Montreal, QC: Lovell.

———. "Song of the Micmac." Publication unknown.

King, Thomas, ed. (1990). *All My Relations: An Anthology of Contemporary Native Canadian Fiction*. Toronto, ON: McClelland & Stewart.

———. (1991). "Interview with Hartmut Lutz." *Contemporary Challenges: Conversations with Canadian Native Authors*, ed. Hartmut Lutz. Saskatoon, SK: Fifth House Publishers, 107–116.

———. (1995). *Medicine River*. 1991. Toronto, ON: Penguin.

———. (1999). *Green Grass, Running Water*. 1993. Toronto, ON: HarperPerennialCanada edition.

———. (2003). *The Truth About Stories: A Native Narrative*. Toronto, ON: Anansi.

Laurence, Margaret. (1964). *The Stone Angel*. Toronto, ON: McClelland & Stewart.

———. (1966). *A Jest of God*. Toronto, ON: McClelland & Stewart.

———. (1969). *The Fire-Dwellers*. Toronto, ON: McClelland & Stewart.

———. (1974). *The Diviners*. Toronto, ON: McClelland & Stewart.

———. (1970). *A Bird in the House*. Toronto, ON: McClelland & Stewart.

Lutz, Hartmut. (1991). *Contemporary Challenges: Conversations with Canadian Native Authors*. Saskatoon, SK: Fifth House Publishing.

Mair, Charles. (1974). *Tecumseh*. Toronto, ON: University of Toronto Press.

Mealing, S. R., ed. (1985). *The Jesuit Relations and Allied Documents: A Selection*. Don Mills, ON: Carleton University Press.

Monkman, Leslie. (1981). *A Native Heritage: Images of the Indian in English-Canadian Literature*. Toronto, ON: University of Toronto Press.

New, William H., ed. (2002). *Encyclopedia of Literature in Canada*. Toronto, ON: University of Toronto Press.

Petrone, Penny. (1990). *Native Literature in Canada: From the Oral Tradition to the Present*. Toronto, ON: Oxford University Press.

Pratt, Edwin John. (1966). *Brébeuf and His Brethren*. Toronto, ON: Macmillan.

Richardson, John. (1987). *Wacousta: Or, The Prophecy; A Tale of the Canadas*, ed. Douglas Cronk. 1832. Ottawa, ON: Carleton UP.

Ryga, George. (1970). *The Ecstasy of Rita Joe*. Vancouver, BC: Talonbooks.

Scott, Duncan Campbell. (1998). "The Onondaga Madonna." In *Labour and the Angel*, Duncan Campbell Scott. Boston, MA: Copeland & Day.

Walton, Percy. (1990). "'Tell Our Own Stories': Politics and the Fiction of Thomas King." *World Literature Written in English, 30:2*, 77–84.

Weaver, Jace. (1993). "Interview with Thomas King." *Publisher's Weekly, 240:10*, 56–57.

Wylie, Herb. (1999). "'Trust Tonto': Thomas King's Subversive Fictions and the Politics of Cultural Literacy." *Canadian Literature, 161:162*, 105–124.

Internet Sources

"Iron Eyes Cody." *Wikipedia*. http://en.wikipedia.org/wiki/Iron_Eyes_Cody [consulted March 9, 2006].

Katarzyna Juchnowicz

Reflections of Oral Traditions in Contemporary Native Writing: Ruby Slipperjack's *Honour The Sun*

> In the contemporary world, our main access to literature is through books or plays or movies, and unless we are a part of those more traditional communities, we see little of the oral. What we see is the written, lying, as it does on the surface, a tip suggesting, as it should, a much larger body just below.
> —King 1996, 354

The Continuous Importance of Storytelling in Native North American Cultures

Storytelling long predates the arrival of the Europeans in North America, and it has always accompanied the lives of Native peoples as it anchors memories, links generations, places, as well as times. In traditional societies, stories form perhaps the most important available model of instruction. The purpose of telling them is "to *integrate,* to *educate,* and to *entertain* all the peoples. The children and the adults of the human, animal, and mythic peoples all depend on the telling of the myths and tales, for within the stories are what is essential and meaningful, what is real" (Frey 1995, 176; emphasis in original). In stories people (can) discover strength and find healing; elders help children find their sense of identity and their place in this world.

The importance of storytelling within a culture is reflected in the status of storytellers, a community's respect for them, and the times assigned to this activity. Stories, traditionally told in wintertime (Frey 1995, 149), carry the history of a people, its cultural beliefs, warnings and advice, as well as a system of values. Leslie Marmon Silko (Laguna Pueblo) explains her usage of storytelling in the following way: "When I use the term *storytelling,* ... I'm talking about something that comes out of an experience and an understanding of that original view of Creation—that we are all part of a whole; we do not differentiate or fragment stories and experiences" (Silko 2001, 160; emphasis in original).

In the post-colonial literary world of Native North America, storytelling has taken the direction of "storywriting," marking a new means for the preservation and continuation of oral traditions. Although seemingly two distinct forms of communication, storytelling and storywriting lie on the same continuum; they are like colours of a spectrum giving a different dimension to the subject of discussion: literature as a transmitter of culture. Renate Eigenbrod put it in the following words: "Remembering orally and remember in writing: the parallel indicates how *litera-ture* is a continuation of *ora-ture,* or the so-called oral traditions" (Eigenbrod 1995, 91; emphasis in original).

Contemporary Native literary outcome is not only influenced by the history of colonization, but it is also closely connected to the traditional worldview and the values of the authors' tribal cultures. "Native literature has been forced to develop as an independent genre, parallel to other 'Canadian literature'" (Grant 1999, 122). Native writers, in search of creative forms of literary expression, often go back to their roots and use oral traditions as a means of cultural identification. Memories that seem to have been lost are given a new shape; stories long forgotten are given a new dimension. The spoken word is transmitted into the written form. To quote Lee Maracle (Métis), "Words are not objects to be wasted. They represent the accumulated knowledge, cultural values, the vision of an entire people or peoples" (Maracle 1992, 87).

The purpose of this paper is to introduce the reader to the world of oral traditions in a contemporary Native literary text, using *Honour the Sun* by Ruby Slipperjack as an example. As a result of the post-contact era, the novel encompasses both traditional elements of the author's Anishinabe background and, obviously, features of a written work. Acting as a reminder of the past, of one's culture and identity, the novel is rich in references to oral traditions. We can trace both explicit and implicit references, and we can distinguish structural, thematic, and topological categories of oral traditions.

Explicit references, which belong to the thematic category, are to be found in stories told directly by various characters, stories of the past (legends), the meaning of names, as well as wisdom, teachings, and traditions passed on usually by members of the older generation to the younger one. The explicit category includes the topological category and thus the presence of Old Man, who represents the Trickster, and the presence of the Memegwesiwag. Implicit references belong to the structural category. Their understanding becomes clear when informed by the background of precious cultural, here Anishinabe, knowledge. The structural category encompasses language (the implied presence of Ojibway) and, specifically, repetition and circularity, as well as the broad meaning of silences.

Presences of Oral Traditions in Ruby Slipperjack's *Honour the Sun*

In her first novel, *Honour the Sun* (1987), Ruby Slipperjack-Farrell (born in 1952), an Anishinabe writer and scholar, attempts to transmit cultural knowledge and strengthen the Native identity of the Ojibway people through multiple layers of oral traditions that are present both explicitly and implicitly. Paula Gunn Allen claims that "structural and thematic elements from the oral tradition, usually from the writer's own tribe, always show up in contemporary works by American Indians" (Gunn Allen 1992, 4).

On the cover of the book, below the title, we find an explanation stating, "Extracted and revised from the diary of The Owl." Even if the diary is a work of fiction and The Owl is a fictional character, the process of writing down is implied here—the main character, The Owl, must have written the diary, which was later extracted and revised. We do not know, however, what was cut out from the original story and what was corrected. The diary encompasses the period between the summers of 1962 and 1968, which means that we get to know The Owl's thoughts and actions from her childhood (when she is eleven) to her teenage years (when she is sixteen). It is divided thematically into twenty-seven chapters, following the seasonal division of particular years. It is written in English, although its implied language is Ojibway.

One of explicit forms of transmitting cultural knowledge is that of sharing oral traditions in the form of stories. In *Honour the Sun* there are two references to traditional stories. The Owl presents them in the following way: "The reading is done and the nightly jokes and stories start. Mom tells a legend of two sisters who went on a journey. They had looked longingly at the brightest star and that star came and took them up to where they found an old woman fishing from a hole in the sky. They asked her to let them back down to earth with her fish line. My eyelids grow heavy as Mom's voice drones on and on…" (Slipperjack 1987, 55). The other traditional story comes to The Owl's head when she is looking at her mother: "[Mom] looks like the girl in the moon. That's a story she told us once about a girl who went out to get water at night and she was not supposed to look at the moon. But she stopped and looked at the moon anyway because she thought the moon was so handsome. The moon came down and took her away and there she was to stay for ever and ever, on the moon, with her pail still in her hand…" (122). Through the presence of many different stories the novel gives an impression that storytelling is a natural everyday activity done by average members of the Ojibway community.

There are also less direct references to traditional knowledge: "There [Mom and I] sat and fished, facing each other about twenty feet apart. She told me stories about Indians of long ago and the magic people who lived inside the rock cliffs" (Slipperjack 1987, 125). We actually do not get to know who these magic people are. Slipperjack explains it in her next novel, *Silent Words*, in a conversation between Danny, its protagonist, and Ol' Jim:

> 'Ol' Jim, is there someone there? Why would you leave tobacco if no one was there to take it?'
>
> 'You are right, son. There is someone there. There are a lot of beings here. The Mimigwesiwag live there. They see us go by. Long ago they were able to communicate with us when there were people who could see and understand them. Now we have lost our communication, so all we can do is know that they are there. It is our fault that we have lost the level of thought and knowledge to be able to see and talk with them. Now all we have left is to acknowledge their existence by leaving them ahsamah.'
>
> ...
>
> 'Well, they looked like us, they spoke the same language as us, but they lived inside the rocks ... They had supernatural powers.' (Slipperjack 1992, 97–98)

Stories shape members of a particular group into a community by stressing cultural values and ideals. They entertain, make people laugh or cry. Laughter has a different meaning and is used in different situations in Native North American cultures than in European ones. In Europe people laugh when a story/situation is funny. Aboriginal people laugh also when a situation is not funny at all, but when it is very difficult or dangerous. Laughter serves as a means of survival, of diminishing the difficulty and supporting a person who is undergoing some difficulties (Fontaine 1993, 53). The Owl, for example, tells a story that entertains and teaches at the same time: "The old man across the tracks told us a story once, about a joker who pulled his pants down and bent over with his butt to the sun one morning, and how the sun got mad and zapped him on the butt so hot, he couldn't sit down for a week! Ha, ha!" (Slipperjack 1987, 114).

Another purpose of telling stories is also that of healing, here with laughter. When The Owl falls and loses all the blueberries she managed to pick, her

Mom tells her a story: "'Once,' she says, looking at me, 'Wess could fill his cup every two minutes, 'til one day, he tripped in front of me and out rolled a wad of moss he had been using to stuff his cup over halfway full.' I start to laugh, and she turns away to continue with her picking" (Slipperjack 1987, 23). Here we are presented with a story whose purpose is to diminish the seriousness of what has happened by providing an example of what happened to somebody else. In this mother-daughter teaching the stress is put on the relationship: older/younger, and, thus, the implied experienced/inexperienced.

In *Honour the Sun* stories are also told by other members of the community, but we do not actually get to know what the stories are about; we only know the fact that they are told. For example, "In slurred sentences, [Ben's mother is] telling Mom a story, only pausing to spit on the floor again" (Slipperjack 1987, 66). Another reference is that to the Town Joker: "He sits down on the porch and eats with us. Amid bursts of laughter, he continues with a story between each mouthful" (70). The Owl's opinion is also influenced by the stories of her community: "Sarah is still my friend but her brother Bobby is getting strange. I've been hearing stories of his weird behavior like torturing animals and always being mean" (166). Later, the young Owl tries to remind herself of stories concerning her deceased father: "I've never heard any stories of my father beating my mother, have I?" (175).

One could ask if it is not important for The Owl to write down exact stories or whether they were, perhaps, extracted from the diary. In the above mentioned examples of storytelling it is not important to know exactly the event the characters are talking about. It is crucial, however, that storytelling is present in everyday life and influences character's behaviour and decisions. Another point to be stressed is the fact that stories are mostly told by the representatives of the grown-up generation like The Owl's mom, Ben's mother, and the Town Joker. The Owl learns storytelling from them, and she tells real life stories of how she swallowed a rock (Slipperjack 1987, 70) or broke one of her ribs (78).

Thomas King wrote about Slipperjack's first novel, "*Honour the Sun* began to move away from focusing on a single alienated Native character (a mark of earlier novels in both the United States and Canada) and dealt instead with the idea of community and communal concerns" (King 1996, 362). In fact, Slipperjack herself continues to develop that idea and in her successive novel, *Silent Words*, it is Danny's father, Daniel, who tells the boy, "'Have you noticed that Native people are generally like one big family? Everyone knows everyone, or someone knows of someone who knows the person in question. You'd be amazed how many relatives you could find if you took it into your head to find out'" (Slipperjack 1992, 244).

In *Honour the Sun* we are exposed to many examples of direct teaching. The Owl is told many times to honour the sun, and, thus, that is the title of the novel. Mom instructs The Owl, "'Wash your face[s] well and comb your hair. There, now stand by the window. The sun is just about to come out. When the sun comes over the horizon, he will see you and be very pleased that you're all ready to greet him and he will bless you'" (Slipperjack 1987, 101). The Owl herself learns this lesson and tells her friend Cora,

> 'Your grandma used to tell us each morning to honour the Sun that it may shine on you again tomorrow, with its blessing.'
>
> ... She looks up at me with a puzzled look.
>
> 'What does that mean?' ...
>
> 'I don't know, except she used to make us wash our faces and comb our hair and stand by the window to watch the sun come up.' (Slipperjack 1987, 199)

Deep inside, The Owl understands the meaning of these words, as she is able to identify herself with nature:

> I lay on my back, staring into the blackness of the room. Everything is alright again. Everything is the way it should be. Smiling, I imagine

> being a blackbird. The warm air gently lifts my breast, filling me, through me, and I become one with the night, only to emerge again as Me, to honour the sun, in the early morning light. (Slipperjack 1987, 39)

The Owl also transmits cultural knowledge to Tony and Brian, who are playing with bloodsuckers by the lake: "'Put those back in water! Remember, Mom says you'll be crippled if you maim any creature! Now, put those back!'" (Slipperjack 1987, 83).

Although traditionally, storytelling time is winter, at The Owl's cabin, the stories are also told in summer time, late in the evening or at night. In *Honour the Sun,* it is recurrent that we, the readers, know that the protagonists are telling a story but actually we do not get to know its details. Only the very telling is stressed as in the following examples: "Mom is telling a story about the time we lived at our trapper's cabin" (Slipperjack 1987, 43) or "Mom's telling us a story, interrupting occasionally when she cracks and pops a nut into her mouth" (119). Slipperjack's repeating of the phrase: "Mom is telling a story again" (23) leads us to the topic of repetition, which is one of the key features of oral traditions.

Since, in essence, all Native pre-contact cultural expression is oral and subject to survival in the minds of (wo)men, it is full of devices to aid memory, and repetition is perhaps most common of all (Eigenbrod 1995, 93). Aside from repetition of entire episodes, it is filled with formulaic expressions. These formulas are matters not only of words but also of structure. The storyteller has at his or her disposal a large variety of conventional motifs and episodes and may use them freely. How appropriately they are made a part of his or her composition depends on the individual's skill, but the audiences are not likely to be very critical as long as (s)he keeps them interested (Gunn Allen 1995, 33). Indeed it is remarkable that in spite of this apparent freedom of improvisation so many rather well-articulated plots have survived for centuries, retaining all their essential features. It is this combination of basic narrative type with a freedom of treatment within traditional limits that makes it possible to identify hundreds of versions of the same tale or song as they appear over long stretches of time and space.

The importance of remembering is stressed in all of Slipperjack's novels. In *Silent Words* Ol' Jim explains that to Danny explicitly: "'It is important to remember exactly what is said so that you in turn, when you are an old man, can tell it to a little person like you'" (Slipperjack 1992, 143–144). In *Honour the Sun* The Owl describes the process of remembering: "Sometimes, we tell old Indian legends with some hilarious mistakes. When we know them well enough, Mom tells us another and we keep repeating it again till we can tell it correctly. I like the story time" (Slipperjack 1987, 15). Rodney Frey explains the difference between remembering and memorizing:

> In the context of storytelling, stories are always remembered, never memorized. Memorization results in a rigidity that can inhibit participation in the story. Remembering encourages spontaneity and thus greater immediacy with the listener. Remembering has an important additional significance. To remember is to return to, to reunite with the reality within the story, to reestablish membership with the characters of the story. The storyteller seeks that membership for the listeners as well as for himself or herself. (Frey 1995, 153)

As The Owl grows up, the situation in the community, and in her family in particular, changes drastically. Although the reader is in no way prepared for such a change, it is presented as if it was a normal thing to happen. The Owl's mother starts to drink, which disrupts the family's transmission of oral traditions. The Owl comments that "Mom doesn't even feel like telling night-time stories, anymore. Nothing's the same" (Slipperjack 1987, 170). Later, she even adds, "I hate it at home now. I have nowhere else to go. I feel like Mom doesn't want me around anymore. She rarely talks to me directly so I avoid her as much as I can. I hardly ever talk to her anymore and she acts as if I'm already gone" (189–190). The Owl also gets to know the oral agreement that was made between her own and Freddy's mom. Freddy informs her,

> 'Did you know that my mother and your mother made an agreement long ago, that I would take you for my wife when I could support

> a wife? Well, I've loved you since you were a little girl. Now you're a beautiful young lady and I'll have you. I'll love you and look after you.' (Slipperjack 1987, 180)

Residential schools as politically programmed institutions to erase Native cultures, plus alcoholism, abuse both physical and sexual, as well as deaths caused by accidents on the railway line, are direct results of colonization. The Owl, when going to a boarding school, symbolically is not allowed to take anything that is close to her heart. Her sister Barbara, who has already been to such an institution, instructs The Owl:

> 'Can't take these! [shiny rocks, a pinecone and a mallard tail feather] What are they going to think, you carrying around things like these? White people are going to be looking after you where you are going, you know?'
>
> I watch my treasure clatter across the floor to the corner behind the stove to be swept up into the garbage later. (Slipperjack 1987, 190)

Sitting in the last row at school in the community means that the next year that child will be sent to a boarding school. No wonder it is avoided by children. "I feel at times like I'm sitting on death row" (Slipperjack 1987, 169), says The Owl. Although in the novel there is no mention of the hardships of life in boarding schools, the very going there means separation from one's family and community, from traditions, stories, Native language, and culture.

The strong bond with the Ojibway culture is represented by the figure of the Medicine Man. In *Honour The Sun* we are presented with two meetings between him and The Owl. While the first meeting shows that The Owl is still a child, when she asks him for medicine for her sore arm, which has been caused by her writing at school all morning, she already realizes the Medicine Man's importance: "It's the sparkling eyes and the smiling face that brings a thrill of excitement, love and respect; it's the Medicine Man" (Slipperjack

1987, 91). The second meeting, at the end of the novel, is of greater importance as it also reveals The Owl's maturity:

> I stop in front of the Medicine Man. He pats the rock at his side motioning me to sit beside him. In silence, we sit together. He is as he always was. I feel his calming presence flood my soul, a rushing warmth of completeness, of knowledge undefined, then calming peace settles over me. I feel like I have just completed a circle; I glance at him thinking that here the medicine man is one person in total harmony with his world. (Slipperjack 1987, 210)

The mention of The Owl's having completed a circle is very significant, as circularity is a direct reference to the Native holistic approach to understanding life and the surrounding world. Whatever happens in nature and in people's lives has its aim; processes are interrelated rather than being separate. The Owl's childhood is over; she has become a young woman. She is also moving from her community to live in the city with Vera and Greg:

> My boxes are all packed. I'm leaving on the train tonight. I take a deep breath of the clean, fresh air and watch the sun's rays dance on the water's surface and think, "The sun will keep coming up till the end of time but the people it shines on are here, then gone. Is that what Mom meant? What was it she used to say? [']Honour the Sun, child, just as it comes over the horizon, Honour the Sun, that it may bless you come another day ....'" (Slipperjack 1987, 211)

The Owl no longer has a place close to her mother, but she has learned how to respect nature, and believes that there is always hope. She can give testimony of her culture and restore her spirit—also one of the purposes of contemporary Native literature.

The second meeting with the Medicine Man brings us to the topic of spirituality. In the "Preface to the First Edition" of *An Anthology of Canadian Native Literature in English*, Terry Goldie and Daniel David Moses discuss this issue:

T. G.: '... I agree with you that the majority of Native writing has something that can be called spiritual.'

D. D. M.: '... I mean spiritual just in the sense of knowing the meaning of your life, what you are doing and why you are doing it.' (Moses/Goldie 1998, xxi)

The conversation between the Medicine Man and The Owl is significantly present at the end of the novel-diary, stressing The Owl's understanding of what is happening, the fact of her maturation, and her way towards a change.

Explicit presences of oral traditions are also shown in people's names, each of which possess special powers and a different story. As we learn from Slipperjack's second novel, *Silent Words*, "The human being is shaped by the name he is given because personality and appearance is attached to a given name and that is how he or she will be treated and expected to behave" (Slipperjack 1992, 95). The Owl in *Honour the Sun* tells the Medicine Man, and thus us, the readers, how she got her name:

> 'An owl hooted several nights in a row outside our cabin before I was born. My brother threatened to go out and shoot it because it kept everyone awake. It went away when I was born but I was a night baby with big round eyes and I made such an awful noise crying all night long, that no one in the cabin could get any sleep ... I don't think my brother was too happy about me, either!' (Slipperjack 1987, 211)

In *Honour the Sun* we also find an explicit reference to Old Man, representing the traditional figure of Trickster, in the conversation between The Owl's mother and the Town Joker: "'Wait, did you have breakfast yet?' asks Mom. The Joker chuckles. 'No. Old Man across the tracks was cooking beaver,' he says, 'and beaver and I don't get along too well in the morning'" (Slipperjack 1987, 102).

Implicit references to oral traditions are present in the form of reference to language. Danny, the protagonist of Slipperjack's second novel, *Silent Words*, is a "city Indian" (Slipperjack 1992, 83). He speaks English, understands Ojibway, but needs practice speaking it. Often he has to speak Ojibway to older members of his community to achieve what he wants, as they pretend not to be listening to him when he speaks English. There is yet another type of language present in *Silent Words*, called a "strange-sounding English" (50). Mrs. Old Indian uses it when she instructs Danny: "'Use your eyes and feel inside you wat da udder is feelin. Dat way, dere is no need for words. Your ears are for 'earing all da udder tings 'round you" (60). In *Honour the Sun*, The Owl, too, speaks about the discrepancy between English and Ojibway:

> My English isn't that good. I wouldn't dare talk English in school. I'd be embarrassed and teased to death if I dared to talk English in front of the whole classroom. So the most we ever say is to answer shyly, "Yes" or "No" to the teacher's questions. Any English I know is only from what I read in my school books and by listening to the teacher talk. I would never dare try to talk to him. If only I saw him by myself, maybe I would try. I sometimes wish I could talk to the teacher easily like I talk Ojibway to Mom. But I wouldn't dare, I'd be too embarrassed. (Slipperjack 1987, 77–78)

Still, she likes English stories (written in the book that she reads at school as opposed to the stories told by her community): "I love the stories in our English lesson. I always leaf through the book far ahead, sometimes to the end when I'm supposed to be writing" (Slipperjack 1987, 92).

In an interview with Hartmut Lutz, Ruby Slipperjack comments on whether her novel *Honour the Sun* is autobiographical:

> Some of the things that are in there were taken out of sequence, things I had seen and heard in different places and times, filled in with fiction to complete the story and make it *seem* real. You know, when you are writing, things pop into your head. It is a part of me. I think when you look at it, it is a part of everybody else because there is one thing that we all have in common. We were all children at one point, so we all feel

> at certain points in our childhood, "Yes, I remember doing that, or I remember feeling like that!" (Slipperjack in Lutz 1991, 204–205)

The novel is based on personal experiences put in the fictional world. Slipperjack succeeds in presenting the world from a child's perspective. In the book we find many descriptions, characteristic for the autobiographical genre, such as that of The Owl's Mom (Slipperjack 1987, 10), family (11), and The Owl herself (14), which are present at the beginning of the novel. Daniel David Moses commented on it in the following way:

> I think our cultures probably allow us to be more autobiographical than the mainstream .... I think it comes from the attitude that everyone is an individual spirit with something unique to say which is important in the life of the entire community. And most Native writers are, as I said before, speaking first to their own community. (Moses/Goldie 1998, xxviii)

As The Owl grows up, she moves from the stage of listening to the stories, both traditional and those told by the members of her community, to listening to silences. It is her mother who introduces her to the world of the silence:

> 'Always listen to the silence. When you feel your emotions all in turmoil inside you, listen to the silence...'
>
> Softly, Mom's voice trails away, as if she were only thinking out loud.
>
> How do you listen to the silence when silence doesn't have a noise? Or does it? I sit and listen. I can hear my heart beat, my breathing, a bird chirp from across the bay, Brian breaking branches somewhere, a slight wind overhead above the trees, a train coming, a dull hum in the air, and always my heartbeats. I smile at Mom. Yes, it is very calming. (Slipperjack 1987, 184)

Although the girl does not understand it at the very beginning, she starts feeling good listening to the silence. She finds it tranquillizing and thus "more and more, [she] spend[s] time sitting by the woodpile, listening to the silence" (Slipperjack 1987, 185). Also here Slipperjack uses repetition as the main structural device repeating the phrase "Silence, listen to the silence" (189, 197). Through the repetition she also stresses the importance of silence and the ability to listen to it.

However, not all of the novel is about the blissful adventures of a teenage girl. In the background we also find references to different forms of danger, represented by alcohol, drunks who attack the vulnerable cabin, kill dogs, and beat up and rape women. The Owl feels hatred inside and claims she could kill the drunks, but her pain is silenced; she feels empty inside (Slipperjack 1987, 36). Experiences like that of residential schools, various relationships, different forms of violence and abuse are presented through the multiple meanings of silence. In Slipperjack's open-ended narrative, the loss of contact between The Owl and her mother resulting in the disruption of the story transmission alludes to the impact of colonization. "Given the many facets and the ambiguity of silence, the question arises: how can individuals decipher meaning when silence is subject to such diverse interpretations?" (Horne 1998, 127).

Underlying the social dimension, spiritual inheritance, and (re-)discovery of one's Native identity, the Anishinabe author Ruby Slipperjack leads her protagonist to recognize the value of the Ojibway culture and perpetuate it as her own. Throughout the novel the character's close relationship to the natural world and Native ways of life is stressed. Through telling the stories of (and for) her people, "Slipperjack ... enacts the role of the traditional Native story-teller by telling the story that is instructive and which communicates cultural knowledge to reaffirm and strengthen Native beliefs and values" (Salat 1996, 76).

Conclusion

Slipperjack's novel is an example of contemporary Native fiction which shows that, despite colonization and its politics of destroying Native cultures, storytelling adjusts to the passing of time. The present understanding of the term "storytelling" is no longer considered as the opposite to the written tradition of the white man. Contemporary Native North American fiction is a hybrid fiction, consisting of both the oral and the written. In fact, a contemporary Native writer becomes a storyteller or rather a storywriter, while a reader is no longer a "reader" but a reader-listener. This opens up a possibility of a dialogue not only between the writer and the reader as it exists between the storyteller and the listener; now the dialogue is also possible between the storyteller and the reader, as well as the writer and the listener, which indicates the contemporary fusion of the oral and the written.

Bibliography

Bowerbank, Sylvia, and Dolores Nawagesic Wawia. (1996). "Wild Lessons: Native Ecological Wisdom in Ruby Slipperjack's Fiction." In *Homemaking: Women Writers and the Politics and Poetics of Home*, eds. Catherine Wiley and Fiona R. Barnes. New York: Garland, 223–238.

Eigenbrod, Renate. (1995). "The Oral in the Written: A Literature between Two Cultures." *Canadian Journal of Native Studies, 15:1*, 89–102.

———. (2000, March). "Reading Indigenity from a Migrant Perspective: Ruby Slipperjack's Novel *Silent Words*—'Log Book' or Bildungsroman." ESC, *26:1*, 79–93.

Fontaine, Phil. (1993). "We Are All Born Innocent." In *Residential Schools: The Stolen Years*, ed. Linda Jaine. Saskatoon, SK: University Extension Press, Extension Division, 51–68.

Frey, Rodney. (1995). *Stories That Make the World: Oral Literature of the Indian Peoples of the Inland Northwest.* Norman, OK: University of Oklahoma Press.

Grant, Agnes. (1999). "'Great Stories Are Told': Canadian Native Novelists." In *Native North America: Critical and Cultural Perspectives*, ed. Renée Hulan. Toronto, ON: ECW Press, 122–134.

Gunn Allen, Paula. (1992). *The Sacred Hoop: Recovering the Feminine in American Indian Traditions.* Boston, MA: Beacon Press.

———. (1995). "Teaching American Indian Literatures." In *Studies in American Indian Literature: Critical Essays and Course Designs*, ed. Paula Gunn Allen. New York: Modern Language Association, 33–37.

Horne, Dee. (1998). "Listening to Silences in Ruby Slipperjack's *Silent Words.*" SCL/ÉLC, 23:2, 122–137.

Hoy, Helen. (2001). "'Listen to the Silence': Ruby Slipperjack's *Honour the Sun.*" In *How Should I Read These? Native Women Writers in Canada.* Toronto, ON: University of Toronto Press, 64–80.

King, Thomas. (1996). "Native Literature of Canada." In *Handbook of Native American Literature,* ed. Andrew Wiget. New York: Garland Publishing, 353–370.

Lutz, Hartmut. (1991). *Contemporary Challenges: Conversations with Canadian Native Authors.* Saskatoon, SK: Fifth House Publishers.

———. (2002). "Native Literatures in Canada Before Oka: An Introduction." In *Approaches: Essays in Native North American Studies and Literatures.* Augsburg: Wißner, 109–125.

Maracle, Lee. (1992). "Oratory." *Give Back: First Nations Perspectives on Cultural Practice.* Women Artists Monographs. North Vancouver, BC: Gallerie Publications, 86–93.

Moses, Daniel David, and Terry Goldie. (1998). "Preface to the First Edition: Two Voices." In *An Anthology of Canadian Native Literature in English,* eds. Daniel David Moses and Terry Goldie. 2nd ed. Oxford: Oxford University Press, xix–xxix.

Salat, M. F. (1996). "Other Words, Other Worlds: Of Ruby Slipperjack." In *Intersections: Issues of Race and Gender in Canadian Women's Writing,* eds. Coomi S.Vevaina and Barbara Godard. New Delhi: Creative Books, 74–89.

Silko, Leslie Marmon. (2001). "Language and Literature from a Pueblo Indian Perspective." In *Nothing but the Truth: An Anthology of Native American Literature,* eds. John Purdy and James Ruppert. Upper Saddle River, NJ: Prentice Hall, 159–165.

Slipperjack, Ruby. (1987). *Honour the Sun.* Winnipeg, MB: Pemmican Publications, l987.

———. (1991). "Interview with Hartmut Lutz." In *Contemporary Challenges: Conversations with Canadian Native Authors,* ed. Hartmut Lutz. Saskatoon, SK: Fifth House Publishers, 203–216.

———. (1992). *Silent Words.* Saskatoon, SK: Fifth House Publishers.

———. (2000). *Weesquachak and the Lost Ones.* Penticton, BC: Theytus Books.

———. (2002). *Little Voice.* Regina, SK: Coteau Books.

PRINT MEDIA AND FILM

Robert Harding

Aboriginal Child Welfare: Symbolic Battleground in the News Media

Foreword

Over the last three decades, dozens of First Nations have negotiated the devolution of delegated responsibility for child welfare, and many more are in the process of negotiating such agreements. A study, conducted in 2004, found that daily newspapers in British Columbia report on Aboriginal management of child welfare services in ways that undermine their aspirations to design and deliver culturally appropriate services to their people. Control over child welfare may be seen as a symbolic battleground where the inherent right and ability of Aboriginal people to govern themselves and exercise control over their own lives is at stake.

This article is based on *selected* findings[1] of a major study on news coverage of Aboriginal child welfare issues that was supported by a Social Sciences and Humanities Research Council Small Universities Grant administered by the University of the Fraser Valley (UFV). This research was made possible by the diligence and hard work of two part-time research assistants, Jeremy Harder and Paul Johnston, who took time out from their studies in the Bachelor of Social Work program at UCFV to assist with data collection.

INTRODUCTION

Aboriginal people in Canada have identified control over child welfare as critical not only to the health of Aboriginal children, families and communities, but also to the survival of diverse cultures and languages. Over the last two decades, many First Nations have negotiated the devolution of delegated responsibility for child welfare, and many more are in the process of negotiating such agreements.

This project builds on research into stereotyping conducted by the 1996 Royal Commission on Aboriginal Peoples (RCAP) and on a more recent study that examines the way in which "common sense" about Aboriginal people is constructed in the press. In its comprehensive assessment of the representation of Canadian Aboriginal peoples in the media, the RCAP concluded that three damaging stereotypes of Aboriginal people are perpetuated in all forms of public discourse: victims, warriors, and environmentalists. In "The Media, Aboriginal People and Common Sense," it was found that newspapers report on Aboriginal child welfare agencies and workers in ways that undermine Aboriginal aspirations to design and deliver culturally appropriate services to their own people (Harding 2005).

Marnie McCall defines child welfare as a "field of social service practice in which the state, operating through specific statutory law, takes over 'functions normally carried out by parents for their children'" (1990, 347). Throughout British Columbia, as in other parts of Canada, First Nations are being delegated authority for Aboriginal child welfare by the provincial governments. Thus, an Aboriginal child welfare news story is one that references Aboriginal people (including "Indian," "Native," "First Nation," "Métis," and "Inuit") *and* is one that involves state child welfare authorities or delegated Aboriginal child welfare authorities. Stories about Aboriginal child welfare issues occurring outside British Columbia, but reported in the province's newspapers, are also included.

Techniques of content analysis are applied to news stories about Aboriginal child welfare issues in the *Vancouver Sun, Vancouver Province* and *Times-Colonist*. The 131 articles considered in this study represent *all news items*, including op-ed pieces, which reference Aboriginal child welfare issues during three complete years—1993, 1998 and 2003. The research is organized around four main questions:

1. What are the dominant patterns in news coverage of Aboriginal child welfare issues?
2. Are the stereotypes that were identified by the 1996 RCAP reflected in news stories about Aboriginal child welfare issues?
3. Are other stereotypes present?
4. How has news coverage of Aboriginal child welfare issues changed?

The first three questions are applied to 2003 news texts, while the last question focuses on continuities and discontinuities in news coverage in the years 1993, 1998 and 2003.

Two types of content are considered in this study. First, elements of *manifest content* that are physically present and countable are analyzed (for example, mentions of a particular topic or number of front page stories). As well, *latent content* is examined through an interpretive reading of the symbolism underlying the physical data (for instance, assessing whether a particular news story contains stereotypes or is sympathetic to Aboriginal interests).

For each newspaper article, a coding form was completed and the results entered into a spreadsheet. The specific research questions are reflected in the structure and design of the coding tool and associated coding protocol (see appendix B). The protocol provides guidelines for coding, definitions of terms used in the coding form, and a selection of choices available for each category. For example, for "Orientation of Aboriginal People to Non-Aboriginal Society/Institutions," the coder is offered the following eight options: "Conflict," "Negotiation," "Collaboration," "Participation in system," "Excluded from system," "Taking advantage of system," "Other—write in," and "Does not apply." The coding sheet is divided into five sections (see appendix A):

Publication Details: headline and sub-headline, date of coding, newspaper, date of coding, story location, page number, month and day of month, year, genre, name of author;

Aboriginal Child Welfare Topics Present: twenty-three Aboriginal child welfare topics are listed; provision is also made for writing in topics not included on the list;

Actors and Roles: up to six actors could be named (three Aboriginal and three non-Aboriginal); six role options for each actor were provided: "none," "victim," "hero," "villain," "survivor," and "other" (which could be written in);

Aboriginal Identity of Aboriginal Actors for all three Aboriginal actors: nine options were available: "First Nation," "Métis," "Inuit," "Canadian Aboriginal person(s) identified as being in one of the above three categories," "Pan-Indian," "Native American(s)," "Other indigenous person—write in," "Unknown," "Does not fit";

Other Attributes of the Article:

Stereotypes of Aboriginal People Present (provision made for up to three stereotypes per article): drawn from a list of five with an "Other" that could be written in;

Main Theme (if not Opinion Piece) or Prescription (if Opinion Piece): provision made for a twenty-word summary;

Sympathetic/unsympathetic to Aboriginal Interests and Issues: options include "Sympathetic," "Unsympathetic," "Neutral," or "Does not fit";

Portrayal of Orientation of Aboriginal People to non-Aboriginal Society/Institutions (check one): this allows the coder to select one of the following eight options: "Conflict," "Negotiation," "Collaboration," "Participation in the system," "Excluded from the system," "Taking advantage of the system," "Other—write in," and "Does not apply";

Photo(s) and Description: allows for up to a fifteen-word description of the photo(s) attached to an article;

Buzz words/phrases: allows for listing up to three key words or phrases used by the author. "Buzz" words and phrases are lexical choices of the journalist that are "loaded," used sarcastically, contain hidden meanings, take poetic license and/or represent "editorializing" —that is, injecting his or her personal opinion into the article;

Comments: allows for up to twenty additional words of commentary by the coder.

Sections A and B are designed to record and count basic manifest features of the content under study, while sections C, D, and E incorporate interpretive analysis of latent content.

Findings

Topics

An analysis of the overall distribution of *primary topics* and *topics mentioned* over significant periods of time may yield insights into what news the media deem significant in the area of Aboriginal child welfare. Topics "mentioned" are those topics that are *referenced* in articles, but not deemed to be primary topics. The most prevalent topics mentioned in 2003 were "foster care" (mentioned in 64 percent of articles), "BC provincial ministry—Children and Family Development" (45 percent), followed by "abuse/neglect of a child" (33 percent). The press was preoccupied with three broad areas of Aboriginal child welfare: conduct of Aboriginal child welfare agencies; interventions and outcomes for children; involvement of the provincial government, including the Ministry of Children and Family Development (MCFD).

Figure 5.1 Top five topics mentioned in 2003

TOPIC MENTIONED	APPEARED IN PERCENT OF NEWS TEXTS
Foster Care	64%
Provincial Ministry (BC) – Children and Family Development	45%
Abuse/Neglect of a Child	33%
Provincial Government (BC) – Generic Reference	31%
Death of a Child	25%

Note: Provision is made for the inclusion of more than one 'topic mentioned' per news item.

An examination of primary topics in news texts illustrates that Aboriginal child welfare agencies have become significant actors in public discourse about child welfare. For example, the active pursuit by Aboriginal child welfare agencies of the repatriation of Aboriginal children from non-Aboriginal care figured prominently in 2003 news texts. While four out of every ten articles (41 percent) focused on repatriation that year, only 5 and 3 percent of news items had this as their primary topic in 1993 and 1998 respectively.

By 2003, 60 percent of all news stories about Aboriginal people focused on the *actions* or *behaviour* of Aboriginal child welfare agencies—either on their role in repatriation efforts or on an appraisal of their performance or management.

Figure 5.2 Top five primary topics in 2003: Percentage of news texts in which a topic was deemed to be the primary topic

PRIMARY TOPIC	APPEARED IN PERCENT OF NEWS TEXTS
Repatriation of Aboriginal Children from Non-Aboriginal Care	41%
Review of an Aboriginal Child Welfare Agency	11%
Other Issue – Management of Aboriginal Child Welfare Agency	8%
Abuse/Neglect of a Child	6%
Death of a Child	6%

Figure 5.3 Emerging child welfare topics: Primary topic as a percentage of total primary topics

PRIMARY TOPIC	1993	1998	2003
Management of Aboriginal Child Welfare Agency	0%	3%	8%
Review of Aboriginal Child Welfare Agency	0%	0%	11%
Repatriation of Aboriginal Children from Non-Aboriginal Care by Aboriginal Child Welfare Authority	5%	3%	41%
Total	5%	22%	60%

It is also interesting to consider *what was not covered* by the press. A number of significant Aboriginal child welfare stories went underreported or unreported altogether in 2003. High profile programs designed to provide healing for victims of abuse in the residential school system were the focus of only two news stories, while traditional child welfare practices of Aboriginal people—supported by First Nations child welfare agencies—were not covered at all. It is difficult to assess whether these "blind spots" are random or systematic. Some media commentators have pointed out that some of the most glaring blind spots in the Canadian media are related to the "consequences of social inequality" (Hackett et al. 2000, 193). Many of the difficulties Aboriginal children, families and communities experience today are directly attributable to over a century of oppressive state policies and practices that created vast material and social disparities between Aboriginal and non-Aboriginal people.

Roles of Actors in News Stories

An examination of the roles of actors in news stories[2] reveals significant differences in the ways Aboriginal actors are treated as compared to their non-Aboriginal counterparts. In all three years—1993, 1998, and 2003—Aboriginal actors were most frequently portrayed as "Victims" (43 percent, 51 percent and 43 percent of Aboriginal actors, respectively). In 1993 and 1998, the second most likely characterization of Aboriginal actors was of "Survivors" and "Heroes" (both at 31 percent). On the other hand, in all three years, non-Aboriginal actors were most likely to be characterized as either "Heroes" or "Villains."

In 2003, Aboriginal actors were much more likely to be cast in the role of "Villain" (28 percent of Aboriginal actors) than in previous years. By comparison, the proportions of Aboriginal actors assigned this role in 1993 and 1998 were negligible (2 and 7 percent respectively). However, in 2003, Aboriginal actors were most likely to be portrayed as "Victims" (43 percent of Aboriginal actors). Only 13 percent of Aboriginal actors were depicted as "Heroes." In contrast, approximately one out of two non-Aboriginal actors was constructed as a "Hero" (49 percent of non-Aboriginal actors). Thirty-one percent of non-Aboriginal actors were depicted as "Villains."

These findings reveal significant differences in the degree to which the news media ascribe *free will* to Aboriginal and non-Aboriginal people. Aboriginal actors *are* accorded *agency* when they act in ways that cause harm to their own people or others ("Villains"). However, the rest of the time, Aboriginal actors are most likely to be cast as *passive recipients* of the consequences of the actions of other actors or events beyond their control ("Victims" or "Survivors"—combined 54 percent). Non-Aboriginal actors, on the other hand, are much more likely to be depicted as active participants in news events (77 percent).

Orientation of Aboriginal People to Non-Aboriginal Society and Institutions

In 1993, the relationship of Aboriginal people to mainstream society was characterized in binary terms. Predominantly, Aboriginal people were portrayed as either in conflict with Euro-Canadian society and institutions (36 percent of articles) or in collaboration with them (23 percent). Five years later, Aboriginal people were still frequently depicted as being in conflict mode. However, they were also seen as engaged in a variety of other types of relationships with non-Aboriginal society. Aboriginal people were alternatively portrayed as "forced into" participating in non-Aboriginal systems and institutions (14 percent); willingly participating in these systems (12 percent); negotiating with non-Aboriginal institutions and systems (12 percent); or engaged in their own parallel systems and institutions (8 percent).

By 2003, binary representations of Aboriginal people in public discourse were being replaced by more complex representations of Aboriginal/non-Aboriginal relationships. Aboriginal people are increasingly seen as being engaged in diverse interactions with Euro-Canadian institutions—which run the gamut from outright conflict to collaboration—some of which are of their own choosing and making.

Furthermore, in nearly six out of ten 2003 news texts, Aboriginal people were portrayed as participating in their own parallel systems (25 percent) or negotiating with non-Aboriginal systems (33 percent). The image of Aboriginal people *in conflict* with Euro-Canadian systems, so prominent in news coverage from 1993 and 1998, had all but disappeared by 2003 (6 percent). These findings suggest that news media are beginning to come to terms with Aboriginal aspirations to negotiate the devolution of services—such as education and child welfare—from non-Aboriginal authorities and to operate their own programs and services in culturally appropriate ways.

Figure 5.4 Changing relationships of aboriginal people to Euro-Canadian society:

Occurrence of relationship mode as a percentage of total news texts

TYPE OF RELATIONSHIP	1993	1998	2003
Conflict	36%	41%	6%
Negotiation	5%	12%	33%
Collaboration	23%	5%	17%
Participation in System	9%	12%	8%
Excluded from System	0%	1%	8%
Taking Advantage of System	0%	4%	3%
Participating in Parallel System	14%	8%	25%
"Forced" Participation in System	14%	14%	0%

Note: Percentages for 1993 do not add up to exactly 100 percent due to rounding off, while percentages for 1998 add up to only 97% because the coder determined that the relationship descriptors did not apply to two news texts.

Sympathy and Antipathy to Aboriginal Issues and Interests in the News

Operationalizing what "sympathetic" is for the purposes of this research inevitably involves an element of arbitrariness and subjectivity. However, it is important to attempt to assess what Richard Ericson, Patricia Baranek and Janet Chan refer to as "sides presented and side favoured" (1991, 168). In their ground breaking study of representations of crime, law and justice in the Canadian media, these researchers found that individual news stories are usually one sided and make no attempt to present two or more sides of issues (172). Rick Ponting and Roger Gibbins place media outlets on an "Indian Sympathy Index" in order to assess the degree to which publications are sympathetic to Aboriginal concerns (1980). Others gauge sympathy to Aboriginal people involved in the news based on whether news stories reflect "anti-Native" or "pro-Native" themes (Skea 1993–94, 20).

In this study, whether or not a news item is sympathetic to Aboriginal interests and issues is determined by assessing the answers to a series of questions about each article:

1. Is a stereotype(s) of Aboriginal people invoked?

2. Does the article have an "anti-Aboriginal" slant? The answer to this question is "yes" if the answers to both the following questions are "no."

3. Are the context and/or history of the issue presented?

4. In news items which present the views of non-Aboriginal people, are the views of Aboriginal people also presented?

The most striking feature of the comparative data from the three years is the dramatic reduction in the proportion of news stories that are sympathetic to Aboriginal issues and interests. In both 1993 and 1998, approximately two-thirds of all news articles (64 percent and 67 percent respectively) were sympathetic compared to less than one-third of 2003 news items. More than half of 2003 news texts were unsympathetic (56 percent), and only one in seven articles were deemed to be "neutral."

The fact that more than half (52 percent) of child welfare news stories in 2003 focused on two contentious issues—repatriation initiatives and reviews of Aboriginal child welfare agencies—may partially account for the high percentage of unsympathetic news stories about Aboriginal child welfare. Efforts by Aboriginal child welfare agencies to repatriate Aboriginal children from non-Aboriginal substitute care are routinely *problematized* in the press. Since reviews of the actions of Aboriginal child welfare agencies are typically conducted after tragic events, such as injuries or deaths of children under care, it may be predicted that the resulting news coverage would be framed in critical terms. Furthermore, as Aboriginal institutions, such as child welfare agencies, begin to assume control over areas of jurisdiction—and their corresponding budgets—previously held by non-Aboriginal authorities, they are increasingly being constructed in news discourse as a threat to Euro-Canadian interests.

Figure 5.5 News stories are increasingly unsympathetic to Aboriginal interests: Percentage of total news texts that is sympathetic, unsympathetic or neutral

RESPONSE	1993	1998	2003
Sympathetic	64%	67%	31%
Unsympathetic	23%	10%	56%
Neutral	14%	23%	14%

Note: Percentages for a given year may not add up to exactly 100 percent due to rounding off.

Stereotyping

The two most significant changes in stereotyping from 1993 to 2003 are the overall increase in stereotyping and the emergence of new stereotypes about Aboriginal people in news coverage. In 1993, only 23 percent of news items contained stereotypes. By 1998, the proportion of articles with stereotypes had declined slightly (18 percent), but by 2003, more than two-thirds of news stories (69 percent) contained stereotypes. What is noteworthy about stereotyping in 2003 is that the stereotypes identified by the RCAP in 1996 were largely absent from news coverage of child welfare issues. Traces of only the

Aboriginal People as Victims stereotype (in 8 percent of articles) were found in 2003 news coverage of child welfare issues. The stereotype of "Aboriginal People as Warriors" was present in only one of thirty-six articles, while the notion of "Aboriginal People as Environmentalists" is wholly absent from 2003 news texts.

However, two emergent stereotypes figured prominently in the news: "Aboriginal Child Welfare Agency as Bully" (33 percent), and "Incompetent or Corrupt Managers/Administrators" (22 percent). The latter stereotype was first identified in 2002 (Harding 2005, 322, 324). The emergence of new stereotypes has occurred during a time in which Aboriginal people have increasingly been challenging the status quo and taking control over institutions that have a decisive impact on their lives. It may be that many Canadians see Aboriginal campaigns for self-governance primarily in terms of the threat they pose to *their* lifestyle and standard of living. John Burrows suggests that when Aboriginal people advocate control of their own affairs, "Canadians obviously feel they have little stake in that message, other than what 'they' think 'we' take from 'them' in the process" (2002, 140).

Figure 5.6 Stereotyping is the "new normal" in 2003: Percentage of total news texts in which stereotypes appear

Stereotype of Aboriginal People	1993	1998	2003
Victim	14%	4%	8%
Warrior	5%	4%	3%
Environmentalist	0%	0%	0%
People who Take Advantage of the System	0%	4%	3%
Incompetent or Corrupt Manager/Administrator	5%	3%	22%
Aboriginal Child Welfare Agency as Bully	0%	3%	33%
Total Percentage of Articles with Stereotypes	23%	18%	69%

It is not surprising that as Aboriginal people continue to assume control over publicly-financed budgets for service areas such as child welfare, they will come under greater scrutiny by the media. However, this alone does not account for the overwhelmingly negative, and even hostile, tone of much of the coverage. Perhaps, contrary to the impression of Aboriginal incompetence and corruption conveyed by emerging stereotypes, it is *competent* and *empowered* Aboriginal people and institutions that pose the greatest threat to the status quo.

Discussion

The nature of discourse about Aboriginal child welfare issues in the British Columbia press looks very different in 2003 than it did in 1993. The focus of news coverage has shifted from *interventions* (e.g., adoption, foster care) and *outcomes* (e.g., injuries, abuse) for Aboriginal children in the child welfare system to the *conduct* of Aboriginal child welfare agencies and workers. Furthermore, Aboriginal child welfare issues are less likely to be portrayed sympathetically than they were in 1993, overall stereotyping of Aboriginal people has increased and damaging news stereotypes have emerged in the press, notably that of "Aboriginal People as Incompetent" or "Corrupt Managers of Child Welfare Services."

Aboriginal Agency

In the three years of news texts examined in the research, there was a high degree of continuity in terms of role assignment. As in 1993, significant differences exist between the types of roles assigned to Aboriginal actors as opposed to non-Aboriginal actors in 2003 news stories. Aboriginal actors are still predominantly constructed as "Victims," while non-Aboriginal actors are typically portrayed as "Heroes." Regardless of whether non-Aboriginal actors are assigned roles that have negative ("Villain") or positive ("Hero") connotations, they are usually given roles that assume they are *active participants* in the events recounted in news stories. The association of Aboriginal actors with victimhood, on the other hand, not only conjures up old stereotypes about Aboriginal people, but it also identifies them as *passive recipients* of the actions of others or events beyond their control.

The myth of the inability of Aboriginal people to exercise control over their lives has informed social policy since early colonial times and is reflected in current legislation such as the Indian Act, which defines Status Indians as "wards" of the state. Mainstream media representations of Aboriginal people as lacking in *agency* perform a strategic function for proponents of the status quo. If a majority of the public can be convinced that Aboriginal people are unable to exercise control over their lives, they may be less likely to support the devolution of authority to Aboriginal institutions or treaty negotiations that lead to the wholesale transfer of significant resources and government powers to First Nations. Canadian governments pay close attention to public opinion about Aboriginal matters, regularly commissioning expensive polling on a wide range of issues (Ponting/Kiely 1997). If opinion polls indicate a lack of public support for self-governance, governments may assign a low priority to negotiations with Aboriginal people and even adopt policies that obstruct their initiatives to gain more autonomy. A major factor in the lack of public support for self-governance and other Aboriginal initiatives is *economic conservatism*, which has been "found statistically to produce antagonism [on the part of the Canadian public] towards aboriginals and their preferred policies" (184).

While it is not possible to determine with any degree of precision the extent to which public opinion influences government policy and action, it is clear that governments are mindful of public opinion, especially on contentious issues, and make every effort to sway public sentiment in favour of government interests. For example, in an effort to manage public opinion during the events at Oka in 1990, the federal government secured the services of National Public Relations, the largest public relations company in Quebec. The result was that "Brian Mulroney conducted the press like a symphony, choosing when to speak and delivering carefully scripted words that were part of a larger public relations campaign" (Winter 1992, 251).

Decontextualization and Public Opinion

Over half the articles analyzed in 2003 are unsympathetic to Aboriginal interests and issues. Many of these news texts focus on attempts by Aboriginal people to deliver culturally appropriate services and strengthen their communities. Yet news stories about the conduct of Aboriginal child welfare agencies are frequently discussed in isolation to the historical context of the state's assimilationist child welfare policies. In many news stories, no Aboriginal sources are quoted at all. The public is best able to make sense of the challenges Aboriginal people face in delivering culturally appropriate child welfare programs to their own people *when* these issues are presented in light of the full context of Aboriginal child welfare. Contextual factors include the history of residential schools; the state's experiments in mass cross-cultural adoption such as the "Sixties Scoop";[3] the challenging nature of developing institutional child welfare expertise and infrastructure with few resources; chronic *underfunding* of Aboriginal child welfare agencies; and the highly complex nature of child welfare work generally, especially in situations of extreme poverty.[4]

In 2003 news coverage, efforts by Aboriginal child welfare agencies to repatriate children from non-Aboriginal foster or adoptive homes were reported on with little or no reference to the residential school system or the widespread apprehension and "adoption out" of Aboriginal children by non-Aboriginal child welfare authorities that occurred in the 1960s and 1970s and is still, to some extent, occurring today. In the latter case, not only were the individual outcomes for thousands of these children disastrous, but many communities lost the majority of their young people, and First Nations sustained considerable damage to their distinct languages and cultures. The determination of First Nations to undo the damage done by over a century of repressive government policies and ensure their cultural *survival* is reflected in their unflinching efforts to take control of child welfare and staunch the flow of their children into non-Aboriginal settings. In the absence of basic information about issues like repatriation, readers may interpret the actions of Aboriginal authorities as heavy-handed, unjust and in violation of "conventional" child welfare principles—such as *the welfare of the child comes before all else*—and prime Western values, such as *each individual receives identical treatment*. Furthermore, simplistic and decontextualized news coverage of complex and emotive issues like repatriation provides fertile soil for emergent stereotypes such as "Aboriginal Child Welfare Agency as Bully." In 2003, headlines frequently set the tone for stereotypical coverage of Aboriginal child welfare authorities (see fig. 5.7).

Figure 5.7 Selected 2003 headlines (British Columbia newspapers)

HEADLINE	NEWSPAPER	DATE
Dead baby's kin riled that dad will duck jail: 'Stupid native healing circle' doesn't wash after plea bargain	The Province	28 January
Toddler's removal highlights worry over native kids' well-being	The Province	18 July
Heartbreak in the name of cultural sensitivity	Vancouver Sun	21 July
Torn between two families	The Province	3 August
Bureaucrats, natives hurting two teens they claim to care for	The Province	5 September
Girls beg band not to make them move	The Province	12 September
Sisters plead to stay with their family: Teenagers caught in cross-cultural dispute	Times-Colonist	24 October
Putting individual rights first	Times-Colonist	25 October
Hundreds of native kids in line to suffer the same fate	The Province	31 October
Sto:lo agency blamed in child's death	The Province	7 November
4,500 aboriginal children in care face an uncertain future	The Province	28 November

Along with lead paragraphs, headlines "summarize what media outlets consider most important ... and are also the most likely aspect to be recalled by the audience to define the situation at a later time" (Lambertus 2004, 6). In this study, Aboriginal child welfare agencies are constructed in news headlines as a threat to non-Aboriginal families and to a prime Euro-Canadian value—that of "individual rights." They are also portrayed as endangering or harming their own children. Finally, even though these headlines reference situations involving a variety of First Nations, only one headline mentions a specific First Nation, and four others conflate diverse cultural identities into "Native."

Decontextualized representations of Aboriginal people have been the norm in the Canadian news media for many years. While Aboriginal people have always represented themselves in the context of their own distinct cultures and histories, "Europeans frequently neglected to inquire about this context and instead assumed it away and substituted a European imperial context" (Lischke/McNab 2005, 4). By further entrenching the communication gulf between Aboriginal people and other Canadians decontextualized representations of Aboriginal issues perpetuates social inequality and may serve to reinforce racist attitudes.

Aboriginal Child Welfare as a Symbolic Battleground

While this study examined news coverage about a wide variety of child welfare topics, three out of five 2003 news texts are preoccupied with the conduct of Aboriginal agencies or workers.[5] This represents a major shift in news coverage. In 1993 and 1998, only 5 percent of articles had the conduct of Aboriginal child welfare agencies or workers as their primary focus. It is almost as if, in news discourse, the very ability of Aboriginal people to run their own lives is on trial.

Undeniably, the eleven-year period covered by the research represents a time of transition in the field of Aboriginal child welfare, one where Aboriginal authorities increasingly began to assume, or more accurately regain, control over child welfare matters. At the very least, the intense scrutiny of Aboriginal child welfare agencies that has emerged in the news indicates that Aboriginal people have experienced some success at putting self-governance issues on the media's agenda. However, news about Aboriginal-run child welfare services and programs is framed predominantly in ways that undercut the credibility of the Aboriginal authorities involved. The majority of 2003 news texts are unsympathetic to the situation of Aboriginal people, and close to two-thirds rely on stereotyping. While approximately eight out of ten articles in 1993 and 1998 contained no stereotypes about Aboriginal people, stereotypes were found in nearly seven out of ten 2003 news texts. The two most prominent stereotypes cast doubt on the ability of Aboriginal people to effectively operate their own programs and services.

Aboriginal control over child welfare and education is essential to the cultural and linguistic survival of Aboriginal peoples. In the 20th century, the practices of coercing parents to send their children to residential schools and "abducting" Aboriginal children and placing them in non-Aboriginal homes and institutions inflicted enormous harm on the identity, culture and language of Aboriginal communities. Control over child welfare is of strategic importance, since it affords Aboriginal people the opportunity to demonstrate their ability to deliver culturally appropriate services to their own people. Effective management of these programs by Aboriginal people advances the case for increased autonomy from non-Aboriginal institutions, and, ultimately, for self-government itself, which has direct implications for the distribution of resources and tax revenue.

The field of child welfare may be seen as a symbolic battleground where the inherent right and ability of Aboriginal people to govern themselves and exercise control over their lives is at stake. Yet the mainstream news media largely ignore the history of state intervention in Aboriginal child welfare and the larger implications of the contemporary contest for control of child welfare, instead focusing on coverage that calls into question the devolution of authority for child welfare from provincial governments to First Nations. While many First Nations have assigned "their highest priority" to "acquiring the legal, social and financial resources to care for their own" (Fournier/Crey 1997, 230), very few news stories explore *why* Aboriginal leaders feel this is so important.

Across Canada, this program of devolution is well under way. Over the last thirty years, numerous First Nations across Canada have negotiated the devolution of delegated responsibility for child welfare services. Unfortunately, many Aboriginal child welfare agencies have experienced difficulty in taking on this responsibility due to the provision of "meagre financial resources and virtually no professional support" by provincial governments (Fournier/Crey 1997, 231). In effect, these child welfare authorities have been set up to fail. Yet the connection between inadequate government support and the difficulties experienced by Aboriginal agencies is not explored in news coverage. Nor are news reports about tragic outcomes of Aboriginal-operated child welfare programs placed in the context of the precarious and problematic nature of child protection work generally.

Evidently, it is not in the best interests of the mainstream media to connect Aboriginal child welfare matters to larger issues. In news discourse, Aboriginal child welfare is routinely discussed in isolation from the question of Aboriginal self-government. Nowhere does the news media provide a forum for the discussion of the historical role played by racism and colonialism in the difficulties being experienced in contemporary Aboriginal families and communities. A debate of this nature would potentially strengthen the case for self-government and create a new discourse about racism in dominant society.

Conclusion

Many of the news texts analyzed in this study, particularly those focussing on the behaviour of Aboriginal authorities, are framed in binary terms, where the relationship between non-Aboriginal and Aboriginal people is characterized as "us" versus "them." In 2003, Aboriginal actors were much more likely to be seen as "villains" than in previous years; emerging stereotypes imply that Aboriginal child welfare workers and managers are either corrupt or incompetent or both, and the tone of most news coverage is decidedly unsympathetic. The empowerment of Aboriginal child welfare authorities represents a challenge to the hegemony of Euro-Canadian values, since these agencies utilize a communal approach to child-rearing rather than the individual nuclear family model favoured by non-Aboriginal child welfare authorities. Successful Aboriginal child welfare agencies also threaten to disrupt the distribution of resources between Aboriginal and non-Aboriginal people, because they strengthen the case of Aboriginal people for jurisdiction over other areas of governance and for self-government as a whole. Sandra Lambertus observes that polarized news reporting of conflicts over resources between Aboriginal and non-Aboriginal people predisposes those Canadians who may be unaware of the "historic context of disputes, are otherwise ambivalent, or have already come to negative conclusions about Native protests" to be unsympathetic to Aboriginal causes (2004, 201).

In news discourse about Aboriginal child welfare, *what is unsaid* in news reports may have as great an influence on the production of meaning as *what is said*. A lack of information about the history and context of complex issues limits the interpretative choices available to audiences, particularly to those audience members who do not already possess or have access to more detailed or nuanced information on those issues. On the other hand, the inclusion of an historical backdrop to contemporary issues would create a genuine opportunity for news audiences to understand the structural inequality facing Aboriginal people in general as well as specific Aboriginal attempts to seek redress, such as the devolution of authority for child welfare to Aboriginal communities.

Future research needs to focus on developing strategies that incorporate Aboriginal voices in mainstream news discourse, challenge dominant representations of Aboriginal people in the press, and ensure that the context and history of important issues is included in news reports about Aboriginal people.

Endnotes

1 While this article is based on content analysis of 131 news texts appearing in three *major daily newspapers* in 1993, 1998 and 2003, the larger project included analysis of 291 newspaper articles in three major daily newspapers *and* five community newspapers in *five* separate years.

2 An individual or any body of individuals, including community, First Nation, organization, government department or ministry, social movement, association and business, may be designated as the "primary actor."

3 The "Sixties Scoop" refers to the adoption practices of non-Aboriginal child welfare agencies in the 1960s and 1970s. During these two decades, child welfare authorities in Manitoba and other provinces dispatched as many as 15,000 Aboriginal children to the "homes of white middle-class couples in Canada and the United States, on the assumption that these couples would make better parents than low-income families on Indian reserves and in Métis communities .... [These children] were submerged in another culture, and their native identity soon disappeared. They became a lost generation" (York 1992, 202–206). Aboriginal communities had virtually no input into the wholesale apprehension of their children by non-Aboriginal social workers acting on behalf of provincial child welfare authorities. The "patronizing" nature of these social workers and child welfare agencies has been compared to that of Canada's early missionaries and colonial government officials (Crey 1991, 155).

4 Many Aboriginal people in Canada live in extreme poverty and have living conditions that resemble those of people in developing countries. Research on child abuse conducted at the University of Toronto School of Social Work indicates that there is a strong, "undeniable link between poverty and disadvantage and the pressure that pushes a small number of parents to hurt their children" (Philp 2001, A3). Due to the low socioeconomic status of many Aboriginal families, attributable in no small part to the legacy of state policies of racism and economic marginalization, Aboriginal people are in a high risk group for child abuse and a variety of other social problems. Yet, in news discourse, problematic outcomes for children under the care of Aboriginal child welfare agencies are rarely discussed in the context of these structural issues.

5 Sixty-one percent of news texts in major daily newspapers in 2003 focused on five primary topics: Financial Management of Aboriginal Child Welfare Agency; Other Issues Relating to the Management of Aboriginal Child Welfare Agency; Review of Aboriginal Child Welfare Agency; Performance of Child Welfare Social Worker (Aboriginal Agency); and Repatriation.

Bibliography

Burrows, John. (2002). *Recovering Canada: The Resurgence of Indigenous Law.* Toronto, ON: University of Toronto Press.

Crey, Ernie. (1991). "The Children of Tomorrow's Great Potlatch." In *In Celebration of Our Survival: The First Nations of British Columbia,* eds. Doreen Jensen and Cheryl Brooks. Vancouver, BC: UBC Press, 150–158.

Ericson, Richard V., Patricia M. Baranek, and Janet B. L. Chan. (1991). *Representing Order: Crime, Law, and Justice in the News Media*. Toronto, ON: University of Toronto Press.

Fournier, Suzanne. (2003, January 28). "Dead Baby's Kin Riled That Dad Will Duck Jail: 'Stupid Native Healing Circle' Doesn't Wash after Plea Bargain." *The Province*, A1.

———. (2003, November 7). "Sto:lo Agency Blamed in Child's Death." *The Province*, A16.

Fournier, Suzanne, and Ernie Crey. (1997). *Stolen from Our Embrace: The Abduction of First Nations Children and the Restoration of Aboriginal Communities*. Vancouver, BC: Douglas and McIntyre.

Hackett, Robert A., et al. (1999). *The Missing News: Filters and Blind Spots in Canada's Press*. Aurora, ON: Garamond Press.

Harding, Robert. (2005). "The Media, Aboriginal People, and Common Sense." *Canadian Journal of Native Studies, 25:1*, 311–336.

Lambertus, Sandra. (2004). *Wartime Images, Peacetime Wounds: The Media and the Gustafsen Lake Standoff*. Toronto, ON: University of Toronto Press.

Lischke, Ute, and David T. McNab. (2005). "Introduction." In *Walking a Tightrope: Aboriginal People and their Representations*, eds. Ute Lischke and David T. McNab. Waterloo, ON: Wilfrid Laurier University Press, 1–17.

McCall, Marnie L. (1990). "An Analysis of Responsibilities in Child Welfare Systems." *Canadian Journal of Family Law, 8:2*, 345–370.

McKnight, Peter. (2003, July 21). "Heartbreak in the Name of Cultural Sensitivity." *The Vancouver Sun*, A6.

McLellan, Wendy. (2003, August 3). "Torn between Two Families." *The Province*, A16.

Mulgrew, Ian. (2003, October 24). "Sisters Plead to Stay with Their Family: Teenagers Caught in Cross-cultural Dispute." *Times-Colonist*, A1.

Philp, Margaret. (2001, March 14). "Poverty Increases Child Abuse Risk, U of T Study Finds." *Globe and Mail*, A3.

Ponting, Rick J., and Roger Gibbins. (1980). *Out of Irrelevance*. Toronto, ON: Butterworth.

Ponting, Rick J., and Jerilynn Kiely. (1997). "Disempowerment. 'Justice,' Racism, and Public Opinion." In *First Nations in Canada: Perspectives on Opportunity, Empowerment, and Self-Determination*, ed. Rick J. Ponting. Toronto, ON: McGill-Hill Ryerson, 152–192.

"Putting Individual Rights First." (2003, October 25). *Times-Colonist*, A10.

Royal Commission on Aboriginal Peoples. (1996). "Renewal: A Twenty-Year Commitment." In *Report of the Royal Commission on Aboriginal Peoples*. Vol. 5, part 4. Ottawa, ON:

Canada Communications Group.

Skea, Warren H. (1993–1994). "The Canadian Newspaper Industry's Portrayal of the Oka Crisis." *Native Studies Review, 9:1*, 15–27.

Thompson, Joey. (2003, July 18). "Toddler's Removal Highlights Worry over Native Kids' Well-being." *The Province*, A5.

———. (2003, September 5). "Bureaucrats, Natives Hurting Two Teens They Claim to Care For." *The Province*, A8.

———. (2003, September 12). "Girls Beg Band Not to Make Them Move." *The Province*, A10.

———. (2003, October 31). "Hundreds of Native Kids in Line to Suffer the Same Fate." *The Province*, A5.

———. (2003, November 28). "4,500 Aboriginal Children in Care Face an Uncertain Future." *The Province*, A5.

Winter, James. (1992). "Showdown at the Oka Corral." James Winter. *Common Cents: Media Portrayals of the Gulf War and Other Events*. Montreal, QC: Black Rose.

York, Geoffrey. (1992). *The Dispossessed: Life and Death in Native Canada*. Toronto, ON: Little, Brown and Co.

Appendix A: Aboriginal Child Welfare Issues Coding Sheet

A. Publication details

Headline ______________________________

Sub-Headline ______________________________

Newspaper ______________________________

Coder ______

Date of coding ______

Story location ______

Page number (s) ______

Day of the month ______

Month ______

Year ______

Genre ______________________________

Name(s) of Author(s) ______________________________

Author #1 ______________________________

Author #2 ______________________________

Author #3 ______________________________

B. Aboriginal Child Welfare Topics Present (00 = Absent, 01 = Primary, 02 = Mentioned)

Provincial government (generic reference) ______

Provincial Ministry – Child & Family Development ______

Provincial Ministry – Community, Aboriginal & Women's Services ______

Other Provincial Ministry

Specify ______________________________

Federal government (generic reference) ______

Department of Indian & Northern Affairs Canada ______

Other Federal Department or Agency

Specify ______________________________

Foster Care ______

Death of child ______

Injury to child ______

Abuse/Neglect of child ______

Financial Management of Aboriginal child welfare agency ______

Other issue re: Management of Aboriginal child welfare agency ______

Review of Aboriginal child welfare agency ______

Government funding of child welfare programs ______

Performance of child welfare social worker (Aboriginal Agency) ______

Performance of child welfare social worker (non-Aboriginal Agency) ______

Aboriginal Healing ______

Traditional Cultural Practices ______

Other Aboriginal Child Welfare Topic ______

Specify ______________________________

Non-Aboriginal Child Welfare Topic ______

Not relevant ______

Repatriation of Aboriginal child by Aboriginal authority ______

C. Actors and Roles

1. Aboriginal Actors

1. Actor #1 ______________________________

Role ______________________________

2. Actor #2 ______________________________

Role ____

3. Actor #3 ____

Role ____

2. Non-Aboriginal Actors

1. Actor #1 ____

Role ____

2. Actor #2 ____

Role ____

3. Actor #3 ____

Role ____

D. Aboriginal Identity of Aboriginal Actors

1. Actor #1 ____

2. Actor #2 ____

3. Actor #3 ____

E. Other Attributes of Article

1. Stereotype(s) of Aboriginal People Present ________ (no = 00, yes = 01)

Stereotype #1 ______

Stereotype #2 ______

Stereotype #3 ______

2. Main Theme (if not opinion piece) or Prescription (if opinion piece)

Summarize: ____

____

3. Sympathetic/unsympathetic to Aboriginal Interests and Issues ______

4. Aboriginal People's orientation to non-Aboriginal Society/Institutions (Check one)

1. Conflict ______
2. Negotiation ______
3. Collaboration ______
4. Participation in system ______
5. Excluded from system ______
6. Taking advantage of system ______

7. Other ______

8. Does not apply ______

5. Photo(s) ______

Description

____

____

6. Buzz words/phrases:

1) ____

2) ____

3) ____

7. Comments:

____

____

Appendix B: Coding Protocol

Aboriginal Child Welfare Issues Research Project
Robert Harding
School of Social Work & Human Services
Winter 04

Part A: Publications Details

1. Headline and Sub-headline

The variable will be completed (not coded) with the full text of the headline and, if applicable, sub-headline.

2. Newspaper Number

Values:

01 Vancouver Sun
02 Vancouver Province
03 Times-Colonist
04 Chilliwack Times
05 Chilliwack Progress
06 Abbotsford Times
07 Abbotsford News
08 Mission City Record

3. Coder

The variable will be completed (not coded) with the initials of the individual coding the article.

4. Date of Coding

The variable will be completed (not coded) for the month and day of the month that the article was coded; for example, Oct. 21.

5. Story Location

Front Page of newspaper	= 01
Pages 2 to 5 of Front Section of newspaper	= 02
Other Location	= 03
Information not available	= 04

6. Page Number

The variable will be completed (not coded) for the **section** of the newspaper, if applicable, and the **first** page number assigned to the article, followed by a comma and the **second** page number. For example, a news item appearing in Section D, beginning on page 1 and continuing on page 4 would be coded as 'D1,4.'

7. Day of Month

The variable will be coded for the value representing the day of the month of the article's publication.

Values:

01 through 31

8. Month

The variable will be coded for the value representing the article's month of publication.

Values:

01. January
02. February
03. March
04. April
05. May
06. June
07. July
08. August
09. September
10. October

11. November
12. December

9. Genre

The variable will be coded for the value representing the type of news item.
Values:

01. hard news
02. soft news
03. editorial
04. named staff columnist
05. named guest opinion writer
06. syndicated columnist
07. named writer but status unknown
08. other – write in

10. Name(s) of Author(s)

The variable will not be coded. The coder is to write in the name of the writers (the names of up to three authors), where this information is available. If the name(s) of a specific journalist is not given, then the coder should record the name of the source to which the news item is attributed (Editorial, Staff, CP, Southam News Service, Reuters, AP, etc.).

Part B: Aboriginal Child Welfare Topics Present

Definition of Child Welfare

"A field of social service practice in which the state, operating through specific statutory law, takes over 'functions normally carried out by parents for their children" (McCall, 1990, 347).

In many parts of BC, First Nations have been delegated authority for child welfare by the provincial government (which in turn has had authority for the child welfare of "Status Indians" delegated to it by the federal government).

Thus, an Aboriginal child welfare topic includes any story involving Aboriginal people (incl. "Indian," "Native," "First Nation," "Métis," "Inuit") in which state child welfare authorities or delegated Aboriginal child welfare authorities are involved, however peripherally. Stories about Aboriginal child welfare issues occurring outside BC, but reported in BC Newspapers, will also be included.

Each topic value will be coded for whether it is absent (00), the primary topic discussed (01), or just mentioned (02) in the piece. The coder must take extra care to code the value 'mentioned' for any explicit mention of the Aboriginal child welfare topic.

Part C: Actors and Roles

The coder should select the role descriptor that best reflects the ***predominant*** role played by the actor in the news item. Thus, selecting "Victim" as the predominant role of the actor does not preclude the possibility that the actor is also, to a lesser extent, being portrayed as a survivor.

Aboriginal Actor and Role

Primary Aboriginal Actor(s)

The variable will be coded for the value representing the position/role held by the **primary Aboriginal actor** mentioned within the central Aboriginal child welfare topic of the article (e.g. Grand Chief – AFN, Treaty Negotiator). Be sure to maintain a log of descriptors of actors that you can share with the other coders to ensure that common language is used by all coders. An individual or any body of individuals, including community, First Nation, Aboriginal organization, government, social movement, association and business, can hold the primary Aboriginal actor role.

Role of Primary Aboriginal Actor(s)

The variable will be coded for the value that represents the role played by the

primary actors directly involved in a past, existing or potential Aboriginal issue within the central Aboriginal child welfare topic. If "Other Role" (05), write in.

Values:
00. None
01. Victim(s) – Individual(s) caused physical, mental, economic, political or social harm with their involvement in an Aboriginal related issue.
02. Hero(es) – Individual(s) improving the physical, mental, economic, political, safety or situation for other individuals with their involvement in an Aboriginal related issue.
03. Villain(s) – Individual(s) causing physical, mental, economic, political or social harm with their involvement in an Aboriginal-related topic.
04. Survivor(s) – Individual(s) improving their own personal physical, mental, economic, political, safety or social situation during their involvement in an Aboriginal related issue.
05. Other Role – write in.

Non-Aboriginal Actor and Role

Primary Non-Aboriginal Actor(s)

The variable will be coded for the value representing the position/role held by the **primary non-Aboriginal actor** mentioned within the central Aboriginal child welfare topic of the article. An individual or any body of individuals, including community, government, government ministry or department, political party, social movement, association and business, can hold the primary non-Aboriginal actor role (e.g., Minister of Indian Affairs, Federal Treaty Negotiator, Premier).

Role of Primary Non-Aboriginal Actor(s)

The variable will be coded for the value that represents the role played by the **primary non-Aboriginal actors** directly involved in a past, existing or potential Aboriginal child welfare issue within the central Aboriginal topic. If "Other Role" (05), write in.

Values:

00. None
01. Victim(s) – Individual(s) caused physical, mental, economic, political or social harm with their involvement in an Aboriginal related issue.
02. Hero(es) – Individual(s) improving the physical, mental, economic, political, safety or situation for other individuals with their involvement in an Aboriginal related issue.
03. Villain(s) – Individual(s) causing physical, mental, economic, political or social harm with their involvement in an Aboriginal-related topic.
04. Survivor(s) – Individual(s) improving their own personal physical, mental, economic, political, safety or social situation during their involvement in an Aboriginal related issue.
05. Other Role – write in.

Part D: Aboriginal Identity of Aboriginal Actors

Values:

01. First Nations (status & non-status Indians, not incl. those identified as Métis)
02. Métis
03. Inuit
04. Canadian Aboriginal person (s) identified as being in one of above 3 categories
05. Pan-Indian (especially for organizations or movements that represent multiple categories of Aboriginal people)
06. Native American (s)
07. Other indigenous person (s) (e.g., transnational Aboriginal person) – write in
08. Unknown
09. Does not fit

Part E: Other Attributes of the News Item

1. Stereotypes of Aboriginal People Present

If stereotypes not present, code 00 for none, if present, code 01. Each news item can have multiple stereotypes present (values 01 through 06)

Aboriginal People as:
01. Pathetic Victims
02. Angry Warriors
03. Noble Environmentalists
04. Incompetent or Corrupt Managers/Administrators – Aboriginal people as incompetent or corrupt at managing finances or services
05. Taking Advantage of the System
06. Other (write down)

The first three stereotypes refer to the typology elaborated in the 1996 Report released by the Royal Commission on Aboriginal Peoples (RCAP). The RCAP concluded that, in most mainstream media, Aboriginal people were portrayed as fitting into one of these three broad stereotypical categories. Stereotypes 04 and 05 emerged out of a pilot study conducted by the researcher in 2002.

2. Main Theme (if not Opinion Piece) or Prescription (If Opinion Piece)
The variable will be completed (not coded) for the coder's summary of the main theme of the article in 20 words or less or a 20 word summary of the prescription or advice offered by the editorialist/opinion writer to address the Aboriginal issue raised in the piece. The prescription is the solution or direction that the writer says should be taken to solve or resolve the problem or issue raised in the piece. If the piece offers no solution or prescription then the coder must write no position.

3. Sympathetic/ Unsympathetic to Aboriginal Interests and Issues
The coder must choose one of the following four options:
Values:
01. Sympathetic
02. Unsympathetic
03. Neutral
04. Does Not Fit

Answers to the following questions will serve as a guide for the coder.

1. Is a stereotype(s) of Aboriginal people invoked?
2. Does the article have an "anti-Aboriginal" slant? The answer to this question is "yes" if the answers to **both** the following questions are "no."

a) Is the context and/or history of the issue presented?
b) In news items which present the views of non-Aboriginal people, are the views of Aboriginal people also presented?

If the answer to ***either*** question #1 ***or*** #2 is "yes," then the article is coded as 02 – unsympathetic. If the answers to questions #1 and #2 are both "no," then the coder needs to decide whether the news items is sympathetic, neutral or "does not fit."

4. Portrayal of orientation of Aboriginal People to non-Aboriginal society/ institutions

Choose (with a check mark) only one of the following descriptors. If more than one applies, select the one that is predominant in the article.

Values:

01. Conflict
02. Negotiation
03. Collaboration
04. Participation in system
05. Excluded from system
06. Taking advantage of system
07. Other – write in
08. Does not apply

5. Photos Attached to Article

Is there a photo or photos attached to the article? Values are 00 for no photo and 01 for photo(s) attached. If there is a photo (s) describe in 15 words or less.

6. Presence of Buzz Words/ Phrases in Article

Buzz words and phrases are the actual words and phrases of the journalist that wrote the article (not the words/phrases of sources quoted in the news item) that

· contain hidden meanings
· are "loaded"
· are used sarcastically
· represent "editorializing" or injecting the writer's personal opinions and views into the article (in news items other than "opinion pieces"
· are subjective or take poetic license

7. Comments

Any other aspect of the news item that the coder considers noteworthy.

Steffi Retzlaff

'The Elders have said' – Projecting Aboriginal cultural values into contemporary news discourse

Introduction

In recent years, it has become obvious that Aboriginal people in Canada are growing stronger in their assertiveness as "nations within," as distinct peoples with a right to self-determination, land and resources, and treaty concessions. The evolving status of Aboriginal people is mediated through a powerful discourse that challenges the existing paradigm. This discourse in the media can be analyzed using various linguistic concepts and models. This article examines how Aboriginal people in Canada represent themselves and their issues in their own media and how they counteract and resist the dominant discourse in Canada by (re)constructing and (re)affirming positive Aboriginal identities.

Using various linguistic concepts and models, a number of strategies can be identified, which Aboriginal people writers of newspaper articles employ to (re)construct and (re)affirm positive identities and specific world views, thereby asserting the status of Aboriginal people as distinct peoples with special rights and a collective memory. I am aware of the danger of talking about "one" Aboriginal discourse. There is no such thing as a monolithic Aboriginal culture but many different Aboriginal nations with distinct histories and cultures and thus with a variety of discursive practices. However, their common history of internal colonialism and discrimination, including destruction or even loss of identity and language, loss of land, and intense suffering, forms part of a collective memory which is reflected in their discursive practice today. Furthermore, in their struggle for self-determination and their efforts to revitalize Aboriginal cultures and languages, Aboriginal people in Canada pursue a variety of common goals and thus employ similar strategies to talk about the world and to create membership categories. I use the term "Aboriginal discourse" to refer to a distinctive discursive practice in contrast to a Euro-Canadian discourse, that is, the hegemonic discourse of Canada.

The Aboriginal discourse is based partly on Aboriginal discursive models; positive self-presentation; and the propagation and consistent use of key items of terminology. This division, however, serves mainly structural purposes. The discursive features of each of these categories necessarily overlap in their (multi)functionality. The three main categories and associated linguistic realizations will be illustrated, in turn, in the following three sections.

Aboriginal Discursive Models

The Aboriginal discourse is shaped by various properties of traditional discourses, which are used for projecting cultural values in contemporary contexts and for positively (re)affirming Aboriginal identities. These properties include, cultural address markers; the concept of family and emphasis on later generations; pronouncements by Elders; the concept of the Medicine Wheel and of Turtle Island.

Explicit references or allusions to these features are linguistically realized through repetition, which has also been identified as a typical discourse feature of Aboriginal text and talk. As Lisa Philips Valentine points out, repetitions are a typical discourse feature of Aboriginal text and talk (1995, 202). In her analysis of orally transmitted teachings and legends in Algonquian languages, she notes that in many narrative texts repetitions of phrases or lines occur. Repetitions are used throughout as a means of adding force to particular parts of the story and also serve as a local structuring device. With regard to repetition in Aboriginal storytelling Roger Spielmann notes, "They appear to be most noticeable at crucial points in the story and thus may be considered to be instrumental in the structuring of the narrative" (1998, 200). Generally, the function of such repetition is quite clear: to enhance and make the repeated proposition more prominent in order to be communicatively more effective.[1]

Cultural Address Markers

I use the term cultural address markers to identify opening or closing formulae in an Aboriginal language, for example, Ojibway, Mohawk and Lakota Sioux phrases such as *Aaniin/Ahnee, Boozhoo, Sago, Onah, Meegwetch/Miigwetch, Nia:wen*, or *Mitakuye Oyasin*:

> *Aaniin*! Greetings everyone. There are very few things in this world today that challenge us more as Nations than the retention and restoration of our First Nation languages. (Fontaine 2000, 5)[2]

> I would like to say *Miigwetch* to all who made this week possible ... Special *Miigwetch* to our Chief and Council, band manager and bookkeeper ... (Stone 2000, 13)

Cultural address markers can be found in many texts in Aboriginal newspapers. *Aaniin*, for example, is Ojibway and considered a greeting and opening formula establishing the right context for an exchange. It is generally translated as "hello." The different spelling alternatives (e.g., "*Ahnee*," "*Aanii*," or "*Aániin*") represent different dialects and are due to the fact that no standard spelling system exists for all Aboriginal languages.

Traditionally, it seemed necessary in encounters between individuals or groups to establish a degree of rapport or solidarity before discussing any matter of substance. Special importance was assigned to the process of establishing and maintaining contact. The cultural address markers identified above can be seen as still fulfilling this contact and relational function of language. This goes hand in hand with Valentine's observations that "members of an English-speaking Algonquian community may include symbolic uses of Ojibwe or Cree in discussions with English-speaking Iroquoian community members, predicated on their assumption that Native language use is a demonstration of aboriginal solidarity" (1999, 341).

However, the Ojibway concept of *Aanii* and *Boozhoo* is broader than that expressed by any simple English translation. It covers not only the conventionalized amenities of greeting, but also symbolizes a more general and, above all, a more spiritual engagement. Uttering *Boozhoo* is a greeting, an invitation, and an agreement, an acknowledgment and thanking of the participants (including the spirit forces) at the same time, meaning "Show me the light of your being." The speakers agree to shed light on their being so that all of their darkness disappears. "We are going to embark on a spiritual journey when our light is one."[3] This "unity of minds," which must be achieved before engaging in any other action, has been identified for the Haudenosaunee as well. Michael K. Foster speaks of a "ritualization of the contact or phatic function of language in certain Iroquois religious and political settings" (1988, 22). He discusses the importance of encounter and welcoming sequences for the Haudenosaunee, through which a "unity of mind" and "goodness of mind" is achieved.

In a circular fashion, many Aboriginal news texts close with a specific cultural address marker. *Meegwetch,* for example, is Ojibway and is translated as "thank you." But again, *meegwetch* suggests a broader range of meaning than that designated by the English verb "to thank." By uttering *meegwetch,* a general feeling of happiness and gratitude over the existence of something or someone is expressed as well as a spiritual connection.

Mitakuye Oyasin is translated as "All my relations." In the *First Nations Messenger* and the *Anishinabek News* it is usually used as both opening and closing marker. *Mitakuye Oyasin* embodies a very important notion for most—if not all—Aboriginal people. It is a core concept in the Aboriginal perspective on life; it reflects awareness that one is related to all things in the universe. This deep spiritual knowledge that all things are related goes back to creation. All things come from the Creator and are endowed with His spirit. As the Ojibway writer Basil Johnston explains, "There are four orders in creation. First is the physical world; second, the plant world; third, the animal world; last, the human world. All four parts are so intertwined that they make up life and one whole existence. With less than four orders, life and being are incomplete and unintelligible. No one portion is self-sufficient or complete, rather each derives its meaning from and fulfils its function and purpose within the context of the whole creation" (1998, 21).

For Aboriginal people the notion of relatives goes far beyond one's own family and even beyond the concept of extended family or community. *Mitakuye Oyasin* includes, for example, the land as relative as well as Mother Earth and everything that sprang from her. This feeling of interconnectedness with Mother Earth and everything else, the stars, the animals, the trees and rivers, the rocks and the winds, creates an immanent sense of respect for everything and everybody because one is in the presence of relatives. The Medicine Wheel (fig. 5.1) is the visual representation of *Mitakuye Oyasin*. *Mitakuye Oyasin* is repeatedly used in Anishinabek ceremonies and in individual prayers. Every ritual is done in the context of "All my relations." By uttering this phrase, one acknowledges all of creation and invites the relatives into the sacred space and time being honoured.[4]

I contend, therefore, that cultural address markers reflect an Aboriginal discourse principle. They are used performatively in that they constitute the act they mean. The speakers or writers of these words are not only saying or writing something; they are actually doing something (Austin 1962, Searle 1969, 1979).[5] Aboriginal terms, such as *Aanii, Boozhoo, Meegwetch, Sago, Onah, Nia:wen,* and *Mitakuye Oyasin,* in the context of print media discourse, still perform their original function. By using them, the writer not only constructs and affirms social identities and relationships because the Aboriginal person is expected to know the underlying spirituality and meanings implied by those words as part of their identity as a member of their nation, but he or she also performs the action of thanking, greeting and acknowledging (in a much broader sense than the English verbs suggest), as well as inviting and communicating with all relatives. Seen as performatives, they are multifunctional in terms of their illocution and contain concepts that are considered semantically distinct in the English language (to thank versus greet versus invite versus acknowledge). It follows that the English language does not provide the concepts needed to communicate with the spirits and the Creator. "The English language takes the people to a certain level but cannot go beyond. It is not a spiritually based language."[6] In summary, cultural address markers contribute to the revitalization of Aboriginal languages, demonstrate Aboriginal solidarity and fill the "concept-gap," by using Aboriginal expressions where the English expressions fail due to the incongruity of Native and non-Native worldviews.

The Concept of Family

The notion of family is very broad and does not only encompass the nuclear family but expands to the community, to the level of individual nations, and includes past and future generations. This is frequently illustrated by phrases such as those in the examples below:

> None of us are to blame for history's effects on *our families, communities, nations* or ourselves. (Wagamese 2000, 6, emphasis added)

> I consider myself fortunate and am extremely grateful to *my parents, grandparents and extended family members* that I am able to speak the Anichinabe language. Because of *my family and community* I have retained the ability to speak my language .... For those of us who can already speak our language, it begins with speaking it at every opportunity we can, especially to *our children and grandchildren* in the home. What is learned and spoken in the family home is the basis upon which *our children and grandchildren* begin their lives and their understanding of the world .... Only by working together as *individuals, families, communities and Nations* will we be able to ensure that our Indigenous languages ... will be completely restored. (Fontaine 2000, 5, emphasis added)

Traditionally, the family was composed of those who worked together and who were bound not only by ties of kinship but also by friendship and responsibility. This extended family was both the largest unit of economic cooperation and the primary system for the socialization of the children. Therefore, by repeatedly using certain words and phrases related to the semantic field of "family" in the (extended) Aboriginal sense of the term, Aboriginal writers establish not only lexical cohesion but also a collective identity among various Aboriginal people, which, in turn, produces a sense of social unity. Collaborative group processes, which include family, extended family, and community members, emphasize traditional Aboriginal values of community that are very much needed in today's individualistic world. As Fyre Jean Graveline notes,

> The knowledge that each person is responsible for his or her actions In-Relation to the larger community is a fundamental shared belief.... We are able to see ourselves and our immanent value as related to and interconnected with other—family, community, the world, those behind and those yet to come .... We are taught that we must, each in our own way and according to the dictates of our own conscience, attend to communal responsibilities. (1998, 57–58)

In projecting traditional values, such as seeing oneself related to and interconnected with others (in family, community, and nation), Aboriginal writers create an awareness that the personal accountability of each individual is important for the welfare of all.

Pronouncements by Elders

Another frequently employed discursive strategy is the appeal to authority by referring to Elders. Linguistically, this is realized by the frequent use of phrases such as "our Elders have always told us," "the Elders have said" or "our Elders tell us":

> *Our Elders have always told us* that our treaties will survive as long as the sun shines, the grass grows and the rivers flow. The treaties are sacred documents that are an expression of our nationhood. *The Elders have also said* the treaties are living, breathing documents and I have always believed this to be so. (Switzer 1999, 4, emphasis added)

> *The Elders have told us* that without our language we might survive, but we will not be whole and we will be cut off from our knowledge, spirituality and our true identity forever. *Some Elders have said* that if effective action is not taken soon, we, as people, will also become extinct. (Fontaine 2000, 5, emphasis added)

The reference to Elders and what they have said is not only significant in terms of textual properties. More important is what is contextual or extra-linguistic—the communicative function—and thus, the social dimension of such a discourse structure. The legacy of Elders, their role and responsibility as teachers and transmitters of culture, which was discouraged and interrupted by imposed Euro-Canadian systems such as the residential schools, is being retrieved and honoured again. The Elders' contributions are very much needed in a time of change and resistance. Their knowledge, advice and teachings still (or continue to) play a significant role in and are part of the Aboriginal discourse in modern-day Canada.

As may have already been noted, there is a stylistic preference to capitalize the word "Elder." This language choice indicates respect towards Elders, their knowledge, wisdom and achievements. Furthermore, the Elders are quoted indirectly and the term "Elders" is used generically, in that no specific Elders are mentioned. This is generally the case when this discourse strategy is used. However, in news reports the credentials of the person stating something are significant. Title and name of the source providing the information are important attributions for the accountability of what is reported (Bell 1991, 190–193).

In Aboriginal news texts, on the other hand, one rather finds the phenomenon of the unnamed source, as in "Some Elders have said," or "Our Elders tell us." As mentioned above, Elders are one of the most important sources of authority and knowledge. They do not have to be named explicitly, since the traditions and the traditional knowledge they pass on have been proven and time honoured. Reporting what the Elders have said thus carries a historic dimension and adds to the force of a collective memory by expressing a proposition that is in line with what "they" have said before. Spielmann has identified the appeal to personal experience and the defusing of contrary opinions with an appeal to authority as an important device within oral Ojibway discourse. He describes the function of this discourse strategy as implying something like, "This isn't just me that believes this and I didn't just make it up. I'm passing down something that has been taught among our people for generations" (1998, 179). Thus, to state the views of Elders in newspaper discourse adds credence and commitment to what the writer intends to communicate.

Medicine Wheel

Aboriginal writers also make use of a traditional concept or symbol that is shared in one form or the other by almost all Aboriginal people of North and South America (Bopp et al. 1985). This concept is known as the Medicine Wheel, the Sacred Hoop or the Sacred Circle. The Medicine Wheel is a teaching tool and a representation of traditional spirituality, philosophy, and psychology. It is usually presented in the form of a circle.

The Medicine Wheel stands for the togetherness of people and nations, for unity and power, for spirit as well as for the cyclical nature of everything. It is the visual presentation of "All my relations," symbolizing the belief that human beings are only one part of the universe and that all things are interrelated. Central to the teachings of the Medicine Wheel is the goal of living a good life, meaning people should try to balance within themselves the facets of all four quadrants of the wheel and respect them equally (Whiskeyjack 2000, online). The Medicine Wheel can be expressed and interpreted in many ways: the four seasons, the four winds, the four elements, the four cardinal directions, the four colours symbolically representing the four different types of people in the world, the four aspects of human nature, and many other relationships that can be expressed in sets of four. There are different but related versions of the Medicine Wheel for different Aboriginal nations.

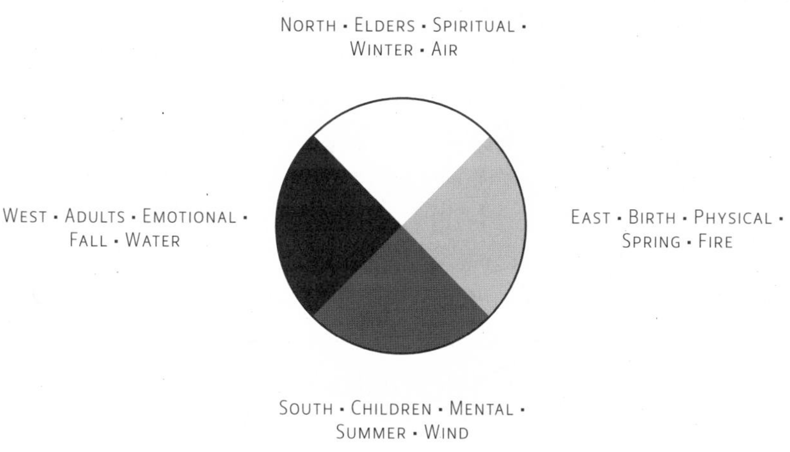

Figure 13.1 Medicine Wheel

Although not explicitly labelled as such, the news excerpts below refer to the notion or idea of the Medicine Wheel:

> It has taken me 36 years of writing to learn something about journalism, but one Anishinabek teaching taught me a lot more about truth ... The teaching deals with the *four original gifts of the Four Directions* we believe the Creator gave to the Anishinabe. (Switzer 2001, 10, emphasis added)

> Our Elders tell us that we must deal with the whole *circle*: the *mental, physical, emotional* and *spiritual* dimensions of health; *the child, the adolescent, the adult* and *the Elder; the individual, the family, the community* and *nation*. All are connected. We must keep the circle strong. (Fontaine 1999, 5, emphasis added)

In latter example, the author directly asserts three dimensions of the Medicine Wheel, namely the four aspects of human nature—the mental, the physical, the emotional and the spiritual, as well as the four stages of life: childhood, adolescence, adulthood and Elders. With the third dimension—individual, family, community and nation—the writer also alludes to the concept of self-in-relation[7] and to the notion of extended family. The author's mentioning of the circle and of the relationships expressed in sets of four, the "Four Directions," as well as the reference to the interconnectedness of it all, is usually associated with the symbol of the Medicine Wheel in many Aboriginal nations. It does not explicitly have to be labelled as such. The elements mentioned are sufficient clues for the culturally initiated to deduce that somebody is talking about the Medicine Wheel.

For Aboriginal people, the circle referred to in the latter example is not just any circle but the expression of a particular world view. It continues to play a central role in Aboriginal cultures and Aboriginal writing of all sorts, specifically in Aboriginal literature. The Okanagan writer Jeannette Armstrong, for example, emphasizes that the parallels between the structure of contemporary Aboriginal novels and the image of the circle are intentional. Talking about her own writing, she remembers being asked, "'Is this accidental that there are four parts [in your novel] and it's like the four Directions, and there are the prologue and the epilogue being the direction above us and below us?'" and Armstrong replied, "'No, it wasn't actually'" (Armstrong in Lutz 1991, 20).

Turtle Island

One key word from the lexical set of Aboriginal people is "Turtle Island." It has a very specific meaning particularly for Aboriginal nations from Eastern Canada, such as the Anishinabek and the Haudenosaunee. In the creation stories of these nations the earth was formed on the back of a giant turtle from a handful of soil scooped from the bottom of the sea by a small, brave animal. The metaphor and related concept of Turtle Island does not exist, for example, on the Northwest Coast or on the Prairies and is therefore rarely used in the discursive practice of the Aboriginal nations of these regions. However, in Aboriginal discourse "Turtle Island" has become a pan-Indian term helping to establish a national identity. As the following examples suggest, it has become a form of imaginative identification with Aboriginal symbols and values that contrast the symbols and discourses of the dominant society:

> When Columbus landed on the shores of what is now the Dominican Republic, there were more than 300 Native American languages. Today 175 of these survive, 53 of them still spoken in *Turtle Island North* (Canada). (Switzer 2000, 10, emphasis added)

> There is diversity among our First Nations. Our cultures are distinctly different. In spite of suppression of successive colonial governments and churches, our uniqueness as original citizens of *Turtle Island* has withstood assimilation and colonialism. (Coon Come 2000, 5, emphasis added)

In the former example, one nation (and identity) is constructed through reference to a national territory: "Turtle Island North (Canada)." Ruth Wodak et al. have pointed out that the discursive construction of "a national body" includes references to a land base, national resources and landscapes as well as to local and geographical borders (1999, 158). The usage of the term "Turtle Island North" implies that a "Turtle Island South" exists. The question then is whether the latter term is used for South America and/or for the territory of the United States. In fact, various examples can be found in Aboriginal (news) discourse in which "Turtle Island" refers to North and South America.[8] More often, however, the symbolic community of "Turtle Island" is constructed in discourse to refer to North America—including Canada, the United States, Mexico and Central America—because the landmass is shaped like a turtle.[9]

By using the phrase "original citizens of Turtle Island" in the latter example, the writer creates a general and unified identity for Aboriginal people in contemporary Canada. The term "citizens" presupposes the existence of a nation. In combination with the prepositional phrase "of Turtle Island," "citizens" is intertextually linked to another area within the Aboriginal discourse, namely to that of treaty-making. Treaties between the Crown and Aboriginal inhabitants were made on an assumed nation-to-nation basis. Therefore, the author's use of the phrase "citizens of Turtle Island" supports the view that Aboriginal people belonged to distinct nations and had governmental structures even before contact; this is a view that is generally held and confirmed by the Aboriginal population in Canada. Moreover, the common element in the construction of "the nation of Turtle Island" is not so much a common culture or language, but a shared history of internal colonialism: "In spite of suppression of successive colonial governments and churches, our uniqueness as original citizens of Turtle Island has withstood assimilation and colonialism" (Coon Come 2000, 5). Regardless of considerable diversity in actual historical experience and tradition on the part of individuals and groups, the notion of a shared past and intense suffering forms part of a collective memory that defines important elements in a pan-Indian identity (Jarvenpa 1992, 129). And as Ovide Mercredi and Mary Ellen Turpel note: "We see ourselves as distinct peoples with inherent rights which exist because of our history on this land, this place we collectively refer to as Turtle Island" (1993, 106).

The nation "Turtle Island" is separated from the state (of Canada). It reflects the status of Aboriginal people as "nations within" and, most importantly, it is an explicit reference to creation reflecting different ways of looking at the world. Using the term "Turtle Island" rather than "Canada" in Aboriginal (news) discourse is thus a choice of signification and an act of resistance as it opposes descriptions and interpretations of the perspective of a cultural outsider, for example the Euro-Canadian account of history that tells of only "two founding nations."

Positive Self-presentation

Positive self-presentation of Aboriginal realities and identities is used to counteract prevailing stereotypes and to valorize Aboriginal life and experiences. This positive self-presentation of Aboriginal people and their issues is achieved through various linguistic means. These include, argumentative structures, attribution of agency and process, foregrounding of positive characteristics, and employment of the high value modals "must" and "will."

Argumentative Structures

In controlling their own media, Aboriginal people ensure that their histories and contemporary issues are told from their own perspectives, particularly when it concerns topics that are handled very differently in the mainstream media. One topic that figures prominently in Aboriginal discourse is the debate about treaties and their implementation. In using linguistic representations, which foreground the validity of the treaties and the inconsistency of argumentation on the Canadian Government's side, Aboriginal people positively affirm their view of history and demonstrate credibility. The example below serves as an illustration where the author employs logical reasoning in the form of an argument-counterargument structure, linguistically realized through the linking of ideas using the coordinating conjunction "but." The author reproaches non-Aboriginal people saying that their arguments are inconsistent. This inconsistency is exemplified by three arguments directly following one another:

> The 1760 treaty between the British Crown and the Mi'kmaq is 'ancient' and should not be binding, they say, *but* still cling to the sanctity of the 1763 Treaty of Paris by which France ceded to Britain most of the eastern mainland of North America after the Seven Years War. Legal contracts are binding, they say, *but* government bean-counters estimate Canada faces $200 billion in contingent liabilities because of its unwillingness to settle its outstanding legal obligations to Aboriginal People. They denounce Indian oral tradition and history as ludicrous fiction, *but* base their values, ethics, and system of justice on the legends of Christianity that are supported by very little in the way of documented historical evidence. (Switzer 1999, 4, emphasis added)

The author's reasoning is based on the argumentative topos of justice (Perelman/Olbrechts-Tyteca 1983). The underlying rule of justice demands that one must treat those things, persons or situations alike that one considers as belonging to the same category. By comparing the 1760 treaty between the Mi'kmaq and the Crown with the 1763 Treaty of Paris between the British and the French, as well as traditional oral history with the legends of Christianity, the author implies an equivalence between them. He also implies, and thus indirectly demands, an equivalent acknowledgment of Aboriginal/Crown treaties and oral history. Or, to put it another way, if the 1760 treaty is "ancient," then the 1763 treaty is ancient too and should not be legally binding. And if Aboriginal oral tradition is nothing but "ludicrous fiction," so too are the legends of Christianity.

The rule or topos of justice, which underlies the author's argumentation, is linguistically realized through parallelism. The example displays a form of grammatical or syntactic parallelism in that it repeats the following pattern:

Clause	Coordinating conjunction	Clause
The 1760 treaty between the British Crown and the Mi'kmaq is "ancient"... they say,	but	still cling to the sanctity of the 1763 Treaty of Paris ...
Legal contracts are binding, they say,	but	government bean counters estimate Canada faces ...
They denounce Indian oral tradition ... as ...	but	base their values, ethics ... on the legends of Christianity ...

Figure 13.2 Parallel constructions

However, more important here is the observation that a formal parallelism, a syntactic one, can signal a parallelism in meaning. By using this argumentative scenario, the author refutes the non-Aboriginal standpoint about the "supremacy of the letter of law" by providing factual evidence where this supremacy is violated.

Attribution of Agency and Process

Positive self-presentation is also achieved by representing Aboriginal people as active agents who deliberately initiate actions and attribute positive images to themselves. The system of transitivity including the notion of different process types is used to explain how people represent or encode experiences of events and activities—"reality"—in grammatical configurations of the clause (Halliday 1985, Halliday/Hasan 1985, Givón 1993). According to systemic functional linguists,[10] the two main elements by which representations of reality can be rendered intelligible are "process" and "participants."

Realities are constructed in terms of what happens, or is the case, and by or to whom, for example, language users can choose from various options to encode their experience of a particular event. They can opt for an active or a passive structure as in, for example, "I broke the window" versus "The window was broken" or "The window broke." All these options are true statements about what happened. However, the first utterance foregrounds the involvement of the agent and, therefore, his or her responsibility. The last two statements feature passive sentences in which agency is deleted. Consequently, involvement and responsibility cannot be attributed to an agent. Even more significantly, the last of these passive constructions gives the impression that the process expressed by this sentence seems to be self-provoked, without any external cause. The choice of whether to include or omit agency from processes as well as to opt for an active rather than passive sentence is a central element in encoding particular views and ideologies and, thus, constructing realities.

Drawing broadly upon the analytical framework of Michael Halliday (1985) and Talmy Givón (1993) and adopting Lütfiye Oktar's view that action processes not only include material processes but also mental and verbal processes (2001, 324), I distinguish between three major processes: actions, events, and states. In an action, an "agent" actively initiates or/and causes an action. It is the participant who is occupying the subject position in a clause, and who is typically human, acting deliberately upon something or somebody. The person or entity affected by the action process is the "patient" or "affected." Such a representation foregrounds the involvement of the agent in a particular event and thus his or her responsibility as these examples suggest:

> During the campaign for national chief, *I crisscrossed* the country. *I visited* your assemblies and communities, *participated* in your debates,

> *responded* to your inquiries and *you shared* your dreams and visions for your people ... *I have listened* to your wise counsel ... *I based* my election platform on what I heard during the campaign. (Coon Come 2000, 5, emphasis added)

> Today, *we teach* university programs, *[we] publish* books, *[we] elect* our own political leadership, *[we] argue* in courts and *[we] struggle* to close the gaps that divide us from our neighbours. (Wagamese 1999, 8, emphasis added)

All clauses in these two examples represent processes of "doing"—action processes. Moreover they are all in the active voice with the speaker ("I" and "we") always occupying the first syntactic position. This kind of representation has a potential ideological function in the sense that it shows how Aboriginal people see themselves in contemporary society, namely, as active and responsible participants and not as passive victims who are affected by the actions of others, that is, the dominant Euro-Canadian society. As Deirdre Burton puts it,

> Once it is clear to people that there are alternative ways of expressing "reality," then people can make decisions about how to express "reality"; both for others and themselves. By this means, we can both deconstruct and reconstruct our realities to an enabling degree (1991, 200).

Foregrounding of Positive Characteristics

Aboriginal people construct a reality not only in terms of action processes but also in terms of "states" and "events." According to Givón, a state is an "existing condition that involves *no change over time*" (Givón 1993, 90; emphasis in original). Events, on the other hand, are defined as involving "*change of state* over time" (90). The participant roles associated with states and events are labelled "patient" and "dative." Patient is a human or non-human participant that is either in a state or somehow affected by an event. Dative is seen as a conscious participant who is typically human but who does not exert intention, action or control, someone who is not a deliberate initiator.

These process types—states and events—encode meanings about states of being, becoming or having (possession), in that persons or things are assigned attributes or identities, as the following examples illustrate:

> I believe *our people are ready. Our nations have the tools* to move forward, *our people are becoming better educated, our business and economic abilities are growing.* (Fontaine 1999, September, 5, emphasis added)

> *We have so many people to be proud of,* from the kindergarten teacher to the university professor, from the carpenter to the medical specialist. *These are our people.* (Fontaine 1999, September, 5, emphasis added)

This representation constructs a positive and motivating reality by assigning positive values and characteristics to Aboriginal people and their achievements (for example, they "are ready," they "have the tools to move forward," they "are becoming better educated," etc.). Consequently, positive attributes and a positive description of themselves lead to positive self-presentation,which is very much needed in a time when negative stereotyping and bias continue to misrepresent Aboriginal people in the mainstream media. As Laura Milliken, a young Aboriginal TV show producer, points out with respect to dominant media representation of Native people and issues, "It was a challenge (growing up) because I wasn't inspired. I wanted to be proud but I never saw any positive representation on television and I never saw any positive stories in the newspaper" (Milliken 2000, 12).

Employment of the High-Value Modals "Must" and "Will"

The analysis of modality complements the results of the process type analysis. In their discursive practice, Aboriginal people predominantly employ high-value modals such as "must" and "will," which are associated with obligation, commitment and certainty.[11] In assuming that the degree of modality matches the level of certainty provided by the evidence, Aboriginal people represent themselves as strongly committed and highly positive—due to evidence and experience—about the things that are and the things to come.

A frequency count of modal verbs in the columns by the National Chiefs Matthew Coon Come and Phil Fontaine in the *First Nations Messenger* affirms this assumption. In the twelve columns that appeared in the *First Nations Messenger* between February 1999 and June 2001, the high-value modal verbs "must" and "will" occurred a 110 times. On the other hand, the medium- or moderate-modal verbs "should," "would," "can" and "ought to" were used only thirty-two times, and the low-value modals "could," "might," "may" and "shall" only seven times (Retzlaff 2005, 198). Aboriginal people are urged to take action, which is realized through highly-modalized directives using "must":

> *We must* develop in our youth the skills and knowledge .... *We must* regain control over our lands and resources as a means of regaining control over our present and future lives. *We must* now develop and commit ourselves in unity .... (Coon Come 2001, 13, emphasis added)

By frequently employing a modal auxiliary from the high-modality scale, Aboriginal writers add considerable force to their utterances since the degree of modality or obligation affects the force of directives. One could describe the general communicative function of a directive speech act modified by "must" as being typically concerned with actions that direct human behaviour, for instance, expressing commands, demands or offers. These speech acts all serve to influence someone else's behaviour. More generally, they serve to set up interpersonal relations, which may lead to what Angela Downing and Philip Locke refer to as a very important function of modality: its power "to intervene in, and bring about changes in events" (1992, 384), and in a broader sense, to bring about socio-political changes. In this respect, the circulation of high-value modalities can help to establish, develop and foster new social identities. This is particularly so in the cases under discussion, since the highly-modalized directives in the above example are accompanied by the first person plural pronoun "we," which induces the readership to conceptualize group identity, solidarity, and a national collective as members of an in-group.[12]

The modal verb "will" constitutes another example of the specific type of modality that is foregrounded in Aboriginal discourse:

> APTN *will* change the face of Canadian communications for the new century. Our faces *will* be beamed across space. I wonder what our ancestors would have thought. Our children *will* grow up watching Nishnawbe Jay Leno or Nishnawbe Sesame Street. Our children *will* be entering a new age. (Rice 1999, 7, emphasis added)

> Our young people *will* become leaders, creators and shapers of a political movement that *will* enshrine all that we have fought for. (Wagamese 1999, 8, emphasis added)

What is important here is the fact that language users have the choice to select from a variety of modal verbs to predict a future outcome, action, result, etc., which vary in degrees of probability. There exists a link between the signification of the future time and the use of modal verbs to indicate degrees of probability along a continuum from certainty at one extreme towards uncertainty at the other. The modal verb "will" expresses certainty. However, other choices for the first proposition in the latter example would have been possible: (a) Our young people *will* become leaders; (b) Our young people *ought to* become leaders; (c) Our young people *should* become leaders; (d) Our young people *could* become leaders; and (e) Our young people *might* become leaders. The writer chooses to modalize the proposition "our young people become leaders" with the high-value auxiliary verb "will." He could have opted for one of the other, though weaker, possibilities available in the system as presented in (b) to (e). "Might" and "could," for example, also express the possibility of the event in the proposition happening, but indicate uncertainty.

The evidence that justifies the high-modality claims in Aboriginal discourse can be seen in the achievements and determination of Aboriginal people since the 1960s and, more specifically, since the beginning of the 1990s. Some major policy and legislative victories, for example, can be credited to Aboriginal people (for example, Supreme Court decisions in favour of Aboriginal people; recognition and affirmation of Aboriginal and treaty rights in the Constitution; land claim settlements, self-government models, and the election of Aboriginal people as members of Parliament, or their appointment as senators).[13] These achievements and successes, the revitalization of Aboriginal cultures and the resurgence of Aboriginal people, are part of the communal value and belief system that is reflected and reinforced in Aboriginal texts. Therefore, the certainty expressed by both the modal auxiliaries "must" and "will" is seen to be a shared certainty; a firm expectation of what will happen based on general wisdom and knowledge; and the "laws" of nature, development and society.

The Creation and Consistent Use of Terminology

The creation and consistent use of terminology constructs collective and national identities and is an important part of the general trend by Aboriginal people to rid themselves of outside domination and, thus, exercise agency. The shifting of membership categories in Aboriginal discursive practices shows that discourses are dynamic, and that these semantic and/or lexical shifts reflect wider processes of socio-political change. In Aboriginal discourse the misnomer "Indian" has been replaced by the terms "Native people," "Aboriginal people," and "First Nations (people)."

The Canadian Constitution (Constitution Act, 1982) refers to, and recognizes, three distinct groups of Aboriginal people in Canada. It uses the generic adjective "aboriginal" to include the Indian, Inuit and Métis people. The preferred alternative at present, however, is to capitalize the terms "Aboriginal" and "Native" and to use them as a modifier, for example, "consultations with Aboriginal people" and not "consultations with Aboriginals." Failing to adhere to these conventions especially in the case of known preferences is not simply a stylistic *faux pas* but a sign of resistance to change, a sign of perpetuating a superior attitude towards Aboriginal people, and is indicative of disrespect and even, in some cases, contempt. A look at the mainstream newspaper coverage of the Assembly of First Nations election in July 2003 shows that both nouns and adjectives denoting Aboriginal groups are consistently represented using lower case letters. The preference for using the terms as modifiers is ignored, too. The following example is taken from *The Globe and Mail,* one of Canada's leading newspapers:

> In a separate interview Tuesday, Mr. Fontaine called the new *native* legislation "regressive" and said the AFN needs to "start all over." New legislation should still protect the rights of *native people* while ensuring open and transparent leadership, he told Newsworld. Another challenge facing *native chiefs* is the fact that Canada has 633 different *native chiefs* and *natives* who speak 80 different languages ... a growing number of *aboriginals* say the national leadership has lost touch with its constituents. (Dunfield 2003, A3; emphasis added)

To capitalize the words "Native" and "Aboriginal" is most likely an editorial decision. However, there exists a capitalization convention in the case of words denoting human groups with respect to nation and nationality, such as "Canadian people" or "German minister." Not complying with those conventions reflects the dominant attitude of the mainstream press; it denies Aboriginal people their status as distinct peoples/nations.

In addition to adopting the labels "Aboriginal" and "Native" as self-referential terms, "First Nation(s)" has become a high-frequency label, inseparable from political mobilization. The designation "First Nation(s)" originally referred to Aboriginal people who fall under the jurisdiction of the Indian Act, that is, Status-Indians generally living in a First Nations community (reserve). In 1981, at the height of the Canadian constitutional debate, the National Indian Brotherhood, which politically represents Status-Indians, changed its name to the Assembly of First Nations as a reaction to the dominant political rhetoric at this time, which kept referring to the "two founding nations" (French and British) of Canada.

Currently, the terms "First Nations," "Native people," and "Aboriginal people" are often used interchangeably and synonymously in Aboriginal discourse and, thus, include all three constitutionally recognized groups of Aboriginal people:

> The march to *First Nation self-government* will be led by a growing army of increasingly better-educated *Native students*. Today nearly 30,000 *Aboriginal students* attend post-secondary institutions ... there is going to be a strong need for *First Nations professionals* in all areas .... We continue to advocate the need for enhanced services and accesses to *First Nations students*. (Goulais 2000, 14; emphasis added)

The ways in which Aboriginal people represent themselves in public (in the news) contributes to the ways in which they see themselves and how others perceive them. Representing themselves as a collectivity is strategic; unity is a precondition to being heard. A shared cultural and/or political identity as First Nations, Aboriginal people, or Native people makes it possible to gain wider attention for their agenda(s) and is a means of making a difference on vital issues such as self-determination, land and resources, education, etc.

To summarize, Aboriginal identities are also (re)constructed and (re)affirmed through the use and circulation of (ethnic) labels. Labelling is a political act since labels include and exclude. Using the term "First Nation" to describe traditionally clan and family-oriented societies is one attempt of Aboriginal people to negotiate their way into the Canadian (political) consciousness. Since legal policies such as the Indian Act still fragment the Aboriginal population, the construction of a homogeneous national identity through collective labels, such as "First Nations" or "Aboriginal/Native people," is one tool to resist outside domination and to empower Aboriginal people. This is particularly so when Euro-Canadian discourses frequently ignore expressed preferences and continue to perpetuate negative stereotypes.[14]

CONCLUSION

There exists a powerful Aboriginal discourse in Canada, which combines traditional and contemporary elements. The evolving status and acknowledgement of Aboriginal people as distinct peoples with a right to self-determination, land and resources, and treaty concessions is mediated through that discourse. Whether the Aboriginal discourse is successful and performative in mainstream discourses in the sense that it "brings into being the very realities it describes" (Bourdieu/Wacquant 2001, 4), can only be assessed through continuous and detailed examination of such discourses. However, various social changes that have occurred over the last twenty years in Canada seem to indicate a socially influential Aboriginal discourse and a process by which Euro-Canada has started to publicly acknowledge that there exists a "third founding nation."

ENDNOTES

1 See, for example, quotations four, five and six in this paper. The former directly repeats the phrase "our children and grandchildren," while the latter two are examples of the frequent repetition of what the Elders have said, for example, "Our Elders have always told us" and "The Elders have said," or "The Elders have told us" and "Some Elders have said."

2 The examples for this analysis are taken from two Aboriginal newspapers, the *First Nations Messenger* (FNM) (formerly *Assembly of First Nations Bulletin*) and the *Anishinabek News* (AN). The former is a bimonthly publication of the Assembly of First Nations (AFN), the political organization that represents Status First Nations in Canada on the federal level but which has increasingly been lobbying not only on behalf of Status First Nations but on behalf of Aboriginal people in general. The *Anishinabek News* is published monthly by the Union of Ontario Indians (UOI)-Anishinabek Nation. With respect to style, emphasis is added in the newspaper examples cited for illustration in this paper. This is realized through *italic print*.

3 Ellen Nowgesic, Ojibway, personal communication, June 17, 2001.

4 Joe Johnson, Mohawk/Ojibway, personal communication, February 2, 2001; see also Bopp et al. 1985.

5 According to the framework of Speech Act Theory (Austin 1962, Searle 1969, 1979), language

in use has a performative dimension. Utterances are used to perform actions as well as to communicate propositions true or false. Explicit performative verbs are, for example, "promise," "declare," "baptize," "name" or "order." Using one of these verbs, in the right context, itself performs the action, for example, I cannot declare anybody man and wife since I am not a marriage commissioner working in a registry office. But to say "I order you to leave" is to give an order, and to say "I promise to come" is to make a promise. Uttering these sentences not only conveys some propositions but also constitutes the action referred to. In a very literal sense it is a speech *act*, not just saying something, but doing it through speaking.

6 Fred Nowgesic, Ojibway, personal communication, March 16, 2000.

7 Fyre Jean Graveline mentions "interconnectedness" and "Self-In-Relation" as some of the values of a traditional belief set. She notes that Aboriginal people are taught a common understanding of interconnectedness, for example, all expressions of life (people, animal, plants, the elements, the planets, etc.) are dependent on each other: "We are like one big family with 'all our relations.'" "Nothing we do, we do by ourselves; together we form a circle" and "We are able to see ourselves and our immanent value as related to and interconnected with others—family, community, the world, those behind and those yet to come" (Graveline 1998, 56, 58).

8 See, for example, the following quote: "We begin this journey in Lower Pertwood, England in Europe and the following years of the June 21st ceremony will be in Africa, Australia, and Japan and then back to Turtle Island (Americas) for a thank you ceremony" (Chief Arvol Looking Horse 2001, 14).

9 In everyday discourse Turtle Island is often used in a similar sense. In an interview that I conducted with an Ojibway/Mohawk friend, he told me, "I use the term Turtle Island sometimes. As I understand it Turtle Island is North America. And in some context they use Turtle Island as all of the land base of Mother Earth. But my understanding is that Turtle Island is North America, and it has been shown before that from certain perspectives North America itself from outer space looks like a turtle. You have to squint your eyes a little bit you know, and imagine a little bit because then you can see how Mexico becomes the tail, California becomes one leg, Florida becomes another leg, up by Alaska becomes the front paw, down by Newfoundland becomes a front paw. And what comes up in Canada on the top, up at Baffin Island almost looks like a head. So, then you understand that our people knew something because they have been talking about Turtle Island for a long time. They knew something about the way the land base looks" (Joe Johnson, Toronto, February 2, 2001).

10 Michael Halliday developed a descriptive and interpretative framework for viewing language as a strategic, meaning-making resource. His approach came to be known as the systemic-functional model or as systemic functional linguistics. It views language as a semiotic system and claims that language cannot be studied without reference to meaning. Underlying Halliday's model are the assumptions that, first, language is multifunctional, in that all language simultaneously performs three social functions and has thus three dimensions of meaning: ideational (representation of "reality"), interpersonal (construction of social relationships and identities), and textual (structure and organization of texts). Second, there are always different ways of saying things or different ways of saying the same thing respectively. Language is regarded as a network of options from which language users can choose. The selections made are ideologically significant (Halliday 1967, 1973, 1978, 1985; Halliday/Hasan 1985).

11 The system of modality provides the language user with different options to encode attitude and opinion in language and thus to construct social relations (Halliday 1985, Huddleston 1988; Eggins 1994). Linguistic structures that are traditionally associated with the expression of opinions are modal auxiliaries ("can," "could," "may," "might," "must," "will," "would," "shall," "should," "ought to," "need"). Some modals are said to be more effective with respect to getting people to do something, in that there exist degrees of obligation (to do or not to do an action) ranging from low to high. Compare, for example, "we must regain control" to "we should regain control" to "we may regain control." "Must" is a modal auxiliary from the high modality scale that is very forceful. The modal verb "should" has median modality and can be interpreted in this context as a recommendation rather than an obligation. The modal verb "may" is considered to have low modality and is consequently much less powerful than "must" and "should."

12 A frequency count of articles in the *First Nations Messenger* and the *Anishinabek News* has shown that the first person plural pronoun "we" and its associated variants "our" and "us" are the most extensively used pronouns in Native news discourse (Retzlaff 2005, 281).

13 Some current Aboriginal Parliamentarians are Nancy Karetak-Lindell (Inuit), Christina Keeper (First Nation), and Gerry St. Germain (Métis).

14 Nevertheless, the term "Indian" is still used in Aboriginal discourse. Using the label "Indian" as a cultural insider can be seen as a marker of group solidarity and as part of Aboriginal peoples' identities, since they have long had definitions of "Indianess" imposed upon them by the dominant society which eventually became internalized and thus accepted as part of their identity (Sawchuk 1992, 140).

Bibliography

Armstrong, Jeannette. (1991). "Interview with Hartmut Lutz." *Contemporary Challenges: Conversations with Canadian Native Authors,* ed. Hartmut Lutz. Saskatoon, SK: Fifth House Publishers, 13–32.

Austin, John L. (1962). *How to Do Things With Words.* Oxford: Oxford University Press.

Bell, Allan. (1991). *Language of the News Media.* Oxford: Blackwell.

Bopp, Judie, Michael Bopp, Lee Brown, and Phil Lane. (1985). *The Sacred Tree. Reflections on Native American Spirituality.* Lethbridge, AB: Four Worlds Development Press/University of Lethbridge.

Bourdieu, Pierre, and Loic Wacquant. (2001). "New Liberal Speak: Notes on the New Planetary Vulgate." *Radical Philosophy, 105,* 2–5.

Burton, Deirdre. (1991). "Through Glass Darkly: Through Dark Glasses." In *Language and Literature,* ed. Ronald Carter. London and New York: Routledge, 195–214.

Chief Arvol Looking Horse. (2001, February). "Spiritual Leader Calls for Urgency, Unity in Helping to Heal Mother Earth." *Anishinabek News,* 14.

Coon Come, Matthew. (2000, August). "New Leader Promises to Listen to the Voices of the People." *First Nations Messenger,* 5.

———. (2001, January). "Regaining Control over Resources Key to Survival." *Anishinabek News,* 13.

Downing, Angela, and Philip Locke. (1992). *A University Course in English Grammar.* London: Prentice Hall International Ltd.

Dunfield, Allison. (2003, July 15). "Opposition to New Indian Act Central in AFN Election." *The Globe and Mail,* A3.

Eggins, Suzanne. (1994). *An Introduction to Systemic Functional Linguistics.* London: Continuum.

Fontaine, Phil. (1999). "Beyond the Numbers: the Federal Budget and Its Message to First Nations." *First Nations Messenger,* 5.

———. (1999, September). "Youth Must Exercise and Embrace Their Right to an Education." *First Nations Messenger,* 5.

———. (1999, December). "Our Nations Must Ensure Treaty Rights are Recognized, Protected and Implemented." *First Nations Messenger,* 5.

———. (2000, February). "Restoration of our Languages is Everyone's Responsibility: Lessons Must Begin in the Home." *First Nations Messenger*, 5.

Foster, Michael K. (1988). "Iroquois Interaction in Historical Perspective." *Native North American Interaction Patterns*, eds. Regna Darnell and Michael K. Foster. Hull, QC: Canadian Museum of Civilization, 22–39.

Givón, Talmy. (1993). *English Grammar: A Function-Based Introduction*. Amsterdam: John Benjamins Publishing Company.

Goulais, April. (2000, December). "Native Student 'Army' Marching toward Self-Government." *Anishinabek News*, 14.

Graveline, Fyre Jean. (1998). *Circle Works: Transforming Eurocentric Consciousness*. Halifax, NS: Fernwood Publishing.

Halliday, Michael. (1967). "Notes on Transitivity and Themes in English, Part 2." *Journal of Linguistics*, 3, 194–244.

———. (1973). *Explorations in the Functions of Language*. London: Edward Arnold.

———. (1978). *Language as Social Semiotics*. London: Edward Arnold.

———. (1985). *Introduction to Functional Grammar*. London: Edward Arnold.

Halliday, Michael, and Ruqaiya Hasan. (1985). *Language, Context, and Text*. Oxford: Oxford University Press.

Huddleston, Rodney. (1988). *English Grammar: An Outline*. Cambridge: Cambridge University Press.

Jarvenpa, Robert. (1992). "The Political Economy and Political Ethnicity of American Indian Adaptations and Identities." In *The First Ones: Readings in Indian/Native Studies*, eds. David R. Miller et al. Piapot Reserve # 75, SK: Saskatchewan Indian Federated College Press, 122–132.

Johnson, Joe. (2001, February 2). Personal communication.

Johnston, Basil. (1998). *Ojibway Heritage*. Toronto, ON: McClelland & Steward.

Lutz, Hartmut. (1991). *Contemporary Challenges: Conversations with Canadian Native Authors*. Saskatoon, SK: Fifth House.

Mercredi, Ovide, and Mary Ellen Turpel. (1993). *In the Rapids. Navigating the Future of First Nations*. Toronto, ON: Viking.

Milliken, Laura. (2000, August). "Show's Roster Reflects the Diverse Range of First Nations Talent in Canada." *First Nations Messenger*, 12.

Nowgesic, Ellen. (2001, June 17). Personal communication.

Nowgesic, Fred. (2000, March 16). Personal communication.

Oktar, Lütfiye. (2001). "The Ideological Organization of Representational Processes in the Presentation of *Us* and *Them*." *Discourse and Society, 12:3*, 313–344.

Perelman, Chaim, and Lucie Olbrechts-Tyteca. (1983). *Traité de l'argumentation, la nouvelle rhetoriqué*. Brussels: Éditions de l'université de Bruxelles.

Retzlaff, Steffi. (2005). *Tradition, Solidarity, and Empowerment: The Native Discourse in Canada. An Analysis of Native News Representations*. Stuttgart: Ibidem.

Rice, Harmony. (1999, April). "Making the World a Better Place for Our Children." *First Nations Messenger*, 7.

Sawchuk, Joe. (1992). "The Metis, Non-Status Indians, and the New Aboriginality: Government Influence on Native Political Alliances and Identity." In *The First Ones: Readings in Indian/Native Studies*, 140–146.

Searle, John R. (1969). *Speech Acts: An Essay in the Philosophy of Language*. London: Cambridge University Press.

———. (1979). *Expression and Meaning*. Cambridge: Cambridge University Press.

Spielmann, Roger. (1998). *'You're So Fat.' Exploring Ojibwe Discourse*. Toronto, ON: University of Toronto Press.

Stone, Evelyn. (2000, September). "Michipicoten First Nations Youth & Elders Gathering." *Anishinabek News*, 13.

Switzer, Maurice. (1999, December). "All You Need to Know about Treaties: A Promise Is a Promise Is a Promise..." *First Nations Messenger*, 4.

———. (2000, February). "Language Key Part of First Nations 'Voice.'" *First Nations Messenger*, 10.

———. (2001, February). "Pursuit of Truth Should be Vision Quest." *Anishinabek News*, 10.

Valentine, Lisa Philips. (1995). *Making It Their Own: Seven Ojibwe Communicative Practices*. Toronto, ON: University of Toronto Press.

———. (1999). "Personal Agency in Systemic Discourse." *Theorizing the Americanist Tradition*. Eds. Lisa Philips Valentine and Regna Darnell. Toronto, ON: University of Toronto Press, 338–350.

Wagamese, Richard. (1999, December). "New Century Presents Great Opportunities for Change and Progress in Our Communities." *First Nations Messenger*, 8.

———. (2000, February). "Residential Schools to Blame for Breakdown of Family's Traditional Lifestyle." *First Nations Messenger,* 6.

Wodak, Ruth, et al. (1999). "The Discursive Construction of National Identity." *Discourse and Society, 10:2,* 145–173.

INTERNET SOURCES

Whiskeyjack, Francis. (2000). "The Medicine Wheel." http://www.ammsa.com/buffalospirit/June-2000/medicinewheel.html [consulted January 11, 2001].

Kerstin Knopf

"Stolen Sisters": Discrimination and Violence against Aboriginal Women as Represented in Canadian Films

Introduction

The 2004 Amnesty International report "Stolen Sisters—A Human Rights Response to Discrimination and Violence against Aboriginal Women in Canada" is a shocking account of cases of horrific sexist violence against Aboriginal women in Canada; violence fostered by racism and discrimination, as well as the systemic social and economic marginalization of a majority of this group. This "human rights tragedy" as Alex Neve, secretary general of Amnesty International Canada, terms it (Neve, online), is happening in a First World country, and thus is all the more despicable. These social phenomena are factors that contribute to the Fourth World status of Canada's Aboriginal people. There is indeed an increasing optimism in relations between Canada and its Aboriginal population at the turn of the century and an overall improvement of the state of Aboriginal Canada, partly as a result of successful land claim settlements (e.g., the Nisga'a Treaty), the partial political autonomy of a large group of Arctic inhabitants (the creation of Nunavut in 1999), the financial compensation package for residential school survivors, and concessions to Aboriginal demands for a self-controlled media system (the creation of APTN in 1999 and a number of radio stations).

In spite of these cautious improvements, the situation of many Aboriginal women is still appalling, and the report reveals cases of sexually assaulted, missing, and/or brutally murdered Aboriginal women that come to the fore again and again. Systemic mishandling of such cases by the police and loopholes in the Canadian justice system account for an alarming number of unsolved missing women and murder cases, not to mention acquitted or not appropriately convicted perpetrators.

Apart from media coverage of such cases (predominantly in the Aboriginal media[1]), the topic of the insufferable poverty of, and sexist and racist violence against, Aboriginal women is increasingly contextualized in literature and film, in examples such as plays by Yvette Nolan (*Blade*) and Marie Clements' *The Unnatural and Accidental Women,* recently turned into the feature film *Unnatural and Accidental* by Carl Bessai. Other films that address this issue in its themes are the feature film *Conspiracy of Violence,* Christine Welsh's NFB documentary *Finding Dawn,* and "Suspicious Love," one part of *Moccasin Flats,* a television series produced by Laura Milliken and Jennifer Podemski. At the ImagineNATIVE film festival in Toronto 2007, two short films premiered that also dealt with the violent death of an Aboriginal woman: Ervin Chartrand's *Sister* and Peter Brass and Helder Mauricio Carvajal's *The Valley.* Tying together this socio-political situation in Canada with its contextualization in film, this article is organized in two parts. It first gives an overview of the distressing situation of Aboriginal women in Canada based upon Amnesty International's report and then discusses how this topic is reflected in Audrey Huntley's documentary *Go Home, Baby Girl,* Nathaniel Geary's feature film *On the Corner,* and Jennifer Podemski's short dramatic film *Laurel.*

The Report as an Indictment of Canada's Human Rights Tragedy

Drawing upon a 1996 Department of Indian and Northern Affairs Canada (DIAND) statistic, Amnesty International's report notes that "Indigenous women between the ages of 25 and 44 with status under the Federal Indian

Act, are five times more likely than other women of the same age to die as the result of violence" (Amnesty International 2004, 23).

The Native Women's Association of Canada (NWAC) estimates that "over the past twenty years more than five hundred Indigenous women may have been murdered or gone missing in circumstances suggesting violence" (Amnesty International 2004, 24). This situation is neither new nor unknown, as Aboriginal women's organizations have for a long time called attention to violence against women and children in predominantly non-Aboriginal communities (23). But only after a considerable number of cases of sexist and racist violence against Aboriginal women were made public and the Royal Commission on Aboriginal Peoples (RCAP), United Nations human rights bodies, and NWAC rigorously called on the Canadian government to address this issue together with the social and economic marginalization of Aboriginal women (2–3, 23) did this issue receive more government and public attention. In line with these concerns, Amnesty International's report examines four factors that, according to them, foster a heightened risk of violence against Aboriginal women:

1. The social and economic marginalization of Indigenous women, along with a history of government policies that have torn apart Indigenous families and communities, have pushed a disproportionate number of Indigenous women into dangerous situations that include extreme poverty, homelessness and prostitution;
2. Despite assurances to the contrary, police in Canada have often failed to provide Indigenous women with an adequate standard of protection;
3. The resulting vulnerability of Indigenous women has been exploited by Indigenous and non-Indigenous men to carry out acts of extreme brutality against them;
4. These acts of violence may be motivated by racism, or may be carried out in the expectation that societal indifference to the welfare and safety of Indigenous women will allow the perpetrators to escape justice. (Amnesty International 2004, 2)

Thus, the report investigates the roles of social and economic marginalization of Aboriginal women, racist and sexist discrimination directed against them, including failures to protect them, and societal indifference to the plight of Aboriginal women as directly related to violent acts committed against Aboriginal women.

Additonally, the report cites a 1993 UN declaration that describes violence against women as a "'manifestation of historically unequal power relations between women and men' and 'a means by which this inequality is maintained'" (Amnesty International 2004, 11). It indicts the latent "blaming-the-victim" concept as being pervasive in many First World male-dominated public discourses and pinpoints such practices of administrators of the criminal justice system, including police, prosecutors, and judges (11); a concept that blames the women themselves, in particular their dress (revealing clothes), conduct and behaviour (suggestive dance and gestures), or consumed substances (drugs and alcohol) as being responsible for violent acts committed against them.

Furthermore, the report places violence against Aboriginal women in the larger context of colonization. The dispossession and drastic reduction of Aboriginal land bases, destruction of traditional gender roles and gender equality, limited participation in political and social decisions in their communities, and cultural alienation all create for Aboriginal women a political and social climate where various forms of racist, sexist, and family violence can breed—a climate that is further supported by the fact that the legislation that governs Aboriginal people has privileged Aboriginal men over Aboriginal women. Section 6 in the 1869 *An Act for the Gradual Enfranchisement of Indians* (which became the *Indian Act* in 1876) deprived Aboriginal women and their children of their Indian status and band membership if they married a non-Aboriginal man or outside of their community (Venne 1981, 12). This law, an infringement on the independence of affected Aboriginal women, pushed them into increased dependence on their spouses, compelled them to leave their communities, and often fostered their alienation from their families, societal contexts, and culture (Amnesty International 2004, 12–13). With Bill C 31 in 1985, the concerned Aboriginal women and their offspring were reinstated, but the devastating consequences of the 1869 discriminatory legislation for many Aboriginal women could not be undone.

The forceful removal of whole generations of Aboriginal children from their homes to have them educated according to Euro-Canadian norms, values, and religion in residential schools became practice between the 1870s and 1960s. In these schools they were exploited as workforce and exposed to psychological, bodily, and sexual abuse. This removal policy similarly contributed to cultural alienation, destruction of self-respect and identity, and loss of parenting and societal skills. The large-scale placement of Aboriginal children into non-Aboriginal foster homes through the Canadian Child Welfare policy, predominantly in the 1960s, 1970s, and 1980s, brought similar results for the affected individuals (Amnesty International 2004, 13–15). These consequences of colonization have created a climate that fosters racist and sexist violence against Aboriginal women; as Amnesty International states, "The painful loss of ties to family, community and culture is a common element of many of the stories of missing and murdered women" (18).

In part owing to the discriminatory legislation, residential school, and child welfare politics, more than half of the Aboriginal population now lives in urban areas. Most of them "live at a disadvantage compared to non-Indigenous people, facing dramatically lower incomes and a shortage of culturally appropriate support services in a government structure that has still not fully adjusted to the growing urban Indigenous population" (Amnesty International 2004, 19). For example, the urban health-care programs, to which urban Aboriginal people have access, "are not necessarily aligned" to their specific needs "or delivered in a culturally appropriate way" (20).[2] Experiences of latent cultural alienation and subtle and overt racism contribute to the relative harshness of urban Aboriginal life. A 2000 status survey of Aboriginal families in Ontario urban areas reports that "'words such as low self-esteem, depression, anger, self-doubt, intimidation, frustration, shame and hopelessness were used to describe some of the crushing feelings of Aboriginal children and parents living in poverty'" (quoted in Amnesty International 2004, 21). Statistically, Aboriginal women earn roughly thirty percent less than non-Aboriginal women (19), and in comparison to Aboriginal/ non-Aboriginal/ immigrant males and non-Aboriginal/ non-immigrant females they are subjected to three-fold discrimination—the nexus of racism, sexism, and classism.

As most of the nine cases outlined in Amnesty International's report show, economic instability, the break up of families, the placement of children in foster and adoptive homes, as well as an ensuing sense of dislocation and loss of individual stability and cultural identity are common features in the lives of those Aboriginal women, who end up as sex workers, often with a substance addiction. These factors are also often common denominators in cases of missing and murdered women (Amnesty International 2004, 48, 51–52, 61). Amnesty International concludes, "A number of the cases recounted in this report demonstrate, in human terms, the disturbing connections among past policies such as residential schools, societal discrimination against Aboriginal people, involvement in the sex trade, and deadly violence" (37).

For many Aboriginal women, prostitution is a last means to sustain themselves, their families, or substance addictions and consequently, they are heavily over-represented among sex workers. A study of sex workers in Vancouver found a share of 30 percent of Aboriginal women working in this trade, as opposed to a share of roughly 3 percent of Aboriginal people in the overall Canadian population (Amnesty International 2004, 21–22). Sex workers in general face a heightened risk of violence because of the social stigmatization and particular conditions of their work (27); Aboriginal women's risk is even greater because of ethnic stigmatization. Stereotypical notions of Aboriginal women, germinated and nourished in colonial discourses, foster disrespect, chauvinism, and sexism. They are also breeding ground for misogynist, culturally hegemonic assumptions that Aboriginal sex workers, and often Aboriginal women in general, are *just* "Indian trash" or "squaw sluts."[3] As Janice Acoose explains, "Stereotypic images of Indian princesses, squaw drudges, suffering helpless victims, tawny temptresses, or loose squaws falsify our realities and suggest in a subliminal way that those stereotypic images are us. As a consequence, those images foster cultural attitudes that encourage sexual, physical, verbal, or psychological violence against Indigenous women" (Acoose 1995, 55). In the same vein, Maureen Matthews revealed in a radio program, "So what you have happening from the first contact is this stereotypical notion that Native women have fewer sexual morals, for example, than European women. It's an unspoken stereotype, but every Native woman I know who's ever walked on a street alone has suffered from that kind of stereotyping" (Matthews 1991, 20).

Not only male offenders but also some members of the police and justice system seem to be operating within this framework of assumptions. As the nine cases of missing and murdered Aboriginal women reveal, in some instances Aboriginal women are inadequately protected by authorities (Amnesty International 2004, 37). The Manitoba Justice Inquiry, established to examine the circumstances of the murder of Helen Betty Osborne in 1971, failed to acknowledge a climate of cultural tensions and a pattern of continual sexual harassment of and threats of violence against Aboriginal women in the The Pas area; it concluded that her life could have been saved if the police had taken appropriate action (39–40). In the case of Shirley Lonethunder, missing since December 1991, the police did not request public assistance through the media, although, according to the Missing Person Policy of the Saskatoon Police Service, they have a responsibility to seek media assistance (43). During the trial of the murderers of Pamela George, the Crown prosecutor and judge reminded the jury that they need to consider that the victim "indeed was a prostitute;" a Regina police officer expressed his disgust by the verdict that considered the murderers as "the boys who 'did pretty darn stupid things,'" indicative of a system where investigators and prosecutors saw Pamela George as "a sex trade worker, not a human being" (47). In the cases of missing women in Vancouver's Downtown Eastside in 1999, the police initially refused to publicly offer rewards for information, although they did so in cases of robberies in affluent neighbourhoods. Family members of murdered Janet Henry and Sarah de Vries assert that in both cases the police were too slow to recognize the larger pattern of serial killings in Vancouver and take concerted action (49, 54). The police investigator in the case of missing and murdered Maxine Wapass in Saskatoon in 2002 informed her cousin, who was phoning the police regularly, that "this case wasn't his priority" (58). The Winnipeg police unnecessarily delayed action in the case of missing and murdered Felicia Velvet Solomon in 2003 because of an alleged forty eight-hour waiting policy; they neither asked for public assistance nor supported the family, who distributed their own missing-person posters (60). In the case of missing and killed Moira Louise Erb in 2003, the Winnipeg police concluded that she was struck by a train, and they failed to investigate the circumstances of her tragic death (62–63).

In some instances, individual police officers showed sympathy and support for the victims and their families, as, for example, in the cases of Shirley Lonethunder, Pamela George, Janet Henry, Sarah de Vries, and Maxine Wapass (Amnesty International 2004, 43–44, 47, 49, 54, 58). Although, because of internal structures and regulations within the police force, they were not effective in solving the cases. Generally, offenders and law enforcement officials seem to work within an ideological framework that is informed by the historically developed colonial trope of a European right to conquest and domination. Consequently, this framework of thought is governed by the ideas of cultural supremacy and male superiority, which are then supplemented by the inherent systemic power position of police and judicial institutions.

Despite the critical situation of an increase in numbers of cases of horrific and deadly violence against Aboriginal women, law enforcers are slow in responding properly to this situation. For example, the Aboriginal Justice Inquiry of Manitoba issued a catalogue of wide-ranging recommendations and reform proposals in order to curb further victimization of Aboriginal people and to ensure their safety. Ten years later, almost none of the 150 recommendations have been followed, the federal government has not implemented any of the suggested reforms that were within their jurisdiction, and the provincial government is still examining which of the recommendations to realize (Amnesty International 2004, 41–42). Similarly, there are "significant gaps in how police record and share information about missing persons and violent crimes," as they do not necessarily record the ethnicity of crime victims and missing persons, resulting in the lack of a comprehensive database about the identities of perpetrators and victims as well as the circumstances of the crimes (25). When asked to provide the number of missing and murdered

Aboriginal women for the United Nations Human Rights Committee in October 2005, the Canadian government could not respond, because that information is non-existent (Amnesty International Canada 2005, 2).

Most often, police officers are assigned to Aboriginal communities with minimal cultural and historical knowledge about Aboriginal people (Amnesty International 2004, 2, 31), which prevents much needed cultural sensitivity. Generally there is not a relationship of trust between Aboriginal people and police, and many (Aboriginal) sex workers "are reluctant to seek the protection of the police for fear of being arrested" (27). In many Canadian cities, there is no specialized personnel for missing persons cases and few police forces have specific protocols for missing Aboriginal women cases (33). Most notably, the Canadian government and public must view the heightened risk of sexual and racial violence that Aboriginal women face as a human rights issue, says Neve (Neve, online). In order to address the severity of this issue and the critical situation of Aboriginal women, the Canadian government needs to ratify the only international human rights treaty that specifically takes issue with violence against women, which it had not done as of October 2005 (Mann, online). Additionally, Michelle Mann critiques social assistance policies in place across Canada and asserts that they violate international human rights law and the Canadian Charter of Rights and Freedoms: "They frequently discriminate against women, entrench gendered economic dependence and hinder women's ability to evade abuse" (Mann, online).

In general, there is a climate of apparent public apathy about the critical and dangerous situation of Aboriginal women in Canada (Amnesty International 2004, 35). This public indifference needs to be drastically changed for the welfare and safety of Aboriginal women, and the relations between Canada and the Aboriginal population improved. A year after Amnesty International's report on the "Stolen Sisters," Amnesty International Canada released a public brief that reviewed Canada's reaction to the report. Besides publicly acknowledging the seriousness of the threats faced by Aboriginal women, the federal and provincial governments launched a number of initiatives and programs to curb causes of this high-risk situation. The NWAC was given five million dollars, as was the Federation of Saskatchewan Indian Nations (FSIN), both received major funding in order to carry out research and analysis on the community level and to take measures to decrease Aboriginal women's high risk of violence. Some police forces are consciously working for better relations with Aboriginal communities. For example, the Saskatchewan government developed an action plan to improve the work of and cultural awareness within the police force by involving Aboriginal police officers and expertise (Amnesty International Canada 2005, 1–4). Nevertheless, many of the police officers interviewed by Amnesty International since the 2004 report's release "continue to deny that risks to Indigenous women and girls require any particular vigilance on the part of the police" (3). Culturally-specific programs operated by Aboriginal organizations are notoriously under-funded and there is a lack of specifically designed programs to assist Aboriginal women in the sex trade (4). The public brief concludes that "despite the number of programs in place, more of which have been announced since the launch of the 'Stolen Sisters' report, serious gaps remain in the provisions of services needed to prevent violence and assist women and girls escape dangerous situations" (4).

Since the release of the 2004 Amnesty International report, this human rights tragedy has gained more and more public appeal, not least through campaigns of Aboriginal organizations, which are designed to confront the climate of general indifference to and apathy about the plight of Aboriginal women. Online appeals to citizens to take action, an online petition asking the federal government for an action plan to take responsibility in this issue, and numerous websites calling attention to singular fates of Aboriginal women and/or listing missing women contribute in this struggle. In 2004, the NWAC launched its "Sisters in Spirit Campaign" with the goal to collect data about each missing Aboriginal woman and to do much-needed research in this area. With a 24-hour Freedom Drum Marathon in Fort Erie, Ontario, in October 2005, Aboriginal members of Amnesty International raised awareness about Aboriginal rights and specifically the "Stolen Sisters" report, in an attempt to put pressure on the Canadian government to respond to Amnesty International's inquiries and to the critical situation of Aboriginal women.[4]

In the same vein, CBC News producer Audrey Huntley with her video project entitled "Traces of Missing Women" brings out the stories of missing and murdered Aboriginal women from the shadows of the mainstream media discourse, and curbs the threat of these stories being lost to public apathy. In the summer of 2005, she travelled for seven and a half weeks to and from Toronto to Western Canada, gathering stories and giving voice to the sorrows and concerns of the victims' families and friends. Her progress report, posted on the Internet, reveals how this project gradually evolved into a memorial collage, how friends and relatives, who had stopped talking to the media, responded eagerly, how the sharing of stories on camera for many became a way of healing, and also how Huntley networked and helped in the search for missing women by disseminating photographs (Huntley 2005, 2–6). As part of the project, Huntley created the film *Go Home, Baby Girl,* which aired on CBC in December 2005.

Go Home, Baby Girl

This forty five-minute documentary relates the story of missing (and murdered)[5] Norma George from Takla Landing First Nation, BC, who disappeared from Vancouver's Downtown Eastside in September 1992. It is a film about her half-sister Claudine Julian's journey to reconnect with her broken family and about the family's struggle to come to terms with their grief and family history. It is a very personal and intense story that required Huntley to build a relationship of trust with Claudine and her family. Claudine (Ceejai) is a good friend of Huntley, and in researching and making the documentary film, Huntley spent six months investigating, talking to the sisters, to the police, and to the people in Norma's life.[6]

Claudine saw Norma last on 28 September 1992 on Hastings Street before she went missing for five and a half days. Her dead body was found in the industrial area of Aldergrove, BC, on 5 October 1992, nude and curled in a fetal position. The police determined exposure to be the cause of her death, which left the family with nagging questions: Who took her there? Where were her clothes and jewellery? Why was she missing for five and a half days before her death when she was otherwise in constant touch with the family?[7] Because Norma's body was badly decomposed, the police strictly advised a closed-casket funeral. However, according to Sekani tradition, the headstone cannot be placed on a grave unless a clan or community member has seen the body. Consequently there is no headstone on Norma's grave and her "spirit is trapped between the two worlds." Thirteen years later, her case remains unsolved. Sekani tradition cannot permit anyone to see the headstone before it is placed. However, Sekani elders agreed to make an exception and to perform a ceremony that allowed the family to safely view the headstones of Norma and her brother Thomas George. Epilogue titles inform the viewers that the RCMP has permitted John David French, husband of Barbara George, to see autopsy photographs of Norma, although her case is not closed. Thus, the family can finally place the headstones of the siblings, release their spirits, and come to terms with their grief.[8]

Claudine grew up in foster homes, group homes, and on the street. She was sexually abused very early in her life, was involved with alcohol and drugs, and had a violent and abusive relationship to a man whom she killed in self-defence. She was sentenced to do time in jail, where she met seventeen other Aboriginal women with the same charge and a similar story. After Norma's death, she repeatedly got caught up in the life of Vancouver's sex and drug trade quarter. Like Norma, she is a mother of two children whom she lost to child welfare during the course of her life; and she says that she "lost everything." The film accompanies her on her journey home to reconnect with her traditional culture and with her family that initially did not acknowledge her as stepdaughter and stepsibling. Interview sequences are complemented with sequences following her on her journey and the film foregrounds Claudine and her narrative of her life story in a number of different locations—Hastings Street in Vancouver, in a plane, in her sister's house, and in a truck on the road.

The film movingly captures the family reunion, the socializing of the women, their road trip from Prince George to Takla Landing First Nation, and the conversations between Claudine and her stepmother Gracie and stepsisters Barb and Mary, which centred mostly on Norma. Barb, Mary, and Gracie also share their life stories on camera; it is especially gripping when Gracie, who was in residential school, speaks about her childhood, her abusive relationship, and her own alcohol abuse and subsequent neglect of her children. She blames herself for being responsible for the fates of her daughters, who partly grew up in foster care, and regrets that she could not give them a better life with high-school degrees and good social standing. The life of these sisters and mother reflects that of many Aboriginal women in Canada and also that of the missing and murdered women described by Amnesty International. Low economic status, residential schools, foster homes, physical and sexual abuse, violence, and alcohol and drug addiction seem to be the blueprint pattern for lives of women who find a violent death. Restricting her own voice input to providing some factual information on Norma's death and the family, Huntley pieces together the tragic story of Norma and the George family through the voices of the mother and sisters.

This personalized telling of life stories gives the film the feel of a bio-documentary, a film that transmits the filmmaker's subjective view of the world, his/her feelings, values, attitudes, and concerns (Worth/Adair 1997, 25). The difference lies in the fact that a bio-documentary shows the filmmaker's subjective view, whereas in this film, Huntley has captured the life stories, sorrows, concerns, grief, and attitudes of a family not related to herself. One could stretch and shift Worth and Adair's definition to include a film that relates someone's individual subjective view as transmitted by someone else, the filmmaker, into the genre, thus distinguish between auto-bio-documentaries and bio-documentaries, similar to the distinction between autobiography and biography. The style of both kinds of films is still opposed to the straight documentary style that objectively examines political, historical, and cultural events, societal phenomena, and the like. Certainly, in this line of argument, *Go Home, Baby Girl* is a bio-documentary.

The film opens with nightly images of a half-overcast moon and of blurred city lights shot from outside the city with leafless branches in the foreground, which elicit feelings of loneliness, alienation, coldness, and exclusion. Then fast, blurred pans and tilts of a brightly lit street introduce Vancouver's sex and drug trade quarter, including the notorious Balmoral Hotel, followed by shots of the street signs of Main and Hastings Streets, a corner that has become known as the emblematic centre of the quarter. By focusing the camera on these two street signs, Huntley creates visual signs for Vancouver's poverty

Figure 14.1 Claudine Julian pictured in the documentary *Go Home, Baby Girl*, Audrey Huntley (dir.), 2005. © AUDREY HUNTLEY

and drug quarter. Also here, the cinematography creates a sense of insecurity, which, in concert with the first shots, produces an atmosphere that appropriately introduces and supports the content of the film. Claudine, first as voice-over and then shot in close-up, recounts that when she saw Norma last on Hastings Street, Norma told her three times "Go home, baby girl." Together with images from Hastings and Main Streets, Huntley in voice-over defines Norma as one of hundreds of missing and murdered Aboriginal women in the past thirty years. She cites the 2004 Amnesty International report that "points to the erosion of Native cultures and asserts that government policies have made Native women especially vulnerable." With newspaper articles covering Norma's story, Huntley visually narrates Norma's death and stresses the connection between Norma and the fate of hundreds of Aboriginal women.

When Claudine recounts where Norma's body was found and the police's conclusions about the circumstances of her death, the film gives nightly images of the same industrial area and location where the body was discovered. With a tracking shot out of a moving car, shaky and rhythmically accentuated low-angle shots of the ground in close-up, and low-angle shots zooming in and out of a streetlight that shines right into the camera, the filmmaker possibly comes close to recreating Norma's psychological state of mind before her death for the viewers, revealing her angst, feeling of insecurity, and inability to (fore)see. Huntley attempts to transmit Norma's subjective position and to align the viewers with it, and she is successfully able to help viewers share similar feelings and empathy for the murdered woman. In a later sequence at a totem pole in Oppenheimer Park in downtown Vancouver, Huntley, in voice-over narration, tells the viewers that Claudine will visit her family for the first time after Norma's funeral. Twice the pole is shot with canted framing, in a close-up and then in a long shot after an unsteady handheld camera moves away from Claudine standing by the pole. The pole in this way comes to symbolize the connection to family and traditional ways that Claudine is about to make, and simultaneously becomes a visual sign for the connection between the Aboriginal community of Vancouver's Downtown Eastside and their home communities and cultural traditions. Yet, this relationship is strained and unstable, hence the unsteady tracking backwards and the canted framing.

Similarly in sequences on the journey home, shaky handheld camera shots, facial close-ups, and background noises from the airport transmit Claudine's subjective position, her insecurity about her life, feelings of instability, and angst about how the family will receive her. Reminiscent of the oral tradition, where storytellers would introduce themselves and the origin of their stories, Claudine names her family she is about to meet; later, the film shows Barb, John, Mary, and Gracie in close-up, introducing themselves before each of the women tells her story. In interview sequences where Claudine speaks about her terrible life experiences, the filmmaker intermittedly inserts a fade to black, as if to respectfully give Claudine the ability to withdraw from the viewers' gaze and gather strength for her talk. These also give the viewers moments to process this deeply affecting information. More often than not, in these interviews the women burst into tears before an unmoving camera as the filmmaker tries to limit her own agency; it seems if as in these moments the women take charge of the film through the strong feelings they express. Huntley also appears to deliberately neglect perfect cinematography as she includes many shots that would otherwise be seen as flaws, shots where somebody moves with her back into the frame, shaky shots inside the truck, handheld shots of the women visiting the graveyard, and inside the small box room where the headstones of Norma and Thomas George are kept and the ritual is performed. At these points, extreme mobile framing with unsteady pans, tilts, zooms, and occasionally canted framing transmit more immediacy and create closeness to the events in the film for the viewers. Also, landscape tracking shots out of the moving truck embed Claudine and her family in their traditional geographical surroundings and create a visual connection to the land.

Throughout the film, Norma is associated with a crow; at first an image of a crow is superimposed on her photograph; later, most of her photographs are complemented with the sound of a cawing crow. With a shot of a decomposing crow, Huntley intensifies the effect of Claudine speaking about the RCMP's order not to open Norma's coffin before the funeral. When Claudine realizes that this has affected the family, in that they cannot achieve a sense of closure, this moment is accompanied by a crow image. A shot in slow motion of the same crow as it flies away is inserted at the end, after the titles have informed the viewers that finally the headstones can be placed, possibly meaning that Norma's spirit will come home. Huntley explains that she chose a crow to represent Norma because the crow and raven are Trickster figures and because she discovered the dead crow in the parking lot where Norma's body was found the day the coroner took the film team there. Later she found out that Norma's nickname was Adama, meaning "mischief" in Sekani, which would associate her with the Trickster;[9] and in this way, verbal and visual symbolism just fell into place.

As suggested by Claudine, the journey to reconnect with her family also meant a journey to reconnect with cultural traditions. Huntley visually supports this journey by presenting Claudine smudging and praying for her family and taking part in the headstone ritual. In her closing monologue, Claudine explains that this trip home meant a new beginning for her and that she is on the way to healing. This is accentuated by the last images showing her at the Carnegie Centre at the corner of Hastings and Main Street, ceremoniously offering tobacco to the Creator and to the brothers and sisters on the "black road." The tobacco on the mosaic[10] on the ground becomes a visual sign for healing and for adhering to tradition and a community spirit in an urban context. Claudine left this "black road" and now works the same streets as a crisis support worker.

On the Corner

Nathaniel Geary's debut feature film *On the Corner*, funded by Telefilm Canada, is an unrelenting portrait of the drug and prostitution scene in Vancouver's

Downtown Eastside. It was listed as one of Canada's Top Ten films by the Toronto International Film Festival Group in 2003, and won the CityTV Western Canada Feature Film Award at the 2003 Vancouver International Film Festival, as well as the Gold Moon of Valencia Award for Best Feature Film at the 19th Cinema Jove International Film Festival in Spain.[11] The film does not primarily focus on the topic of missing and murdered Aboriginal women (in fact, it is a non-Aboriginal woman that is missing), but it fictitiously traces possible life stories of Aboriginal people on Vancouver's skid row. It thus recreates the social environment of Aboriginal women walking the "black road," as Claudine Julian has termed it, and that of the sixty women who went missing from this area over the last decade, sixteen of whom were Aboriginal (Amnesty International 2004, 23).

The principal idea was not to centre on Aboriginal individuals but to "accurately portray the neighbourhood," which involved having Aboriginal characters in the story; as Geary says, "And if I have Native people in the story, then why can't they be leads?" (Linekin, online). As such, the film runs the risk of being criticized for contextualizing only a serious and negative side of Aboriginal life and by that upholding stereotypes that involve poverty, criminality, violence, substance abuse, and prostitution. But then, films like Chris Eyre's *Skins*[12] and the television series *Moccasin Flats*, both largely created by Aboriginal talent, run the same risk. The critical point is that Geary comes from Canada's non-Aboriginal middle class with a degree from Concordia's film school, and as such, creates fictitious Aboriginal stories from an outsider perspective. In terms of the milieu, however, he is no outsider, as he worked as a social worker at the government-run Portland Hotel in Downtown Eastside Vancouver for seven years. He portrays Aboriginal reality as part of a societal section, the cancerous character of which is all too often overlooked by the mainstream. He thus depicts and humanizes the indescribable, and he gives life and soul to people at the margins of Canadian society, people who tend to be statistical numbers only and are considered outcasts and a burden to society at large.

The film tells the story of Patty (Angel), who leaves her reserve and carves out a living in Vancouver's Downtown Eastside as a prostitute and is a heroin addict. She teams up with Stacey, who lives just down the hall of the same

Figure 14.2 "Angel" in the film *On the Corner*, Nathaniel Geary (dir.), 2003. © GEARFILMS INC.

cheap hotel with her pimp boyfriend, Cliffie. Angel's life story is similar to that of numerous Aboriginal women in Canada. Raised in a broken family and while coping with the abandonment of her father and with the neglect and alcoholism of her mother, she takes responsibility for her younger brother, Randy, who later ends up in foster care. When Randy runs away from his foster home in Prince Rupert and shows up at Angel's door, she is not too happy about this visit. Nevertheless, she tries to assume responsibility for Randy and urges him into the care of Floyd, a former drug addict and friend of the siblings' father who managed to get clean and survives by binning bottles and cans. Randy also comes to search for his father who died on the mean streets of this quarter, but Angel and Floyd keep his death a secret. As much as she tries, Angel cannot prevent Randy from starting smoking rock (crack cocaine). Pressured by Randy, who gets tired of bottle collecting and wants to make quick money, and still believing he only smokes weed, she sets him up with her supplier, Wade. Sadly, this move is motivated by the siblings and Stacey's dream to make money and move into a nice apartment together, which shows the twisted and vicious laws of this quarter. Having entered the drug trade, Randy becomes quickly swallowed up in this maelstrom until he ends up becoming a "junkie whore" himself. Angel is compelled to get clean on methadone in the hospital when she is thrown down the stairs by a jealous Cliffie, in a fight over drugs and Stacey. Cliffie beats up Randy in a public bathroom to get his drugs and then, is later stabbed by him. In her worries about Randy and Stacey (who is missing), Angel realizes what is happening to Randy and herself and resolves to get both of them out of the Downtown Eastside. She organizes bus tickets for them to go home—but it is too late: Randy has lost trust in her and is too deeply involved in the scene.

With this story, Geary has created a film that is emotionally compelling but establishes "this world without its depressing nature to dominate" (Nusair, online). He takes his time to introduce the milieu and characters, only to quickly intensify the plot with gripping scenes, accelerating to the climactic end of Randy stabbing Cliffie and overdosing. Unflinchingly, he recreates the harsh reality and harrowing way of life in the quarter. At the beginning of the film, Angel is introduced as a prostitute when she walks up the stingy hotel stairs with a lecherous old man only to rob him in her room, with the landlord sharing in the profit. Immediately afterward she shoots up in the bathroom and is strolling with Stacey minutes later. In the morning, she is so desperate for a fix that she spends whatever money she has on drugs. With this introduction, Geary expertly illustrates the vicious hand-to-mouth life that such individuals go through day after day. At various times, Angel is seen performing oral sex, shooting up, and being brutally handled by Wade. In such scenes, the film robs her of her dignity, but reconstructs it most often in the following scenes, showing her smiling or doing profane things. With this interplay, the film actually pinpoints the fact that these are not simply some dehumanizing experiences from which one could slowly recover but that such individuals are trained to be emotionally numb and to rebuild their dignity on a daily basis. Similarly, Randy is shown performing sexual acts, smoking rock, and shooting up, and Cliffie, constantly hyper and high on drugs, gives examples of the various ways to take cocaine and heroine and their effects.

Whereas in movies about the drug and sex trade milieu these acts are most often only hinted at, Geary brutally presents them to the viewers. It is difficult to evade these pictures, and one holds one's breath when the characters fight, mostly about drugs, in states of withdrawal, when the line between friend and foe becomes alarmingly blurred. The film very effectively brings out the anger, agony, and misery of the characters, primarily due to brilliant acting. Only the here and now counts, and there is no forgiveness. There is none for Charlotte, who comes to Vancouver desperately looking for her son Randy and has the courage to face her daughter, who feels only contempt for her. There is none for Stacey's father, who continually leaves messages begging Stacey to call home. And there is none for Cliffie, who considers himself a friend but nevertheless is left out of the plan to move into a nice apartment. It is from these scenes and character studies that the film derives its uncompromising realism.

Geary casts a well-balanced set of characters from Aboriginal and non-Aboriginal cultures, each with an approximate counterpart from the other culture: Angel and Stacey, prostitutes and junkies, and Randy, gradually turning into a dealer, junkie, and prostitute, and Cliffie, junkie and pimp. There is the elder Floyd, looking after and partly assuming a fatherly role for Angel and Randy, and Bernie, landlord of the Pennsylvania Hotel, who is both an exploitive businessman and a father figure for his tenants. Angel and Randy's aunt Glenda and her friend Dolly are their sole connection to home and family, and Wade, who (sexually) exploits Angel and Randy, drawing them deeper into their misery and away from family and a healthy life. Finally, there is the mother, Charlotte, and Stacey's father, whose existence is realized through the messages he leaves for his daughter. In that configuration, the Aboriginal characters are actually drawn in a more positive light than the non-Aboriginal characters. In the end, Angel, Floyd, and Charlotte overcome their addiction, and while Floyd, Glenda, and Dolly give ersatz family support, they are not exploitive as Wade and Bernie are. Stacey gets hit by a client and has to jump out of his car, as bruises on her face visually make clear. At the end, Wade is in trouble because he owes money to his providers, he is not safe in his shabby apartment anymore, and his brutal machismo almost turns into a wimpiness. Floyd, in contrast, is content binning cans and bottles. He lives in his homely hotel room, having made peace with the ghosts of his earlier life, and carves out a dignified life with the means he has. Of the four main characters, Angel, Stacey, Randy, and Cliffie, only Angel makes it, and the film suggests that the other three die.

The film also works with oppositions to better paint its characters. Despite her distressing situation, Angel tries to make her little room homely with a red couch, flowered curtains and bedsheets, and a little teddy bear she keeps in her bed. The teddy bear in itself signifies her longing for warmth and security and her childlike insecurity in the space of her home, as opposed to the toughness she exhibits in the space of her work. A beautiful scene with Angel in the bathtub can be read in the same vein. It is a very calm scene, with Angel and Stacey chatting about love and dating and their plans of getting an apartment—like teenage girlfriends to whom these are the most pressing problems. This peacefulness stands in stark contrast to their agitated and hyper conduct when they are on drugs and working the streets. The unfulfilled dream of a nice apartment, contextualized again and again, works to pinpoint the opposition between the characters' life and an "ordinary" life that they will not achieve (except possibly Angel). Randy buys a pair of rollerblades, which he never takes off. To him, these blades mean independence, whereas in reality they help him to become more and more entangled in the drug and prostitution scene; as Wade aptly says, "He is my only dealer with wheels on his feet." The film plays with the supposed independence, which in the end becomes lethal dependence. The fact that his binning money is not enough to buy him the blades and illusionary independence, and he needs prostitution money from Angel, reveals the warped laws of street life.

In two cinematographic character studies of Angel and later Randy on the street, Geary parallels their life situations. He first portrays Angel at the corner of Hastings and Main, smoking one cigarette after the other, waiting for and speaking to clients, and getting into cars. Later Randy is seen at the same corner waiting for clients, dealing drugs, smoking rock and cigarettes. These one-minute and forty-four-second visual portraits are realized from various camera perspectives and with various camera distances (close-ups, medium shots, long shots) at a steady editing rhythm, each with the same musical soundtrack. Both studies end with a longer take that shows both characters alone in a long shot at the corner in the busy street life. These studies, as well as the film's title, emphasize this corner as emblematic for Vancouver's poverty and drug quarter. At another point, Geary shows Angel and Stacey waiting for clients and a homeless person walking in front of an advertisement with luxury liners in Vancouver's port and people waving,[13] which again neatly emphasizes the contrast between their dream life and their reality.

With the exception of these two studies and the bathtub scene, Geary leaves no room for contemplation. He works with brief, intense scenes cut together at a fast pace. Most scenes are shot at night, and the filmmaker does not use classical (three-point) lighting. He thus underlines oppositions between bright and shadowy spaces, reminiscent of a *Dogma* film style. Most often he works with a handheld camera that in agitated situations becomes shaky and unsteady, such as when Angels walks up the stairs with the old man, when she shoots up in the bathroom, when she and Stacey work the streets, when Angel desperately looks for drugs in her room, and during the fights in the hallway of the hotel and in the public bathrooms. This style lends the film more immediacy and corresponds with the fast-paced lives of the people it portrays. With some salient stylistic means, Geary highlights certain scenes, for example when he casts the public bathroom where Cliffie beats up Randy in a greenish, cold light. Randy smoking rock is framed before a red wall employing the symbolism of red and alarm to visualize Randy's condition. Similarly, a tracking shot with canted framing of the streets refers to Randy's gradual deteriorating condition: he is a junkie, has started to prostitute himself, and owes a lot of money to Wade. Again, at the end, a shaky handheld camera in a night scene shows him sitting on the sidewalk, taking off his rollerblades, and then shooting up. The last shot is taken from a very low angle framing his rollerblades and bare feet in the foreground and thus highlighting the fact that he has taken them off for the first time in the film. Whereas before in street scenes, Randy was only shown standing or rollerblading, here he sitting for the first time. In this way, the scene suggests that he shoots up an overdose and will stay and die where he is.[14]

Through repetition Geary also emphasizes visual motifs that characterize the filmic environment. A few times there are close-ups of tables with cigarettes and items needed for drug consumption. Drugs and cigarettes are items seen again and again in the film. The Kraft Dinner that Angel makes for Randy (not for herself) and that he says is not very good, also signifies the relative poverty of the characters. In fact, there are more scenes with characters consuming drugs than consuming food, which serves to underline their priorities. The streets buzzing with buses, cars, and rather poor people is the most consistent motif, and the streets become a character in themselves, representing the lethal climate

Figure 14.3 "Randy " in the film *On the Corner*, Nathaniel Geary (dir.), 2003. © Gearfilms Inc.

of the quarter. They are the antagonist maelstrom with the threats of violence, death, and psychological isolation against which the protagonists constantly struggle. After their big fight in the hotel hallway, all four main characters are framed somewhere alone: Angel in the hospital, Stacey at the entrance of the hotel, Cliffie in a doorway, and Randy rollerblading along a street. In other moments, Randy is seen spending the night alone under the freeway and in street niches. Geary thus creates isolation and loneliness as a characterizing visual motif.

The missing posters for Stacey that her father has brought are a visual sign that denotes the heightened risk of violence that women in the sex trade face "because of the circumstances in which they work, and because the social stigmatization of women in the sex trade provides a convenient rationale for men looking for targets for acts of misogynistic violence" (Amnesty International 2004, 27). After the big fight, when the film shows her alive for the last time getting into a car, Stacey seems rather nervous and is looking back. As a team Angel and Stacey had been taking down the licence plate numbers of each other's clients[15]—a fact that could serve as safety advice for women working on the street. Working alone Stacey feels insecure and transmits the angst that many women in her profession consistently deal with. In the hospital, the doctor does not take Angel's worries that Stacey and Randy might be missing seriously. Her reaction—she asks whether or not they are a couple, suggesting they might have run off together—is reminiscent of many missing women cases where police officers did not properly address missing women's reports by family members and friends. Thus, Stacey's fate is an analogous cinematic contextualization of that of the "Stolen Sisters."

Despite the human life tragedies that unfold in the film, its end gives a positive outlook as Angel is determined to free herself from drug dependency and a life of prostitution. When Bernie asks her to stay, she declines: "No thanks, Bernie." Her upper body is framed before the dingy hotel wall, and the frame highlights her clear determined look. The shot suggests that she will make it on her own, despite the surroundings that have almost swallowed her up. The film ends at the same street corner as *Go Home, Baby Girl*. The last two shots, as long takes, show Angel alone standing with her bags at the corner of Hastings and Main, first in a long shot from behind emphasizing her loneliness, and then in close-up with the camera calmly panning around her crying face and thus underlining her pain and suffering. With this open ending, Geary does not lend the film final closure and he also avoids delivering an "obvious message" and "a prescription for social change" (Linekin, online). Kim Linekin aptly states "Geary spends more time setting up the world his characters live in than raining down lessons on it, which makes the film revolutionary in its own, quiet way. We're invited to get to know these people rather than draw conclusions about them" (Linekin, online). What Geary does is grant the people in Vancouver's Downtown Eastside the humanity that their representation in public discourse often lacks. And he also calls for attention and awareness for this section of society so easily hidden from public conscience.

Laurel

The 24-minute film *Laurel,* produced by Jennifer Podemski and Laura Milliken in association with APTN, is a surreal noir drama depicting the death and former life of an Aboriginal prostitute through recollections of her mind. It screened at the ImagineNATIVE Film Festival in Toronto, at the American Indian Film Festival in San Francisco, and aired on APTN in 2002. The film has an intricate plot à la David Lynch and only a second viewing allows one to reconstruct what and how the film narrates. The staged situation is a psychological interview of the mind of this woman by a "collector of thoughts and memories in the moment of death." This "being" appears disguised as a client, a neat bookkeeper type, who she takes up to her hotel room. He is not interested in sex, but in talking, which for her becomes an exhausting and horrific trip into her repressed mental state of mind. That this is not simply a conversation between prostitute and client is suggested by the surreal atmosphere of the film, created with disharmonious jazz music, distorted piano music, and alienated sound, in concert with inserted colour-enhanced and posterized shots. It is furthermore achieved with lagged and superimposed images, intercut dream sequences, blurred and distorted images of characters, and an often unsteady camera.

The film opens with a mix of images of city streets, cars, and faces, defamiliarized with the means as described above. They are followed by a brief sequence of a man walking up to a prostitute, Laurel, and attacking her. With a succession of split-second images—the attack, posterized in white and light blue, and her point of view from the ground as he kills her and takes her picture with a blinding flash—the film narrates her death. Quick, colour-enhanced shots of a lit skyscraper, a room, a white mask, and the back of a man in a green coat lead to the next scene, where the "collector" solicits the same woman. By alienating the sound and lagging and superimposing several images of her on the screen, this sequence introduces the following hotel sequence as an unreal encounter. During the conversation in Laurel's hotel room, this effect is upheld by the often distorted sound, the vanishing of her purse, and the bathroom door being ajar with bright light and strange noises coming from inside. The client's job remains a mystery; and he continually refers to but insufficiently explains it. Pretending to be the shy inexperienced type, he harmlessly starts a conversation about two serial killers in the city, one stabbing men randomly and the other killing prostitutes and leaving their Polaroid pictures at the location of death. The client continues his interview by asking whether or not Laurel is afraid of becoming a victim, how many clients she had, why she is a hooker, if she is happy, and if she respects herself. He has a calm demeanour, a highly sophisticated language and form of expression and behaviour, and a superior and derisive attitude. With this conduct and his specific questions and well-administered insults, the client constantly provokes strong reactions of Laurel and drives her to face well-repressed memories. He forces her to face her unhappy childhood and her present situation with its physical and psychological consequences. Her reactions are partly violent, as she is increasingly mentally driven into a corner.

Some part of their conversation stands in for a critical verbal exchange between the mainstream and the marginalized inferior group of prostitutes. It is an analogy that expresses each group's view of the other as it is seen by the filmmakers:

He: Now human culture and customs being as they are
dictate that your type is the lowest form of life
in any society.

She: Yeah, well society sucks, who gives a fuck what society
thinks. Most of society is made up of ugly rich
men who come to see girls like me cause they
make their wives wanna puke ...

He: I do have a theory though ... I believe that society is
made up of a reflection of many many many
individuals like you, sort of a collage of tragic
...

He [later]: I don't think that the police will have much
sympathy for the plight of someone like you
...

Through this conversation, the film accuses the mainstream of not recognizing low social status and poverty among women and their subsequent prostitution as systemic failure of the larger society, and of simply dismissing these factors as generating single tragic fates. At the same time it pinpoints the fact that police forces often fail to adequately protect Aboriginal women and men, specifically Aboriginal women in the sex trade as Amnesty International has repeatedly stated (Amnesty International 2004, 2–5, 27, 29–30, 37).

The client continues his cruel unrelenting interrogation that further leads into the horrid depths of her psyche by bringing up the death of her mother, her father's drinking and sexual abuse, and how she eventually kills him. In this way, her inability to brush aside the dehumanizing attitude of her clients towards her resurfaces. Consequently, the interview sequence is spiked with surreal images of a girl with a white mask, which represents her own younger self that continually confronts her, and which she desperately tries to avoid. There are also, sometimes distorted or superimposed, images of young Laurel with her mother, of her father drinking, of her younger self handing her a knife, and of Laurel stabbing her father. All of these create a visual link between the tormented adult and young Laurel. Colour-enhanced images of her having sex with a client in a car and later stabbing him, and of the man in the green coat killing and mutilating a woman's body in her bathroom give further clues. So do images of blood stains on a wall and of her picking up the Polaroid photograph the killer took of her. The red flashing exit sign, which has come to be almost a clichéd filmic symbol denoting, among other things, repressed mental states, trapped psyches, or cornered states of being,[16] in addition to the narrative style, is reminiscent of Lynch's *Lost Highway*.

In the last scene the client confronts Laurel with her own dead bloody body in the bathtub of her bathroom. The extremely bright light in the room with a greenish glare lends the scene coldness and enhances the impression of this encounter as the biblical last judgement before death. When Laurel asks, "So this is what happens when you die?" the client replies,

> No, this is what happens when *you* die, people like you. You've heard the stories right? How people have had near-death experiences on the operating table? These people later swear that while they lay on the table dying, they're drawn towards a tunnel of beautiful white light. You see, people who have done the types of things that you have done later don't see the tunnel of white light while they go or hear the angels sing, people like you they see me.

Here, the client divides people into two groups and clearly counts prostitutes as second-class citizens. In biblical semantics he suggests that other people would go to heaven and she would go to hell. In a way, Laurel reflects this, as she goes through hell with his psychological humiliation and dehumanization of her. The client thus embodies the latent superior position of the mainstream and humiliating and marginalizing practices toward sex trade workers. The last scene strings together the plot: she is the killer of the men, and she is the sixth victim of the serial killer who has murdered her in her hotel bathroom. She was already dead when the mystical client approached her and this psychological interrogation happened in her mind in the last seconds of her life. With the questions he asks, he may represent her own conscience that critically examines her life. He may also, as mentionned earlier, represent the hegemonic and exclusionist position of the larger part of society against which she has to defend herself.

As suggested above, Podemski and Milliken extensively work with colours. Colour posterization and colour enhancement give the intercut shots a surreal character and help to distinguish these from the main sequence in the hotel room, which is shot in rather natural subdued colours; however, the colours also serve to establish symbolic associations. The red dress of young Laurel, who is often framed before a reddish background here, implies demise or death and connects her to the dead body of adult Laurel covered in blood. The red of the exit sign roots Laurel's psychological traumas in her younger life. The white and light blue colours of the posterized shot of the attack at the beginning are repeated in the split-second posterized shots right after she has killed her father with imagery of blood stains and her younger self with white mask. These shots link physical and sexual violence and blur clear lines between victim and offender, as it is often the case when victims become offenders. Green, in the scene with her and the client in the car shot with greenish light, the green coat of the murderer, and the greenish glare in the last scene, associates these scenes with death.

The framed newspapers, with the headlines "Serial Killer's Grip on the City Continues" at the beginning and "Photo Killer Claims Sixth Victim" with her photograph underneath at the end, is a means by which the film connects its surreal atmosphere to an outer reality. Like the missing woman poster in *On the Corner* and the newspaper headlines of Norma's death in *Go Home, Baby Girl,* the headlines become a visual sign of the string of missing and murdered women cases in Canada. The film is a bizarre, surreal picture that nevertheless relates to pressing issues in Canadian

Figure 14.4 "Laurel with her client" in the film *Laurel*, Laura J. Milliken and Jennifer Podemski (prods.), 2002. © Big Soul Productions

society. Much less than *Go Home, Baby Girl* and *On the Corner*, this film does not present solutions to the critical situation of Aboriginal prostitutes, nor does it give advice on how to cope with life on the streets. It does not moralize about the plight of Aboriginal women on the streets, nor does it criticize self-defence. With the catalogue of questions the film might ask concerned women to reconsider their lives, their choices, their possibilities, and their self-respect. At the same time it lends humanity to women in the sex trade and simply asks viewers to revise their own attitudes towards people in such life situations.

Conclusion

Different in genre, style, and approach, the three films all address topics of Aboriginal women's poverty and prostitution, the threat of misogynist violence that prostitutes live with, and the social stigma of prostitution. In various ways they contextualize tragic fates of missing and murdered (Aboriginal) women, and the mishandling of such cases by officials. The films similarly unravel the women's harrowing life stories that eventually led to them becoming prostitutes (and drug addicts) and to live such degrading lives. By translating these issues into film, the filmmakers battle against the public apathy and indifference towards the plight of Aboriginal sex trade workers. Like Amnesty International's "Stolen Sisters" report, they attempt to give life and a human face to statistic numbers and abstractly described social problems as they often appear in public discourse. In this way they appeal to the public Canadian conscience and call for awareness about the human tragedies that happen daily at the margins of a rich First World country.

Endnotes

1 The discussion of the covering of such cases in the mainstream media (or the lack thereof) would exceed the limits of this article.

2 See Brede "The Commission on the Future of Health Care in Canada: A Case Study of Aboriginal Health" in this edition.

3 The murderers of Pamela George hurled these racist slurs at an Aboriginal woman before they encountered their victim. This woman was later to become witness in the trial. The same offenders confided to a friend that they had picked up an Indian hooker and beat her (to death); one said, "'She deserved it. She was an Indian'" (Amnesty International 2004, 46, online).

4 See "Canada: Seven Ways to Stop Violence against Indigenous Women," at http://www.amnesty.ca/take_action/actions/canada_stolen_sisters_7ways.php; "Canada: Stolen Sisters - Help Break the Silence," at http://www.amnesty.ca/take_action/actions/canada_stolensisters_2005.php; "Aboriginal Women Many Missing: Many Murdered," at http://www.turtleisland.org/news/donnajoe.htm; Sisters in Spirit Campaign, at http://www.sistersinspirit.ca/engmissing.htm; "Freedom Drum: A 24-hour Marathon in Support of Indigenous Rights," at http://www.amnesty.ca/campaigns/sisters_midnight_messenger.php.

5 It was never proven conclusively that Norma George was murdered (personal email from Audrey Huntley); hence the parentheses. However, the facts surrounding her death indicate that she was, thus this paper refers to her as being murdered.

6 Personal email from Audrey Huntley and Huntley, "Traces of Missing Women: Progress Reports," at http://www.cbc.ca/sunday/progressreports.html

7 "Traces of Missing Women," at http://www.cbc.ca/sunday/missingwomen.html.

8 The above and the following information are taken from Huntley's film *Go Home, Baby Girl.*

9 Personal email from Audrey Huntley.

10 The mosaic features the Carnegie Center, a community center that provides a number of services to the community such as a food program, a library, and cultural activities (personal email from Audrey Huntley).

11 "Canada's Top Ten," at http://www.topten.ca/content/archive.asp; "*On the Corner* – Official Website," at http://www.onthecorner.ca/html/home.html; "NSI: Canada, in Association with Telefilm Canada, Announces Call For Entries for NSI Features First," at http://www.nsi-canada.ca/news/2004/media071504.html.

12 *Skins* does not contextualize prostitution.

13 This fact came to my attention in a personal conversation with André Berg.

14 This reading came up in a personal conversation with Thomas Rüdell.

15 This fact came to my attention in a personal conversation with André Berg.

16 See Herzogenrath 1999, online.

Bibliography

Acoose, Janice. (1995). *Iskwewak. Kah' Ki Yaw Ni Wahkomakanak: Neither Indian Princesses Nor Easy Squaws.* Toronto, ON: Women's Press.

Bahn-Coblans, Sonja. (1996, Winter). "Reading with an Eurocentric Eye the 'Seeing with a Native Eye': Victor Masayesva's *Itam Hakim, Hopiit.*" *Studies in American Indian Literatures, 8:4,* 47–60.

Bordwell, David, and Kristin Thompson. (1997). *Film Art: An Introduction.* 1979. New York: McGraw-Hill Companies.

Clements, Marie. (2005). *The Unnatural and Accidental Women.* Vancouver: Talonbooks.

Matthews, Maureen, et al. (1991, December 11–12). *Isinamowin: The White Man's Indian.* CBC: Toronto. Transcript from radio program.

Nolan, Yvette. (1992, Winter). "Blade." *Theatrum, the Theatre Magazine, 31,* 1–5.

Worth, Sol, and John Adair. (1997). *Through Navajo Eyes: An Exploration in Film Communication and Anthropology.* 1972. Albuquerque, NM: University of New Mexico Press.

Venne, Sharon Helen. (1981). *Indian Acts and Amendments 1868–1975, An Indexed Collection.* Saskatoon, SK: University of Saskatchewan Native Law Centre.

Filmography

Brass, Peter, and Helder Mauricio Carvajal, dirs. (2007). *The Valley.* First Nations University of Canada.

Bessai, Carl, dir. (2006). *Unnatural and Accidental.* Writ. Marie Clements. Unnatural Films.

Chartrand, Ervin, dir. (2007). *Sister.* National Film Board of Canada.

Eyre, Chris, dir. (2002). *Skins.* Writs. Jennifer D. Lyne and Adrian C. Louis. First Look Media.

Geary, Nathaniel, dir./writ. (2003). *On the Corner.* Gearfilms Inc.

Huntley, Audrey, dir./prod. (2005). *Go Home, Baby Girl.* Canadian Broadcasting Corporation.

Mankiewicz, Francis, dir. (1991). *Conspiracy of Silence.* Writs. Suzette Couture and Lisa Priest. Canadian Broadcasting Corporation.

Podemski, Jennifer, and Laura Milliken, prods. (2001). *Laurel.* Writ. Patrick Tenascon. Big Soul Productions.

Stewart Curtis, Stacey, dir. (2003). "Suspicious Love." *Moccasin Flats.* Television Series. Season 1, episode 2. Writs. Penny Gummerson and Darrell Dennis. Prods. Laura Milliken and Jennifer Podemski. Big Soul Productions.

Welsh, Christine, dir. (2006). *Finding Dawn.* National Film Board of Canada.

Internet Sources

Amnesty International Canada. (2004, October). "Canada: Stolen Sisters: A Human Rights Response to Discrimination and Violence against Indigenous Women in Canada." http://www.amnesty.ca/stolensisters/amr2000304.pdf [consulted February 12, 2006].

———. "Canada: Stolen Sisters: Help Break the Silence." http://www.amnesty.ca/take_action/actions/canada_stolensisters_2005.php [consulted February 28, 2006].

———. (2005, October 26). "'How Many More Sisters and Daughters Do We Have to Lose?': Canada's Continued Failure to Address Discrimination and Violence against Indigenous Women." http://www.amnesty.ca/campaigns/resources/sisters_brief_oct2005.pdf [consulted February 12, 2006].

———. (2005). "Freedom Drum: a 24-hour Marathon in Support of Indigenous Rights." http://www.amnesty.ca/campaigns/sisters_midnight_messenger.php [consulted February 28, 2006].

———. (2006). "Canada: Seven Ways to Stop Violence against Indigenous Women." http://www.amnesty.ca/take_action/actions/canada_stolen_sisters_7ways.php [consulted February 28, 2006].

Canada's Top Ten Archive. "Canada's Top Ten Films of All Time." http://www.topten.ca/content/archive.asp [consulted March 8, 2006].

Herzogenrath, Bernd. (1999, January). "On the *Lost Highway*: Lynch and Lacan, Cinema and Cultural Pathology." *Other Voices, 1:3.* http://www.othervoices.org/1.3/bh/highway.html [consulted May 2, 2004].

Huntley, Audrey. (2004). "Traces of Missing Women: Progress Reports." *CBC News.* http://www.cbc.ca/sunday/progressreports.html [consulted February 28, 2006].

Linekin, Kim. "East Side Story: On the Corner." *Eyeweekly.com.* http://www.eye.net/eye/issue/print.asp?issue_06.17.04/film/onthecorner.html [consulted February 28, 2006].

Mann, Michelle. (2005, October 21). "Time to Make History on Gender Equality." CBC *News Viewpoint*. http://www.cbc.ca/news/viewpoint/vp_mann/20051021.html [consulted February 12, 2006].

National Screen Institute. (2004, July 15). "Canada, in Association with Telefilm Canada, Announces Call For Entries for NSI Features First." http://www.nsi-canada.ca/news/2004/media071504.html [consulted March 8, 2006].

Neve, Alex. "An Interview with Alex Neve." CBC *News*. http://www.cbc.ca/sunday/alexneve.html [consulted February 12, 2006].

Nusair, David. (2004, June 17). "On the Corner: Reel Film Reviews." http://www.reelfilm.com/oncorner.htm [consulted February 28, 2006].

On the Corner. "*On the Corner*: Official Website." http://www.onthecorner.ca/html/home.html [consulted March 8, 2006].

Seah, Gilbert. (2004). "Review: On the Corner." http://www.cinemaeye.com/index/reviews/rev_more/on_the_corner_1_2/ [consulted February 28, 2006].

Sisters in Spirit. "Campaign." http://www.sistersinspirit.ca/engmissing.htm [consulted February 28, 2006].

Turtle Island Native Network. "Aboriginal Women: Many Missing, Many Murdered." http://www.turtleisland.org/news/donnajoe.htm [consulted Feburary 28, 2006].

Appendix A: Glossary

canted framing: A view in which the frame is not level; either the right or left side is lower than the other, causing objects in the scene to appear slanted out of an upright position.

close-up: A framing in which the scale of the object shown is relatively large; most commonly a person's head seen from the neck up, or an object of a comparable size that fills most of the screen.

intercutting: Editing that alternates shots of two or more lines of action occurring in different planes, usually simultaneously.

long shot: A framing in which the scale of the object shown is small; a standing human figure would appear nearly the height of the screen.

long take: A shot that continues for an unusually lengthy time before the transition to the next shot.

medium shot: A framing in which the scale of the object shown is of moderate size; a human figure seen from the waist up would fill most of the screen.

mobile frame: The effect on the screen of the moving camera, a zoom lens, or certain special effects; the framing shifts in relation to the scene being photographed.

motif: An element in a film that is repeated in a significant way.

pan: A camera movement with the camera body turning to the right or left. On the screen, it produces a mobile framing that scans the space horizontally.

posterization: A technique that involves restricting the vibration of light waves on the film strip so that they have different amplitudes on different planes and, therefore, show distorted outlines and distorted colors (Bahn-Coblans 1996, 55).

POV shot (point-of-view shot): A shot taken with the camera placed approximately where the character's eyes would be, showing what the character would see; usually cut in before or after the character looking.

scene: A segment in a narrative film that takes place in one time and space or that uses crosscutting to show two or more simultaneous actions.

sequence: Term commonly used for a moderately large segment of a film, involving one complete stretch of action, in a narrative film, often equivalent to a *scene*.

shot: 1. In shooting, one uninterrupted run of the camera to expose a series of frames. Also called a take. 2. In the finished film, one uninterrupted image with a single static or *mobile framing*.

style: The repeated and salient uses of film techniques characteristic of a single film or a group of films (for example, a filmmaker's work or a national movement).

superimposition: The exposure of more than one image on the same film strip.

three-point lighting: A common arrangement using three directions of light on a scene: from behind the subjects (*backlighting*), from one bright source (*key light*), and from a less bright source balancing the key light (*fill light*).

tilt: A camera movement with the camera body swiveling upward or downward on a stationary support. It produces a mobile framing that scans the space vertically.

tracking shot: A mobile frame [camera movement] that travels through space forward, backward, or laterally.

Note: If not specified, the definitions are taken from the glossary of Bordwell/Thompson 1997, 477–482.

List of Contributors

Marlene Atleo, PhD (ʔeh ʔeh naa tuu kʷiss or "a person that can say the same thing in a lot of different ways") is a member of the Ahousaht First Nation of British Columbia. For the first half of her life she worked in the salmon fishing industry, and now she is a professor of adult and higher education at the University of Manitoba specializing in diversity, Aboriginal education, storywork, and phenomenological orienteering. Marlene Atleo has worked at "home" in social, health, wellness, and consumer education through adult programming promoting an "across the kitchen table" style of interaction. She is a grandmother of six, and lives with Umeek, her husband of forty years, in Winnipeg, Manitoba.

Falko Brede earned his PhD in the Department of Political Science at the University of Augsburg, Germany, in 2006. His main research interests are in the areas of health policy-making, comparative public policy, and the relationship between science and politics. He is currently working as personal assistant for a member of the German Parliament and teaches political science at the University of Augsburg. In his doctoral thesis, he analyzed the influence of advisory commissions on health policy-making in Canada and

Germany. His thesis, *Gesundheitspolitik und Politikberatung,* was published in 2006 (Deutscher Universitäts-Verlag).

MANSELL GRIFFIN is a Nisga'a citizen from Gitwinksihlkw, British Columbia, Canada. He completed his Bachelor of Arts in First Nations Studies in 2000 and is currently completing his MA in Environment and Management. Mansell Griffin is a member of the Wolf Phatry of the Nisga'a Nation and bears a hereditary title in his family's house. He currently works as the Lands Manager for the Nisga'a Lisims Government in New Aiyansh, British Columbia.

NANCY GRIMM studied at the University of Potsdam, Germany, and at the State University of New York at Potsdam, New York. Currently, she is a research assistant at the Department of English and American Studies of Friedrich-Schiller-University Jena, Germany. Her doctoral thesis in progress is titled "Beyond the 'Imaginary Indian': Eine interkulturelle Studie zur Entstehung und Omnipräsenz stereotyper 'Indianerbilder' in der euro-amerikanischen Imagination und deren Dekonstruktion durch ausgewählte indigene Texte Nordamerikas." Her research interests and fields of publication focus on North American ethnic literatures and cultures. Other research interests and fields of publication—which always take into consideration their implementation in the EFL classroom—range from film and intertextual/-medial studies to the domain of E-Learning and the Internet.

EVA GRUBER studied English and Biology at the Universities of Heidelberg and Constance, Germany, and at the University of Guelph, Canada. She completed her PhD exams in February 2006 and is currently assistant professor of American Literature at the University of Constance. She has published on Thomas King's short fiction, on translating Native Canadian Literature into German, and on Native American adaptations of the road movie genre. Her research interests include Native North American literature, "race" and the novel of passing, and life writing/intersections of autobiography and fiction. *Reimagining Nativeness: Humor in Contemporary Native North American Literature,* her PhD thesis, is scheduled for publication in 2008 (Camden House, New York).

ROBERT HARDING moved to British Columbia from Quebec in 1997 to help a local university college and the Stó:lö First Nation develop a social work program based on Aboriginal principles. He received his PhD from Simon Fraser University with a dissertation on media discourse about Aboriginal self-governance issues. His latest publications include "Historical Representations of Aboriginal People in the Canadian News Media" in *Discourse and Society*, and "The Media, Aboriginal People and Common Sense" in the *Canadian Journal of Native Studies*. Robert Harding also teaches social policy, community development, and Aboriginal social work at the School of Social Work and Human Services at the University of the Fraser Valley in Abbotsford, British Columbia.

KATARZYNA JUCHNOWICZ graduated from Nicholas Copernicus University in Toruñ, Poland in the field of English Philology. In 2001 she was awarded second prize for the best MA thesis written in Canadian Studies in Poland by the Polish Association for Canadian Studies. At present she is a doctoral student with Professor Hartmut Lutz at the University of Greifswald, Germany. The working title of her dissertation is "Presences of Oral Traditions in Contemporary Anishnabe Writing."

KERSTIN KNOPF holds an MA in American, Canadian, Hispanic, and Scandinavian Studies from the University of Greifswald in Germany. She also studied in Los Angeles (US), Gothenburg (Sweden), and Regina and Ottawa (Canada). Twice, she spent six months at the First Nations University of Canada in order to do research for her MA thesis, "Aboriginal Women and Film in Canada," as well as for her PhD *Decolonizing the Lens of Power: A Study of Indigenous Films in North America*, which is forthcoming with Rodopi Press in Amsterdam. Kerstin Knopf is assistant professor to the chair of North American Studies at the University of Greifswald. Her main research interests are Aboriginal literature, film and media, women's studies and Canadian 19th century women's literature. Currently she is working on her habilitation thesis, entitled "The Female Gothic in Canada: Nineteenth-Century Women's Literature at the Interface between Romance and Horror."

TRICIA LOGAN is currently a master's student at the University of Manitoba, Winnipeg. Her research interests include Métis history and Residential School histories in Canada. She is also currently working for the Métis Centre at the National Aboriginal Health Organization in Winnipeg, Manitoba. Originally from Kakabeka Falls, Ontario, Tricia Logan is daughter of Métis and German parents, and she has always been encouraged by them to explore history, both personally and academically.

STEFFI RETZLAFF is an assistant professor in the Department of Languages and Linguistics at McMaster University in Hamilton, Canada. She earned her PhD in Linguistics from the University of Potsdam, Germany. Her major areas of research are in the field of Critical Discourse Analysis and include culture and society, racism, stereotyping and identity (re-) presentations in various cultures and contexts. She is also interested in various action-oriented approaches to the teaching of languages and literature such as drama pedagogy.

THOMAS RÜDELL studied English, Teaching German as a Foreign Language (DaF) and Media Studies at the University of Trier, Germany and the University of Manitoba, Winnipeg. His thesis, "Modernizing the 'Indian'—Literary Constructions of the Native in Selected Novels by Thomas King," earned him an MA from the University of Trier. During his stay in Winnipeg he took classes in Canadian Literature and Native Studies, where he got to know the works of Thomas King. He is a regular contributor to, and editor of, the online cultural magazine *Hunderttausend.de* (www.hunderttausend.de), which publishes concert reviews, news articles, and interviews with rock musicians. In October 2006, he began working as press and public relations officer for the Chat Noir, an old-school vaudeville-style theatre in Trier's newly-built Petrisberg district.

SIOBHÁN SMITH is the registrar for the Morris and Helen Belkin Art Gallery, University of British Columbia (UBC) in Vancouver, Canada. She is a graduate of the History and Curatorial Studies MA program at York University, Toronto (2005). Previously she completed a diploma in Studio Art at

Capilano College (1998) and obtained a bachelor's degree in Art History and Women's Studies at UBC (2003). Her research interests cover a wide range of studies in Canadian art history, feminist theory, and museum practice. In 2004, she was awarded a Social Sciences and Humanities Research Council (SSHRC) Canada Graduate Scholarship.

GENEVIÈVE SUSEMIHL studied English and American Studies, Sociology and Educational Sciences at the University of Rostock in Germany, at Connecticut College, and at the Long Island University in the United States. In 2003 she received her PhD completing her dissertation entitled "The Assimilation and Integration of German-Jewish Hitler Refugees in New York and Toronto." From 1998 to 2005, she worked as an assistant professor in the English Department at the University of Rostock, researching and teaching in the fields of North American culture and literature. Since 2003, she has been a visiting professor at different institutions, the University of Greifswald, the Radboud Universiteit Nijmegen, in the Netherlands, and the Humboldt-University of Berlin, among others. Geneviève Susemihl has received various honours and awards. She is a DAAD and Fulbright-Alumnus, the recipient of the John G. H. Halstead-Memorial Fellowship of the *Stiftung für Kanada-Studien,* and a member of the Canada Meets Germany—A Forum for Young Leaders. Her main areas of research are Jewish and Native American Studies, popular and visual culture, and media studies.

BARBARA WALBERG is professor at Negahneewin College of Access and Community Development at Confederation College, Thunder Bay, where she has taught for twenty-one years. Presently, she is the coordinator of the Aboriginal Law and Advocacy Program, as well as member of the development team for the Indigenous Leadership and Community Development Degree of Applied Learning. Barbara Walberg has an undergraduate degree in Anthropology from Lakehead University, Thunder Bay, and a teaching certification in both British Columbia and Ontario. She recently completed her MA in Integrated Studies at Athabasca University, Alberta in June 2007. Her research interests include Community Studies, with a focus on the Aboriginal issues of Northwestern Ontario.

Index

Composed by Sandra Friesen in Arno, a typeface created by Robert Slimbach in 2007. Arno is based on the early humanist types of the 15th and 16th century Italian Renaissance. The typeface is named after the river that runs through Florence.

The paper used in this publication is Rolland Opaque. It contains FSC certified 30 percent post-consumer and 70 percent virgin fibre, is certified EcoLogo and FSC Mixed Sources and is manufactured using biogas energy.